Barlow's Cohabitants and the Law

Barlow's Cohabitants and the Law

4th Edition

David Josiah-Lake
Solicitor and Collaborative Family Lawyer

Advisory Editor: Professor Anne Barlow
University of Exeter

Bloomsbury Professional

LONDON • DUBLIN • EDINBURGH • NEW YORK • NEW DELHI • SYDNEY

BLOOMSBURY PROFESSIONAL
Bloomsbury Publishing Plc
41–43 Boltro Road, Haywards Heath, RH16 1BJ, UK

BLOOMSBURY and the Diana logo are trademarks of Bloomsbury Publishing Plc

First published in Great Britain 2018

British Library Cataloguing-in-Publication Data

A catalogue record for this book is available from the British Library.

ISBN: PB: 978 1 52650 304 6
ePDF: 978 1 52650 306 0
ePub: 978 1 52650 305 3

Typeset by Compuscript Ltd, Shannon

To find out more about our authors and books visit www.bloomsburyprofessional.com. Here you will find extracts, author information, details of forthcoming events and the option to sign up for our newsletters

Preface

I should start by extending my thanks to Professor Anne Barlow for entrusting me to update this (fourth) edition of her work, putting together in one place, as much as it is possible to do, discussion of the laws affecting unmarried/co-habiting families. Anne kindly proofread the chapters in this new edition, offering advice and asking questions to aid better explanation of the law. Her support and input has been invaluable and it is only fitting that the title of the book makes reference to the fact that, whilst she has handed over the reins to me, this is still her work.

As one would expect, there have been enormous (and hugely progressive) advances in the area of family law since the last edition of this book in 2001.

Ever-growing acceptance of and legal recognition for same sex relationships has seen the passing of the Civil Partnership Act 2004 enabling same sex couples to register as civil partners (with rights akin to marriage) which came into effect on 5 December 2005. As at December 2016, 64,372 civil partnerships had been registered in England and Wales.

The Marriage (Same Sex Couples) Act 2013 came into force on 13 March 2014 with the first same sex marriages taking place on 29 March 2014. Between 29 March 2014 and 30 June 2015 there were 7,366 same sex marriages in England and Wales. Over that period, there were also 7,732 conversions of civil partnerships to marriage.

In the context of same-sex co-habiting couples, the effect of the passing of the civil partnership legislation was that the legal definition of cohabitants as offered by FLA 1996, s 62(1) was amended to include 'two persons who are neither married to each other nor civil partners of each other but are living together as husband and wife or as if they were civil partners'. Likewise, the Adoption and Children Act 2002 definition of a couple includes 'two people (whether of different sexes or the same sex) living as partners in an enduring family relationship' (s 144(4)). Thus, same sex couples who do not marry or enter into a civil partnership are subject to the same limited remedies as opposite sex cohabiting couples, in contrast to the position as at the date of the last edition of this work when same sex couples were expressly excluded from such limited remedies.

The number of cohabiting couples (whether of the same or opposite sex) continues to grow. The Office of National Statistics, in its Statistical Bulletin on *Families and Households: 2017*, reported that in 2017 the second largest family type was the cohabiting couple with 3.3 million such families in existence (a huge increase on the 1.5 million families recorded in 1996). Notwithstanding this, there has been little or no attempt by lawmakers to consider legislation affording rights to co-habiting couples. The latest incarnation of the Cohabitation Rights Bill 2017–19 had its first reading in the House of Lords on 5 July 2017 but has been stalled ever since. There is still no cohesive body of law which constitutes 'a divorce law equivalent' for cohabitants in England and Wales with the law affecting them still ranging over many areas of expertise and Resolution (formerly, the Solicitors Family Law Association) continues to advocate for the rights of cohabitants.

Whilst in England and Wales lawmakers have been reluctant even to consider the passing of legislation to confer legal rights and obligations on cohabitants, in Scotland cohabitants can look to the Family Law (Scotland) Act 2006, which at least provides a limited set of rights for cohabitants, including the ability to bring potentially significant financial claims against their partner. Indeed, s 28 provides the basis for cohabitants to make an application to the court for financial provision within one year of separation. In such situations, the court can make certain orders, namely: an order for the payment of a capital sum to the applicant; an order requiring the respondent to pay a sum in respect of any economic burden of caring for a child of the family; or any interim order the court considers appropriate. Section 29 also enables a surviving cohabitant (who was living with their deceased partner at the date of death) to make an application for provision from the intestate estate of the deceased within six months of their death, provided that the deceased cohabitant was domiciled in Scotland immediately before his/her death.

Once again, the purpose of the book is to draw together the disparate areas of law affecting cohabitants and to highlight the progress made and the progress yet to be made in the increasingly important area.

The original structure of this book has been retained in this fourth edition, with Part I (Chapters 1–6) examining the law which affects cohabitants/the 'unmarried family' when living together as a unit. One significant development since the last edition (discussed at Chapter 2) is that on the birth of a child the joint registration by the parents of that child will confer on the unmarried father parental responsibility. There has been legal recognition of the fact that the desire to be a parent is not specific to gender or sexual orientation, such that the Human Fertilisation and Embryology Act 2008 now enables a child born to a same sex couple (whether through assisted reproduction or surrogacy) to be treated as the child of both parents. In Chapter 3 we highlight that local housing authorities are now under a duty to provide the statutory homeless with permanent accommodation (HA 1996, s 193(3) as amended by the Homelessness Act 2002, s 6, which abolished the minimum period (of two years) for which a local authority was subject to a duty to rehouse). The changes to the benefits system and the introduction of Universal Credit are examined in Chapter 4. Chapter 5 looks at the developments in the law where a cohabitant dies, noting that same sex cohabitants were only included as a separate category of applicant entitled to apply for provision under the Inheritance (Provision for Family and Dependants) Act 1975 with effect from 5 December 2005.

Chapter 6 continues the discussion of the position of and impact on a cohabitant or his or her partner involved in divorce or dissolution proceedings.

Part II deals with the impact of relationship breakdown. Developments in the law relating to domestic abuse are discussed in Chapter 7, together with reforms to the homelessness legislation affording better protection for victims of such abuse. Domestic Violence Protection Notices (DVPNs) and Orders (DVPOs) – an alternative to requiring the victim to apply for an injunction – were brought into effect by the Crime and Security Act 2010, ss 24–27 and implemented across England and Wales from 8 March 2014. Chapter 8 explores the effect on and the arrangements for children following their parents' break up. Residence and Contact orders are no longer made, the courts now encouraged to make child arrangements ('lives with' or 'spends time with') orders. The Child Maintenance Service (taking over the responsibility of child maintenance issues from the Child Support Agency) is discussed at Chapter 9, as well as the fact that access to justice/to legal assistance is of real concern as legal aid has been removed from such family matters (save in respect of mediation) unless the applicant for legal aid has been a victim of domestic abuse. Some attempt has been made to resolve the practical difficulties highlighted in Chapter 10 of the last edition in respect of the transfer of tenancies under Pt IV of the Family Law Act. Whilst the recent decisions in the cases flowing from *Stack v Dowden* [2007] and *Jones v Kernott* [2011] have sought to give clarity with regard to the position of express, resulting and constructive trusts as discussed in Chapter 11, the fact remains that only Parliament can properly afford rights to cohabitants in respect of a home in which they have no clear, express, settled interest, the Cohabitation Rights Bill 2017–19 (as discussed in Chapter 11) if enacted would enable a cohabitant to apply for a financial settlement order including the transfer, sale or settlement of property.

With Brexit sucking all the air out of the room (well, out of the legislative chamber in Parliament), it is unlikely that there will be any significant developments with regard to the law affecting unmarried families and no 'divorce law equivalent' affording rights to cohabitants for some time. It has been 18 years since the last edition of this book and the profession as well as many of the 3.3 million unmarried families/co-habiting couples desperately need Parliament to step up and address the continuing lack of clarity and certainty in many areas of the law affecting such family relationships.

As before it is hoped this book will be a useful resource for those teaching family law, as well as those continuing to practice in this area.

Last but not least, I would like to thank my family, Jeremy and Ryan, and my partner in law Rebecca Gardiner for allowing me the time and support needed to do justice to this work.

Contents

Table of Statutes

Table of Statutory Instruments

Table of Cases

C

E

F

G

I

J

K

Q

R

S

X

PART I

Living together

CHAPTER 1

The cohabitation relationship

1 Introduction

1.01

As the number of cohabiting couples continues to rise, it makes sense to revisit Anne Barlow's work, to assess what if any further protections are now (or proposed to be) extended to couples who choose not to marry or to enter into civil partnerships and whether the rights afforded to cohabiting couples (and the children of such families) are satisfactory. On 8 November 2017, the Office of National Statistics released its Statistical Bulletin on *Families and Households: 2017*, in which it reported that in 2017 the second largest family type was the cohabiting couple with 3.3 million of such families in existence (a huge increase on the 1.5 million families recorded in 1996). It concludes that 'this may be explained by an increasing trend to cohabit instead of marry (or for same sex couples to register as civil partners) or to cohabit before marriage (or civil partnership), particularly at younger ages'. Since the last edition of this book was published, perhaps the greatest expansions of the law relating to families and family relationships have been the Civil Partnership Act 2004, which came into effect on 5 December 2005, enabling same sex couples to register as civil partners of each other and endowing on them such rights, obligations and protections enjoyed by married (opposite sex) couples, and the Marriage (Same Sex Couples) Act 2013, under which, from 29 March 2014, same sex couples are now permitted to marry and to enjoy the same rights as opposite sex married couples.

1.02

The word 'cohabitation' has come to denote the situation where two people live together as husband and wife or as civil partners in a family framework analogous to marriage or civil partnership, without actually having gone through a ceremony of marriage or entering into a civil partnership. The parties involved in such an arrangement are often described as 'cohabitees', although the words mistress, common law husband/wife, *de facto* spouse and spouse equivalent are among a wealth of alternatives, none of which is completely satisfactory or legally correct. Despite its common usage, it has often been pointed out that the word 'cohabitee' is grammatically incorrect and as in previous editions the term 'cohabitant', first used in Part IV Family Law Act 1996 (FLA 1996) is adopted here.

1.03

There is no one formal definition of 'cohabitants', but as offered by s 62(1) FLA 1996 cohabitants are 'two persons who are neither married to each other nor civil partners of each other but are living together as husband and wife or as if they were civil partners'. The Adoption and Children Act 2002 definition of a couple includes 'two people (whether of different sexes or the same sex) living as partners in an enduring family relationship' (s 144(4)). It should be noted that same sex couples who do not marry or enter into a civil partnership are subject to the same limited remedies as opposite sex cohabiting couples, in contrast to the position as at the date of the last edition of this work when same sex couples were expressly excluded from such limited remedies.

It seems to be assumed, at least by Parliamentary draftsmen, that where a phrase such as 'living together as husband and wife' is used in statutes, such a situation is easily recognisable and thus not worthy of detailed definition. Whether or not such an assumption is justified is debatable, particularly as the definitions do vary from statute to statute. In the case of *Kimber v Kimber* [2000] 1 FLR 383, HHJ Tyrer considered the various factors that would tend to show that a couple were living together as husband and wife and concluded that 'the matter should be determined by asking whether, in the opinion of a reasonable person with normal perceptions, it could be said that the two people in question were living together as husband and wife' (or by extension as same sex spouses or civil partners). From a practitioner's point of view, however, for the moment each case has to be examined on its own facts in the context of the situation in which advice is sought. Thus, for present purposes, attention is merely drawn to the fact that statutory definitions do vary and will be examined where appropriate in the chapters that follow.

1.04

It is worthy of note here that the European Court of Justice has held that the definition of the term 'spouse' does not include heterosexual cohabitants for the purposes of European Community Law (see *Netherlands v Reed*: 59/85 [1986] ECR 1283). However, and significantly, given the implementation in October 2000 of the Human Rights Act 1998 (HRA 1998), there has been an increasing recognition in Strasbourg of the unmarried cohabiting family. Thus in *X, Y and Z v United Kingdom* 20 EHRR CDG, a case involving the relationship between children born by AID to a mother whose cohabitant and the children's 'social father' was a female-to-male transsexual, the European Court of Human Rights held that whether or not a relationship amounting to 'family life' protected by Article 8 of the European Convention existed was a question of fact. Relevant factors to consider included whether the couple live together, the length of their relationship and whether they have demonstrated their commitment to each other by having children together, or by any other means. Nonetheless, the position of same-sex cohabitants is not currently assisted by Strasbourg case law. Indeed, in the case of *Kerkhoven v Netherlands*

(Application 15666/89) (19 May 1992, unreported), it was held that Article 8 does not oblige a State to confer parental rights on a woman who was living with a child's mother. Thus, the decision of the European Court of Human Rights that where same-sex couples cohabit in a stable relationship, this does not fall within the scope of Article 8 of the Convention remains good law (see *X and Y v United Kingdom* (Application 9369/81), 32 Decisions and Reports 220), although this of itself did not prevent the House of Lords finding that a surviving partner of a long-standing same-sex relationship was a member of his deceased partner's family for Rent Act tenancy succession purposes (*Fitzpatrick v Sterling Housing Association* [2000] 1 FLR 271). Even though 'under the Strasbourg case law same sex partners still do not fall within the scope of family life' (per Lord Nicholls of Birkenhead in *M v Secretary of State for Work and Pensions*) [2006] UKHL 11), it is anticipated that future decisions of the European court will reverse its currently stated position. In *Karner v Austria* (Application No 40016/98) [2003] 2 FLR 623, the Court did emphasise that discrimination on the basis of sexual orientation required particularly serious reasons by way of justification.

1.05

In a cohabiting relationship, each member of the couple, during the currency of the relationship, would normally regard the other member of the couple as their 'next of kin' – the person they would wish to succeed to their estate or part of it if they were to die without leaving a Will, and the person to be notified in case of an accident or other emergency. Such couples organise themselves and live as one unit in society, which often involves purchasing or renting accommodation together and jointly purchasing household goods. It may be that no provision for contingencies such as the death of one of the parties or breakdown of the relationship is made. In addition, there are common misconceptions about the legal consequences of cohabiting or joint ownership, upon which couples may erroneously rely. It is telling that, despite numerous attempts to curb this practice, in 2018 tabloids and many of their readers still continue to refer to unmarried cohabiting couples as 'common law spouses', which phrase implies rights that do not exist in law. Indeed, a poll conducted by Resolution during the Cohabitation Awareness Week (27 November to 1 December) 2017 found that two-thirds of cohabitants were unaware that there is no such thing as 'common law marriage'.

1.06

As is often the case, popular expectation and the true legal position of cohabitants may not coincide. For example, unless specific provision is made, the law does not as a rule allow people to appoint a person of their choosing as their next of kin for any purpose, whereas upon marriage a spouse automatically assumes this role.

1.07

This state of affairs means that cohabiting couples (not married or in a civil partnership) are in much greater need than their married (or civil partner) counterparts of legal advice on the consequences of joint enterprises undertaken or proposed by them. Certainly, where advice is sought on breakdown of the relationship or on death, the emotional effects and social consequences as well as the legal implications may be far more complex where the relationship involved cohabitation than otherwise would be the case. It is therefore crucial that advisors are aware of this, not only when instructed to advise at a time of crisis, but also when advising during the currency of the relationship, for example in the joint purchase of a house. If clear advice as to the legal implications is given at that stage, and a record kept or a document drawn up setting out the parties' respective shares, or at least the stated intentions as to their beneficial interests, this may avoid a dispute in the future. It may also be a good time to mention the possibility of making Wills and the unsatisfactory nature of the law on intestacy with regard to cohabitants, who are in effect the chosen next of kin of the other.

1.08

By and large, UK domestic law has always recognised differences in its treatment of cohabitants and married couples or civil partners. Those differences are seen in particular with regard to property rights, rights in relation to the child and rights on the death of one partner. In an increasing number of situations, legal rights or restrictions similar to those applicable to married couples (or civil partners) have been extended to cohabiting couples. This has principally been done by statute. Examples include the right to succeed to an assured tenancy under s 17 Housing Act 1988, the right to claim financial provision against a deceased partner's estate (s 1(1)(ba) and 1(1A) Inheritance (Provision for Family and Dependants) Act 1975); and the right to apply for the transfer of the family home on relationship breakdown (Sch 7 FLA 1996). In other situations, the law totally ignores the cohabitation relationship.

1.09

The trend has been for legislation to extend rights of cohabitants whilst continuing to privilege marriage and civil partnership by giving lesser rights to cohabitants.

2 Social background and the impetus for reform

1.10

Marriage has always been society's preferred method of structuring family life and the rhetoric of past governments has been to reassert its importance, but with growing social awareness and acceptance of diversity and the increasing rejection of any concept of social stigma attaching to children born or raised in *non-traditional* families, as noted above, the number of cohabiting couples is continuing to increase.

1.11

Some couples cohabit rather than marry (or enter into a civil partnership) because one of them remains married to (or in a civil partnership with) another person, some because they have fundamental concerns about what marriage represents, some (opposite sex couples) because they are unable to enter into civil partnership which arguably does not carry with it the historical baggage of church and patriarchy.

1.12

Certainly, a large proportion of people now cohabit before marriage or civil partnership. Further, the age at which opposite sex couples marry has risen sharply in the 20 years to 2014. In 1994, the average male was aged 32.7 years old and the average female aged 30.3. By 2014, this had risen to 37 for men and 34.6 for women. Marriage rates provide a better indication of trends than simply looking at the number of marriages. This is because they take account of changes in the size of the unmarried adult population, as well as the number of marriages. Marriage rates show the number of marriages per 1,000 unmarried men and women aged 16 and over. Over this same period, the rate declined from 36.3 for men and 30.6 for women to 23.0 for men and 20.9 for women (Office for National Statistics Statistical Bulletin: Marriages in England and Wales: 2014 released on 14 March 2017).

1.13

Research on cohabitation that looks at the reasons why people choose to cohabit tends to confirm the reasons proffered by commentators or based on small-scale surveys. These reasons include: an ideological objection to marriage by one or both partners; a belief that a relationship is a private matter and not something which needs to be licensed by the state; a reluctance to marry following a previous failed marriage; a desire to avoid divorce on relationship breakdown and/or to avoid the legal consequences of divorce, such as payment of maintenance to a former partner; and freedom to vary the terms of a relationship without providing grounds for divorce. Perhaps a further, more troubling, contributory factor is the so-called 'common law marriage myth' whereby there is evidence that people falsely believe that heterosexual cohabitation carries with it the same legal implications as formal marriage (see eg Barlow and Duncan, 'New Labour's Communitarianism, Supporting Families and the "Rationality Mistake": Part II' [2000] *JSWFL*, vol 22(2), p 129).

1.14

For whatever reasons, there has been a marked increase in the number of couples who have decided to live together outside marriage or civil partnership and an increase in the number of children who live with parents who are not married (or civil partners). Whether or not the cohabitation is intended to endure in the short, medium or long term, such periods of cohabitation engender legal consequences about which lawyers are increasingly consulted, and in respect of which there is no neat body of law. Unless and until this situation changes, lawyers must search out disparate case law and be aware of which statutory provisions recognise the existence of cohabitants. They must, for example, distinguish those which include them in definitions as a member of their partner's family, from those which ignore the relationship and treat the partners as two unconnected individuals.

1.15

On 31 July 2007, the Law Commission consultation paper (Law Com 307) 'Cohabitation: The Financial Consequences of Relationship Breakdown' dealing with the termination of cohabitant relationships (whether by breakdown or death) was published by the Law Commission for England and Wales. In 2008, a Private Member's Bill was prepared with the aim of giving a measure of legal protection to cohabiting couples and family members, but it stalled in March 2009 after its second reading in the Commons. Although, in an interview reported in *The Times* on 3 February 2011, the then President of the Family Division, Sir Nicholas Wall, declared himself to be 'in favour of cohabitees having rights because of the injustice of the present situation', it was not until 9 October 2013 that another Private Member's Bill (the Cohabitation Rights Bill 2014–15) received its first reading in the House of Lords. As with its predecessor, it fell at the first hurdle. It was subsequently reintroduced as the Cohabitation Rights Bill 2015–16, receiving its first reading in the House of Lords on 4 June 2015 after which it too failed to progress. Reintroduced yet again as the Cohabitation Rights Bill 2016–17, it had its first reading in the House of Lords on 13 June 2016 and once again went no further.

1.16

The latest incarnation, the Cohabitation Rights Bill 2017–19, had its first reading in the House of Lords on 5 July 2017. As at the date of writing, no date has been announced for its second reading in the House of Lords. Although, history tells us that it is unlikely to progress further, not least because there is no appetite for reform in this area and it is not seen as a priority when the current government and Parliament are mired in the wrangling over Brexit, it is still necessary to highlight the (property and other financial) rights and protections potentially to be afforded to cohabitants under this Bill.

1.17

Cohabitants are defined as any two people whether of the same sex or the opposite sex in a relationship who live together as a couple and:

(i) are each treated in law as being mother, father or parent of the same minor child; or

(ii) there is in force in respect of a minor child either a joint residence order in respect of both of them or a child arrangements order stipulating arrangements such as when a child is to live, spend time or otherwise have contact with them; or

(iii) they are the natural parents of a child as yet unborn at the date when they ceased living together as a couple; or

(iv) they have lived together as a couple for a continuous period of three years or more.

Former cohabitants are two people who were cohabitants in a relationship but who have ceased living together as a couple.

1.18

Under s 8 the court may make a *financial settlement order* if satisfied that the applicant and the respondent have ceased living together as a couple, that the respondent has retained a benefit or the applicant an economic disadvantage as a result of qualifying contributions made by the applicant and having regard to the discretionary factors the court considers that it is just and equitable to make an order. Such an application can be made within 24 months of the date on which the cohabitants ceased living together as a couple (although in exceptional circumstances the court would be permitted to consider an application made after that date). A financial settlement order includes payment of a lump sum, the transfer, sale or settlement of property and a pension sharing order. Maintenance is not however one of the options available to the court.

A 'retained benefit' is a financial benefit which has been acquired, retained or enhanced by or for the respondent during the parties' cohabitation or in contemplation of the parties' cohabitation whether in the form of capital assets of any kind, income whether actual or potential, or earning capacity.

An 'economic disadvantage is a past, present or future financial loss, burden or cost sustained by the applicant during the parties' cohabitation or in contemplation of such cohabitation, or likely to be sustained by the applicant following its breakdown.

A 'qualifying contribution' is any financial or other contribution made by the applicant to the parties' shared lives or to the welfare of members of their families during the parties' cohabitation or in contemplation of such cohabitation or likely to be made by the applicant following its breakdown.

If the court determines to make a financial settlement order it may by its order adjust any retained benefit by reversing it insofar as it is reasonable and practicable to do so having regard to the discretionary factors. Similarly, any economic disadvantage may be shared equally between the parties.

In making a decision, the first consideration must be the welfare of any child who is still under 18.

The discretionary factors which must also be considered include:

(i) the welfare while a minor of any child of both parties who has not attained the age of 18;

(ii) the income, earning capacity, property and other financial resources which each of the parties has or is likely to have in the foreseeable future (including any pension, allowance or benefit paid or to be paid to either party or the eligibility of either party for a pension, allowance or benefit);

(iii) the financial needs and obligations which each of the parties has or is likely to have in the foreseeable future;

(iv) the welfare of any children who live with or might reasonably be expected to live with either party;

(v) the conduct of each party if but only if it is of such a nature that it would be inequitable to disregard it;

(vi) the circumstances in which the applicant made any qualifying contribution in particular if the respondent shows that the applicant made such contribution despite the respondent's express disagreement that it should be made.

1.19

Couples are permitted to opt out of such financial settlement orders and such *opt out agreement* must be in writing, signed as a deed and contain a statement by each of the persons entering into it to the effect that each of them:

(i) has separately received legal advice from a qualified practitioner as to the effect of the opt-out agreement and understands its effect;

(ii) agrees that a financial settlement order should not be available in the event that they cease living together as a couple; and

(iii) specifies whether there are any circumstances in which a financial settlement order may be available (eg only in relation to certain assets).

Such agreements can be varied or revoked by the parties at any stage. The court may vary or revoke an agreement if the court determines that the agreement is manifestly unfair to the applicant because of the circumstances in which the agreement was entered into or varied or any change in the circumstances of either party which was unforeseen at the time the agreement was entered into or varied. Similarly, cohabitation agreements or deeds of trust entered into by cohabitants may be varied or revoked by the court on application by one of them for a financial settlement order.

1.20

The Bill also extends rights on the death of a partner. A qualifying cohabitant would be entitled to a share of the estate of the other just as a spouse or civil partner would and could similarly make an application under the Inheritance (Provision for Family and Dependents) Act 1975 for provision from a deceased's estate.

3 Characteristics of the cohabitation relationship

1.21

The legal consequences of cohabitation can be far reaching, but unfortunately, cohabiting couples rarely seek direct legal advice about their situation until a crisis, commonly in the form of death, relationship breakdown or perhaps possession proceedings is upon them. There is a common misconception amongst cohabiting couples that rights equivalent to marriage (or civil partnership) are acquired after a certain period of cohabitation. Although the precise legal consequences of the various aspects of cohabitation will be dealt with in detail in the following chapters, a few illustrations of the possible pitfalls of cohabitation are appropriate here. They also underline the advisability of prevention, in the form of agreements or contracts, Wills and declarations of trust in relation to property, rather than the only cure available – litigation.

1.22

It is common for people to enter into joint mortgages or other loans without realising the full implications of joint and several liability. This problem is not exclusive to cohabiting couples, but they are often faced with the consequences. There is no maintenance available to either partner of a formerly cohabiting couple, no matter how long the period of cohabitation. Maintenance is available only to any children of the relationship and this will usually now be administered through the Child Maintenance Service (see Chapter 9). Where a property has been bought jointly by a couple, unless, as unfortunately is often not the case, there has been an express declaration of their respective beneficial interests in the conveyance, or in the form of a declaration of trust which sets out their shares, there is ample room for expensive litigation on relationship breakdown to resolve a dispute.

1.23

A cohabitant living in a property owned or rented in the sole name of his or her partner may be in a precarious position should the relationship end either through breakdown of the relationship or death of the partner, unless provision has previously been made. Similarly, if Wills are not made, then on the death of one of the couple, all his or her property, including personal belongings and savings not jointly held, and in the absence of any children, will pass to an estranged spouse not yet divorced, a parent, brother or sister, rather than the partner, although where there has been cohabitation for two years prior to death and in some other limited circumstances an application may be made to the court for some provision to be made out of the estate (see Chapters 3 and 4).

1.24

Before looking at the possibility of cohabitation contracts as a means of providing for at least some of the contingencies which may arise during the course of or at the end of cohabitation, it is proposed to look at certain of the consequences of cohabitation which do not fall easily into the specific subjects covered in the following chapters and in relation to which advice is often sought.

(a) Changing names

1.25

There is nothing to prevent a cohabitant from changing his or her surname so as to be known by the same name as his or her partner. Change of name by an adult can be achieved by means of a short statutory declaration, declared pursuant to the provisions of the Statutory Declarations Act 1835; or a deed setting out details of the original name and the new name which must be substituted for all purposes thereafter. It is advisable to have a deed witnessed by a solicitor to ensure acceptance by all authorities. The original declaration or deed is then sufficient proof for banks, building societies, the Passport Office and most other purposes, to ensure that official documentation is transferred into the new name.

1.26

It is possible to change one's name merely by common usage, and some argue that this is all that is required to legally change one's name, but for official purposes evidence of the change is normally required and thus a simple deed or declaration is advisable to avoid unnecessary complications and delay.

1.27

Names can also be changed by enrolled deed poll. The advantage of this is that there is an official record of the change, as the change of name is enrolled at the Filing and Record Department at the Central Office of the Supreme Court. However, the procedure is longer, including verification of the person's identity by means of a declaration from a Commonwealth citizen and householder resident in the UK who has known that person for ten years, an advert in the

London Gazette and payment of both the advertisement costs and a fee to the Court. (See the Enrolment of Deeds (Change of Name) Regulations 1994.) It is also a procedure which is open only to citizens of the UK, Commonwealth and the Republic of Ireland.

1.28

There are still some purposes for which an enrolled deed poll is the only acceptable option to effect a change of name. In particular, some professional bodies such as the General Medical Council require enrolment before the change of name will be accepted, and thus advisors should check whether the change needs to be registered with any body likely to have such a requirement.

1.29

Changing a child's name may present more difficulty and the right, or lack of right, to do so is inextricably bound up with the law relating to children. Even where the parents of a child were never married to each other, the father has not jointly registered the birth and no court order or recognised agreement has been made granting the father parental responsibility, it is not clear that the mother can now safely change the child's surname, or indeed any of the child's names, without reference to the father or an order of the court (see *Dawson v Wearmouth* [1999] 2 AC 308). Where the father's identity is unknown to the mother or where his consent is forthcoming, the change can be achieved by an adapted form of statutory declaration or deed executed by the mother. Similarly, where one of the parents dies without appointing a testamentary guardian, and there has been no previous court order, a surviving parent *with parental responsibility* is free to change a child's names if he or she so wishes. Otherwise, a specific issue order under s 8 Children Act 1989 (CA 1989), where there is no child arrangements ('lives with') order in force, can be sought to authorise any change of name (s 13(1) CA 1989). This will be discussed further in Chapter 2.

(b) Making wills

1.30

The position of cohabitants on intestacy (when the deceased dies without leaving a valid Will) renders them particularly vulnerable on their partner's death. As there is no blood or legal relationship between cohabitants, they do not come within any of the categories of person entitled to inherit on intestacy under s 46 Administration of Estates Act 1925. Thus, even where a cohabitant dies leaving no surviving relatives whatsoever, his or her estate will pass *bona vacantia* to the Crown rather than to the surviving partner. It is worthwhile noting that the Crown may be prepared to make an *ex gratia* payment to a cohabitant in such circumstances. Section 46(1)(vi) gives a discretion to make payments for dependants and 'other persons for whom the intestate may have been expected to make provision'. It is entirely discretionary but in fact may provide for a cohabitant who cannot make any other type of claim as they had neither lived with their partner for two years prior to the death, nor were they dependent upon them. As is detailed in Chapter 5, if reasonable financial provision has not been made for a cohabitant of two years' standing, then a claim under the Inheritance (Provision for Family and Dependants) Act 1975 as amended by the Law Reform (Succession) Act 1995 for maintenance may be made. An alternative claim exists for dependants of the deceased. Such an application is not without difficulty. It is bound to be costly and may well be resisted by those who would otherwise inherit under the terms of a Will or on intestacy. As discussed above, the Cohabitation Rights Bill 2017–19 would, if it becomes law, put cohabitants (as defined in the Bill) in the same position as spouses and civil partners.

1.31

Nonetheless, cohabitants must be advised of the advantages of Mutual Wills and the hazards of not making them. Mutual Wills, however, while avoiding the laws on intestacy, will not necessarily solve all cohabitants' problems, and much will depend on any responsibilities they have towards others. The following matters should be borne in mind when advising cohabitants in relation to Wills:

(i) Marriage and civil partnership always revokes a Will. Thus, if Mutual Wills have been made and the cohabiting partners marry each other, new Wills must be considered.

(ii) Wills can be revoked or changed at any time by a testator (or testatrix) and it is not possible to bind a partner to the terms of a particular Will.

(iii) Without a Will, a partner will not be entitled to anything belonging to the other partner on his or her death, not even personal belongings. Only jointly owned property which has not been declared to be beneficially owned in specified shares will pass to the surviving joint owner. Thus, as discussed in Chapter 3, if property is owned jointly as tenants in common, a deceased's partner's beneficial interest will pass to the joint owner only if bequeathed to him or her by Will.

(iv) Where a partner has a former spouse or civil partner and/or children who are still dependent upon him or her, they have a right to make a claim under the Inheritance (Provision for Family and Dependants) Act 1975 that provision be made for them out of the estate. This will inevitably mean that the surviving cohabiting partner who is a beneficiary under the Will, is forced to concede or compromise the claim; or become involved in expensive litigation if advised to resist the claim, which would undoubtedly deplete the estate. Thought therefore needs to be given as to how best to balance these competing claims on the estate in a Will, in a way which would be held to be fair if challenged. Life assurance may well provide the answer in a situation where there may not be enough to provide for everyone adequately.

(v) It is important to correctly identify a cohabitant beneficiary in a Will. A testator who refers in a Will to his or her cohabitant as their spouse or civil partner, may unintentionally defeat the gift, although case law has tended to give effect to the testator's intentions where these are clear (see, for example, *Re Brown, Golding v Brady* (1910) 26 TLR 257 and *Re Lynch, Lynch v Lynch* [1943] 1 All ER 168).

(c) Life assurance and pensions

1.32

Where cohabitants enter into joint debts such as a mortgage, attention should be drawn to the implications of joint and several liability on the death of one of the partners. The financial difficulties that this causes can be circumvented by taking out a mortgage protection policy, which would guarantee to pay off the debt in such a situation. Where one partner is financially dependent upon the other, life assurance is even more important to avoid the risk of losing the home on the death of the breadwinner. Strong advice should be given as to the consequences of failing to make appropriate provision, even where a Will has been made making the surviving dependent partner a beneficiary. Any life policy aiming to protect the surviving partner from sole or joint debts should either be assigned to the creditor such as the mortgagee or be written in trust for the other partner. The proceeds of the policy will not then form part of the estate of the deceased partner and so will escape potential Inheritance Tax (at 0% on the value of the deceased's estate up to £325,000 and then at 40% on such assets over £325,000).

1.33

Similarly, where there are likely to be competing claims on an estate from other dependants, a life policy written in trust for a cohabitant, has the advantage of not forming part of the deceased's estate, and thus could not be made subject to a claim under the Inheritance (Provision for Family and Dependants) Act 1975. If, on the other hand, the benefit of any such policy is bequeathed by Will, it forms part of the estate and could be diverted to other dependants by virtue of the provisions of the 1975 Act.

1.34

It should be noted that life assurance can only benefit a person who has an insurable interest in the assured's life pursuant to s 1 Life Assurance Act 1774 and will otherwise be void. Unlike spouses, civil partners and engaged couples, cohabitants are not deemed automatically to have such a financial interest in their partner's life but it is arguable that a financially dependent partner does have such an interest, which must be valued in accordance with the loss they are likely to suffer on the insured's death. Cohabitants are already recognised by several insurance companies as possessing such an interest, and on taking out life insurance it is important to clarify the position of the insurance company involved. Where there are joint liabilities such as a mortgage, there is obviously no difficulty in proving the financial interest in any event. The Cohabitation Rights Bill 2017–19, if it were to become law in its present form, would give clarity and certainty to this issue as s 16 states that 'each cohabitant in a relationship is to be presumed for the purposes of section 1 of the Life Assurance Act 1774 (no insurance to be made on lives, etc, by persons having no interest etc) to have an interest in the life of the other cohabitant in the relationship'.

1.35

A recent case offers hope to a cohabitant whose partner may have failed to nominate them to receive survivor's benefits under a pension scheme in the event of his or her death. In *Re an application by Denise Brewster for Judicial Review* [2017] UKSC 8, [2017] All ER (D) 74 (Feb), the appellant and her partner had lived together for about 10 years before becoming engaged two days before her partner suddenly died. The appellant's case was that her partner had completed a form in which he nominated her for payment of a survivor's pension, but as the form had not been received by the pension company it refused to pay out to her. The appellant argued that the absolute requirement of nomination imposed on unmarried cohabitants as a condition of eligibility for a survivor's pension constituted unlawful discrimination contrary to art 14 of the European Convention on Human Rights. The Supreme Court declared that such requirement should be disapplied and that the appellant was entitled to receive a survivor's pension under the scheme.

4 Cohabitation contracts

1.36

Couples who live together are able to regulate their (primarily financial) affairs by entering into cohabitation contracts. It is popularly thought that such a contract would be binding upon the parties in the event of breakdown of the relationship, as is indeed the case in other jurisdictions. At one time, such contracts would have been held to be void on public policy grounds as they arguably encouraged sexual immorality/pre-marital sex (see *Gammans v Ekins* [1950] 2 KB 328, [1950] 1 All ER 140, *CA and Diwell v Farnes* [1959] 2 All ER 379), but as living together before marriage became more and more commonplace the attitude of the courts has rightly changed with the times as society accepts the reality (and normalcy) of cohabitation.

1.37

Contractual freedom is one of the boasts of the English legal system. In 1938 Lord Atkin endorsed the following statement made by Lord Jessel in 1875:

> 'If there is one thing more than another public policy requires it is that men of full age and competent understanding shall have the utmost liberty of contracting and that their contracts when entered into freely and voluntarily shall be held sacred and shall be enforced by the Court of Justice: therefore you have this paramount public policy to consider, that you are not lightly to interfere with their freedom to contract.' (Lord Atkin in *Fender v St John-Mildmay* [1938] AC 1 citing Lord Jessel in *Printing and Numerical Registering Co v Sampson* (1875) LR 19 Eq 462 at page 465)

1.38

Whether or not a contract will be considered valid by the courts may depend on its contents as well as on a number of other factors. A cohabitation contract is a matter of a private rather than a public agreement, and thus the starting point is that the parties are free to agree the scope and nature of the terms themselves. Whether or not all or any of the terms of such a contract will be upheld by the courts may in any event not be the parties' only motive for having an agreement drawn up. In the case of *Sutton v Mischon De Reya and Gawor & Co* [2003] EWHC 3166 (Ch), [2004] 1 FLR 837, a 'deed of cohabitation' was entered into by a same sex couple who intended to cohabit in a 'master and slave' relationship. It was held that, although a cohabitation agreement might be valid, this agreement was an attempt to express a sexual relationship in property terms and was therefore invalid.

1.39

Cohabiting couples are likely to want a cohabitation contract to cover their rights and obligations both during cohabitation and on breakdown of the relationship in much the same way as couples who choose to enter into pre- (or post-) nuptial or pre- (or post-) civil partnership contracts seeking to regulate what is to happen about their property and finances if they subsequently separate. Although, in the marital/civil partnership context, such agreements are not strictly enforceable as contracts, they may be regarded as a very relevant factor to be considered with regard to the correct resolution of financial and property matters between the separated couple, with the burden shifting to the party seeking to resile from the agreement to satisfy the court that (because it is unfair to them) they should not be held to it. The Cohabitation Rights Bill 2017–19 makes reference to the validity of cohabitation agreements and, if it becomes law, would only in specified circumstances enable the court to vary its terms. Recently, in *Ely v Robson* [2016] EWCA Civ 774, [2016] All ER (D) 140 (Jul), the Court of Appeal even enforced an oral agreement! These developments bode well for the likely enforceability of cohabitation contracts made by consenting couples, where they are limited to issues of property; but before discussing enforceability in detail, the range of matters which cohabiting couples may wish to include in their contracts is considered.

(a) Contents

1.40

The exact content of each cohabitation contract is obviously a matter for the couple concerned. The advantage of drawing up a contract is that it requires the partners to consider, before there is any dispute, their respective expectations, both during the relationship and, in so far as can be foreseen, on breakdown.

1.41

It is also possible to have a contract that deals only with the eventuality of breakdown, without regulating the terms of the relationship itself. Some couples may wish to commit to writing every aspect of the agreements between them, down to the minutiae of the washing-up rota, whilst others may find this unnecessary yet see the value of discussing, agreeing and recording in advance their respective rights in relation to property, maintenance and any children. The more romantic may wish instead to trust their partner sufficiently to feel sure that in the event of breakdown, a satisfactory agreement would be reached. However, sadly, the bitterness that breakdown usually engenders often means that such trust is misplaced.

1.42

Some argue that to ask or advise couples to agree such matters in a formal legal document may raise problems within a relationship that were not previously present, and that accordingly matters are best left undocumented. However, it is submitted that if such an exercise reveals different understandings about the implications of a couple's arrangements, then surely this is a matter which merits discussion during the currency of the relationship where possible, rather than on breakdown when compromise or re-evaluation of the position may be much more difficult.

1.43

What should be the main tenets of a cohabitation contract? The agreement must be freely and voluntarily entered into. Both parties must have had access to independent and competent legal advice (whether or not they ultimately choose to seek or accept such advice). It would be better if such agreement was in writing but in so far as it deals with interests in land there is no reason why it cannot be made orally (*Ely v Robson* [2016] above). Further, and crucially, both parties will need to make full disclosure of all relevant financial and other circumstances. It is perfectly possible to include the agreed rules upon which the cohabitation is founded; these include whether or not other relationships are permitted; how the household chores should be shared; and the amount of leisure time the parties will spend together. However, no court would ever compensate a breach of any such terms with an order for specific performance (see *Balfour v Balfour* [1919] 2 KB 571, CA), as is the general rule with contracts for personal services. It is unlikely that a court would compensate a breach of the rules of the relationship (as opposed to the terms contained in the contract relating to property division), with damages, as it may be felt that the parties did not intend to be legally bound by such rules other than to provide evidence of breakdown of the relationship. Their inclusion can never be more than a record of the parties' intentions in those areas and should only be expressed as such in the contract.

1.44

Providing the contract meets the general criteria for an enforceable contract as set out above, contract terms which detail how property which is brought into the relationship or subsequently purchased individually or jointly by the parties, is to be treated on breakdown, may well be enforceable. At the very least it will be strong evidence of the parties' intentions at the time of the contract and will be valuable in case of dispute. Similarly, if a property is bought for occupation by the couple as a family home, a clause indicating that it is property which is to be beneficially jointly owned in stated shares may negative any contrary indication on the title documents, providing the cohabitation contract is executed as a deed. Provision can also be made for giving notice under the agreement to terminate the relationship and to provide for the agreed division of property at that juncture. A clause to pay maintenance on breakdown of the relationship to a partner who would otherwise have no right to maintenance will also prove enforceable if the contract is executed as a deed. Other relevant matters to be considered for inclusion in a cohabitation contract are:

(i) its duration – eg for the life of the relationship, a fixed period or until a specified event (eg marriage or civil partnership or the birth or adoption of a child);

(ii) treatment of property held at inception by either party – how this is to be treated;

(iii) treatment of property acquired during cohabitation – whether to be treated as joint property or not;

(iv) whether life insurance is to be taken out, how/by whom it is to be funded and who is to be nominated as beneficiary;

(v) whether a nomination is to be made to enable the other to receive survivor's benefits under an occupational pension fund;

(vi) children – whether or not to have any and if so, how to bring them up;

(vii) inheritance and Wills – what if anything they will leave to each other;

(viii) resolving disagreements – such as through relationship counselling or mediation; and

(ix) variation or renewal of the contract – parties are always able to vary their agreement, so preferably in writing.

(b) Enforceability

(i) Illegality on grounds of public policy

1.45

Contracts for immoral purposes, which of course include sexual immorality, are illegal and consequently unenforceable. In *Diwell v Farnes* [1959] 2 All ER 379, CA, Ormerod LJ stated at page 384E that 'such joint venture must depend on a contract express or implied between the parties which being founded on an immoral consideration, would not be enforceable'. As stated above, recently, in *Sutton v Mischon De Reya and Gawor & Co* (above), a master/slave sexual relationship set out in a cohabitation agreement rendered it invalid.

1.46

Any term that provides for the payment of maintenance or some other form of financial provision by one cohabitant to the other during their relationship is unlikely to be enforced (unless this agreement is made by deed). The courts have held that a similar agreement between married partners lacks the intention to enter into legal relations (*Balfour v Balfour* [1919] above). However, if the agreement provides for such payment to be made following the breakdown of their relationship, that may not be subject to the same objection, but the court may still hold such an agreement to be void on public policy grounds. It is worth noting here that of the financial remedies being mooted for former cohabitants under the Cohabitation Rights Bill 2017–19, maintenance is not one of them.

1.47

Given that cohabitation is now so socially accepted and even affords parties statutory protection in some areas, would a cohabitation contract be found void on the grounds that it is prejudicial to the institution of marriage? Cohabitation agreements cannot be said to undermine the institution of marriage and are unlikely to prevent cohabitants subsequently choosing to marry (or in the case of same sex couples to become civil partners).

1.48

Even if the cohabitation contract expressly stated that the parties would not subsequently marry (or in the case of same sex couples become civil partners), it would not be unenforceable on this ground alone, as it is possible to sever the offending part of the contract leaving the remainder of the terms, for example, those dealing with jointly owned property, intact and enforceable.

1.49

A more positive view regarding the enforceability of cohabitation contracts, despite the lack of modern judicial authority on the point, is given weight by recent decisions which will be more fully discussed in Chapters 3 and 11 in relation to housing and property. In these cases the courts have enforced promises made to 'mistresses' by their partners. Promises to continue to provide accommodation on breakdown of the relationship have been enforced by imputing a licence for life (see *Tanner v Tanner* [1975] 1 WLR 1346 and *Chandler v Kerley* [1978] 1 WLR 693). The courts have also found resulting and constructive trusts where cohabitants have purchased a property in the sole name of one of them, but their actions showed it was clearly intended as a joint venture (see, for example, *Hammond v Mitchell* [1992] 2 All ER 109; *Oxley v Hiscock* [2004] EWCA Civ 546, [2004] 3 All ER 703 for consideration by the court of parties' intentions where there is no written agreement; also *Stack v Dowden* [2007] UKHL 17, [2007] 2 AC 432 and *Jones v Kernott* [2011] UKSC 53, [2011] 3 FCR 495). In none of these cases has there been any mention that such agreements may be illegal or void on public policy grounds, although in cases relying on trusts, such a consideration is irrelevant as the courts apply the law of trusts rather than the law of contract.

1.50

Where there is a child of an unmarried relationship, the courts have endorsed the making of binding agreements for maintenance for mother and child. It was said in *Horrocks v Forray* [1976] 1 WLR 230, at page 239: 'when an illegitimate child has been born, there is certainly nothing contrary to public policy in the parents coming to an agreement which they intend to be binding in law, for the maintenance of mother and child'. Of course, where there are children, it is not possible to oust the jurisdiction of the Child Maintenance Service or the court with regard to maintenance or financial provision, but certainly a clause providing for the payment of maintenance to one or other of the partners for a child on relationship breakdown would seem to be enforceable providing the other ingredients for a valid contract are not wanting and no application has been made to the Child Maintenance Service for an assessment of liability.

(ii) Absence of intention to create legal relations

1.51

There is a rebuttable presumption that parties to an agreement regarding domestic arrangements do not intend to be legally bound. The principle was set out in the case of *Balfour v Balfour* [1919] 2 KB 571 where a promise by a husband who worked abroad, to his wife who had to stay behind on medical grounds, that he would pay her £30 per month was held to be unenforceable both because she had provided no consideration and also because the domestic nature of the agreement showed that there was no intention to create legal relations. Atkin LJ at page 578 said:

> 'Those agreements, or many of them, do not result in contracts at all ... even though there may be what as between other parties would constitute consideration for the agreement ... They are not contracts ... because the parties did not intend that they should be attended by legal consequences.'

However, where there is a written agreement, especially if it has been drawn up by a legal advisor, this should be enough to rebut the presumption, as parties do not have agreements drawn up unless there is an intention that they should be legally binding (see *Merritt v Merritt* [1970] 1 WLR 1211, CA).

1.52

The case of *Layton v Martin* [1986] 2 FLR 227 provides a word of warning to cohabitants who indicate that they wish to draw up their own agreements without taking legal advice. In that case, the man wrote to the woman asking her to live with him, and offering her 'financial security during my life – and on my death'. A few months later she went to live with him; they stayed together for eight years, although they separated two years before his death. However, the court refused to enforce the alleged contract against his estate and Scott at page 239 underlined the difficulty faced:

> 'In family or quasi family situations there is always the question whether the parties intended to create a legal binding contract between them. The more general and less precise the language of the so-called contract, the more difficult it will be to infer that intention.'

1.53

The content of a contract may also influence the court's view. Thus the less domestic detail that is contained, and the more terms there are relating to more legalistic matters, such as a statement of respective interests in jointly owned property, the more likely a court would be to infer the requisite intention. In any event, this is a hurdle easily overcome by cohabitants who do wish to create a binding contract; an advisor drafting a contract can, to ensure the intention is unambiguous, specifically recite the intention to be bound.

(iii) Contract void for uncertainty

1.54

As with any contract, if the terms are so vague and uncertain that they are incapable of enforcement, then this will either be a term which the court ignores, or, if the uncertainty comprises terms which are fundamental to the operation of the contract, may vitiate the whole contract. Thus, a term agreeing to make financial provision without any indication of the nature or extent or the rules according to which such provision could be ascertained would be void for uncertainty. Thus, advisors drafting a cohabitation contract should have this potential problem in mind.

(iv) Absence of consideration

1.55

As with any contract, there must be consideration for a cohabitation agreement to be enforceable. In the case of cohabitation agreements, the consideration for one party's agreeing to make financial provision for the other could be argued to be the act of cohabiting with the other party or perhaps one party giving up a secure tenancy. If the agreement is in the form of a deed, no consideration for the bargain is necessary. Thus, if there is any doubt about consideration, the agreement should be by deed. Advisors should therefore always recommend that a deed be executed.

(v) Contract voidable for undue influence

1.56

A finding of undue influence exercised by one party over the other inducing that person to enter into the contract will vitiate the contract in its entirety. If the terms of a contract are heavily weighted in favour of one of the parties, it may be susceptible to such a finding. If it can be established that the agreement was freely and voluntarily entered into, that both parties had access to independent and competent legal advice (whether or not they ultimately choose to seek or accept such advice) before signing and that both parties have made full disclosure of all relevant financial and other circumstances, this will help counter any allegation of undue influence. As advisors may advise only one party to a contract (to avoid potential conflict of interest), it is obviously desirable, where there is any hint of inequality of bargaining power, to ensure that the less favoured party is urged to seek independent legal advice.

5 Conclusion

1.57

In her Briefing Paper to the House of Commons entitled *'Common law marriage' and cohabitation*, dated 9 March 2017, Catherine Fairbairn reported that Advicenow has published a useful guide which is available on its website on 'How to make a living together agreement' which also includes a template of an agreement. It offers the following:

> 'Living together agreements have a slightly odd status in law. They aren't binding unless you write them as a formal legal deed, but the court will usually follow them as long as what you agreed is fair, and you were both honest about your finances when you made the agreement. A court is even more likely to uphold the agreement if both of you also had some legal advice about what you were doing before signing the agreement. If you want to ensure it is binding, take your completed agreement to a solicitor and ask them to write it as a legal "deed".'

1.58

What are the advantages and disadvantages of entering into a cohabitation agreement, and how should clients be advised? It seems clear that where there are children, subject to not ousting the jurisdiction of the court, agreements between parents are welcomed. Furthermore, as long as the provision of sexual services is not explicit consideration, the contract is executed as a deed and the other requirements for a valid contract discussed above are met, there seems a strong chance that the English courts would enforce a contract which contemplates the division of property and financial support on relationship breakdown. In any event, if there is an agreement between parties, regardless of whether or not one would in fact seek to enforce it against the other on breakdown, it must be evidence of the parties' intentions at the time of the agreement. As such, at the very least, it provides the starting point either on separation, or on death, when there is a risk of a dispute with relatives.

1.59

An agreement may confer on a party rights he or she could not otherwise acquire; from the other party's point of view, this binds them to something they did not have to concede, yet in happier times actually wanted to give to their partner. Advisors of course need to point out the possible future disadvantages. Another potential disadvantage of entering into a cohabitation contract is the fact that it is of course impossible to cover every eventuality. A comprehensive agreement with some omissions may imply that their absence means they were deliberately excluded and so are not to be implied by a court. This again underlines the need either to make the contract clear in its limitations, for example, by confining it to maintenance and without prejudice to any other claims against property; or to be as comprehensive as possible. The best result may be achieved by a series of separate agreements dealing individually with maintenance and property during the relationship and on breakdown. These could then be amended as circumstances changed.

1.60

It is important to remember that most cases concerning relationship breakdown are settled out of court. A cohabitation agreement will always provide a starting point, or provide for mediation before resorting to court proceedings. In this sense, providing the potential conflict of interest between the parties is kept firmly in mind by advisors at the drafting stage, there is much to be said for encouraging cohabitants to set down their affairs in an agreement, despite the doubts surrounding its legal enforceability. As is always the case when advising a client about a Will, advisors must emphasise the need to keep the situation under review, and to vary the contract from time to time as circumstances change.

CHAPTER 2

The status of children

1 Parental status (Parentage)

2.01

Until comparatively recently, problems over parentage were largely concerned with proof of the identity of the (biological) father. Now, however, the question of who the legal parent is can be more complex when considering the status of children born through artificial insemination, *in vitro* fertilisation, ova and embryo donation and surrogacy.

2.02

Unless the child is an adopted child, the legal mother is the woman who has given birth to the child. The Human Fertilisation and Embryology Act 2008 (HFEA 2008), s 33(1) provides that 'the woman who is carrying or has carried a child as a result of the placing in her of an embryo or of sperm and eggs, and no other woman, is to be treated as the mother of the child'. The legal father is the man whose sperm fertilised the egg (although if the legal mother is married then the rebuttable presumption is that her husband is the legal father). Despite the removal of legal discrimination towards children born outside marriage, the Children Act 1989 (CA 1989) does nothing to alter the position of any category of unmarried father on the birth of his child. Thus the legal situation of the father of a child born in a stable relationship between cohabitants is identical to that of the father of a child born of a more casual encounter, with neither acquiring any automatic legal parental responsibility for their children. This discriminatory effect of the legislation on unmarried fathers (held to be 'Human Rights Act compliant' (*B v United Kingdom* [2000] 1 FLR 1)) takes no account of the fact that particularly cohabiting fathers play exactly the same role as married fathers in their child's life. In July 2017, the Office for National Statistics reported that in 2016 two-thirds of the babies born outside marriage or civil partnership have parents who were living together (at the date of their birth or registration). Since 1998, over 60% of all births registered outside marriage or civil partnership each year have been to a cohabiting couple; in 2016 the figure was 67%. This is consistent with increases in the number of couples cohabiting rather than entering into marriage or civil partnership.

2.03

Before the CA 1989, when a child was born to parents who were not married, all the legal rights relating to the child vested solely in the mother. Section 4 of the CA 1989 replaced and assimilated parental rights orders with 'parental responsibility orders' and also enabled both parents to agree to share parental responsibility for the child. A parental responsibility agreement avoids the need for a court order, provided it is recorded in a document in the prescribed form and registered in accordance with the regulations made under the Act. Yet the unmarried father's status at the time of the child's birth remains unaffected, whatever the nature of the relationship between the parents. As things currently stand, there is not even a presumption of paternity where unmarried parents were living together at the date of a child's conception, as exists in some other jurisdictions. Thus, if both parents wish the father to have legal recognition, then various steps have to be taken so that he acquires parental responsibility and these will be considered in the following sections. Similar concerns arise over the acquisition of parental responsibility by an unmarried woman in a same sex relationship whose partner by virtue of giving birth to their child is treated in law as the legal mother.

2 Registering the birth

2.04

The birth of any child must be registered within 42 days and this legal duty rests on the mother alone where the parents are unmarried (Births and Deaths Registration Act 1953 (the 1953 Act), s 10). Unfortunately, where the parents are not married and both wish to be recorded as parents on the birth certificate, the procedure is not as simple as for married parents. Strictly, in the absence of any specific issue order concerning the child's name (s 8 CA 1989) or of an order or formal agreement granting the father parental responsibility (s 4 CA 1989), the choice of name to be registered for the child lies with the mother. However, there is nothing to prevent her from registering the child with the father's surname if she wishes, or indeed with any other surname. It should perhaps be noted here, however, that where there is a dispute as to the name in which the child is to be registered and the mother is aware of this, the House of Lords (now, the Supreme Court) have endorsed the view that the matter should be referred to the court regardless of whether or not the father has parental responsibility (see *Dawson v Wearmouth* [1999] 1 FLR 1167, per Lord Mackay of Clashfern at p 1173B).

2.05

The unmarried father is under no *duty* to register the birth and is not automatically recorded as the child's father on the register even if his surname is being given to the child. A record of the father's identity on the register can only be achieved in one of the following ways. First, and most simply, a joint request by the mother and father (who must both attend in person to sign the birth register together) that the father's name be recorded will be sufficient. If this is not possible, then the identity of the father can be recorded by either the mother or father alone if one of them completes a statutory declaration of parentage form (as to the child's paternity) and the other takes the signed form to register the birth. Otherwise, the father's name can be recorded on the written request of either the mother or the father, providing one of the following documents is produced: a parental responsibility agreement made between the parents in proper form or a parental responsibility order from the court. In addition a declaration that the order or agreement is still subsisting is needed. It is also possible, by virtue of s 10A of the 1953 Act, to re-register the birth at a later stage to include the father's name. The requirements and procedure remain exactly the same and thus any of the methods described will achieve this end. However, once the child has reached the age of sixteen, their consent to the re-registration is also needed. Registration of the identity of the father of a child of unmarried parents on the birth certificate, is *prima facie* evidence of paternity and shifts the burden of proof onto the father if he later wishes to dispute it. Registration of the father's identity on the birth certificate does not of itself, however, confer any rights or duties upon the father.

3 Parental responsibility

(a) The general position

2.06

This is defined in s 3(1) as: '... all the rights, duties, powers, responsibilities and authority which by law a parent of a child has in relation to the child and his property.' Parental responsibility exists for the benefit of the child and not for the benefit of the parent. In *Re H-B (contact)* [2015] EWCA Civ 389, Munby P reiterated that 'first and foremost, and even more importantly, parental responsibility involves duties owed by each parent to the child'.

2.07

As has been detailed previously, only the mother in an unmarried family automatically acquires parental responsibility on the birth of a child (s 2(2) CA 1989), leaving unchanged the unmarried father's position of initial disadvantage, although by virtue of s 2(2)(b) CA 1989 as amended by the Adoption and Children Act 2002, s 111(5) he can subsequently acquire it. Questions of with whom the child should live or spend time with (formerly residence and contact) and parental responsibility following breakdown of an unmarried relationship will be explored in Part II (see Chapter 8) and will not therefore be discussed in this chapter.

2.08

Unmarried parents can share parental responsibility, but even where no order or agreement has been made, some minimum standards are imposed upon the unmarried father. Where the father (or indeed any person) lives with a child, limited duties are found in s 1 Children and Young Persons Act 1933 to ensure the child receives an education and is not neglected or maltreated. Section 3(5) CA 1989 provides that any person who does not have parental responsibility but who has care of the child may do what is reasonable in all the circumstances of the case for the purpose of safeguarding or promoting the child's welfare, for example, consenting to emergency medical treatment for the child.

2.09

In addition, as with married parents, where one or both unmarried parents have acquired parental responsibility, all parental rights which exist only for the child's protection diminish as the child increases in age and understanding as was decided in the case of *Gillick v West Norfolk and Wisbech Area Health Authority* [1986] AC 112.

2.10

Whilst it is now possible for unmarried parents to share parental responsibility without obtaining a court order, s 4(1)(b) CA 1989 requires an agreement between parents to share parental responsibility to be in prescribed form and recorded in a prescribed way. Joint registration of the birth vests parental responsibility in the unmarried father, if the child was born after 1 December 2003.

(b) The advantages and disadvantages of sharing parental responsibility

2.11

The parental responsibility agreement which must be made in the prescribed form [C (PRA1)] requires each parent's signature to be witnessed by a lay justice or officer of the court (Family Proceedings (Amendment No 4) Rules 1994) and must be recorded thereafter at the Central Family Court.

2.12

Before considering the procedure, it must be pointed out that, as matters currently stand, a mother who agrees to share parental responsibility pursuant to s 4 CA 1989 is giving up her right to sole parental responsibility of the child unless and until another court order is made restoring it. Once parental responsibility is conferred on the father, it cannot be unilaterally withdrawn by the mother. Thus, a decision to share parental responsibility at an early stage in the child's life may on the face of it have important ramifications if the relationship later breaks down and the arrangements for the child or children cannot be agreed between the parents. The existence of a parental responsibility agreement or order will be a factor to be taken into account when making orders relating to the child on breakdown and may influence how the court views the father's role in the child's life. Any mother agreeing to share parental responsibility should accordingly be advised that, in effect, she is placing herself in a position much more akin to that of a married mother *vis-à-vis* her rights over her child. In a stable relationship, she may well be happy to take such a step, but should know at the outset the possible ramifications. As the law confers parental responsibility on unmarried fathers who jointly register the birth, the weighing of these factors will need to be done initially at the point of birth registration. These considerations also reveal a possible conflict of interest between the parents, and separate advice may be desirable where the father seeks an agreement or intends to apply for an order. Having said this, however, case law has shown the courts to be very willing indeed to grant parental responsibility orders, even on opposed applications, as discussed below.

2.13

How much real difference a parental responsibility order or agreement makes in practice to unmarried cohabiting parents who later separate is debatable. Wherever there is a dispute, the child's interests are paramount, and thus it is likely to be the degree of parental involvement and the respective circumstances of the parents which will be critical. An unmarried father who has joint parental responsibility, but who has otherwise shown little interest in the child, will not succeed in a dispute on breakdown to any greater degree than a comparable father without parental responsibility. However, it is conceivable that an unmarried father who has had the major role in bringing up a child may find it easier to obtain an order that the child live with him on breakdown (a child arrangements 'lives with' order) if the mother has legally acknowledged joint parental responsibility. In *Re P (a minor) (parental responsibility order)* [1994] 1 FLR 578 and in *Re S (minor) (parental responsibility)* [1995] 2 FLR 648, it was determined that a parental responsibility order does not give the father the right to interfere in day-to-day issues, nor override the mother who had a residence order. Such an order confers status, rather than power. Section 4(3) also gives the court power to discharge a parental responsibility order or agreement on the application of a person with parental responsibility for the child concerned where the court has given leave for the application to be made. However, this course of action would have to be in the child's best interests and overcome the no order presumption laid down in s 1(5) CA 1989, and it seems clear that a court would be unlikely to take a father's parental responsibility away without very good reason, once it had been given. In *Re P (termination of parental responsibility)* [1995] 1 FLR 1048, the court did revoke a parental responsibility agreement made without the mother's knowledge that the father had abused the child, stating that it would be wrong in these circumstances for the parents to have equal status in respect of the child. More recently, in *Re D (a child)* [2014] EWCA Civ 31 the Court of Appeal upheld a decision to terminate parental responsibility acquired by joint registration of the birth of a child, where the father had been convicted of sexually abusing children of a previous relationship.

2.14

The most common way for unmarried fathers to acquire parental responsibility for their child is now by joint birth registration Where this is done or where a parental responsibility agreement is entered into, unlike the position in relation to the making of a parental responsibility order by the courts, there is no judgment made on whether giving the father parental responsibility for the child is in the child's best interests. The mother's consent is all that is needed to effect this important change in legal status. Indeed, although a court has power to refuse to make an order even if both parents consent, it has no jurisdiction to prevent parents from either jointly registering the birth or entering into a parental responsibility agreement even where the child is in care and the Local Authority oppose the agreement (see *Re X (minor) (care proceeding: parental responsibility)* [2000] 1 FLR 517). The advantage from the mother's point of view is that a parental responsibility order, like a parental responsibility agreement (or the joint registration of the child's birth), ostensibly extends parental duties, as well as rights, to the father. Whilst such duties (including the duty to maintain a child) usually exist regardless of whether or not a father has parental responsibility, entering into a parental responsibility agreement (or making a joint registration) is a public declaration of commitment to the child.

2.15

A parental responsibility order or an agreement under s 4 CA 1989, like a joint registration, also means that should the mother die, the father automatically becomes the child's guardian, as happens where a child's parents are married. However, without any of these, unless the mother has appointed the father (or some other person) testamentary guardian in accordance with the provisions of s 5(3) and (5) CA 1989 (see para 2.26), the child will be left without a legal guardian. The father who wanted to be responsible for his child would have to apply to the court for a s 4 order at that stage, or for a s 8 child arrangements ('lives with') order, or for an order appointing him guardian pursuant to s 5(1) CA 1989.

2.16

Conversely, where a s 4 order exists, s 5(7) provides that any appointment by the mother of a testamentary guardian other than the father does not take effect until after the death of the father with parental responsibility, unless there was a child arrangements ('lives with') order in favour of the mother at the date of her death. Thus, from the mother's point of view, the joint registration of the child's birth, a s 4 order or the entering into of a parental responsibility agreement will mean that the father will automatically become the child's guardian on her death even if this is against her wishes. Where the parents are still living together at the time of the mother's death, this would seem to be appropriate. The situation is more difficult where the parents have joint parental responsibility but the child has lost touch with the father following breakdown, as discussed in Chapter 8 below.

2.17

A s 4 agreement, or order, in the same was as a joint registration, is also recognition by the father of paternity and of his duties towards his child, including the duty to maintain, although a parental responsibility order was not withheld by the court to force a father to meet his maintenance obligations in *Re H (minor) (parental responsibility order)* [1996] 1 FLR 867. It enables a father to consent to medical treatment and jointly take decisions about, for example, schooling, or change of surname, which are otherwise in law, at least in principle, the sole province of the unmarried mother. It should be noted that even where there is no joint parental responsibility, s 2(9) and (10) CA 1989 enable a person who has parental responsibility to arrange for some or all of it to be met by one or more persons acting on his or her behalf, although parental responsibility cannot be surrendered or transferred to another person.

2.18

It is thought that where parents are cohabiting in a stable relationship, they may both wish to place themselves as nearly as possible in the position of married parents and this is the intention and effect of both joint registration and of a s 4 agreement. Nonetheless, some distinctions, although not necessarily disadvantages, remain. The citizenship of a child of unmarried parents is still transmitted through the mother rather than the father, and a child will acquire his or her domicile of origin from the mother not the father. It should be noted though that since 1 July 2006 the unmarried father who has not acquired parental responsibility has the right to pass on UK citizenship to his child (see Nationality, Immigration and Asylum Act 2002, s 9, amending the British Nationality Act 1981, s 50; the Nationality, Immigration and Asylum Act 2002 (Commencement No 11) Order 2006, SI 2006/1498, and the British Nationality (Proof of Paternity) Regulations 2006, SI 2006/1496). Although it is important for both parties to understand the consequences of joint registration and of a s 4 agreement or order, unless breakdown or irreconcilable differences relating to the child are foreseen, such joint registration, agreement or order will enable parenthood to be shared in the same way as it is by married parents and be proof that both parents are keen to share with the other the associated rights and duties.

(c) Orders and agreements for joint parental responsibility

2.19

As discussed above, a parental responsibility agreement (conferring parental responsibility on the unmarried father, which he will then share with the mother) must be made in the prescribed form (ie C(PRA1)) which must be formally executed and duly recorded/registered at the Central Family Court. These formal requirements are intended to minimise the prospect of pressure being applied to the mother to enter into the agreement and to eliminate the risk of the mother's signature being forged. There is no express rule preventing a parent under 18 from entering into such an agreement. It is also possible for parents to make an agreement in respect of their child who is the subject of an interim care order and of an application in care proceedings (*Re X (parental responsibility agreement: children in care)* [2000] 2 All ER 66, [2000] 1FLR 517). It is still the case that the annual number of agreements registered since the Children Act 1989 came into force in 1991 remains very small, not least because parental responsibility can be acquired by the joint registration of the child's birth and the father's inclusion on the birth certificate.

The Family Court and the High Court both have jurisdiction to hear applications for parental responsibility orders under s 4 CA 1989, although the need to apply for an order seems most likely to arise upon breakdown or, perhaps, on the death of the mother, as there should be no need to issue proceedings if the parents agree, as the parties can achieve the same end by entering into an agreement as described above. Only the father himself can apply for an order and the court cannot of its own motion make such an order. An order can be made as long as the child is still under 18. Applications are made by the father's completing form C1. This is then issued by the court and the applicant must serve copies on the mother and on every other person whom the applicant believes may have parental responsibility for the child whether at the date of the application or previously where the child is the subject of a care order (Family Procedure Rules (FPR) 2010, 12.31). Written supporting evidence takes the form of signed statements containing a declaration that the maker believes them to be true. In addition, the starting point for the court when asked to make a s 4 order is that it must not make any order under the Act unless it considers that to do so would be better for the child than making no order at all (s 1(5)).

2.20

Accordingly, in deciding whether or not to make such an order, the court must apply the principle that the child's welfare is paramount and it must be satisfied that making the order sought would be better for the child than making no order. Where the applicant has shown commitment to the child there is a presumption that a parental responsibility order should be made (providing there was no evidence that it would adversely affect the child's welfare) *(Re G (a minor) (parental responsibility order)* [1994] 1 FLR 504, CA; *Re E (a minor) (parental responsibility:*

blood tests) [1995] 1 FLR 392, *CA*; *Re H (parental responsibility: maintenance)* [1996] 1 FLR 867; *Re P (parental responsibility)* [1997] 2 FLR 722, CA).

2.21

Case law gives guidance on when parental responsibility orders under s 4 CA 89 should be granted. In *Re H (minors) (illegitimate children: father: parental rights) (No 2)* [1991] 1 FLR 214, Balcombe LJ set out some of the factors to be considered by the court when asked to make a s 4 order. These include the degree of commitment shown by the father to the children; the degree of attachment between the father and the children; and the father's reasons for applying for an order. In this case, although the children were in care and the subject of an application that they be freed for adoption, a parental rights order was made giving him *locus standi* in the application. So, if the father has played an important part in the child's life and is devoted to the child, the facts may justify granting him a parental responsibility order *(Re J-S (a child) (contact: parental responsibility)* [2002] EWCA Civ 1028, [2003] 1 FLR 399).

2.22

In *D v Hereford and Worcester County Council* [1991] 1 FLR 205, Ward J expanded on the text in *Re H* (above) and suggested that the test should be, has the father, or will he, 'behave with parental responsibility for the child'. Here again the child was in care. In *S v R (parental responsibility)* [1993] 1 FCR 331, FD, it was held that the court should expressly consider the matters in the judgment of Balcombe LJ in *Re H* (above) and in *Re H (a minor) (contact and parental responsibility)* [1993] 1 FCR 85, CA, in which a parental responsibility order was granted to a father, even though it was appropriate to refuse him contact, in order to give him the right to be consulted before adoption of the child. The Court of Appeal in *Re C and V (minors) (parental responsibility and contact)* [1998] 1 FLR 392 emphasised that the making of an order was designed to confer status and it would normally be in a child's best interests for an order to be granted. The court did, however, refuse to make a parental order in *Re T (a minor) (parental responsibility: contact)* [1993] 2 FLR 450, where a father had shown total disregard for a child's welfare and attacked the mother while holding the baby and then detained it for nine days after a two-hour contact period. Similarly, in *Re C and V* (above) the court made clear that an order should be refused where a father's motives for seeking an order are improper as occurred in *Re P (parental responsibility)* [1998] 2 FLR 96, in which case it was found that the order was being sought to interfere inappropriately with the exercise of the mother's parental responsibility, against whom he had made unfounded allegations and as occurred in *Re M (handicapped child: parental responsibility)* [2001] 2 FLR 342 in which it was held that the order was intended to interfere with and possibly undermine the mother's care for the child. The court may however take the view that such improper interference may be effectively controlled by s 8 orders in which case parental responsibility may be granted (see *Re S (a minor) (parental responsibility)* [1995] 2 FLR 648.

2.23

Where the parents are living apart, the father may want the child to live with him. If the court grants the child arrangements ('lives with') order sought, then it must also make a s 4 parental responsibility order (s 12(1) CA 1989). If the father is granted a child arrangements ('spends time with') order the court 'must decide whether it would be appropriate … for him to have parental responsibility for the child and, if it decides that it would be appropriate … must also make an order under section 4 giving him … that responsibility' (s 12(1A) CA 1989, as amended by the Children and Families Act 2014).

2.24

Where a s 4 order or agreement has been made, s 2(7) CA 1989 provides that each person who has parental responsibility may act alone without the other in meeting that responsibility. On the face of the Act, there is no right of veto where the other person with parental responsibility disagrees with an action to be taken in relation to the child, although either parent is entitled to apply for a 'specific issue order' under s 8(1) CA 1989 (see Chapter 8 below) to determine a specific question which has arisen in relation to any aspect of parental responsibility. The only limits on the independent exercise of parental responsibility provided by the Act are that nothing incompatible with any order made under the provisions of the Act must be done; and the right of independent action does not override the need to obtain the consent of another person if this is required by statute, such as for the purposes of adoption. However, despite its plain language, the courts have not always given s 2(7) its literal meaning and seem to take the view that a parent with parental responsibility has the right to be consulted even where there is no statutory duty to do so. In *Re H (parental responsibility)* [1998] 1 FLR 855 Butler-Sloss LJ indicated that a father with parental responsibility had 'the right to be consulted on schooling, serious medical problems and other important occurrences in the child's life'. And in *Re J (specific issue orders: child's religious upbringing and circumcision)* [2000] 1 FLR 571d, the Court of Appeal agreed that 'circumcision must join the exceptional categories where disagreement between holders of parental responsibility must be submitted to the court for determination'. Thus, despite the ostensible power to use parental responsibility jointly and severally given in s 2(7), this has been interpreted to imply a duty to consult on at least some issues.

2.25

An agreement or an order conferring parental responsibility automatically ends when the child reaches the age of 18 (CA 1989 s 91(7) and (8)), if the father subsequently marries the mother (when the father then has parental responsibility by operation of law – CA 1989 s 2(1)) or if the child is adopted (Adoption and Children Act 2002, s 46). Otherwise, only a court can bring a parental responsibility order or agreement to an end. The application may be made by one of the persons who has parental responsibility; or, with leave of the court, by the child providing he or she has sufficient understanding to make the application (s 4(3) and (4)).

2.26

The unmarried father may also acquire parental responsibility as a guardian. This can occur where the mother has appointed him guardian on her death (CA 1989 s 5(3)) or the father may, after her death, apply to the court to be appointed a guardian (CA 1989 s 5(1)), instead of applying for a s 4 order. The CA 1989 procedure can be used to vary any appointment previously made by Will. In any event, where there is a surviving parent with parental responsibility in whose favour a child arrangements ('lives with') order is in place, the appointment of a testamentary guardian takes effect only on the death of the surviving parent.

2.27

To summarise, if unmarried cohabiting parents wish to share parental responsibility this can be done by means of their joint registration of the birth of their child or by entering into a parental responsibility agreement which meets the requirements of s 4 CA 1989. Where there is no agreement, the father can apply to the court for an order and must show that to make an order is better for the child than making no order at all. This has not proved difficult even where the mother does not agree but is the child's prime carer, although the attitude of the courts to this issue may vary. In *Re A (minors)* [1993] Fam Law 464, FD, the judge made a parental responsibility order despite the mother's opposition. The father had been present at the birth, was registered as the father on the child's birth certificate and had lived with the mother for three months before their relationship deteriorated. Having not seen the child for a year he applied for both contact and parental responsibility orders, both of which were made, with the judge commenting that he had shown considerable commitment to the child and loved the child as a married father would have done. In practice, it is now clear that a father who has lived with the mother and child and who has been or is likely to be granted a child arrangements order, whether 'lives' with or 'spends time with', were the relationship to break down is unlikely to be refused an order granting parental responsibility.

2.28

Nonetheless, where cohabitants have children, and seek advice, consideration should be given to the question of the benefits and possible disadvantages of parental responsibility agreements and orders. Even more important, perhaps, is the need for the parent or parents with parental responsibility to appoint a testamentary guardian for their children and such appointments should be kept under review and amended if circumstances change.

(d) Children of previous relationships

2.29

Many unmarried families include children of one of the parties by another relationship. Where the adults of a new family marry each other, their children are recognised as children of the family (s 52 Matrimonial Causes Act 1973 (MCA)). Where the adults remain unmarried no duty to maintain them will arise under the Child Support Act 1991 as amended (by the Child Maintenance and Other Payments Act 2008 and the Child Maintenance and Other Payments Act 2008 (Commencement No 11 and Transitional Provisions) Order 2013) or otherwise and their legal status will be governed solely by the position of their natural parents and any orders made in proceedings between these parents.

2.30

Section 2(9) CA 1989 provides that any person who has care of a child may do what is reasonable to safeguard or promote the child's welfare, and accordingly where a child of a previous relationship lives with cohabiting adults, this provision covers the relationship between a child and the adult who is not the child's parent. The natural parent's cohabitant will not normally be able to acquire parental responsibility under the Act, unless he or she successfully applies for a child arrangements ('lives with') order, which will be discussed below, or unless he or she is appointed the child's guardian. The cohabitant may be appointed by the natural parent as the child's testamentary guardian (as outlined above); and upon the death of the natural parent, if the deceased parent had a child arrangements ('lives with') order in his or her favour, the testamentary appointment of a guardian will take effect even though the other natural parent still retains parental responsibility (s 5(7)). The surviving natural parent could however apply to the court to be appointed a guardian and such an appointment would take effect jointly with the testamentary guardian. Similarly, if the child's other parent does not have parental responsibility, which will arise in the case of unmarried fathers only, then the mother could appoint her cohabitant as guardian and this will take effect on her death.

2.31

Where no testamentary guardian was appointed but there was a child arrangements ('lives with') order in favour of the deceased natural parent, the cohabitant could apply to the court to be made the child's guardian whether or not the surviving parent has retained parental responsibility. The surviving natural parent can make a similar application (see s 5(1) CA 1989). Where there is no child arrangements ('lives with') order, and the surviving parent has retained parental responsibility, the deceased parent's cohabitant will not be able to apply to be appointed guardian by the court, and any testamentary appointment is postponed until the death of the surviving parent with parental responsibility. If the child's father never had parental responsibility, the mother's cohabitant, as well as the child's father, could apply to the court to be appointed guardian, in the absence of an appointment by the mother before her death.

2.32

This again highlights the importance of making arrangements for children. Section 10(2) CA 1989 enables *any* person, with leave of the court, to apply for a s 8 order. Section 8 orders will be discussed in Chapter 8, but include child arrangements ('lives with' and 'spends time with') order. Thus, a non-parent cohabitant who has built up a good relationship with their partner's child could apply for leave on breakdown or on the death of the partner. Where the child has lived with the non-parent for three years more, or where the applicant has the consent of the parent(s) with a child arrangements ('lives with') order or of both parents with parental responsibility, then CA 1989, s 10(5) gives them a right to apply for a s 8 order. This right can be exercised at any time, not only in the context of breakdown or death. Thus, a non-parent cohabitant living with the child and one of his or her natural parents could in theory apply for a child arrangements ('lives with') order jointly with the resident natural parent. Section 12(2) then provides that if a child arrangements ('lives with') order is made in favour of a non-parent, the court must make an order giving that person parental responsibility for the duration of the order. However, s 1(5) of course provides that in addition to applying the welfare principle, the court should not make any order unless to do so is better for the child than making no order at all. If such an order is likely to make the child's relationship with their other natural parent difficult, the court may well fall back on the 'no order' presumption.

4 Change of name

2.33

The right to change the name of a child of unmarried parents ostensibly rests with the mother alone, unless a court order affecting her parental responsibility has been made or unless the father has acquired parental responsibility. Generally, though, unmarried fathers will be unable to change their child's name unless they have parental responsibility by virtue of s 4 CA 1989 or obtain a court order. Where parental responsibility is shared, either parent can exercise it independently of the other (s 2(7) CA 1989) yet the courts have been reluctant to endorse the seeming ability of one parent to change the child's name without the other's knowledge. Any dispute can only be finally settled either by a specific issue order or where there is a child arrangements ('lives with') order by an application under s 13 CA 1989. A specific issue order can be sought by either parent to resolve a change of name dispute, providing no order to determine with whom the child should live has been made or is being applied for. The House of Lords in *Dawson v Wearmouth* [1999] 2 AC 308,

[1999] 1 FLR 1167, HL laid down the principle that a court should not make an order to change a child's surname unless there is some evidence that it would lead to an improvement in his welfare. In *Re W, Re A, Re B (change of name)* [1999] 2FLR 930, CA, the Court of Appeal further clarified the law to confirm that if the parents are unmarried the mother has the sole duty and power to register the child's name. The initial choice is hers and she can change the surname; but the father has the right to challenge both choice and change under s 8 CA 1989. That said, it has since been urged that 'parents and courts should be much more prepared to contemplate the use of both surnames in an appropriate case, because that is to recognise the importance of both parents' (Hale LJ in *Re R (surname: using both?)* [2001] EWCA Civ 1344, [2001] 2 FLR 1358). It is of course now commonplace for many children of unmarried parents to have hyphenated surnames.

2.34

In *Dawson v Wearmouth* [1999] 1 FLR 1167, the House of Lords confirmed the appropriateness of an application for a specific issue order in relation to change of name applications where no residence order *(now, child arrangements order)* was in force and of the consequent application of the welfare checklist (s 1(3) CA 1989) and no order presumption (s 1(5) CA 1989) in such cases.

2.35

Where a child arrangements order has been made, then s 13 of the 1989 Act provides that a child's surname cannot be changed without the written consent of every person who has parental responsibility or leave of the court. Thus, leave will have to be sought under s 13. As we have seen, the Act generally provides that no order should be made unless it would be better for the child than making no order at all. In addition, it specifically provides, in relation to contested s 8 applications, for the child's wishes and feelings, in the light of his age and understanding, to be taken into account. This would seem to make it imperative to apply to change a child's name only if the child agrees or is not of an age to express his or her feelings. However, in *Re B (minors) (change of surname)* [1996] 1 FLR 791, CA, the application to change the surname of children aged 12, 14 and 15 was refused despite their clear wishes for the change and the fact that they had already informally adopted the new name. It is worthy of note that where child arrangements orders are made as between unmarried parents, the restriction on changing a child's surname following the making of such order will still apply where the parent with whom the child does not reside retains parental responsibility following breakdown. Whilst in *Re B* the status quo argument did not prevail, it was held in *Re C (minors) (change of surname)* [1998] 1 FLR 549, CA that it was not in the interests of the children to continue to carry their unmarried mother's surname, given that she no longer used it and that they had for some time been living with their father and had informally adopted his surname. In *Re P (minors) (parental responsibility: change of name)* [1997] 2 FLR 722, in which case the children of unmarried parents were registered in the father's name and the mother had subsequently changed their surname to hers, the Court of Appeal refused to restore this in part due to the passage of time. Thus, it is difficult to argue for a change in the status quo in these change of surname cases.

2.36

Some children who come to form part of an unmarried family may be the children of one of the cohabitants born during a marriage, and thus cohabitants may also seek advice if they wish to change these children's surnames. On divorce, s 13 CA 1989 always applies to changing the names of children of married parents where a child arrangements ('lives with') order has been or will be made, as married parents each have and will retain parental responsibility. However, the no order presumption means that few such orders are made on divorce and these are certainly not made automatically. Generally, where parents agree arrangements for their children, no s 8 orders will be made, leaving both parents with unrestricted parental responsibility. Thus, in these cases, whilst there is no clear statutory impediment to either parent changing the child's surname (see s 2(7) CA 1989), *Dawson v Wearmouth* (above) has made it clear that where there is not agreement between the parents, an application must be made to the court.

2.37

In *Re H (child's name: first name)* [2002] involving married but separated parents the Court of Appeal held that the mother as primary carer of the child was entitled to use her choice of forenames, as whereas the child's registered surname is 'of particular significance in so far as it denotes the family to which the child belongs', forenames 'have a much less concrete character. It is commonplace for a child to receive statutory registration with one or more given names and subsequently to receive different given names, maybe at baptism or maybe by custom and adoption.' The fact that there have been no reported cases since suggests that in light of this decision it is accepted that it would be difficult to envisage circumstances in which restrictions can or would be imposed on parental choice of forenames, as a child may well be called one name by family members and another at school.

5 Adoption and infertility treatment

2.38

The Adoption and Children Act 2002 (ACA 2002) permits adoption by single persons (aged over 21), cohabiting couples (whether same- or opposite-sex living as partners in an *enduring family relationship*), married couples and couples in a civil partnership (s 49(1)). Thus, if a couple wish to adopt jointly, so that they share parental responsibility, they need not be married or civil partners. It is possible for one of a cohabiting couple to apply to adopt but of course detailed investigations are carried out by the local authority in relation to all members of the prospective adopter's household before a child is placed for adoption. Some local authorities may not be prepared to recommend adoption by a single person who is cohabiting, the obvious question then being why this is being done alone if the couple are in a settled and enduring family relationship, although there is nothing in the Act or the Regulations which prevent this course of action. The investigation procedure is and is likely to remain very thorough and the initial placement of a child can take place only if the local authority or approved adoption agency (registered under the Care Standards Act 2000, Part 2) recommends the placement.

2.39

The ACA 2002 provides that the paramount consideration of the court or adoption agency must be the child's welfare throughout his life (s 1(2)). The court or adoption agency must at all times bear in mind that in general any delay in coming to a decision is likely to prejudice the child's welfare (s 1(3)). A welfare checklist is set out at s 1(4), which provides that the court or adoption agency must have regard to the following:

(i) the child's ascertainable wishes and feelings regarding the decision (considered in light of the child's age and understanding);

(ii) the child's particular needs;

(iii) the likely effect on the child (throughout his life) of having ceased to be a member of the original family and become an adopted person;

(iv) the child's age, sex, background and any of the child's characteristics which the court or agency considers relevant;

(v) any harm (within the meaning of the CA 1989) which the child has suffered or is at risk of suffering;

(vi) the relationship which the child has with relatives, and with any other person in relation to whom the court or agency considers the relationship to be relevant, including:

  (a) the likelihood of any such relationship continuing and the value to the child of its doing so;

  (b) the ability and willingness of any of the child's relatives, or of any such person, to provide the child with a secure environment in which the child can develop and otherwise to meet the child's needs; and

  (c) the wishes and feelings of any of the child's relatives, or of any such person, regarding the child.

2.40

The courts are placed under a duty not to make any order under the ACA 2002 unless doing so would be better for the child than not doing so (s 1(6)). The European Convention on the Adoption of Children (Revised) 2008, Article 5(1), as cited in *R and H v United Kingdom (Application 3548/06)* [2001] 2 FLR 1268, provides that an adoption shall not be granted without the consent of the mother and father (or, if there is neither father nor mother to consent, the consent of any person or body entitled to consent in their place), the child if considered by law to have sufficient understanding (which may not be an age greater than 14) and of the spouse or registered partner of the adopter. A court cannot dispense with the consent of any parent or guardian of a child to the child being placed for adoption or to the making of an adoption order in respect of the child unless the court is satisfied that the parent or guardian cannot be found or is incapable of giving consent or that the welfare of the child requires the consent to be dispensed with (see ACA 2002, s 52(1) and *Re P (children) (adoption: parental consent)* [2008] EWCA Civ 535, [2008[2 FCR 185).

2.41

An adoption order confers parental responsibility for the child upon the adopter(s) (s 46(1)) and extinguishes the parental responsibility which any other person had for the child immediately before the making of the order (s 46(2)(a)–(d)). The adopted child is treated in law as if born as the child of the adopters' (s 67(1)).

2.42

To become parents, some couples have opted for human assisted reproduction. Such treatment is, at least in theory, available to any woman, whether married, single, heterosexual or homosexual. There is no bar on who can apply and there are certainly no rigorous investigation procedures to discover the suitability of the household for the child, although some counselling is usual. However, the availability of treatment varies from health authority to health authority. The legal status of the child born as a result of human assisted reproduction, or rather the status of the parents, will vary depending on the nature of the treatment. In the case of AIH treatment, where the mother is artificially inseminated with her cohabitant's sperm, the child will be the genetic child of the parties, although as the parents are unmarried only the mother will have parental responsibility at birth, unless the father's name is entered on the register/birth certificate. The father can, however, apply for a parental responsibility order or enter into a parental responsibility agreement in the same way as any unmarried father as described above.

2.43

If the AID method is used, whereby the mother is artificially inseminated by the sperm of an anonymous donor, the mother will of course have parental responsibility from birth, and her cohabitant by virtue of s 36 HFEA 2008 will be treated as the legal father if the mother became pregnant in the course of treatment services provided by a UK licensed clinic for her and him *together* and they have both given written consent in this regard (HFEA 2008 s 37). Thus, if cohabitants have a child as a result of artificial insemination, which treatment was provided by a licensed body for the man and woman together, then the man is treated as the father of the child. He can then obtain parental responsibility by virtue of a s 4 agreement or order in the same way as any other unmarried father. It should be noted that if the treatment is carried out by an unlicensed body, such as a hospital abroad, the father may not apply for parental responsibility and will not be the legal father of the child for any purpose, including the Child Support Act (see *U v W (A-G intervening)* [1998] Fam 29).

2.44

Where a cohabiting couple has a child by virtue of the *in vitro* fertilisation method (IVF) and the egg is donated anonymously and fertilised by the male cohabitant's sperm, then by virtue of s 33(1) HFEA 2008, the mother in whom the egg is placed is regarded as the child's mother and if she is unmarried then she alone will have parental responsibility of the child at birth. However, her cohabitant can by s 36 HFEA 2008 as discussed above be treated as the legal father of the child if the conditions for such have been met or he could obtain parental responsibility by virtue of a s 4 agreement or order as if the child were conceived naturally as set out above. If the mother is married, s 35(1) provides that the child will be treated as a child of the marriage unless the husband is shown not to have consented. If both the egg and the sperm are donated, then the mother in whom the embryo is placed is treated as the mother of the child. Her cohabitant is in exactly the position described above in relation to AID. Providing the treatment was provided by a licensed body for the man and woman together, s 36 states that he is to be treated as the father of the child. He can therefore obtain parental responsibility in accordance with s 4 CA 1989.

2.45

If a child is born to a same sex female couple as a result of assisted reproduction services provided by a UK licensed clinic for them *together* and they have both given written consent in this regard, the mother may agree that her partner is to be treated in law as the other parent (HFEA 2008, ss 43 and 44).

2.46

If a female co-habitant is not able to or chooses not to carry a child to term and for gay male couples wanting a child together which carries the DNA of one of them, surrogacy is probably the only course and is fraught with legal and practical difficulties. The child is deemed to be that of the surrogate mother even if both the egg and sperm were donated (s 33(1) HFEA 2008). The couple can in this circumstance though apply for a parental order under s 54 of the

Human Fertilisation and Embryology Act 2008 (HFEA 2008), which states that the court is empowered to make an order providing for a child to be treated in law as the child of two applicants who are married or civil partners or living together in an enduring family relationship where:

(i) the child has been carried by the woman who is not one of the applicants, as a result of the placing in her of an embryo or sperm and eggs or her artificial insemination;

(ii) the gametes of at least one of the applicants were used to bring about the creation of the embryo; and

(iii) prescribed conditions apply.

Where informal sperm donation arrangements are made between gay and lesbian couples, the birth mother will be the legal mother and if she is married to or the civil partner of her same-sex partner, the birth father now acquires no legal status as the child's father under the provisions of the HFEA 2008. The mother and her partner are recognised as the child's parents under ss 2, 45, and 48 HFEA 2008. However, in *Re G (a minor); Re Z (a minor)* [2013] EWHC 134 (Fam) leave was granted to the donor fathers to apply for orders under s 8 CA 1989 to spend time with their children.

2.47

A finding as to whether the parents are in an enduring family relationship is a question to be determined by the court at its discretion on the facts specified in the particular case. An enduring relationship is not to be defined in terms of its length (see *Re F and M* [2016] EWHC 1594 (Fam) also reported as *P and B v Z* [2016] EWHC 1594, [2016] Fam Law 1098 in which case one of the parents had entered into the surrogacy agreement before meeting the other in April 2014 and cohabiting from June 2014. The child was born in January 2015 and they jointly applied for parental orders in May 2015).

CHAPTER 3

Housing

1 Introduction

3.01

At some point in their relationship, cohabitants have taken a conscious decision to share accommodation with one another. This could have involved one of them moving into their partner's accommodation and giving up their own; or they may have decided to rent accommodation jointly, or buy a property together.

3.02

Legal consequences flow from each of these possibilities. Yet few couples seek, or even think of seeking, legal advice before they take the critical step, unless they happen to be in contact with an advisor about another matter. If legal advice was to be sought by cohabitants in relation to the legal and financial implications of living together prior to doing so that would enable each of them to safeguard his or her interests as far as possible in advance of any crisis. Some cohabitants may feel that the arrangement is, at first, very much on trial and is not something on which legal advice need be sought. More commonly, in the early stages, each cohabitant trusts the other and does not want to be seen questioning their faith in the relationship. There may be a rather vague intention to look into the position later. All too often, it is only on breakdown of the relationship, or in the context of another crisis, such as threatened possession proceedings by a landlord or mortgagee, that the legal implications of a decision to rent or buy accommodation together will become apparent. Difficult housing market conditions across the private, public and independent sectors in most parts of Britain make it vital for cohabitants to know at the outset how a decision to share accommodation will affect each party's housing and property rights if the relationship comes to an end. It may of course not be possible or appropriate for a solicitor, who should generally take instructions rather than seek out problems, to take the initiative. Yet there are situations where an indication of the effects of cohabitation on housing rights may be welcomed and may elicit a request for more comprehensive advice.

3.03

Some of the more common problems can be illustrated. For example, where cohabitants purchase a property they will do so either in their joint names or in the name of just one of them; this will have important ramifications if it becomes necessary to define their respective interests, either on breakdown of the relationship or on death. A non-owner cohabitant who has given up other accommodation may have little or no beneficial interest in the accommodation which he or she regards as home. Thus, there may be no legal rights to live there once the owner withdraws consent unless action can be taken to obtain an occupation order pursuant to s 36 (Family Law Act 1996 FLA 1996), as discussed in Chapter 7. Such cohabitants often believe that the act of cohabitation over a period of time will protect them from being forced out of their 'homes', but this is not of course currently the case. If it were to become law, the Cohabitation Rights Bill 2017–19 (discussed at Chapter 1) would give cohabitants property and other financial rights as against the other where (*inter alia*) they have lived together as a couple for a continuous period of three years or more. Where cohabitants live in rented accommodation, their positions during cohabitation will depend on in whose name the tenancy is vested; and on whether the accommodation is rented in the private, public or independent sector. Problems may arise on breakdown of the relationship, on the death of the partner or the granting of a possession order. Even where a property is jointly purchased, negative equity may prevent an agreed solution being put into effect, or the death of one cohabitant may jeopardise the home of the other. Cohabitants may also find themselves homeless. In some situations, they may be eligible for rehousing by the local housing authority under their duties to the homeless as set out in the Housing Act 1996 Part VII.

3.04

This chapter will consider the implications for cohabitants of the various forms of tenure in all contexts other than breakdown, and consider the situations in which cohabitants may be assisted by the provisions of the homelessness legislation (Housing Act 1996 Part VII as amended by the Homelessness Act 2002).

2 Rented accommodation

(a) Private rented accommodation

3.05

This area of law is highly complex and it is not proposed to attempt to give anything other than a broad outline of the position as it affects cohabitants, and to detail specific problems that cohabitants are most likely to encounter. At present there are two statutory schemes which govern private sector tenancies. If a tenancy was granted before 15 January 1989, it will be governed by the provisions of the Rent Act 1977 and it will be a protected tenancy (contractual or statutory). After 15 January 1989 all residential tenancies granted (with limited exceptions where the tenant was previously a Rent Act protected tenant of the landlord) fall within the provisions of the Housing Act 1988 as amended. They will be either assured or assured shorthold tenancies where the landlord may charge a market rent and, in the latter case, there is only very limited security of tenure. Indeed, tenancies created on or after 28 February 1997 will normally be assured shorthold tenancies unless the landlord expressly states otherwise (Housing Act 1988, Pt 1, Chapter 2, s 19A as inserted by the Housing Act 1996, s 96). A cohabitant's housing rights thus depend on when the tenancy was entered into, and the type of tenancy granted under the relevant statutory provisions.

3.06

As with any rented accommodation, another important factor which will determine a cohabitant's position is whether the tenancy is in joint names, or vested in the sole name of one of them. The importance of this distinction is discussed in (d) below. A joint tenancy is more likely to have been granted if the cohabitants jointly looked for and found the accommodation. However, even where this has happened, many private landlords insist on putting the tenancy in the sole name of one of them, probably because this may prove advantageous if possession is ever sought. Where the tenancy is in writing it is easy to establish whether or not there is a joint tenancy by looking at the tenancy agreement itself. In some cases the tenancy may have been granted orally, and whether it is a joint tenancy or not is something that will only ever be specifically determined if it becomes necessary at a later stage. The matter will be decided by the court with reference to the parties' intentions at the time they reached agreement, and any other evidence (such as correspondence, the name or names on the rent book or which person paid the rent) available.

(b) Public sector secure tenancies

3.07

Cohabitants living in local authority accommodation are secure tenants, and their tenancies are governed by the Housing Act 1985 as amended. This is also the case with housing association tenancies granted before 15 January 1989. The advantages and disadvantages of a joint tenancy are discussed below. Public sector landlords are generally fairly willing to grant or transfer tenancies into the joint names of cohabitants.

3.08

An assignment of a secure tenancy is generally prohibited, save in certain circumstances as set out in the Housing Act 1985 at s 91(3) including where the assignment is to someone who is entitled to be a successor to the tenancy, and, as set out below, a cohabitant may come within this definition providing he or she has lived in the accommodation for 12 months. Thus, where these conditions are fulfilled the tenant cohabitant may assign the secure tenancy into joint names by deed.

3.09

Local authority secure tenants have a right to buy their accommodation at a discount providing they fulfil certain conditions (see Part V, Housing Act 1985), and although a non-tenant cohabitant has no right to require to be a joint proprietor, a tenant has the right to require that up to three members of his family who are not joint tenants, but who occupy the accommodation as their principal home, purchase the property jointly with the tenant. Thus, at the request of the tenant cohabitant, providing the non-tenant partner has resided in the property for the past 12 months, or providing the landlord consents, cohabitants can jointly purchase accommodation under the right to buy provisions, even if only one of them was the secure tenant. Conversely, a joint tenant has the right to buy the premises but could not do so without at least the consent of the other joint tenant. Cohabitants purchasing accommodation under the 'right to buy' scheme must of course be advised of the implications of purchasing the property and the relevant considerations are set later in this chapter.

(c) Independent sector tenancies

3.10

Since the introduction of the assured tenancy by the Housing Act 1988, housing associations have been unable to grant public sector secure tenancies, but must instead grant assured tenancies governed by Part I of the Act. Where a tenancy was granted by a housing association before 15 January 1989, it is likely to be a secure tenancy and the considerations set out above apply. Any tenancy granted after this time by a housing association (with limited exceptions where the tenant was previously a secure tenant of the association) will be an assured tenancy. Housing associations are not prevented by statute from granting assured shorthold tenancies for fixed-term periods with little security of tenure, as is common in the private sector. They are at first sight entitled to charge a market rent. However, as a matter of policy, housing associations have been given the role in the housing market of providers of 'social housing'. Despite a statutory right for landlords granting assured tenancies to charge a market rent, the Home and Communities Agency's Rent Standard Guidance (issued April 2015), which applies to all housing associations registered with it, provides that rent levels should be kept within the reach of those in low-paid employment and assured shorthold tenancies should be granted only where, exceptionally, this is the only means of fulfilling the Association's housing objectives. Nonetheless, housing association tenants now generally come within the statutory provisions of the Housing Act 1988 and are granted assured tenancies. Thus, there are different rules relating to assignment and succession for those who, after 15 January 1989, became tenants of housing associations as opposed to local authorities; this is discussed below (see paras 3.35–3.42). It should also be noted that s 16 Housing Act 1996 (HA 1996) has given assured tenants of 'registered social landlords' (which currently mainly comprise housing associations) the right to acquire the dwelling of which they are a tenant. This scheme mirrors the 'right to buy' and applies wherever the dwelling was provided wholly or in part by public money.

(d) General implications of joint tenancies for cohabitants

3.11

If cohabitants enter into a joint tenancy of private rented accommodation, or indeed any residential accommodation, then they both acquire under the terms of the tenancy agreement the right to occupy the accommodation specified in that agreement. Neither is at liberty to exclude the other from the accommodation save by court order obtained, for example, under the domestic violence legislation (see Chapter 7). Both are jointly and severally liable to perform the obligations under the tenancy agreement. Thus if one joint tenant who normally pays the rent fails to do so, the landlord can look to the other joint tenant to pay the whole of the rent, regardless of any arrangement made between the tenants. Failure to meet the rent demands will ultimately lead to possession proceedings which, in the case of joint tenants, must be taken against each of them.

3.12

Whatever the nature of the tenancy in other respects, where a joint tenancy has been granted and one of the joint tenants dies, the other will automatically become the sole tenant by survivorship. However, if one joint tenant leaves the accommodation permanently, then the remaining joint tenant, whilst continuing to have the right to occupy the accommodation, will need to take legal action (as discussed in Chapter 10 below) to have the tenancy transferred into their sole name either under Sch 7 FLA 1996, or alternatively, where there are children of the relationship under para 1(2)(e) Sch 1 CA 1989.

3.13

Generally, a joint tenancy gives each cohabitant security. Both have equal rights to occupy the accommodation and should therefore each be notified of alleged breaches of the terms of the tenancy agreement, or other statutory grounds for possession. There can be no challenge to the right of the survivor of joint tenants to continue to occupy the accommodation on the death of the partner, as, by operation of law, the survivor becomes the sole tenant. In addition, although not of personal concern to joint tenant cohabitants themselves, a joint tenancy which is protected by the Rent Act (in contrast to an assured joint tenancy under the 1988 Act), has the effect of enhancing statutory succession rights by permitting two further successions to resident members of the tenants' family following the death of the second joint tenant. Cohabitants now have the statutory right to succeed to the tenancy of their deceased sole tenant partners (Housing Act 1985, s 86A, Rent Act 1977, Sch 1, Pt 1, para 2, Housing Act 1988, s 17 in respect of assured tenancies).

3.14

Conversely, as will be seen in the context of breakdown, there are situations where a joint tenancy may work to the disadvantage of a cohabitant. Both remain jointly and severally liable to pay the rent regardless of who remains in occupation, and as will be seen in Chapter 10, a valid notice to quit the accommodation by one joint tenant will be sufficient to determine the whole tenancy even if the other cohabitant wishes to remain in occupation and such determination may not even breach an occupation order (see *Hammersmith and Fulham London Borough Council v Monk* [1992] 1 AC 478, *Harrow London Borough Council v Johnstone* [1997] 1 All ER 929 and *Newlon Housing Trust v Alsuaimen* [1999] 1 AC 313). It is also possible that, if rendered homeless where previous accommodation vested in joint names has been given up, both cohabitants may be more readily found intentionally homeless if fault can be attached to the loss of the previous accommodation (see para 3.93 ff).

3.15

Whether a joint tenancy will prove more or less advantageous to a cohabitant than a sole tenancy on breakdown of the relationship depends on which of them ultimately seeks to remain in the accommodation and whether or not that person is the tenant. At the outset it is not usually possible to foresee the circumstances which may arise, and of course the scenario which benefits one cohabitant is likely to disadvantage the other. Nonetheless, it seems that overall the advantages of a joint tenancy outweigh the disadvantages for cohabitants in terms of achieving security. Such disadvantages as there are usually occur on breakdown of the relationship. Many of the disadvantages can be overcome, but security for a non-tenant cohabitant in accommodation which he or she regards as home, particularly if deserted by the tenant partner, or sometimes on death, may be more difficult, if not impossible, to achieve. Section 53 and Sch 7 to Part IV FLA 1996 enables both joint tenant cohabitants and non-tenant cohabitants whose partner is a tenant to apply for a transfer of tenancy order on relationship breakdown. Nonetheless, it is submitted that whilst cases will vary according to individual circumstances, a joint tenant is likely to generally be in a stronger position than a non-tenant cohabitant. As will be discussed further in Chapter 10, this view is reinforced by the Court of Appeal's decision in *Gay v Sheeran* [1999] 3 All ER 795 where a former cohabitant was denied the right to seek a transfer of tenancy on the grounds that her former partner had left the property and was no longer 'entitled to occupy' it as required by Sch 7 FLA 1996.

3.16

All legal advisors can do is outline the implications of the options. Where appropriate, a written agreement or a Will drawn up in advance of any difficulties can be suggested.

(e) Cohabitants and sole tenancies – the general position

3.17

Where cohabitants occupy accommodation the tenancy of which is vested in the sole name of only one of them, the non-tenant cohabitant is vulnerable. This is even more so where the tenant cohabitant is in fact a joint tenant with a third party, such as a former partner, who has abandoned the home but not formally assigned the tenancy into the sole name of the remaining tenant cohabitant. In the case of spouses or civil partners, a non-tenant spouse/civil partner has the right to occupy the family home of which the other is the sole tenant (or indeed a joint tenant), by virtue of s 30 FLA 1996. A non-tenant cohabitant, on the other hand, is usually no more than his or her partner's licensee in law. They have no right at all to occupy the accommodation, no matter how long he or she may have lived there, once the partner revokes the licence to occupy or leaves the accommodation without an intention to return or even, in some situations, dies. Although the situation seemed to have been greatly improved by the transfer of tenancy provisions in s 53 and Sch 7 FLA 1996 in the context of relationship breakdown, the non-tenant cohabitant or former cohabitant still has no occupation rights, nor even a right to pay the rent, unless and until the court is prepared to make either an occupation order pursuant to s 36 FLA 1996 or a transfer of tenancy order in their favour. In addition, as noted above, following the decision in *Gay v Sheeran* [1999] 3 All ER 795 there are still significant difficulties in a non-tenant cohabitant obtaining a transfer of tenancy order where their tenant partner has left the home thereby relinquishing entitlement to occupy and it now seems necessary for the remaining non-tenant partner to obtain an occupation order in order to be eligible to apply for the tenancy of the home to be transferred (see further Chapter 10).

3.18

It may be possible to ameliorate this position by creating a joint tenancy, either by a grant of a new joint tenancy by the landlord, or in some cases by way of assignment by the sole tenant to the cohabitants as joint tenants. Much will depend on the nature of the tenancy and the situation may be more complicated where the tenancy of the home was originally granted to the tenant cohabitant and a third party who cannot be traced or is not willing to co-operate. Although on relationship breakdown a transfer of tenancy application can now be made pursuant to Sch 7 FLA 1996 (providing occupation by the tenant and thus security of tenure has not been relinquished or a s 36 occupation order has been made), whilst cohabitation is ongoing a non-tenant cohabitant does not have any right to insist that the tenancy be transferred into joint names. So here the consent of the partner, any third-party joint tenant and, where appropriate, the landlord, will be needed. Advisors should be alert to the possibility of conflict of interest between the partners and any third-party joint tenant would clearly need to be advised to take independent legal advice.

3.19

Broadly, statutory tenancies governed by the Rent Act 1977 and periodic assured tenancies arising under the Housing Act 1988 cannot be assigned without the landlord's express written consent (see Chapter 10). Contractual Rent Act tenancies and fixed-term assured tenancies can be assigned during the fixed-term period providing the terms of the tenancy permit assignment. Secure public sector tenancies can be assigned to a person entitled to be the statutory successor to the tenancy. Thus a tenancy can be assigned as between cohabitants providing the non-tenant cohabitant has been living with the tenant at the accommodation for the previous 12 months. If such a tenancy is still in the names of the tenant cohabitant and a third party, the situation is more complex as here there would need to be an assignment by the third party to the tenant cohabitant. They in turn would be able to assign it to their cohabitant as soon as they qualified as a successor following a further 12 months' cohabitation. In the case of local authority or housing association tenancies, it is usually possible to obtain the landlord's agreement to an assignment, or to a grant of a new tenancy in joint names. In the private sector, particularly where a Rent Act tenancy is concerned, a landlord's consent to an assignment or new tenancy which would retain Rent Act protection (see s 34 Housing Act 1988) is unlikely to be forthcoming and the parties may have little choice but to retain such security as is available to the sole tenant.

(f) Succession to tenancies on death

3.20

Where cohabitants are joint tenants, the survivor of them will automatically succeed to the tenancy on the death of his or her partner. Where cohabitants have lived together for a period of time in a private sector tenancy in the sole name of one of them, it may be possible for the surviving cohabitant to succeed to the tenancy. Succession to tenancies on death is now governed by statute and the position of non-tenant cohabitants again varies according to the nature of the tenancy.

(i) Rent Act tenancies

3.21

The surviving spouse, civil partner or cohabitant of an original tenant automatically succeeds and becomes the statutory tenant of the accommodation on the tenant's death, providing he or she was residing with the tenant in the accommodation at the time of the tenant's death (Rent Act 1977, Sch 1, Pt 1, para 2). Providing it is the first succession, the statutory tenant will remain protected by the Rent Act 1977 as long as they continue to occupy the accommodation as a residence. There is now no qualifying period.

3.22

Additionally, Sch 1 to the Rent Act 1977 provides an alternative means of succession to a tenancy for anyone who can prove they are 'a member of the tenant's family' who has resided with the tenant in the accommodation for the two years prior to the tenant's death (para 6). A 'member of the tenant's family' includes some non-blood relatives. Thus, it was held to include a woman who had been brought up by the tenant but never formally adopted (*Brock v Wollams* [1949] 1 All ER 715), although a *quasi* aunt and nephew relationship was not considered a sufficient familial relationship even though they had shared accommodation for 18 years and the 'nephew' had looked after the 'aunt' during her failing health (see *Carega Properties SA (formerly Joram Developments Ltd) v Sharratt* [1979] 2 All ER 1084).

3.23

As noted above, in the absence of a spouse, civil partner or cohabitant, a member of the tenant's family may succeed on the death of the original tenant providing the family member was living with the tenant in the accommodation for two years immediately before the tenant's death. More generally, it should also be noted that where there has already been one succession of a Rent Act tenancy by the original tenant's spouse, civil partner or cohabitant (the first successor as defined at para 4), that successor's spouse, civil partner or cohabitant can succeed to an assured tenancy (para 5), as can someone who is a member of both the original tenant's and the first successor's family, providing that person lived in the accommodation with the first successor for two years immediately before the first successor's death (para 6).

(ii) Succession of assured tenancies

3.24

An assured tenancy held in a tenant's sole name remains an interest in property even on the tenant's death and thus, subject to the statutory provisions governing succession, will devolve according to the terms of any Will, or, in the absence of a Will, according to the intestacy rules. At first sight this appears to have a significant adverse effect upon cohabitants who are not joint tenants as the survivor of joint tenants succeeds to the tenancy by operation of law. Indeed, where a fixed-term tenancy of not more than two years (of a home of which the landlord is a private registered provider of social housing), as opposed to a periodic tenancy, is still in existence on the death of the tenant, the tenancy will indeed devolve in accordance with any Will or the rules of intestacy and will vest in the tenant's personal representatives under the Administration of Estates Act 1925. They should then vest the tenancy by a simple assent in the beneficiaries, who may or may not include a cohabitant. Where there is no Will, a cohabitant will not be a beneficiary and a claim under the Inheritance (Provision for Family and Dependants) Act 1975 may be the only means of attempting to vest the tenancy in the surviving cohabitant, notwithstanding that the accommodation is that person's home. Even then, an application is fraught with difficulties. As shall be seen in Chapter 5, the court can look only to whether 'reasonable financial provision' has been made. This phrase has been narrowly interpreted in the case of claims by non-spouse dependants; arguably it may not extend to tenancies which have no intrinsic financial value.

3.25

The situation for a surviving cohabitant is much better where there is a periodic assured tenancy, be it a statutory periodic tenancy arising on the expiry of a fixed term or a periodic tenancy from the outset. Section 17 Housing Act 1988 provides that the spouse, civil partner or cohabitant living with the tenant at the time of the tenant's death, who was not himself or herself a successor to the tenancy (s 17(1D)), is entitled to succeed to the tenancy providing he or she occupied the accommodation as their only or principal home immediately before the tenant's death, notwithstanding the terms of any Will (s 17(1), (4)). The definition of 'successor' includes a tenant who became a sole tenant by virtue of the Will or intestacy of the previous tenant or by the right of survivorship under a joint tenancy. This contrasts with the Rent Act position where a joint tenancy prolongs the potential succession rights. No other member of the tenant's family is entitled to succeed to a periodic tenancy, although where the tenant does not have a spouse, civil partner or cohabitant, a tenancy which was periodic from the outset can be left by Will. However, unless the implied absolute covenant against assignment has been specifically overridden by the terms of the agreement, the personal representatives will, it seems, be unable lawfully to assign the tenancy to the beneficiary and the new tenant would not obtain security of tenure.

3.26

The right of succession also applies in respect of assured tenancies for a fixed term of not less than two years where the landlord is a private registered provider of social housing (s 17(1B)).

3.27

It is worth noting that in order to succeed by statute to an assured periodic tenancy, the requirement is for residence in the accommodation *by* the tenant's spouse or civil partner, not residence *with* the tenant. So, for example, if the sole tenant has been removed by court order or has voluntarily vacated the property (perhaps even to live with another partner) and dies before giving up the tenancy the spouse/civil partner left in occupation of the property would still be able to succeed to the tenancy. However, as a cohabitant is defined as a person who was living with the tenant as his or her wife or husband or as civil partners, it may be that in this scenario, the cohabitant left in occupation might not be able to succeed to the tenancy. Where, for example, a tenant has been in hospital for a long time, leaving the partner in occupation of the accommodation, a landlord could argue that they do not meet the 'living with' requirement as they are no longer living together as spouses or civil partners. There is though in the statute no requirement that the cohabitation should immediately precede the death, and it is hoped that should this issue come before them, the courts will not interpret the criterion too narrowly, but look to whether the nature of the relationship was akin to that of spouses or civil partners without also requiring the partners to have lived together in the accommodation immediately before the tenant's death where circumstances other than breakdown of the relationship prevented this.

(iii) Succession to public sector secure tenancies

3.28

A housing association tenant will now normally be granted an assured periodic tenancy. Accordingly, succession rights for such non-tenant cohabitants are as set out above in relation to private sector assured tenancies, and are significantly less favourable than those which apply to both protected and secure tenants. Where cohabitants are living in local authority accommodation they will normally be secure tenants and their tenancies are governed by Housing Act 1985. This is also the case with housing association tenancies granted before 15 January 1989. It should be noted that s 124 HA 1996 enabled local housing authorities and housing action trusts to elect to operate introductory tenancy schemes, under which all new periodic tenancies granted by a local authority or housing action trust operating the scheme will be for a period of one year in the first instance. Thus, in this situation the tenancy will not be secure or assured, although a cohabitant who is not a joint tenant may succeed to the introductory tenancy on death providing they have resided with the tenant for the 12 months prior to the death (see ss 131, 133 and 140).

3.29

There can be only one succession to a secure tenancy under the terms of the s 89 Housing Act 1985 and this can be to either the tenant's surviving spouse, civil partner, cohabitant or a member of the tenant's family (save that in England the tenancy must make provision for that family member to succeed – s 86A (2)). A 'member of the tenant's family' includes children, parents, grandparents, siblings, aunts, uncles, nephews, nieces, step-and half relations (s 113).

3.30

On succession, the tenancy ceases to be a secure tenancy (s 89(4)). Where there was originally a joint tenancy, on the death or surrender of the last surviving joint tenant, there can be no statutory succession. In order to succeed to the tenancy, the successor must have been living in the accommodation as his or her only or principal home. There is no prior period of qualification but the successor must have been living with the deceased tenant at the time of death.

3.31

Accordingly, succession and, to some extent, assignment possibilities for cohabitants depend on the nature of the tenancy granted and the law of landlord and tenant, which, across different types of tenancy, is far from consistent in its treatment of cohabitants. Advisors need therefore to establish the nature of the tenancy before attempting to advise on cohabitants' housing rights.

3 Owner occupied property

3.32

Of the various courses open to cohabitants, purchasing a property together is the most likely to lead them carefully to consider their respective positions and to seek legal advice. They will usually instruct a solicitor, who would usually advise them to take separate and independent legal advice on the implications of buying a property in their joint names, particularly where only one is contributing to the purchase price or the couple are making unequal contributions. This places a heavy burden on advisors as judicial warnings abound as to the careful advice needed from solicitors in this type of transaction in order to avoid negligence claims. The courts have justifiably become increasingly critical of inadequate advice given to joint purchasers which has in turn led to costly and unnecessary litigation between cohabitants on relationship breakdown. In *Walker v Hall* [1984] FLR 126, the Court of Appeal found that a solicitor who failed to find out the beneficial interests of joint purchasers for whom he was acting and had declared a tenancy in common without declaring any shares was guilty of negligence. Such practice was further lamented in the case of *Springette v Defoe* [1992] 2 FLR 388, where property had been transferred to the parties as joint tenants in law without any declaration as to their beneficial interests in the property having been made in the transfer. Clearly, the lesson for advisors here is that prevention is better than cure.

3.33

If the property is being purchased in the name of one of them alone, then the partner may not have access to advice, even if contributing to the purchase price. In this situation an advisor may still be required to take instructions from both cohabitants, but should always invite the partner to obtain separate and independent legal advice. Most building societies and banks who lend money secured by mortgage on residential property require, from all occupiers over the age of 18, signed consents agreeing to postpone any interest in the property they may have or acquire, to that of the mortgagee. This is so that any person in occupation (in the absence of undue influence being proven) cannot prevent the mortgagee from realising its interest should the mortgagor default (see *Williams & Glyn's Bank Ltd v Boland* [1981] AC 487). An advisor who discovers that the purchaser's cohabitant will be living in the property must explain why the consent is required by the mortgagee. This provides an opportunity to indicate the legal implications of the whole transaction to both cohabitants, even though the property is to be in the sole name of one of them. Only one of the cohabitants would in fact be the advisor's client, but a duty is owed to the mortgagee to obtain consent for its charge to have priority over any interest of the other cohabitant. A letter to the non-client cohabitant should be written, outlining the consequences of the required consent and suggesting separate legal advice should they be concerned about the position. A legal advisor is clearly in a difficult professional position here, but it may be appropriate for a declaration of trust (see 3.54 ff) to be suggested.

(a) Purchase in joint names

3.34

As with rented accommodation, if a property is purchased in the joint names of cohabitants each has the right to occupy it. Neither can lawfully exclude the other without having first obtained a court order to do so. In addition, as both names are on the title deeds, one joint owner cannot sell, mortgage or charge the property without the consent of the other, whose signature will be required to effect the sale or create the legal charge. This also means that if one co-owner wished to sell and the other refuses, an application has to be made to the court for an order to resolve the dispute. The court will either order the sale or agree to a postponement of the sale in certain circumstances. This situation usually arises on breakdown of the relationship between cohabitants and is explored in more detail in Chapter 11.

3.35

All joint purchasers hold the legal estate of their property as joint tenants in law. By virtue of s 5 and Sch 2 Trusts of Land and Appointment of Trustees

Act 1996 (TLATA 1996) where there is joint ownership, a statutory trust of the land is implied. Co-owners are therefore trustees, and hold on trust for themselves as either joint tenants or tenants in common in equity. As the law allows joint owners to hold their beneficial interest in the property either as joint tenants or as tenants in common, all co-owners should be advised at the time of purchase on the broad implications of both options, so they can make an informed decision as to which properly reflects their intentions. Indeed, the Land Registry Transfer Form TR1 requires a statement as to whether the property is held by the purchasers as joint tenants, tenants in common in equal shares or tenants in common in other specified shares. This is of tremendous importance to all co-owners, and particularly to cohabitants. Failure to explain and keep a record of the legal advice given at the time of purchase is likely to amount to negligence on the part of a solicitor (see eg *Walker v Hall* and *Springette v Defoe* (discussed above)).

3.36

When purchasing a property, cohabitants may make different contributions to the purchase price. They may agree to make unequal contributions to the mortgage repayments or other outgoings. They may decide to apply one partner's income towards the mortgage repayments and the other income towards all the other outgoings. Very often, however, the agreement reached is not set out in any legal document. Many do not appreciate that these agreements may affect their beneficial interests in the property, and that these arrangements can prove critical. Some joint purchasers may not even expressly discuss with each other their understanding of the implications of the agreed arrangements they have made to contribute to the purchase price and to the mortgage repayments, as was the case in *Springette v Defoe* (above). Yet, as was decided in that case, in the absence of a completed TR1 dealing with this issue, unless there is a common intention which has been communicated as to how the parties intended to hold their respective beneficial interests, then the presumption of a resulting trust whereby the joint owners are presumed to hold beneficially in proportion to their respective contributions, may not be rebutted. This is so even if they each shared the same intention. As Steyn LJ commented at page 394, 'Our trust law does not allow property rights to be affected by telepathy'.

3.37

The effect of this decision has been significantly modified by *Midland Bank plc v Cooke* [1995] 2 FLR 915, from which it was distinguished on the facts on the basis that the former case involved middle-aged cohabitants whose purchase of their home was akin to a commercial partnership arrangement (see Chapter 11 below). Nonetheless, the uncertainties within the law make it all the more imperative that clear advice is given on purchase and that this is translated into documentation giving effect to the true intentions of the parties. As (pretty much) all purchases will be effected by TR1, if completed correctly, the statement of the terms of the trust on which it is held will be clear and determinative and if not the likely remedy may be in damages against the legal adviser for negligent advice rather than the co-owner, in the absence of a subsequent provable agreement made as regards the division of the beneficial interest in the property.

3.38

Solicitors are often criticised for failing to explain clearly to joint proprietors, at the time of purchase, the options and their implications. Where the advisor is on notice that the joint purchasers are cohabitants, the implications of purchasing in joint or sole names, and of purchasing as beneficial joint tenants or tenants in common, must be explained to both parties so that an informed and joint decision is taken. The legal documentation should then be drawn up to reflect and record the intentions of the co-owners at the date of the purchase, and to provide an accurate starting point to determine any future dispute. It may also be appropriate at this time to ask the cohabitants to consider whether they wish to reflect arrangements relating to other property in a written agreement, or to consider a cohabitation agreement or Wills.

3.39

In any event, in order to avoid negligence claims and disputes between cohabitants at a later stage, it is important when taking instructions on a purchase to ask crucial questions about the source of the purchase money, the proposed contributions to the mortgage and intentions as to beneficial ownership. All the options and implications need to be carefully explained, including the implications of relationship breakdown and death. It is important for advisors to discover whether there are any other potential beneficiaries who would be adversely affected by the right of survivorship in the case of a beneficial joint tenancy and, if appropriate, to suggest the need for the drawing of new Wills and explain the ramifications of the Inheritance (Provision for Family and Dependants) Act 1975 if one or both cohabitants have former spouses or civil partners or minor children by other relationships.

3.40

Another issue that needs to be addressed is whether the life assurance usually offered to cohabitant joint purchasers on standard terms is appropriate to their individual circumstances. So-called 'joint life, first death' policies (typically designed to pay out on the first death a sum equal or close to the amount of any mortgage or other debt secured over the home) can give unexpected results where death of both cohabitants takes place within a short space of time, particularly if, as is now common practice, the mortgagee does not take an assignment or notice of deposit of the policy, as the right of survivorship applies to the proceeds, potentially not protecting the estate of the longest surviving cohabitant. Consideration needs to be given to whether a mortgage protection policy or policies taken out by each purchaser on their own life might be more appropriate. One other option to help sidestep a potentially large inheritance tax bill would be to put the life insurance 'in trust' so that it does not fall into the deceased's estate for tax purposes.

3.41

The relative merits of the main considerations to which both advisors and purchasers should apply their minds will now be considered.

(b) Joint tenancy or tenancy in common?

3.42

Regardless of their actual contributions to the purchase price, joint proprietors, whilst being obliged to hold as joint tenants in law under a statutory trust of land, have the option of declaring that they hold their beneficial interests either as joint tenants or as tenants in common. One of the most important effects of this decision is seen on the death of one of the joint tenants. If the couple are beneficial joint tenants and neither has severed the joint tenancy thereby creating a beneficial tenancy in common, the survivor of them will succeed to the deceased joint tenant's legal and equitable interests by operation of law, and become the sole owner of the property, notwithstanding the terms of the deceased joint tenant's Will. However, where there is a beneficial tenancy in common, then the deceased co-owner's share will form part of that person's estate on death and devolve according to the Will, or the rules on intestacy in the absence of a Will. If there is no Will, the intestacy rules provide that the deceased cohabitant's share of the property will be inherited by his or her next of kin, and not by the partner. The surviving partner will have to rely either on the proceeds of any life policy to purchase the other share of the property from the partner's beneficiary; or apply for provision under the Inheritance (Provision for Family and Dependants) Act 1975, which would not necessarily enable the applicant to remain in the home (see Chapter 5 below).

3.43

What, therefore, should determine whether cohabitants should be joint tenants or tenants in common in equity, and how should this be reflected in TR1? Where the contributions made by each of the cohabitants are broadly equal, and it is intended that they should contribute to the mortgage in roughly equal shares, and they agree that their interests in the property are equal and expressly wish them to remain equal, even if these circumstances change, the crucial issue is whether they wish the right of survivorship to apply. If they decide that they wish the other to inherit their share of the property without having to make a Will to that effect, then a beneficial joint tenancy should be created.

3.44

However, it could be argued that, given the reluctance of the courts to intervene and adjust shares of cohabitants on relationship breakdown, it might never be appropriate to recommend a beneficial joint tenancy to cohabitant joint purchasers in case the relationship breaks down, and the original desire to share the property equally becomes inappropriate from the perspective of one of the parties. From an advisor's point of view, the safest course of action is a declaration of a tenancy in common (potentially in unspecified shares) together with mutual Wills in relation to the property being purchased. Yet there is often a formidable, if not altogether logical, reluctance on the part of cohabitants to make Wills, and a beneficial joint tenancy is seen as a means of dealing with succession to the family home without having to make difficult decisions about the destination of other assets. Another potential difficulty is that a beneficial tenancy in common expressly declaring proportionate beneficial interests based on actual and intended contributions to capital and mortgage at the time of the purchase, may not provide a flexible enough assessment of the parties' true intentions about their interests in the property. Where one is providing mainly capital and the other mainly mortgage repayments, these issues may be magnified in the effects they produce. Often, parties feel that the fairest method of assessing respective interests in the home is a retrospective one at the date the property is to be sold, taking into account the actual contributions made and not just the promise of, for example, mortgage repayments made at the date of the purchase. There is judicial approval (see *Passee v Passee* [1988] 1 FLR 263, particularly at pages 270–272) for such deferred ascertainment of the beneficial interests, where it can be inferred that this was clearly intended by the parties and this approach was approved by Slade LJ in *Springette v Defoe* (above). It therefore seems that a possible solution to the practitioner's dilemma is a declaration which creates a beneficial joint tenancy until severance by either party, whereupon a beneficial tenancy in common is created, to be held in shares specified with reference to the parties' contributions. This possibility will need careful thought by both parties and their advisors and will be discussed further below.

3.45

It falls to the practitioner acting for the purchaser to record the intentions about how the beneficial interests are to be held on the TR1 (in section 10 headed 'Declaration of Trust'). Prior to the TR1 being used, probably the majority of solicitors did no more than complete the declaration on the old standard form of transfer stating that the survivor can give a valid receipt for capital monies arising on disposition of the land and cases may still arise where this is all that is formally recorded to assist in determining the manner in which the property is held. For many years it was not clear whether this declaration would be sufficient to create an express beneficial joint tenancy. In *Bernard v Josephs* [1982] 3 All ER 162, the Court of Appeal held that where property had been transferred to two cohabitants jointly, without any express declaration as to the nature of the beneficial ownership, there was no presumption that the parties held the property in equal shares. Instead, a court should look at all the evidence, such as respective contributions, and see whether it indicates any intention to hold the property other than in equal shares. In that case, it was decided that the parties did have equal interests in the property, but much time and expense would have been saved if the transfer had indicated the parties' intentions at the time of purchase. In the decision of *Huntingford v Hobbs* [1993] 1 FLR 736, a majority of the Court of Appeal rejected the contention that the standard declaration on the transfer form, that the survivor of the two cohabitant joint proprietors could give a valid receipt for capital money arising on the disposition of the land, constituted a declaration of trust that they held the property as beneficial joint tenants. They found that because such wording could equally have been employed to indicate that they were holding the beneficial interest as trustees on behalf of a third party, it did not constitute a declaration of their beneficial interests in the property. Furthermore, extrinsic evidence was not admissible in this context and thus the interests fell to be decided in accordance with the principles of resulting, implied or constructive trusts.

3.46

Thus, to create a beneficial joint tenancy, an express declaration of trust unambiguously to this effect must be entered into by the joint purchasers as recorded on the TR1 in which the respective parties' shares must be indicated. Where the transfer does not include a declaration of the beneficial interests but has indicated joint ownership, a separate declaration of trust document, executed by both parties, should be drawn and kept with the title/ownership documents. Once there is an express beneficial joint tenancy, then each party will be deemed to have an equal interest in the proceeds of sale even if the joint tenancy is subsequently severed (see *Goodman v Gallant* [1986] Fam 106) unless, as suggested above, each party's beneficial interest on severance has been specified in the original declaration. Thus, if it is intended to pursue this option, a beneficial joint tenancy should be indicated on the transfer but made subject to the terms of the separate declaration of trust which becomes effective on severance of the joint tenancy. Where there is an initial joint tenancy, it can later be severed by either of the joint tenants, by service of a notice of severance on the other party or by course of dealing. As soon as a joint tenancy is severed, a tenancy in common arises and the right of survivorship no longer applies. Each co-owner's share will then devolve separately with his or her estate. If instructed to sever a joint tenancy, the client should be advised to make a new Will.

3.47

Even if the parties have contributed in unequal shares to the purchase price of the property, they may still choose to purchase as beneficial joint tenants. However, as has been seen (*Goodman v Gallant*, above), even after the tenancy has been severed, they will normally still hold the property in equal shares, although where separation takes place some adjustment may be made to reflect varying contributions made after the separation.

3.48

Where there are unequal contributions to the purchase price and on purchase the parties wish this to be reflected in their respective interests in the property, then a beneficial tenancy in common is needed. To create a beneficial tenancy in common, the appropriate box in section 10 of the TR1 should be ticked and if in unequal shares so specified in the box provided or in a separate declaration of trust document, clearly stating the proportions in which the property is held by the co-owners. Express declarations of trust can be simple documents and must be in writing following the requirements of s 53(1) Law of Property Act 1925 (see eg Appendix II).

3.49

Where advisors are acting for joint purchasers, it should be standard practice to ask whether they wish to hold the property as joint tenants or tenants in common. It is arguable that a beneficial joint tenancy is never appropriate in the cohabitation context. Whatever the answer, an express declaration should be made at the time as it should avoid future disputes. It may well be appropriate to set out in a separate trust, not only the capital contributions to the deposit, but also any credit to be given for a 'right to buy' discount; the parties' proposed present and future contributions to the mortgage and other outgoings; and the planned use of the property as a family home. In effect, a small-scale cohabitation agreement dealing specifically with the parties' intentions in relation to the home could be drawn up.

3.50

To summarise, any advisor instructed to create a tenancy in common should immediately advise on the position of each cohabitant on death. Without a Will leaving their interest in the property to the other, a partner's share will devolve according to the intestacy rules on their next of kin, which may not reflect his or her true wishes. As discussed above, the relative shares of tenants in common either on purchase or following severance of a beneficial joint tenancy, must in any event be recorded on the transfer and/or in a separate declaration of trust.

3.51

Those purchasing as tenants in common, specifying fixed shares, should also be advised that the declaration of trust can be varied in the future, but only by agreement. If joint purchasers' true common intention is reflected by declaring neither a beneficial joint tenancy nor a beneficial tenancy in common in specific shares, there are two further possibilities to consider. First, it may be possible to create a beneficial tenancy in common which builds in flexibility in the way in which the shares are calculated. A deferred ascertainment clause recording the common intention of the method in which the beneficial interests are to be calculated could be a way of achieving this. The advantage is that important issues like the value of contributions in kind, such as home improvements or perhaps child care, could be built into the method of assessment. A method of dealing with negative equity if this was considered in need of different treatment to the proposed division of positive equity could also be addressed. The potential difficulty with this approach is that it is open ended and risks leaving the couple with too much to argue over should the relationship breakdown. However, it does at least leave the couple with a clear common intention which with careful drafting could provide a couple with the flexibility to take future events into account, yet provide them with a fixed framework for determining their interests on relationship breakdown.

3.52

Secondly, there seems to be no reason why cohabitants who are purchasing a property jointly and who wish during the currency of the relationship to be beneficial joint tenants, taking advantage of the right of survivorship – yet who, should the relationship break down, do not necessarily want to hold the property in equal shares on severance of the joint tenancy – should not be able to enter into an effective 'hybrid' declaration of trust. The declaration should make clear either the proportions in which the beneficial interest is to be held on severance, or the method of calculating them if deferred ascertainment is preferred.

3.53

Both of these options should only be used where they clearly coincide with the joint purchasers' intentions at the time of purchase. Thought does need to be given to these options when the parties are not satisfied that either of the two more straightforward options meet with their true intentions. They both have the advantage of flexibility and the disadvantage of lack of immediate certainty. It could be argued that, framed in the right way, they can effectively achieve for cohabitants a fairer method of dividing property on relationship breakdown in accordance with principles decided by the couple when they were at one, and which they may accordingly be happy to agree to abide by with the minimum of dissension on breakdown.

(c) *Purchase in sole name*

3.54

If for tax or other *bona fide* reasons, cohabitants who are both contributing to the purchase of a property wish it to be purchased in the sole name of one party, it is still possible to have a declaration of trust as to how the equity is held. Although this would give only an equitable rather than a legal interest in the property to the non-purchaser cohabitant, it would still be clear evidence of the parties' respective interests in any subsequent dispute between them. A non-owner partner who has contributed in money or money's worth is likely in any event to be able to prove a beneficial interest in the proceeds of sale and can make an application under s 14 TLATA 1996; see Chapter 11. Accordingly, although such situations are likely to be rare, where a beneficial interest is acknowledged or apparent from the outset, a declaration of trust should be drawn up, setting out the respective interests under the resulting trust and reciting the contributions made by each party.

3.55

Where an advisor is acting for a mortgagee as well as a sole purchaser, enquiries must be made in respect of others who will be occupying the property. If the existence of a cohabitant is thereby revealed, then the cohabitant will be required to sign a declaration that any interest in the property that they may have does not have priority over that of the mortgagee. Enquiries as to whether the cohabitant is contributing to the purchase price should be made of both parties, and, if a contribution is confirmed, further questions as to the basis upon which this is being done would seem to be entirely appropriate. Such a revelation would in any event provide an opportunity, if not always a duty, to discuss the possible consequences of cohabitation in a home purchased by one cohabitant, and to advise on the merits of drawing up full documentation to record the parties' intentions with regard to the property which is to be the family home. Following decisions on undue influence in the marital context such as *Barclays Bank plc v O'Brien* [1994] 1 AC 180 and *Midland Bank v Cooke* (above), independent legal advice will always be appropriate for the non-purchasing cohabitant. Such advice at an early stage may prevent the need for litigation later, and to that extent must be of benefit to all concerned in the proposed transaction. Enquiries may reveal that the proposed contribution takes the form of a loan or a gift, and not a contribution to the purchase price, in which case the loan agreement or deed of gift should be drawn up as appropriate, and the desirability of independent advice clearly explained.

3.56

The need for a declaration of trust may arise where parties agree to cohabit in a property already owned by one of them, and the incoming partner pays for improvements to the property or contributes to the mortgage repayments. It is open to them to transfer the property into joint names, but this may involve obtaining a mortgagee's consent, and possibly paying stamp duty, land registration fees, legal costs and disbursements as on a new purchase. Some cohabitants may prefer to make a declaration of trust, although from the non-owner cohabitant's point of view this would confer only an equitable rather than a legal interest and would be enforceable against their partner only. The need for Wills to be drawn up should be considered, as, if they hold the property as tenants in common, their shares will devolve with their respective estates. A later purchaser for value of the property would normally raise enquiries about the interests of any other adult occupier of the property, and where the cohabitant is in actual occupation of the property, the owner cohabitant will not be able to give vacant possession without the partner's co-operation, and a purchaser is likely to be put on notice. The partner would in any event have an overriding interest where the title is registered (s 70(1)(g) Land Registration Act 1925). At the very least, a declaration of trust gives the non-owner cohabitant documentary evidence of his or her interest in the property which will prove helpful on relationship breakdown.

3.57

Unfortunately, express declarations of trust in these circumstances are rare. Where there is no declaration of trust, and a dispute arises on the breakdown of the relationship, the onus is on the non-owner cohabitant to prove that he or she has a beneficial interest in the property. The courts have in some cases been prepared to find implied, constructive or resulting trusts in a property of which only one cohabitant is the legal owner, deeming the owner to be holding the property in trust for both cohabitants. Another possibility where only one cohabitant is the owner is to find that a licence for life has been granted to the non-owner. This is only likely to arise in special circumstances and will never be easy to prove. These issues, which usually arise in the context of breakdown of the relationship, or, possibly, on death, are dealt with in detail in Chapter 11.

3.58

It should also be borne in mind that a non-owner cohabitant, or indeed in some situations a joint owner cohabitant, may wish to assert rights of beneficial ownership or occupation as against a mortgagee. The home may be mortgaged by one partner without the other's knowledge or consent; usually the mortgagee's rights will prevail, unless, there was actual occupation of the land before the creation of the charge (*Williams and Glyn's Bank v Boland*, above).

3.59

There has been a plethora of cases considering the issues of misrepresentation and of undue influence where one partner is asked by the other to consent to a mortgagee's charge against the family home to secure the business debts of that partner. This will occur during the currency of the relationship and may apply whether or not the home is vested in their joint names. The House of Lords in *Barclays Bank v O'Brien* (above) recognised that where one partner could show that she generally trusted and had confidence in her partner in financial matters a presumption of undue influence arises, placing a heavier burden on the mortgagee. If, in rare cases, the husband acts as the mortgagee's agent, then they will be unable to enforce the charge against the wife's equity. Otherwise, the ability to enforce would depend on whether or not the mortgagee was fixed with actual or constructive notice of the undue influence. The House of Lords made it clear that these principles would apply as much to cohabiting couples, whether heterosexual or homosexual. The case of *CIBC Mortgages plc v Pitt* [1994] 1 AC 200 where, unlike in *O'Brien*, the matrimonial home was in joint names and as far as the mortgagees were aware, the loan was purportedly for a joint holiday home, emphasised that in the *O'Brien* situation, where the home was in the man's sole name and the loan was for his business, the risk of undue influence was greater. In *Massey v Midland Bank plc* [1995] 1 All ER 929, CA it was confirmed that *O'Brien* applied to the cohabitation context, although the bank here were entitled to rely on the fact that they had required Ms Massey to seek independent advice. Furthermore, in *Barclays Bank plc v Boulter* [1999] 2 FLR 986, HL, it was confirmed (reversing the decision of the Court of Appeal) that it was for the wife to prove the bank had constructive notice of the undue influence, not for the mortgagee to disprove it, and that whether the land was registered or unregistered was irrelevant in cases of this nature. The question was whether the creditor had actual or constructive notice of the facts on which the equity to set aside the transaction was founded.

3.60

Thus, advisors need to be aware both of the potential conflict of interest between cohabitants and of their own professional position when advising in these situations and may find the decision in *Royal Bank of Scotland v Etridge (No 2)* [1998] 2 FLR 843 in which helpful guidelines are set out as to the effect of legal advice in such cases particularly valuable.

GOOD PRACTICE CHECKLIST FOR ADVISORS OF COHABITANTS PURCHASING PROPERTY

- Take very full instructions as to the relationship, the contributions to the deposit, details as to whom any right to buy discount is attributable, anticipated contributions to the mortgage repayments, implications of any proposed improvements to the property.
- Ensure that a firm conclusion is reached in relation to the holding of the beneficial interests, whilst bearing in mind that certainty does not rule out flexibility. Complete the declaration on the TR1, making reference to a separate declaration of trust where a more complicated calculation of the beneficial interest is preferred. This may be particularly appropriate where one party is contributing mainly capital and the other intends to take prime responsibility for the mortgage repayments. Be aware that the communicated common intention of the purchasers at the time of purchase is critical, although deferred ascertainment of the beneficial interests is a permissible common intention.
- Consider the appropriateness of the life assurance arrangements in the light of anticipated contributions to the mortgage repayments and any dependency by one partner upon the other as well as the effect on other potential beneficiaries.
- Advise on the need to draw up Wills, where appropriate, and the possibility of a cohabitation agreement.

4 Homelessness

3.61

The law governing the statutory duties owed to the homeless by local housing authorities is contained in Part VII Housing Act 1996 (HA 1996), as amended by the Homelessness Act 2002. Local housing authorities are now under a duty to provide the statutory homeless with permanent accommodation (s 193(3) HA 1996 as amended by the Homelessness Act 2002, s 6, which abolished the minimum period (of two years) for which a local authority was subject to a duty to rehouse).

3.62

Regardless of the tenure of their previous accommodation, cohabitants may find themselves, either as a family unit or, following breakdown of their relationship, as a single person (possibly with young children) without any accommodation at all. Homelessness arises in different ways, and how that situation arose may often determine whether or not a local authority has a duty to secure accommodation. Unfortunately, as will be seen, rooflessness of itself does not necessarily guarantee that a person is entitled to be found accommodation, even where there are dependent children. Homelessness has developed into a complex area of law and much of the case law under the previous 1985 statutory scheme remains relevant now. Only an outline of the main provisions and cases relevant to cohabitants is attempted here. Further details of provisions relevant to homelessness caused by domestic violence are given in Chapter 7 (see 7.124 ff).

(a) Procedure

3.63

Applicants must show that they are eligible for assistance and not excluded by being an asylum seeker or a person from abroad subject to immigration control (see ss 183(2), 185 and 186). This is in addition to having to show they are homeless or threatened with homelessness (s 175), that such homelessness is unintentional (see s 191) and that they are in priority need (s 189). A local authority must make enquiries under s 184 to see whether a duty is owed to secure accommodation. Where there is an apparent priority need, there is a duty to provide accommodation pending their enquiries (s 188). A victim of domestic abuse in need of urgent accommodation, regardless of whether or not they are the tenant or owner of accommodation, may still be homeless within the meaning of the Act and given that the homelessness legislation now provides a direct route into permanent accommodation, applicants should no longer be forced to pursue a remedy in relation to the former family home in any event. HA 1996, s 193(7C) and (7D) as inserted by the Housing and Regeneration

Act 2008 specifically confirm that an offer of an assured shorthold tenancy from a private landlord (which offers very little security to a tenant) will not be sufficient to discharge the duty to a homeless person unless they specifically agree to accept the offer in the knowledge that they are under absolutely no obligation to do so. Further, s 193(7F) imposes duties on Local Authorities to only offer eligible homeless applicants accommodation which is suitable for them.

3.64

Under the 1996 Act (as amended), to be eligible to be permanently housed, the applicant must:

(i) be eligible for assistance;

(ii) be homeless or threatened with homelessness;

(iii) have a priority need;

(iv) not be intentionally homeless.

3.65

If a local authority has reason to believe an applicant is eligible for assistance, homeless and in priority need, it must provide temporary accommodation pending a final decision (s 188) whilst it completes its enquiries and decides whether all four conditions are met. Fortunately, the once widespread use of bed and breakfast accommodation as temporary accommodation has largely disappeared, other than as a very short-term measure, and has been replaced with private sector accommodation, often leased to the local authority. The Homelessness (Suitability of Accommodation) (England) Order 2003 provides that B&B accommodation is not suitable accommodation for families with children and households that include a pregnant woman, unless there is no alternative accommodation available and then only for a maximum of six weeks.

3.66

Where cohabitants find themselves homeless or threatened with homelessness, they should be advised to apply to their local housing authority for accommodation pursuant to Part VII HA 1996. Where the authority has reason to believe that the applicant is homeless or threatened with homelessness, it has a duty to make enquiries (s 184(1)) and consider whether they are eligible for assistance and whether it owes a duty to secure them accommodation. If they also appear to be in priority need within the meaning of s 189 (see below), for example if they have dependent children who reside with them, the authority also has a duty to provide temporary accommodation pending completion of its enquiries (s 188). Thus, making an application can of itself provide a family with immediate help. There is no particular application form but most authorities normally require an applicant to attend their offices for an interview. However, their duties take immediate effect and cannot be avoided by closing the offices; and in the cities at least, they are expected to provide a 24-hour service (*R v Camden London Borough, ex p Gillan* (1988) 21 HLR 114).

3.67

The Act sets out various steps to be followed by the local authority, and hurdles which the applicant must clear before proving entitlement to accommodation. In addition the authority must also have regard to the current Department for Communities and Local Government Homelessness Code of Guidance for Local Authorities published 24 July 2006 (s 182), which sets out matters to be taken into account. However, providing they have had regard to it, failure to comply with it will not of itself provide a basis for a valid challenge to an authority's decision (see *De Falco v Crawley Borough Council* [1980] 1 All ER 913).

3.68

The current edition of the Code of Guidance to Local Authorities can be found on gov.uk website at www.gov.uk/government/publications/homelessness-code-of-guidance-for-councils-july-2006. It is a useful aid in negotiating cases with local authorities and has gone some way to soften the edges of the 1996 Act. Applicants must be advised in writing of the local authority's decision and the reasons for the decision where a duty to secure accommodation is denied pursuant to s 184(3) of the Act. The letter must also inform the applicant of their right to request a review under s 202 within 21 days of notification of the decision (s 202(1A)(3)).

3.69

Significantly, the 1996 Act introduced a right to request a review of any decision of the local authority under this Part of the Act (s 202) and, subject to having done this, a right of appeal on a point of law to the county court (s 204). The right to review is a prerequisite to the right of appeal to the county court under s 204 on a point of law. This in effect means that the vast majority of decisions are no longer challengeable by way of judicial review, although the grounds for challenge and the remedies available to the court remain broadly the same. Here the court may quash, confirm or (unlike in judicial review) vary the decision (s 204(3)). It is still the decision letter which will form the basis for the appeal, subject to the review procedure having been unsuccessfully pursued. Advisors should ensure that they request copies of the information on the local authority's file to which the applicant or advisor is entitled and from which the strength of the review or legal challenge can be assessed. Procedure on review is governed by s 203 and the Allocation of Housing and Homelessness (Review Procedures) Regulations 1999 (SI 1999 No 71) and is considered in the Code of Guidance (Chapter 19). An application for review must be made within 21 days of notification of the decision (s 202(3)). Reviews are undertaken on the basis of written representations in most cases, although local authorities may hear oral representations if they wish (and must do so in some situations (see paras 19.10–19.14 Code of Guidance)) and should normally be carried out within 56 days (para 19.15). Legal aid in the form of (means tested) Legal Help is available to applicants requesting review of a decision.

(b) Eligible for assistance

3.70

This is a controversial hurdle inserted by s 183 HA 1996 and those who are not eligible are defined in ss 185 (persons from abroad not eligible for housing assistance) and 186 (asylum seekers and their dependants). Annex 9 of the Code of Guidance gives further details of those who are ineligible. Effectively, s 185(2) provides that persons from abroad subject to immigration control within the meaning of the Asylum and Immigration Act 1996 are ineligible and only British citizens, citizens of a European Economic Area country (and Switzerland) or Commonwealth citizens with the right of residence in the UK can effectively be eligible for assistance. A dependent partner or child who is an ineligible person from abroad will not be taken into account in determining whether their partner or parent is homeless or has priority need (s 185(4)). Section 186 goes on to indicate that an asylum seeker (and any dependants) who are not ruled out by s 185, will still be ineligible for assistance if they have any accommodation in the UK, however temporary.

(c) Homeless or threatened with homelessness

3.71

Persons are regarded as 'homeless' if they have no accommodation in the UK or elsewhere which they, together with any person who normally resides with them as a member of their family or such other person for whom it is reasonable to reside with them, are entitled to occupy (s 175(1)).

3.72

The applicant's entitlement to occupy accommodation may take the following forms:

(i) an entitlement to occupy by virtue of an interest in it or by virtue of an order of the court;

(ii) an express or implied licence to occupy;

(iii) occupation as a residence by virtue of any enactment or rule of law giving him the right to remain in occupation or restricting the right of another to recover possession.

3.73

Section 177(2) provides that the accommodation must be such as is reasonable for the applicant to occupy and in determining this the local authority may have regard to the prevailing housing conditions in the local area. This is considered further in relation to the test for intentional homelessness (see para 3.82).

3.74

Accommodation will not constitute 'available accommodation' if it is available to the applicant only and not to other members of the family or other persons normally and reasonably residing with him (s 176).

3.75

Thus, a cohabiting couple's needs as a unit should be taken into account in determining whether accommodation is available for occupation. Similarly, where a finding is made to secure accommodation for an applicant, the suitability of the accommodation should be assessed according to their joint needs. Current policy and practice as noted above is to place any tenancy granted in joint names. It has been held that occupation by way of licence of a women's refuge and a night shelter, which could refuse admission if the shelter were full did not amount to accommodation (see *R v Ealing London Borough Council, ex p Sidhu* (1982) 2 HLR 45 and *R v Waveney District Council, ex p Bowers* [1983] QB 238). These examples predate the decision in *R v Brent London Borough Council, ex p Awua* (above), in which Lord Hoffmann (at page 461) stated that the word 'accommodation' must mean a place which can fairly be described as such. A night shelter, which is available only if there are bed-spaces and which excludes people during the day, would seem to fail this test. A women's refuge may not now be so clear cut.

3.76

An applicant will also be homeless if unable to secure entry to the accommodation (s 175(2)(a)) or at risk from domestic violence or other violence from a person residing there (s 177(1)), as discussed in Chapter 7 below. A person is 'threatened with homelessness' if they are liable to be made homeless within 28 days (s 175(4)), and, for the purpose of the subsequent duties imposed on the authority, there is no distinction made between these two categories of people.

(d) Priority need

3.77

Victims of domestic violence are arguably always in priority need in their own right on account of being vulnerable within the meaning of s 189(1)(c) as a result of a 'special reason' and s 177(1). However, an applicant can also establish priority need under s 189 if they are pregnant; have dependent children residing with them or who might reasonably reside with them; or are vulnerable as a result of old age, mental illness or handicap or physical disability or other special reason, or if such a person might reasonably reside with the applicant.

Additional applicants in priority need include:

(i) a person who is homeless or threatened with homelessness as a result of an emergency such as a fire or flood;

(ii) someone within a group of persons described as having priority need by the Secretary of State.

3.78

If homeless as a result of an emergency, cohabitants will automatically be considered to be in priority need although the nature of the emergency must be such as to cause physical damage. An illegal eviction is not an emergency (*R v Bristol City Council, ex p Bradic* (1995) 27 HLR 584, CA). A homeless cohabiting couple has nothing to lose from applying to the housing authority to see whether they can be classified in any of these categories. It has been held that it is not lawful for an authority to have a policy of excluding childless couples from falling within priority need (see *A-G (ex rel Tilley) v Wandsworth London Borough Council* [1981] 1 All ER 1162).

3.79

'Dependent children' normally means children under the age of 16 and all children aged 16 to 18 who are in, or are about to begin, full-time education or training or who for other reasons are unable to support themselves and who live at home. The test is a question of fact: are there dependent children who reside or ought reasonably to reside with the applicant? An authority cannot, where the parents are separated, insist that the applicant produces a court order before accepting that a priority need exists (see *R v Ealing London Borough Council, ex p Sidhu*, above). In *R v Lambeth London Borough Council, ex p Vagliviello* (1990) 22 HLR 392 the Court of Appeal confirmed that even a partial *custody* arrangement could indicate a priority need, as the test is one of whether children could reasonably be expected to reside with the applicant, not whether the applicant had sole custody. Since the advent of the Children Act 1989 (CA 1989) both these issues have increased significance. The 'no order presumption' in CA 1989 means that cohabitants are less likely to have child arrangements ('lives with') orders in effect relating to children of previous relationships, yet such children may still give cohabitants a priority need for accommodation. In addition, s 11(4) CA 1989 specifically envisages that child arrangements ('lives with') orders may be made in favour of two or more persons who do not live together and, thus, what would previously have been described as a shared residence or shared care situation, has become more common, as discussed in Chapter 8. Indeed the Code of Guidance does now recognise this type of situation may give one or both parents a priority need and that each case must be carefully considered (paras 10.6–10.11).

3.80

The House of Lords decision in the joined cases of *R v Oldham Metropolitan Borough Council, ex p Garlick; R v Bexley London Borough Council, ex p Bentum; R v Tower Hamlets London Borough Council, ex p Begum* [1993] AC 509 decided, *inter alia*, that 'dependent children' were not normally capable of being 'applicants' and did not have a priority need in their own right through their vulnerability.

3.81

To show vulnerability, an applicant must be of retirement age, or vulnerable in some other way. This has been defined as being less able to both find and keep accommodation (see *R v Lambeth London Borough Council, ex p Carroll* (1987) 20 HLR 142, and *R v Kensington and Chelsea London Borough Council, ex p Kihara* (1996) 29 HLR 147). In *Carroll* the court indicated that an authority must reach its own decision on vulnerability and not merely rubber stamp a medical opinion unless that is decisive on the only relevant issues. Accordingly advisors should in appropriate cases advise the applicant to submit independent medical evidence to the local authority. Regard should also be had to the Code of Guidance (paras 10.12–10.35) which gives examples of the different categories of priority need and of vulnerability. The local authority must provide interim accommodation where there is a *prima facie* priority need, but thereafter they should make further enquiries to see if there is in fact such a need. Only if this is established will applicants proceed to the next hurdle.

(e) Intentional homelessness

3.82

It is this final hurdle which has spawned the most case law under the old law and undoubtedly causes hardship to people who fulfil the other criteria but are deemed to be the authors of their own misfortune. Where there is a finding of intentional homelessness, but that the applicant has a priority need, a local authority will not owe any duty to secure permanent accommodation for the applicant, but 'shall secure that accommodation is available for his occupation for such period as they consider will give him a reasonable opportunity of securing accommodation for his occupation and provide him with (or secure that he is provided with) advice and assistance in any attempts he may make to secure that accommodation becomes available for his occupation' (s 190(2)). If the applicant is considered not to have a priority need, the duty is just to 'provide him with (or secure that he is provided with) advice and assistance in any attempts he may make to secure that accommodation becomes available for his occupation' (s 190(3)). A person is intentionally homeless if he or she deliberately does or fails to do anything which leads them to cease to occupy accommodation which is available and reasonable for them to occupy (s 191(1)). The definition of becoming intentionally 'threatened with homelessness' is subject to a similar test. An act or omission in good faith by a person unaware of a relevant fact such as security of tenure, the availability of assistance with rent or mortgage payments, or the validity of a notice to quit, is not to be treated as deliberate (s 191(2)). Section 191(3) is responsible for widening the ambit of intentional homelessness. It states:

> 'A person shall be treated as becoming homeless intentionally if—(a) he enters into an arrangement under which he is required to cease to occupy accommodation which it would have been reasonable for him to continue to occupy; and (b) the purpose of the arrangement is to enable him to become entitled to assistance under this Part; and there is no other good reason why he is homeless.'

Section 191(4) goes on to include as intentionally homeless persons who have received advice and assistance under s 197 as to where they can find suitable accommodation, but who have failed to secure this when they should reasonably have been expected to. These provisions aim to avoid collusion between friends, relatives, landlords and tenants with a view to obtaining accommodation, encouraging them instead to stay in 'unsettled' accommodation, for example with relatives, whilst they await accommodation through the housing register route. In addition, they can be seen to push people into making greater use of the private rented sector.

3.83

The issue of good faith (see s 191(2)) arose in *R v Hammersmith and Fulham London Borough Council, ex p Lusi* (1991) 23 HLR 260, where a couple who gave up their London flat in order to pursue a business venture in Turkey which subsequently failed were found to be intentionally homeless upon their return. The Divisional Court found, however, that the local authority had misdirected itself in law by equating ignorance of relevant facts with bad faith and consequently quashed the decision, remitting it for further investigation of what was actually known or ought to have been known by the applicant. This approach was endorsed by the Court of Appeal In *R v Exeter City Council, ex p Tranckle* (1993) 26 HLR 244.

3.84

A person is not intentionally homeless if they give up accommodation which is not available for both the applicant and any person with whom they might reasonably be expected to reside (s 175(3)). Thus, in *R v Peterborough City Council, ex p Carr* (1990) 22 HLR 206, QBD, a pregnant woman who left her accommodation with her sister due to her sister's refusal to allow her prospective child's father to live with her was not intentionally homeless. In *R v Westminster*

City Council, ex p Bishop (1993) 25 HLR 459, the Court of Appeal found that accommodation was only available for the applicant's occupation if both the applicant and those members of her family who normally reside with her can reasonably be expected to occupy it. Thus, a finding of intentionality against an applicant who surrendered her tenancy on a problem estate where there was strong evidence of adverse effects from living there upon the applicant's daughter was quashed.

3.85

Where one cohabitant has done an act, such as giving up a job, which has meant the loss of tied accommodation, then it may be possible for their spouse, civil partner or cohabitant or another adult who usually and reasonably resides with them, to make the application under the Act in order to avoid a finding of intentionality (see *R v North Devon District Council, ex p Lewis* [1981] 1 WLR 328 and *R v Swansea City Council, ex p Thomas* (1983) 9 HLR 64). Each case will depend on its own facts, but to be successful the applicant must not have acquiesced in the act which led to the loss of accommodation. Thus, in *Lewis* above, although it was accepted that a cohabitant was entitled to make an application following her partner's quitting his job and losing accommodation, she was equally found to be intentionally homeless because she had acquiesced in his decision to leave. It would have been otherwise if she had done all in her power to prevent him from resigning.

3.86

Cases of mortgage and rent arrears may lead to intentionality findings, as do possession orders granted on the basis that the applicant has caused nuisance and annoyance to other occupiers. The Code of Guidance (see para 11.18–11.19) suggests that a lenient view may be taken where arrears arise due to ignorance of the availability of welfare benefits or where the applicant was genuinely unable to keep up the rent or mortgage payments even after claiming benefits, and no further financial help was available. Where one party has spent the rent money on alcohol or caused nuisance and annoyance despite the attempts by the other to prevent it, the 'innocent' cohabitant or spouse/civil partner can argue that they are not intentionally homeless, particularly if financially dependent on their partner, or for other reasons were not in a position to prevent the situation. It is submitted that this should be the case regardless of whether the parties are joint tenants or the tenancy is vested in the other's name. It has been held that mere knowledge of rent or mortgage arrears by a partner is not necessarily enough to constitute intentionality as they may not have learned of the situation until it was too late to forestall. However, where there is a joint tenancy, lack of knowledge may be difficult to uphold as both parties should be communicated with and served with proceedings. Many couples in severe financial straits may decide that what money is available should be spent on food rather than housing costs. They may be helped to some extent by the case of *R v Hillingdon London Borough Council, ex p Tinn* (1988) 20 HLR 305 where it was held that it could not be reasonable to occupy accommodation where to meet the mortgage repayments the family had to go without food and the other necessities of life. This approach was endorsed by the Court of Appeal in *R v Wandsworth London Borough Council, ex p Hawthorne* (1994) 27 HLR 59, where a mother was evicted for rent arrears which had accrued as a result of her electing to spend her benefit entitlement on food for the children rather than the rent after the imposition of a housing benefit ceiling. Indeed, the authority had considered the failure to pay rent a deliberate act without having applied itself to the question of what had caused the failure to pay rent as required by the Code of Guidance and consequently the intentionality finding was quashed. The Homelessness (Suitability of Accommodation) Order 1996 (SI 1996 No 3204) requires the housing authority to consider the affordability of the accommodation for the applicant. The Order specifies, among other things, that in determining whether it would be (or would have been) reasonable for a person to continue to occupy accommodation, a housing authority must take into account whether the accommodation is affordable for him or her and must, in particular, take account of:

(i) the financial resources available to him or her;

(ii) the costs in respect of the accommodation;

(iii) maintenance payments (to a spouse, former spouse or in respect of a child); and

(iv) his or her reasonable living expenses.

3.87

Whether or not it is reasonable for an applicant to continue to occupy accommodation involves many questions, but an authority must take into account the housing conditions in its area in reaching a decision on reasonableness (s 177(2)), and the worse these conditions are, the more an applicant is expected to put up with before quitting accommodation. In *R v Tower Hamlets London Borough Council, ex p Monaf* (1988) 20 HLR 529, it was held that the authority must perform a balancing exercise between the reasons for departure and housing conditions in that area. However, the authority must compare the applicant's actual housing conditions with those in the *authority's* area and not with the conditions of residents in the area or country where the applicant had left the accommodation (see *R v Newham London Borough Council, ex p Tower Hamlets London Borough Council* (1990) 22 HLR 298). Another important factor is that the authority can look beyond the immediate cause of homelessness to see if the real cause of the homelessness is intentional.

3.88

The House of Lords decision in *Awua* (above) removed the concept of 'settled accommodation' developed under the 1985 legislation and the fact that accommodation lost is not settled or permanent will not save an applicant from a finding of intentional homelessness unless the tenure was so precarious it rendered them liable to leave within 28 days.

3.89

In *Din v Wandsworth London Borough Council* [1983] 1 AC 657, where a family ignored advice to remain in accommodation until the court order for possession expired, although it was accepted that by the time they applied to the authority they would in any event have been homeless unintentionally, the act of leaving available accommodation before being required to leave was sufficient to render them intentionally homeless in the view of the House of Lords. However, the latest Code of Guidance now suggests that 'authorities should note that the fact that a tenant has a right to remain in occupation does not necessarily mean that he or she is not homeless. In assessing whether an applicant is homeless in cases where he or she is a tenant who has a right to remain in occupation pending execution of a warrant for possession, the housing authority will also need to consider whether it would be reasonable for him or her to continue to occupy the accommodation in the circumstances'.

3.90

Accordingly, it might well be considered unreasonable for local authorities to require mortgagors or tenants to fight possession actions where the mortgagee or landlord has a certain prospect of success. In *R v Newham London Borough, ex p Ugbo* (1993) 26 HLR 263, an assured shorthold tenant who ignored the council's advice to stay in the accommodation until after the possession order had been made, had a finding of intentionality made against her quashed by the Divisional Court, which found that the advice she had been given by the council was wrong.

(f) Duties of local authorities; local connections; other routes to accommodation

3.91

Once an authority has made its decision it must notify the applicant, giving reasons if it finds no duty to secure accommodation (s 184(3)) or that there is a local connection elsewhere (s 184(2)). If the authority finds that there is no priority need, but that the applicant is not intentionally homeless, then advice and assistance must be provided (s 192(2)), although secure accommodation could still be offered (s 192(3)). If there is priority need but the applicants are judged intentionally homeless, then accommodation must be provided for such period as will allow them to find other accommodation (typically 28 days) (s 190(2)(a)) and advice and assistance should also be provided (s 190(2)(b)). At this point, a family is often left unable to afford, or even find, private sector accommodation, yet nothing further has to be done by the local authority.

3.92

The harsh effects on a family of an intentionality finding, produced some imaginative attempts to secure housing under the 1985 Act by extending the principle established in *R v North Devon District Council, ex p Lewis* (above). The House of Lords decision in *R v Oldham Metropolitan Borough Council, ex p Garlick*; *R v Bexley London Borough Council, ex p Bentum, R v Tower Hamlets London Borough Council, ex p Begum* (above) was the result of three such attempts. They each sought to argue that a duty to house the families involved in each case arose where in the cases of both *Garlick* and *Bentum*; a dependent four-year-old child, and in *Begum*, a severely mentally handicapped adult daughter, neither of whom were 'tainted' with the intentionality of their parents (the original applicants), made fresh applications in their own names under the Act. However, the House of Lords rejected this argument on the basis, *inter alia*, that a degree of understanding sufficient to appreciate the nature of the application was implicitly required by applicants under the Act, who needed to be able to decide whether or not to accept the accommodation offered. In the cases of the four-year-old dependent children, they were far too young to achieve this threshold and, in any event, had no priority need. Thus they could not be applicants under the Act. In the case of *Begum*, further evidence of her level of understanding would be required in order to determine whether she had the capacity to be an applicant.

3.93

In its deliberations, the court took the view that Parliament could not have intended intentionally homeless families to be housed 'through the back door'. It also took into account the fact that there were other statutory provisions which would assist in providing accommodation for children or a vulnerable person, namely s 20 CA 1989 and s 21 National Assistance Act 1948 respectively (although the latter provision has been omitted from the Act by virtue of the Social Services and Well-being (Wales) Act 2014 (Consequential Amendments) Regulations 2016).

3.94

In cases involving applicants who have children under 18 where the housing authority are satisfied that the applicant is ineligible for assistance, the housing authority must alert the social services authority, or social services department, as appropriate, to the case (s 213A). Cohabitants with dependent children who find themselves in this situation, and who do not wish their children to be accommodated under s 20, may be able to obtain assistance by a request for assistance by Social Services under s 17 CA 1989. This places a duty on social services departments to safeguard and promote the welfare of children 'in need' within their area and to promote the upbringing of such children *by their families* where this is consistent with their welfare. This is to be done by providing a range of services including under s 17(6) 'providing accommodation and giving assistance in kind or cash'.

3.95

Providing a child can be shown to be 'in need', as defined by s 17(10), which involves showing that the child's health or development is likely to be significantly impaired or to fall below a reasonable standard without the provision of services, then the duty to provide assistance arises. It must be strongly arguable that any child who is literally roofless is 'in need' and that the assistance required to remedy this is accommodation. Unfortunately, social services departments no longer have their own housing stock. If they accept the need for assistance they may either provide cash for a deposit for private rented accommodation. Nonetheless, this may result in practice in the whole family being given emergency accommodation pending an assessment of the child's needs. However, in *R v Barnet LBC, ex parte Foran* (1999) 31 HLR 708, the Court of Appeal confirmed there was no absolute duty on Social Services to house homeless children together with their families. Furthermore, in *R (G) v Barnet LBC* [2001] EWCA Civ 540, the Court of Appeal confirmed that the duty in s 17(1) CA 1989, to promote the upbringing of children by their families, could be met by financing the family's return to their home country. Thus, whilst there is power to accommodate, there is no duty to house a family, but only the children under s 20 CA 1989. Local Authority Circular 2003(13): *Guidance on accommodating children in need and their families* provides further guidance to social services authorities on the effect of s 17.

3.96

Prior to the Housing Act 1996, the House of Lords had been asked in *R v Northavon District Council, ex p Smith* (1994) 26 HLR 659 to consider whether the duty contained in s 27 CA 1989 requiring local housing authorities to co-operate with social services in carrying out functions under the 1989 Act, unless it is incompatible with their own duties and functions, extended to the provision of accommodation for a family previously found intentionally homeless, but whose children had subsequently been identified as 'in need'. They held that the housing authority were under no duty to provide permanent accommodation following the intentionality finding and that the applicants had no priority over others awaiting accommodation, either through the homelessness legislation or the waiting list route. All they therefore had to do was consider whether they could assist in preventing the children from suffering from lack of accommodation without prejudicing their other functions. If they could not, then it fell to social services to protect the children, either by financial assistance or by exercise of their other powers. Section 10 of the Children Act 2004 established a duty on local authorities to make arrangements to promote co-operation between the authority, relevant partners (including district authorities) and other persons or bodies engaged in activities in relation to children, to improve the well-being of children and young people in the authority's area. Where an applicant is eligible for assistance and unintentionally homeless, and has a priority need because there is one or more dependent child in his or her household, the housing authority will owe a main homelessness duty to secure that accommodation is available to them.

3.97

Thus, following eviction from temporary accommodation, intentionally homeless families' best hope of assistance lies with social services, whose policies will vary from area to area and whose ability to assist them in finding and financing accommodation as a family is likely to be limited. Nonetheless, the duty in s 17(1) to promote the upbringing of children by their families is a powerful argument for advisors to use in favour of financial assistance, especially given the high cost of providing accommodation for children under s 20 CA 1989. Another possibility, where a family is on income support or income-based jobseeker's allowance, is for assistance to be provided in applying for a social fund budgeting loan for rent in advance (see Chapter 4).

3.98

If an applicant has succeeded in overcoming the hurdles contained in the homelessness legislation and described above, then the authority has a duty to secure suitable permanent accommodation (s 193(3)). The duty is brought to an end only on securing such accommodation for the applicant or where the applicant refuses an offer of accommodation which the authority is satisfied is suitable for him/her on the authority notifying the applicant that it regards itself as having discharged its statutory duty under (s 193 (5), (6), and (7)).

3.99

In assessing suitability, which is governed by s 210 HA 1996, space and arrangement will be key factors, but other matters, such as affordability of the rent and location, may be material. Housing authorities will need to consider carefully the suitability of accommodation for applicants whose household has particular medical and/or physical needs. Under the 1985 legislation, the Court of Appeal has found that the physical structure of the building is not the only test and a vulnerability to violence in that location could be a factor (*R v Broxbourne Borough Council, ex p Willmoth* (1989) 22 HLR 118). In addition, personal factors of the applicant and those expected to reside with them are relevant (see *R v Brent London Borough Council, ex p Omar* (1991) 23 HLR 446). Accommodation at a rent which the applicant cannot afford from their own resources or with state assistance was not suitable (*R v Tower Hamlets London Borough Council, ex p Kaur* (1994) 26 HLR 597). It seems clear that assured shorthold private sector accommodation will be regarded as suitable, although it would still seem to be good law that the tenure or time element of suitability should reflect the circumstances of the case (*R v Wandsworth London Borough Council, ex p Wingrove* and *ex p Mansoor* [1997] QB 953, CA). Account will need to be taken of any social considerations relating to the applicant and his or her household that might affect the suitability of accommodation. Any risk of violence or racial harassment in a particular locality must also be taken into account. The Code of Guidance at Chapter 17 provides more detailed guidance on the factors to be taken into account when determining the suitability of temporary accommodation secured under the homelessness legislation.

3.100

If there is no local connection with the authority to whom they have applied, but there is with another authority, then s 198 provides that the applicant can be referred back to the authority with whom he or she has a local connection, providing the applicant does not run the risk of domestic violence (or abuse) in that area. Section 199 defines 'local connection' in terms of periods of residence (past or present), employment, family associations and special circumstances. Where an applicant does not have a local connection with any area but fulfils the other criteria, then the local authority to whom he or she has applied must secure suitable accommodation, although this may be done through another authority or housing body (see *R v Hillingdon London Borough Council, ex p Streeting* [1980] 3 All ER 413).

3.101

Section 177(1) specifically indicates that a person is homeless if they have accommodation which it is not reasonable for them to occupy because it is 'probable' that this will lead to domestic violence against them or a person who might reasonably be expected to reside with them. In determining whether it would be reasonable for the person to continue to occupy accommodation regard may be had to the general circumstances prevailing in relation to housing in the area (s 177(2)). In addition, s 175(2) treats a person as homeless if they have accommodation but cannot secure entry to it. Homelessness on family breakdown due to domestic violence is a problem often affecting cohabitants with children, and is dealt with in Chapter 7.

CHAPTER 4

Tax, pensions and social security

4.01

It is in the areas of tax, pensions and social security that some of the greatest anomalies in the legal treatment of cohabitants become apparent. Whilst all taxpayers, whether married, in a civil partnership, cohabiting, separated, divorced or single are taxed as independent taxpayers on their own income and capital gains, spouses and civil partners are still treated preferentially in limited tax-related ways. A spouse or civil partner is for example able to transfer 10% of their personal income tax allowance to the other provided that neither of them is a higher rate taxpayer. Cohabitants are not treated in the same way as a married couple or civil partners except for the purposes of the high income child benefit charge (see 4.38), childcare top-up payments (see 4.17) and when claiming tax credits (see 4.06 ff).

4.02

It is not proposed here to look at the substantive law in any great detail, but to outline the general principles, and points of particular relevance to cohabitants.

1 Income tax and tax credits

4.03

There are now very few differences between spouses/civil partners and cohabitants as far as income tax is concerned. Instead the focus is on those with children and particularly on those working parents on low incomes. Income, apart from dividends and savings income, is taxed at the basic rate, the higher rate and the additional rate. The standard personal allowance (ie the amount of income on which no tax is paid) is £11,500 (2017/18, rising to £11,850 for 2018/19). The basic rate of 20% is charged on income up to £33,500 (2017/18, rising to £34,500 for 2018/19). The higher rate of 40% is then charged on income from £35,501 to £150,000 (2017/18, but from £34,501 to £150,000 for 2018/19). The additional rate of 45% applies to income over £150,000. No personal allowance applies in respect of income of £123,000 or over (2017/18, rising to £123,700 for 2018/19).

4.04

Child tax credit (CTC) and working tax credit (WTC) were introduced from April 2003 as part of the then Labour government's programme to halve child poverty by 2010. Figures published in February 2010 showed that tax credits were awarded to 5.92 million families (roughly 87.5% of all families with children). This number fell sharply from April 2011, as the Conservative-led coalition government made numerous changes to the regime which reduced entitlement for many middle income households, so that in 2014/15 just 4.43 million families were in receipt of such benefits. Further significant changes to child tax credit were introduced by the current Conservative government from 6 April 2017, including a two-child limit which applies where a family has a child or children born after that date. Tax credits and the current system of means-tested working age state benefits are currently being phased out and replaced with Universal Credit, such that it is intended that new claimants may be obliged to claim Universal Credit rather than tax credits and existing claimants will be transferred over between July 2019 and March 2022 (see 4.14 ff).

4.05

Tax credits do not count as taxable income and are paid directly by HMRC. Claims are made jointly by cohabitants (who are both aged 16 or over and present in the UK) and awards are reviewed annually (or earlier on separation) and cease should one party no longer reside (save for temporary absences) in the UK. A claim form TC 600 can be ordered directly at www.gov.uk/quakify-tax-credits by following the simple instructions. The Tax Credit Helpline is open daily from 8am (9am on a Sunday) to 10pm and its number is 0345 300 3900.

2 Tax Credits (including Universal Credit)

(a) Child Tax Credit

4.06

Child Tax Credit (CTC) may be claimed by cohabitants in respect of a 'child' or a 'qualifying young person' for whom they are responsible (the Tax Credits Act 2002 (TCA 2002), s 8(1)). The principal rule is that a claimant is responsible for a child or young person who normally lives with the claimant and each member of a cohabiting couple qualifies in respect of children or young persons who normally live with them. The TCA defines a 'child' as someone under the age of 16 (s 8(3)). A child becomes a 'qualifying young person' on 1 September following his or her 16th birthday. A qualifying young person is someone who is not a child but who is under 20 and continuing in ordinary or further education at a school or college (excluding advanced education/university degree course and education provided as part of employment) or is undertaking approved training which is not being provided for him/her as part of his/her employment and is not engaged in remunerative work, is not on a relevant training programme for which payment may be made and is not in receipt of income support or income-based jobseekers allowance. Full-time education at a school or college must be for at least an average of 12 hours a week during normal term time (the Child Tax Credit Regulations 2002, reg 5(5)).

4.07

CTC consists of four elements:

(i) Family element (subsequently withdrawn from 6 April 2017 in respect of families with children born on or after that date – s 9(2) TCA 2002 as inserted by the Welfare Reform and Work Act 2016, s 13(2)(a));

(ii) Child/Young Person's element (limited to a maximum of two children or young people born on or after 6 April 2017 – s 9(3A) TCA 2002 as inserted by the Welfare Reform and Work Act 2016, s 13(4));

(iii) Disability element for a disabled child of young person;

(iv) Disability element for a severely disabled child or young person.

4.08

The maximum child tax credit award is the aggregate of all the elements that the claimant is entitled to. The Family element is presently worth £545 per annum. For the tax years ending 6 April 2018, 2019 and 2020 the Child/Young Person's element is frozen at the 2015/16 rate of £2,780 per annum. Children with disabilities receive the Disability element according to their needs regardless of their date of birth and irrespective of the number of children in the family. For the year 2017/18 the disabled child element is £3,175 per annum with an additional £1,290 if a child is severely disabled.

(b) Working Tax Credit

4.09

The elements of working tax credit (WTC) are:

(i) *Basic element* – at the rate of £1,960 per annum for tax year 2017/18;

(ii) *Couples and lone parent element* – at the rate of £2,010 per annum for tax year 2017/18;

(iii) *30-hour element* – at the rate of £810 per annum for tax year 2017/18;

(iv) *Disabled worker element* – at the rate of £3,000 per annum for tax year 2017/18;

(v) *Severe disability element* – at the rate of £1,290 per annum for tax year 2017/18; and

(vi) *Child care element* – variable (presently, for the tax year 2017/18, a maximum of £122.50 per week or £6,370 per annum for one child; for two or more children the maximum weekly amount is £210 which equates to £10,920 per annum) as it requires the claimant to have incurred expenses on childcare materially greater than the amount of the tax credit in order to be payable. It should be noted however that this element cannot be claimed in addition to child care 'top-up payments' made by HMRC under the Child Care Scheme introduced by the Childcare Payments Act 2014.

4.10

In order to claim the other elements, the claimant must first establish an entitlement to the basic element ie s/he must be in qualifying remunerative work on the date of the claim or must have an offer of work to begin within seven days of the date of the claim. If a claimant is cohabiting and both partners satisfy the WTC entitlement conditions only one of each of the basic, couples and 30-hour elements can be claimed per couple (ie a maximum of £4,780 for a couple). However, if each claimant satisfies the necessary conditions, two disability or severe disability elements may be claimed.

4.11

In order for joint claimants to qualify for WTC where neither cohabitant is responsible for a child or qualifying young person, each must:

(i) be aged at least 16, work for not less than 16 hours per week, have a physical or mental disability which puts him or her at a disadvantage of getting a job; or

(ii) be at least 25 years old and work for at least 30 hours per week; or

(iii) be at least 60 and work for not less than 16 hours per week.

4.12

In the case of a joint claim by cohabitants where one is responsible for a child or qualifying young person, it is enough to show that the partner responsible for the child:

(i) is at least 16 years old and is a member of a couple where at least one partner works for not less than 16 hours per week and the aggregate number of hours for which the couple work is not less than 24 hours per week;

(ii) is aged at least 16 and works for not less than 16 hours per week and has a physical or mental disability which puts that person at a disadvantage in getting a job;

(iii) is at least 16, works for at least 16 hours a week and that person's partner is incapacitated, an in-patient in a hospital, in prison or entitled to carer's allowance; or

(iv) is at least 60 and works for not less than 16 hours per week.

4.13

If a joint claim is made, the payments in respect of CTC and the child care element of WTC will be made to only one of the claimants (TCA 2002, s 24(2)). The intention is that payment should be made to the main carer of the children or young persons in respect of whom the claim was made. If the couple are living together at the same address they may jointly nominate the main carer. If there is a change in circumstances which means that the claimant(s) ceases to be entitled to tax credits or the change would decrease the rate of entitlement there is a specific requirement to notify HMRC within one month of the change or if later one month after the person is aware of the change. A notification may be given orally or in writing. HMRC presently requires notification by following the instructions on its website in this regard at www.gov.uk/ and/or by calling the Tax Credit Helpline. Notification of a change must normally be given by the claimant but in the case of a joint claim may be given by either claimant.

(c) Universal Credit

4.14

Universal Credit (UC) is a single integrated means-tested benefit for people of working age who are on a low income. It is being rolled out gradually over a number of years and replaces the primary means-tested benefits including CTC, WTC, income support, income-based jobseekers allowance, income-related employment and support allowance and housing benefit. It is intended that these benefits will in time cease to be payable and that all existing claimants will be transferred to UC by 2022. The principal legislative provisions for UC are the Welfare Reform Act 2012, Part 1 and the Universal Credit Regulations 2013 (as amended).

4.15

To qualify for UC a claimant must meet the basic conditions which are to be aged 18 or over (or aged 16 or 17 in specified circumstances), under the qualifying age for pension credit, present in the UK and not subject to immigration control, not in education and have accepted a 'claimant commitment' to meet certain work-related conditions. A claimant must also meet the financial conditions. In contrast with tax credits, there are no in-work or out-of-work hours considerations (as you can continue to receive UC regardless of hours worked) and UC is subject to a capital limit and will only be payable if a claimant (and their partner if a joint claim is made) has capital of less than £16,000. As for tax credits however a joint claim must be made by cohabitants. A claimant can find out if they are eligible to claim UC by starting the online application process for UC at www.gov.uk or using the postcode checkers at www.universalcreditinfo.net or www.entitledto.uk. UC is calculated by adding together a standard allowance and set amounts for different financial needs to arrive at the maximum amount of UC. In addition to the standard allowance, amounts can be claimed in UC for children, housing costs (for assistance with rent, mortgage interest, some service charges and interest on a loan secured on a home), limited work capability, carers and childcare costs. A Benefit Cap (see 4.45) applies in respect of UC and to obtain an estimate of how much of the benefit will be capped, the gov.uk website offers a benefit cap calculator at www.gov.uk/benefit-cap-calculator.

4.16

The elements of the monthly award are set out in the Universal Credit Regulations 2013, Part 4 and are (as per the tax year 2017.18) as follows:

1.	*Standard Allowance*	
	Single claimant aged under 25	£251.77
	Single claimant aged 25 or over	£317.82
	Joint claimants both aged under 25	£395.20
	Joint claimants where either is 25	£498.89
2.	*Child Element*	
	First child or qualifying young person if born before 6 April 2017	£277.08
	Second child or qualifying young person (or first child born on/after 6 April 2017)	£231.67
	Each subsequent child or qualifying young person	£ 0
3.	*Additional Amount for Disabled Child or Qualifying Young Person*	
	Lower rate	£126.11
	Higher rate	£372.30
4.	*Limited Capability for Work Element (for claims made before 3 April 2017)*	£126.11 per calendar month.
5.	*Limited Capability for Work and Work-related Activity*	£318.76
6.	*Carer Element*	£151.89

7. *Child Care Costs Element*

   Maximum amount for one child £646.35 (or 85% of actual costs whichever is lower)

   Maximum amount for two or more children £1108.04 (or 85% of actual costs whichever is lower).

(d) Childcare Payments Act 2014

4.17

This Act enables parents and carers to receive money from HMRC towards the cost of childcare.

If a person makes a declaration of eligibility to childcare top-up payments, any tax credit award (made singly or jointly) terminates automatically and immediately as tax credit claimants are not entitled to child care payments (Childcare Payments Act 2014, s 30). The same applies in respect of Universal Credit (s 31). The amount of the top-up payment is 25% of the amount of the qualifying payment (s 1(4)), which essentially means any payment made into a childcare account (s 19(1)) over a three-month period (s 5) up to a maximum of £4,000 in the case of a disabled child and £2,000 in the case of any other child (s 19(5)).

3 Capital gains tax

4.18

The Taxation of Capital Gains Act 1992 (TCGA 1992) provides that capital gains tax is payable on all chargeable gains made in respect of chargeable assets, after deduction of all allowable losses and subject to an annual exemption/tax-free allowance of £11,300 for the tax year 2017/18. Cohabitants are taxed as independent persons and disposals between cohabitants do not attract any special treatment and are thus chargeable either as a gain or a loss as appropriate, unlike transfers between spouses or civil partners which are made free of any capital gains tax implications.

4.19

The main asset of most cohabitants is likely to be the home, in respect of which a principal private residence exemption applies, so that a sale would not attract capital gains tax, and any profit made on a sale is not considered a gain (ss 222–224 TCGA 1992). Spouses or civil partners can have only one principal private residence, whereas cohabitants may have one each. Accordingly, providing one property is vested in each of their names, and they can each satisfy the residence condition, it is possible to avoid paying capital gains tax on either property no matter when they are sold.

4 Inheritance tax

4.20

While no inheritance tax is payable on gifts or transfers made to a surviving spouse or civil partner from the deceased's estate, there is, again, no like treatment of cohabitants, who are basically treated as strangers. Inheritance tax is payable on 'transfers of value', that is those which reduce the value of the transferor's estate, made either *inter vivos* or on death. However, there is a threshold of £325,000 (which has remained unchanged since 2010/11) below which no tax is payable in respect of transfers made. Although (outside of London and surrounding counties) this may seem a fairly large sum of money, there is, unlike capital gains tax, no exception in respect of the transferor's residence, and thus the value of the deceased's share of his or her property will be taken into account in calculating when the threshold is reached. Where jointly owned property is held as tenants in common in equity, the deceased's share forms part of the estate and tax will be payable in accordance with the terms of the Will.

4.21

Where there is an equitable joint tenancy, the deceased's share in the property will pass to the co-owner in accordance with the right of survivorship who will not be liable for any inheritance tax due in respect of the deceased's share.

4.22

After the first £325,000, tax is payable, currently at 40%, either by the estate or by the beneficiary. Thus where a cohabitant is the only beneficiary, his/her inheritance will be subject to tax where the total value exceeds this threshold. Where gifts are made before death, and providing the transferor lives for seven years after the making of the gift, then no inheritance tax is payable on such a gift and its value will not form part of the transferor's estate on death. Even if the transferor dies within the seven-year period, liability to tax will normally be reduced on a sliding scale, although if death occurs within three years of the gift, then tax is still payable at the full rate. If the donor survives three years but less than four, then 80% of the full rate of tax is payable; tax is payable at 60% of the full rate if the death occurs after four years but less than five; at 40% of the full rate after five years but less than six; and at 20% after six years but less than seven. In addition, there is an annual exemption of £3,000 which reduces liability on *inter vivos* gifts.

4.23

Cohabitants making Wills, perhaps even more than other clients, need to be advised of the inheritance tax implications of their proposed gifts, and to consider the advantages of making use of the annual exemption and of effecting life assurance for the benefit of their partner, as discussed in Chapter 1.

5 Council tax

4.24

Council tax is a local tax levied on each 'dwelling' (see s 3 Local Government Act (LGA) 1992) and is based on the assumption that the dwelling is occupied by two adults. It is payable by one or more of the residents (who must be over 18), where the dwelling is occupied as their sole or main residence. Where there is no such resident, council tax becomes payable by the non-resident owner. There is a hierarchy of residents, and the adult resident(s) liable for the tax will be the first to fall into the highest of the following categories (see s 6(1) LGA 1992):

- freeholder;
- leaseholder;
- statutory or secure tenant;
- contractual licensee;
- any other resident.

4.25

Two or more residents falling into the same category (or owners in the absence of a resident) will normally be jointly and severally liable for the tax (s 6(2)). This will obviously affect cohabitants who are joint owners or joint tenants of a property. Furthermore, even where only one partner is ostensibly liable, s 9 provides that the partner of a liable person is (with the exception of a severely mentally impaired partner) also jointly and severally liable for the period of their residence if they are married, civil partners or living together as if they were spouses or civil partners. The consequence of this for cohabitants is that, on separation, it is vital for the cohabitant who leaves to inform the local authority that they are no longer resident in the property to avoid future liability.

4.26

The amount of council tax payable depends on the valuation band into which the property has been placed and liability may be reduced if the dwelling is exempt, has less than two residents, is occupied by residents who are disregarded or are entitled to a status discount, or there is entitlement to council tax benefit (see ss 11, 11A and 12 and Sch 1 LGA 1992 and SI 1992/552, SI 1992/2942, and SI 1993/149). Those people not considered to be adults for the purposes of council tax liability include 'children' under 18, 18- and 19-year-olds in full-time education, people on some apprenticeship schemes, full-time college and university students, people under 25 who get funding from the Skills Funding Agency or Young People's Learning Agency and student nurses.

4.27

It should be noted that with regard to properties in multiple occupation, liability normally falls on the owner and not the individual residents. However, this entitles the owner landlord to include an element for council tax in the rent charged to tenants, which, although not reclaimable through council tax benefit, should form part of the rent eligible for housing benefit payments as discussed below.

4.28

In April 2013, Council Tax Benefit was replaced by Council Tax Reduction (or Council Tax Support), which could result in a council tax bill being reduced by up to 100%. The amount of the reduction depends on where the claimant lives (as each local authority runs its own scheme), their household income, the presence or absence in the household of children, whether they/their partner has any savings and whether they/their partner is in receipt of benefits.

6 Welfare benefits and pensions

4.29

The law is by no means even-handed in its treatment of cohabitants in the area of welfare benefits and once again it is not possible here to do more than give a summary of the main points relevant to cohabitants. As has been noted in respect of imputed joint liability for council tax, there is a tendency to treat cohabitants in the same way as spouses and civil partners where this is to the advantage of the state purse, but not when this would involve extra cost.

(a) Contributory benefits

4.30

Contributory benefits are those which are payable upon condition that sufficient National Insurance contributions have been made; they are not means tested. In some circumstances, contributions by a person's spouse or civil partner are taken into account in assessing entitlement to a contributory benefit, but this is never the case for cohabitants.

4.31

At the present time, a person entitled to a contributory benefit may in addition often need to claim either income based jobseeker's allowance (JSA) or income support (see para 4.41 ff) to supplement his or her income; these are non-contributory and means-tested benefits. It is most likely to be appropriate where the claimant has dependants for whom the contributory benefit does not provide or where the claimant is liable for mortgage repayments, which may be provided by income-based JSA or income support. If accommodation is rented, then a claim for housing benefit (see para 4.52 ff) should be made to cover rent payments. Council Tax Reduction, as noted above, may also be applied for to cover Council Tax payments. Again, these are both non-contributory and means tested, and are administered by the local authority rather than the DWP.

(i) Contribution-based jobseeker's allowance and other contributory benefits

4.32

Jobseeker's allowance (JSA) may be either contribution-based or means tested (or income-based). Entitlement to contributory JSA (otherwise known as 'new style' JSA) depends upon the claimant's having paid sufficient class 1 National Insurance contributions, which are payable by those in employment only, and not by the self-employed. Other conditions of entitlement include being available for work, actively seeking employment and establishing that the unemployment is not voluntary. Once entitlement has been established, the claimant is paid contributory JSA for a period of up to six months at an age-differentiated rate. The weekly rates for 2017/18 are up to £73.10 for those aged 25 or over, up to £57.90 for those aged 18 to 24 and for couples (where both are aged over 18) up to £114.85. At the end of the six-month period, JSA becomes entirely means tested.

4.33

To claim JSA, claimants must not be in remunerative work of more than 16 hours per week, although their partner's earnings (and savings) will not affect entitlement to contributory JSA. Claimants must be 'capable of work', be under pensionable age and be in Great Britain. In addition, claimants are required to 'sign on' at the jobcentre and participate in an interview, involving making a declaration (a 'Jobseeker's Agreement') as a condition of receiving such benefit that they have been available for work and actively seeking work since the date of the last declaration and that there has been no change to their circumstances in that time.

4.34

Contributory Employment and Support Allowance (ESA) (known as 'new style' ESA if the claimant is also eligible for Universal Credit) is available to claimants who have paid sufficient National Insurance contributions, are affected by a health condition or disability and as a result are not required to work (due to either *a limited capability for work* or *a limited capability for work-related activity*). It is usually paid for a maximum of 12 months, unless the claimant is deemed to have a limited capability for work-related activity when payments when payments will continue.

4.35

Other contributory benefits include the state retirement pension and maternity allowance (payable where the claimant has recently stopped working, is not in receipt of statutory maternity pay from an employer or is self-employed and pays Class 2 National Insurance payments and which is payable for up to 39 weeks).

(ii) Widows' benefits

4.36

No payments of any of the benefits to which widow(er)s are entitled can be made to cohabitants on the death of his or her partner, no matter how long they have lived together. A bereavement allowance (and a widowed parent's allowance where there are dependent children) was formerly paid to a claimant whose spouse or civil partner died before 6 April 2017 for a period of 52 weeks. This has been replaced by a bereavement support payment payable to a claimant (who is under the state pension age) whose spouse or civil partner died on or after 6 April 2017, provided that the deceased had paid sufficient National Insurance contributions or died because of an accident at work or a disease caused by work. It contains a one-off lump sum payment of either £2,500 or £3,500 and 18 monthly payments of either £100 or £350 (the higher rate payable to pregnant women and those entitled to child benefit). It is important to note that the payments will continue for the full period of up to 18 months even if a widow(er) receiving such bereavement support payments cohabits.

(iii) Pensions

4.37

Perhaps the biggest anomaly in the treatment of cohabitants and one about which people are least aware concerns the Additional State Pension which is made up of three separate schemes – the State Earning Related Pension Scheme (SERPS) which operated from 1978 to 2002, the State Second Pension which operated from 2002 to 2016 and the State Pension Top-Up operating between 12 October 2015 and 5 April 2017. If a spouse or civil partner dies, the widow(er) may be able to inherit part of their Additional State Pension, but this does not extend to cohabitants, no matter how long the relationship may have lasted. This means that cohabitants are severely disadvantaged at this stage in the life-cycle and where each partner has not made their own pension arrangements, then the survivor's only option is to apply for means-tested income support to top-up their other income (see below). Since 6 April 2001, it has been possible to take out a stakeholder pension which most employers (with five or more staff) were required (before 1 October 2012 when the automatic enrolment legislation was introduced) to set up where no occupational pension existed. Now, under the Pensions Act 2008 as amended by the Pensions Act 2011, every employer in the UK must put certain staff into a pension scheme and contribute towards it. This is what is meant by 'automatic enrolment'. Again, cohabitants need to check their entitlement under both a stakeholder or auto-enrolment scheme.

(b) Non-contributory benefits

(i) Child benefit

4.38

Child benefit is a benefit payable regardless of means in respect of all children under the age of 16 and those under the age of 20 in approved non-advanced (ie not a degree course or equivalent) full-time education or training. The benefit is payable to the person who is responsible for the child and does not necessarily have to be a parent. From 7 January 2013, an income tax charge known as *a high income child benefit charge* has applied to recipients of child benefit whose annual 'adjusted net income' exceeds £50,000 and those with income over £50,000 whose partner receives child benefit (Income Tax (Earnings and Pensions) Act (ITEPA) 2003 s 681B as inserted by Finance Act (FA) 2012, s 8 and Sch 1, para 1). For taxpayers with income between £50,000 and £60,000, the income tax charge is 1% of the child benefit received for every £100 of income in excess of £50,000; and for taxpayers with income above £60,000, the tax charge is equal to the amount of child benefit received (ITEPA 2003 s 681C as inserted by FA 2012, s 8 and Sch 1).

4.39

Responsibility comprises either having the child living with the claimant; or contributing to the expenses of the child at a rate no less than the weekly benefit payable (s 143(1) SSCB Act 1992). However, where one person contributes and another has the child living with him or her, the person with whom the child resides will be the person entitled to claim.

4.40

Cohabitants with children will normally be entitled to child benefit for each child living with them. Either parent is entitled to claim. From April 2017, £20.70 is payable weekly in respect of the eldest (or only) child, and £13.70 for each additional child. Where cohabitants each have children from previous relationships, as there cannot be two eldest child payments, just the eldest child in the new family qualifies for the £20.70 rate.

(ii) Income support and income-based JSA and ESA

4.41

JSA remains the principal benefit claimed by those who are not working, but as Universal Credit is rolled out across the country this position is likely to change. To claim JSA, the applicant must either be unemployed or employed for less than 16 hours per week on average, aged between 18 and the state pension age, not in full-time education and available and actively looking for work. For joint claimants (only one of whom needs to be 18 or over), whilst the principal claimant can only be in paid employment for less than 16 hours per week on average, the partner is able to work for up to 24 hours per week on average. Both must usually also 'sign on' unless one partner is responsible for a dependent child (under the age of 5). The claimants must have no more than £16,000 of savings. There is a general rule that full-time students cannot get JSA. The weekly rates for 2017/18 are up to £73.10 for those aged 25 or over, up to £57.90 for those aged 18 to 24 and for couples (where both are aged over 18) up to £114.85.

4.42

Income Support is similar to income-based JSA but without the signing on requirement and is available to those on a low income, unemployed (or working less than 16 hours per week on average) and exempt from looking for work, aged between 16 and state retirement age and with no more than £16,000 in savings. This includes single parents with young children (ie under the age of 5), some (usually vulnerable) young people and carers of people affected by a long-term health problem or disability. A partner's income and savings are taken into account. The weekly rates for 2017/18 are up to £73.10 for those aged 25 or over, up to £57.90 for those aged 18–24 and for couples (where both are aged over 18) up to £114.85.

4.43

Income-related Employment and Support Allowance (ESA) is available to those on a low income who are affected by a health condition or disability (due to either *a limited capability for work* or *a limited capability for work-related activity*) and as a result are not required to work and who have savings of less than £16,000. It cannot be claimed if the cohabitant works for 24 hours or more each week on average. A partner's income and savings are also taken into account in assessing the claimant's eligibility. ESA has an initial assessment phase (during which for 2017/18 the claimant will receive weekly payments of £73.10) to enable the DWP to collect information and evidence about the claimant's health problem or disability and how it affects his or her ability to work. If a claimant is deemed to have a limited capability for work he or she is not then expected to work but will still have to undertake work-related activity (eg taking a course of training, writing a CV and getting appropriate experience) and is placed in the work-related activity group, receiving for 2017/18 weekly payments of up to £102.15. If deemed to have a limited capability for work-related activity, the claimant is placed in the support group, receiving for 2017/18 weekly payments of £109.30.

4.44

In respect of JSA, ESA and Income Support, claimants may be entitled to claim additional support for mortgage interest (SMI) where appropriate, providing they satisfy the means test. Help is available with the interest payments on up to £200,000 of a mortgage or home loan (£100,000 if receiving Pension Credit). The effect of this is that borrowers may be required to take out private insurance against unemployment at the time of taking out their mortgage. In any event, the mortgagee should be notified of the situation and a (capital and interest) repayment mortgage potentially switched to an interest only one. Even then the monthly interest payment payable to the mortgagee may be greater than the amount of the SMI and thus repossession could ensue unless an arrangement is made. SMI as a benefit is however ending on 5 April 2018, after which date it will be replaced by a loan. For all applications made on or after 7 July 2017, SMI as a benefit is no longer available, so if eligible an SMI loan can be provided to assist with the mortgage interest payments. The loan offers the same support for paying the mortgage interest. However, the loan attracts interest and both the loan amount and the accrued interest will need to be repaid when the claimants sell or transfer ownership of their home.

4.45

For means-testing purposes, cohabitants are treated in exactly the same way as married couples and civil partners. The rationale for this is that to do otherwise would be to discriminate against spouses and civil partners. On the other hand, spouses and civil partners have a mutual and legally enforceable duty to maintain each other, whereas this is not the case as between cohabitants. From April 2013, a Benefit Cap restricts the total income that non-working households can receive. The Cap is applied by local authorities for those in receipt of housing benefit subject to certain exceptions, so people who do not qualify for housing benefit or who receive SMI through an unemployment benefit (such as JSA, ESA and Income Support) are not affected at all until they are moved onto Universal Credit. If receiving housing benefit, the Cap on weekly income for single claimants is £296.35 in London/£257.69 outside London; and for couples and child carers £442.31 in London/£384.62 outside London. Housing benefit will be reduced by the amount of the excess (ie the total income inclusive of benefits less the amount of the cap).

4.46

Whilst only one partner can be paid income-based JSA or income support on behalf of a couple, if one cohabitant fails to support the other from the benefit received, the partner has no legal redress. Similarly, if one partner is employed, earning more than the JSA or income support that would be paid if the family had no income, but fails to support the partner, the unsupported partner may not claim JSA or income support. Co-operation is presupposed between the partners as it is between spouses and civil partners, but cohabitants cannot bring pressure to bear by applying for a maintenance order. In this situation, where the couple has been jointly assessed for JSA or income support, the aggrieved partner can either apply for the benefit to be paid directly to him or her instead of to the partner on the grounds of failure to maintain; or commence living in a separate household to gain individual entitlement to benefit. For those whose partners are in employment, the latter is the only option.

4.47

Where a couple do not admit to being cohabitants/living together as spouses or civil partners, it is for the DWP to show that the couple cohabit in this sense and are more than just friends living at the same address/in the same household. The factors to be taken into account have been developed through case law and guidance. In *K v K (Enforcement)* [2000] 1 FLR 383, the court enumerated a list of factors based on s 137(1) Social Security Contributions and Benefits Act 1992 and other authorities which were of assistance in determining whether the couple are cohabitants. These were:

- *Living together in the same household* – this did not mean they always had to live under the same roof, although this was the normal meaning (see *Mouncer v Mouncer* [1972] 1 WLR 321 and *Broxtowe Council v CS (HB)* [2014] UKUT 0186 (AAC)); liability for separate housing costs was held to be enough to show two separate households, regardless of living arrangements (*R(SB)* 13/82); and the mere fact of marriage to another person does not prevent a person being a member of a household with a cohabitant (*R(SB)* 35/85).

- *A sharing of daily life* – in *Broxtowe Council v CS (HB)*, the Judge of the Upper Tribunal, in rejecting the appeal by the local authority which had refused to award housing benefit to a JSA recipient, upheld the First-tier Tribunal's conclusion that 'the couple had two separate homes and each stopped with the other at weekends when possible. (They) were separately liable for their own accommodation and had completely separate living arrangements so cannot be members of the same household'.

- *Stability and a degree of permanence* – a passing relationship such as a holiday romance is not sufficient, but cohabitation of a few weeks may be sufficient evidence of a couple's having formed a relevant relationship.

- *Shared finance* – although it is not at all unusual for couples to maintain separate bank accounts they must pool their resources to some extent even if it just in the sharing of outgoings or one providing financial support for the other.

- *Children* – where there are children of the relationship, or children of one of the parties who are cared for or have been maintained by the other, there is a strong presumption of cohabitation.
- *Intention and motivation.*
- *The opinion of the reasonable person with normal perceptions* (see *Kimber v Kimber* [2000] 1 FLR 383).

4.48

If it is determined that the couple are indeed cohabiting, then only one couple's allowance for income-based JSA or income support can be made for the household, and any other benefit will be withdrawn. In the case of single claim couples, either of the partners may make the joint claim. Joint claim couples must both apply and nominate one of them to receive the couple's payment.

4.49

Where a couple wishes to dispute a decision by the local authority (in the case of housing benefit) or DWP, they may appeal within one month of the decision, and are entitled to reasons for the decision maker's decision. It is for the decision maker to prove that there is cohabitation. It is also possible to ask for the decision to be reviewed, and this will be particularly appropriate where the reasons for refusal show that an important fact has not been properly taken into account.

4.50

If partners separate, a new claim will have to be made. In practice, if they continue to live at the same address, it may be difficult to show that they are now living in separate households. In the case of married couples or civil partners, the fact that a solicitor has been approached with a view to matrimonial/civil partnership proceedings will often back up the contention that a *de facto* separation has taken place. With cohabitants, this is, ironically, sometimes more difficult to prove, and separate arrangements for cooking, sleeping, shopping, washing and payment of bills may need to be shown to convince the decision maker of a change in the arrangements.

4.51

Where a cohabitant in receipt of JSA, ESA or Income Support is liable for child support for a child not living with him or her, he or she will be expected to pay a flat rate of child maintenance. If the maintenance payable has been calculated by the Child Support Agency, the flat rate is £5 a week. If by the Child Maintenance Service case, the flat rate is £7 a week. This sum will be collected from the non-resident parent and will be deducted automatically from their benefit. Child maintenance payments will likewise be deducted from the monthly Universal Credit payment if the paying parent has no 'earned income'. See Chapter 9 for a fuller discussion of child support.

(iii) Housing benefit

4.52

This is another means-tested benefit available to help pay rent and only available where the claimant's savings do not exceed £16,000. It is administered by the local authority, although the DWP will automatically notify the authority of a claimant's eligibility for housing benefit if they are in receipt of income support or JSA. Those on low incomes, or claiming WTC or any benefit other than income support or JSA, must apply directly to the local authority for housing benefit (HB). Once again, cohabitants are entitled to make only one claim in respect of their household, and their capital and income will be aggregated. The amount of such benefit will depend on the claimant's 'eligible rent', whether they have a spare room, their household income and other relevant circumstances (eg the ages of people in the house or someone in the house with a disability). A benefits calculator is available on the gov.uk website at www.gov.uk/benefits-calculators. Eligible rent means the reasonable rent for a suitable property in the area. If the cohabitants live in council or social housing and have a spare bedroom, the housing benefit is reduced by 14% of the eligible rent for one spare bedroom and 25% of the eligible rent for two or more bedrooms.

4.53

From April 2013, a Benefit Cap restricts the total income that non-working households can receive. The Cap is applied by local authorities for those in receipt of housing benefit, subject to certain exceptions. The Cap on weekly income for single claimants is £296.35 in London/£257.69 outside London; and for couples and child carers £442.31 in London/£384.62 outside London. Housing benefit will be reduced by the amount of the excess (ie the total income inclusive of benefits less the amount of the cap).

(iv) Council tax benefit

4.54

Help with payment of council tax was previously by means of council tax benefit (CTB), which was administered by the local authority. In April 2013, Council Tax Benefit was replaced by Council Tax Reduction (or Council Tax Support), which could result in a council tax bill being reduced by up to 100%. The amount of the reduction depends on where the claimant lives (as each local authority runs its own scheme), their (low) household income, the presence or absence in the household of children, whether they/their partner has any savings and whether they/their partner is in receipt of other benefits.

Applications can be made online via the gov.uk portal at https://ww.gov.uk/apply-council-tax-reduction.

4.55

If the cohabitants separate, the one remaining in what was their family home will be entitled to a 25% reduction on the amount of the Council Tax payable for their home.

(v) The social fund

4.56

There were two categories of Social Fund in the UK, but the discretionary social fund (a form of welfare benefit provision payable for exceptional or intermittent needs, in addition to regular payments such as JSA or income support) was abolished with effect from April 2013, by means of legislation contained in the Welfare Reform Act 2012, by the Conservative-led coalition government.

4.57

The regulated fund continues to operate. Its payments include the Sure Start Maternity Grant (of £500 for each baby), the annual Winter Fuel Payment, the Funeral Expenses payment and the Cold Weather Payment (of £25 each time the local temperature is less than 0 degrees Celsius for seven consecutive days between 1 November and 31 March), of which only the Winter Fuel Payment is not means tested.

4.58

The Maternity Grant is payable where the claimant or his/her partner is getting Universal Credit, Income Support, income-based JSA, ESA (income-related), Pension Credit, Working Tax Credit where a disability or severe disability element is included in the award or Child Tax Credit at a rate higher than the family element. Funeral expense payments are intended to help the claimant pay for a funeral if they are on a low income and are the person responsible for arranging the funeral. It is recoverable from the deceased person's estate if they have left one. The cold weather payments are available only to households claiming income-based JSA, income-related ESA, Universal Credit or income support.

4.59

Budgeting Loans are available only to those who have been in receipt of income-based JSA, income-related ESA, Universal Credit (if also claiming Pension Credit) or income support for at least 26 weeks to meet intermittent and specified categories of expenses, including furniture and household equipment, clothing, rent in advance and removal expenses to secure accommodation, improvement, maintenance and security of the home. There are strict criteria, and any loan is repayable, although interest free. Such a loan will not be made unless the claimant is able to repay it. Where a loan is made, it can be recovered both from the person to whom it was made, and from a person for whose benefit it was made. This may be of particular relevance to cohabitants. It is not possible to secure a Budgeting Loan if in receipt of Universal Credit, when an application for a Budgeting Advance (which also has to be paid back) will need to be made.

4.60

The gov.uk website at www.gov.uk is again a useful resource for claimants and advisers alike, although in challenging any decisions made in respect of welfare benefits, the Child Poverty Action Group's *Welfare Benefits and Tax Credits Handbook 2017/2018* is invaluable.

CHAPTER 5

Inheritance and succession

5.01

The desirability of making Wills and taking out life assurance has been discussed in Chapter 1. Cohabitants, whether of the same or opposite sexes, are vulnerable on the death of their partners if no provision has been made by Will to cover such an eventuality. Where a cohabitant dies intestate (ie without leaving a Will), the distribution of the estate is governed by s 46 Administration of Estates Act 1925 (AEA 1925). Any children of the deceased, including those of the relationship, will inherit from the estate under these provisions unless there is a surviving spouse or civil partner and the value of the estate is less than £250,000, in which case the whole estate passes to the spouse or civil partner who must survive the deceased by at least 28 days in order to inherit. Although the Family Law Reform Acts 1969 and 1987 have effectively given children of unmarried parents the same succession rights as those of married parents, the deceased's partner will never be a beneficiary on intestacy under s 46 and may not take out letters of administration in respect of the estate. As noted in Chapter 1, the Cohabitants Rights Bill 2017–19 which has at the date of writing had its first reading in the House of Lords would extend rights to cohabitants on the death of a partner. A qualifying cohabitant would be entitled to a share of the estate of the other just as a spouse or civil partner would (ie all personal possessions, the first £250,000 of the estate and one half of the remainder).

5.02

The surviving cohabitant may, however, have a claim under the Inheritance (Provision for Family and Dependants) Act 1975 (I(PFD)A 1975) for financial provision to be made out of the deceased's estate. However, even where a Will has been made, benefiting a cohabitant and any children of the relationship, should the deceased also leave behind a spouse, civil partner, former spouse or former civil partner who was being maintained by the deceased, or any children by other relationships, they may all, by virtue of the same statute, have a claim against the deceased's estate. This could of course substantially reduce the provision the deceased believed would be available for his or her partner and their children. If the deceased had had the necessary means, life assurance could have ensured provision was made for all those to whom the deceased owed financial responsibility. Unfortunately, such foresight is rare. The first part of this chapter will therefore deal with the claims that can be made under I(PFD)A 1975, either by or against a deceased cohabitant's partner.

5.03

The cause of death may have a bearing on the financial provision available to those left behind. Where it can be shown that death resulted from the fault of a third party, then the partner may well, and any children of the relationship certainly will, have a claim for compensation against the third party under the Fatal Accidents Act 1976 (FAA 1976) as amended. As will be seen, a minimum period of cohabitation of two years is required by the statute as a prerequisite for a claim. The second part of this chapter will therefore consider the law relating to FAA claims, as it affects cohabitants. Similarly, the Criminal Injuries Compensation Authority entitles cohabitants of two years' standing to claim following a partner's fatal injury as discussed below.

1 Inheritance Act claims

5.04

Following recommendations made by the Law Commission in *Distribution on Intestacy* (Law Com No 187, Part III), opposite sex cohabitants were included by the 1995 amendments as a separate category of applicant entitled to apply for provisions under the 1975 Act. Same sex cohabitants were only included as a separate category of applicant entitled to apply for provisions under the 1975 Act with effect from 5 December 2005 (I(PFD)A 1975, s 1(1B) as inserted by the Civil Partnership Act 2004, Sch 4, Pt 2). However, it should be borne in mind that the inheritance situation will always be more complex where the deceased partner has left a surviving spouse or civil partner or children from outside the cohabitation relationship. In broad terms, the I(PFD)A 1975 enables claims to be made by specified categories of person against a deceased's estate, where either the deceased's Will or the law on intestacy does not make satisfactory provision for them. The rules as to what sort of provision should be made vary according to the category of person. It should be remembered that on intestacy, although cohabitants never inherit from their partners (s 46 AEA 1925) and may therefore need to make a claim under the 1975 Act, any children of that relationship will usually inherit on a parent's intestacy regardless of the fact that their parents never married.

5.05

Where there is no surviving spouse or civil partner, the deceased's estate will be divided equally between his or her children, regardless of whether those children were born inside or outside the marriage or civil partnership. Thus account will be taken of all the deceased's children. If there is a surviving spouse or civil partner (and significantly this definition includes a spouse or civil partner in the process of dissolving the marriage or civil partnership but where the decree absolute or dissolution order has not yet been made), then the first £250,000 of the deceased's estate will go to the spouse or civil partner, who will also receive one half of the remainder of the estate (s 46(1) AEA 1925 as amended by the Inheritance and Trustees' Powers Act 2014 and with effect from and affecting deaths on or after 1 October 2014). The other half of the residuary estate is held upon the statutory trusts for the deceased's children in equal shares. These rules apply regardless of the ages of the children. Only where the deceased's estate passes *bona vacantia* to the Crown because there are no beneficiaries at all on the deceased's intestacy, may a surviving cohabitant, at the discretion of the Crown (see Chapter 1), receive provision out of the deceased's estate without having to apply under the 1975 Act.

5.06

Should the deceased's children have been omitted from their parent's will as beneficiaries, if they are to receive provision out of the estate, they also must make a claim under the Act; in this situation whether or not they are minors is significant, as will be discussed below.

(a) Claims by cohabitants

(i) Eligible applicants

5.07

Providing a cohabitant can show he or she is an eligible applicant under the Act, the claim will proceed to be considered on the merits. Cohabitants who have lived with the deceased as his or her spouse or civil partner in the same household for at least two years immediately prior to their death may apply to the court for reasonable provision to be made out of their estate for their maintenance (see ss 1(1)(ba) and (1A) and (1B)). The biggest change to the law is that cohabitants who meet the two-year cohabitation requirement will no longer have to show dependency upon the deceased in order to obtain provision. The wording of the added subsection follows that included in the amendments to the Fatal Accident Act 1976 and is part of a trend where a period of cohabitation is stipulated by statute as a qualification for rights resulting from a cohabitation relationship. However, proof of cohabitation throughout the two-year period is required and this itself could in some cases create difficulties if for any part of the requisite two-year period the couple were living apart. As the evidential burden is on the applicant (see *Patel v Vigh and another* [2013] EWHC 3403 (Ch), [2013] All ER (D) 81 (Nov)), a helpful case to cite is *Kaur v Dhaliwal* [2014] EWHC 1991 (Ch), [2014] All ER 164 (Jun), in which the court held that the appropriate test when determining the period of two years is whether there is a settled relationship creating a tie between the parties, evidenced not simply by their 'living under the same roof but by the public and private acknowledgment of their mutual society and the mutual protection and support that binds them together' and if so whether that relationship had irretrievably broken down or rather was merely suspended with any interruption being transitory. It should be noted that a period in which parties intended to cohabit and gradually drifted towards doing so would not be included within the two-year period required (see *Kotke v Saffarini* [2005] EWCA Civ 221, [2005] 2 FLR 517). The Court of Appeal has held that the requirement of two years' cohabitation as a means of limiting certain statutory claims for cohabitants is compliant with the European Convention on Human Rights (*Swift v Secretary of State for Justice* [2013] EWCA Civ 193, [2013] All ER (D) 155 (Mar)).

5.08

This extension of the categories of eligible applicants was recognition of the growing numbers of couples who choose to cohabit rather than to marry or enter into civil partnerships. In the case of *Re Watson (Deceased)* [1999] 1 FLR 878, the Chancery Division considered what could amount to 'living as husband and wife' in the heterosexual context. Here a couple who had in their youth been romantically involved and sexually intimate had never married or cohabited at that time preferring instead to care for their respective elderly parents. Some 20 years later, the applicant (the woman), moved into the deceased's home as a companion and also kept house for him. Her own home remained unoccupied and she paid half the household bills arising out of the shared occupation of the deceased's home until he died some 10 years later. As he had no surviving relatives and had made no Will, on his death, his estate passed *bona vacantia* to the Crown. Subsequently the applicant applied under the 1975 Act claiming she had lived with the deceased as his wife and was entitled to provision. Neuberger J allowed her claim, stressing that in order to judge whether a couple were living as husband and wife, the court should ask whether they would be considered so to be in the opinion of a reasonable person with normal perceptions. He stressed that consideration of that question should not ignore the multifarious nature of marital relationships, but listed the cooking, cleaning and washing tasks performed by the applicant alongside the mutuality of life shared by the couple despite the lack of both shared bedroom and sexual relationship, which he found would not be unusual for a married couple in their mid to late 50s. Thus here, the lack of any sexual relationship during cohabitation was not fatal to the claim and companionship plus performance of 'wife-like' housekeeping tasks coinciding with the patriarchal expectations of the marital relationship were sufficient, at least for a couple in this age group. On the facts, the applicant could not easily claim to have been financially dependent on the deceased under s 1(1)(e) (discussed below) and thus her only possibility of a claim was as a cohabitant.

5.09

If a cohabitant's claim is successful, the provision available is still limited to 'maintenance' and is therefore less generous than the provision that can be made in favour of a spouse or civil partner where no such limitation applies. In *Ilott v The Blue Cross* [2017] UKSC 17, the Supreme Court considered the definition of 'maintenance' and held that '(whilst) the concept of maintenance is no doubt broad it cannot extend to any or every thing which it would be desirable for the claimant to have. It must import provision to meet the everyday expenses of living'. Nonetheless, where there has been a long-term cohabitation relationship with children of the deceased forming part of the family unit, the courts have scope to give substantial weight to these factors, which mirror those to be taken into account in respect of applications by (former) spouses and (former) civil partners (see s 3(2)). These must still be considered in the light of the other factors set out in s 3 (discussed below), such as the size of the estate, the financial needs and resources of the applicant and any other applicant or beneficiary under the estate.

5.10

If the couple are not able to satisfy the court that they were living together in the same household as spouses/civil partners, then the applicant must show that, immediately before the death of the deceased, he or she was being maintained, either wholly or partly by the deceased (s 1(1)(e)) which requires an element of dependency by the survivor on the deceased.

5.11

Thus, cohabitants can make a claim under this subsection only if they can show that they were financially dependent upon the deceased, and such dependence must have existed immediately before the death. It was considered by Megarry V-C in *Re Beaumont, Martin v Midland Bank Trust Co Ltd* [1980] 1 All ER 266 (at page 272b) that a temporary interruption of maintenance just before death would not necessarily defeat the claim, as what the court had to decide was whether there was in existence a settled arrangement between the deceased and the claimant at the time of death. Section 1(3) as amended by the Inheritance and Trustees' Powers Act 2014 states that:

> 'For the purposes of subsection (1)(e) above, a person is to be treated as being maintained by the deceased (either wholly or partly, as the case may be) only if the deceased was making a substantial contribution in money or money's worth towards the reasonable needs of that person, other than a contribution made for full valuable consideration pursuant to an arrangement of a commercial nature.'

5.12

In considering whether a person was being maintained, 'the court must use common sense and remember that the object of Parliament in creating this extra class of persons who may claim benefit from an estate was to provide relief for persons of whom it could truly be said that they were wholly or partially dependent on the deceased' – Griffiths LJ in *Jelley v Iliffe* [1981] Fam 128 at 141, in which case the Court of Appeal held that rent-free accommodation provided for the applicant by the deceased was capable of being a substantial contribution to his needs. Whether or not this was for full valuable consideration depended on whether the applicant's contribution to household expenses equalled or outweighed the value of the deceased's contribution by virtue of the accommodation. Thus, where cohabitants make equal contributions, or indeed where the surviving partner was maintaining the deceased, no claim is available under this subsection. A degree of financial dependency must be established.

5.13

In *Re B* [2000] 1 FCR 385, CA, Robert Walker LJ suggested that 'whether one person makes a substantial gratuitous contribution to another person's needs is essentially a question of fact, and the benefactor's motives or intentions are irrelevant except so far as s 3(4) makes them relevant to the court's task in deciding whether to make provision for the claimant, and if so in what form and on what scale'. Section 3(4) as amended by the Inheritance and Trustees' Powers Act 2014 provides that:

> 'where an application for an order under section 2 of this Act is made by virtue of section 1(1)(e) of this Act, the court shall, in addition to the matters specifically mentioned in s 3(1) paragraphs (a) to (f), have regard (a) to the length of time for which and basis on which the deceased maintained the applicant, and to the extent of the contribution made by way of maintenance; and (b) to whether and, if so, to what extent the deceased assumed responsibility for the maintenance of the applicant'.

5.14

In *Bishop v Plumley* [1991] 1 All ER 236, the Court of Appeal held that in order to decide whether the deceased had been making a substantial contribution, the matter had to be looked at in the round, and a common-sense approach applied, avoiding fine balancing computations involving the value of normal exchanges of support in the domestic sense. Interestingly, Butler-Sloss LJ commented that it could not have been Parliament's intention to place an applicant who was less devoted and contributed less to the deceased partner's needs in a more advantageous position than a more caring applicant. Thus, although the wording of the Act appears to be capable of leading to an anomalous position, in this case, the applicant was allowed to proceed and have her application considered on the merits. She was herself in poor health and 64 years of age, and had lived in a property owned by the deceased with whom she had lived for ten years, performing the domestic chores and caring for him during years of bad health.

5.15

Given that the duration of the cohabitation relationship is a factor which the court must specifically weigh in relation to applications made under s 1(1)(ba), the court may be reluctant to make orders where the period of cohabitation is less than two years. A claim under this head may however assist a dependant and very recently deserted cohabitant or a former cohabitant who was being voluntarily financially supported post-separation by their former partner.

(ii) Criteria relevant to the claim

5.16

The next hurdle an applicant must overcome is to show that the distribution of the deceased's estate, either in accordance with any Will or pursuant to the law on intestacy, 'is not such as to make reasonable financial provision for the applicant' (s 2(1)). In the case of a cohabitant this has to be considered in the light of s 1(2)(b) which defines reasonable financial provision as 'such financial provision as it would be reasonable in all the circumstances of the case for the applicant to receive for his maintenance'. This is deliberately less generous than the test applicable to spouses and civil partners, where provision is not limited to that needed for maintenance (see below). In addition, it will not be sufficient for a cohabitant to show that he or she needs maintenance, but also that it was objectively unreasonable in the circumstances of the case for the deceased to have failed to make provision. Thus in *Re Coventry, decd; Coventry v Coventry* [1980] Ch 461, the Court of Appeal held that an adult son who was undoubtedly in need of maintenance and whose father died intestate, resulting in a fairly small estate devolving to his wife, received an award of only £2,000. It was stressed that each case will depend on its own facts, but it is not for the court to decide how the deceased's assets should have been fairly divided, but rather whether it is unreasonable that the estate does not provide reasonable maintenance for the applicant.

5.17

Section 3(1) sets out the principal factors to be taken into account by the court in deciding whether the estate has provided 'reasonable financial provision'. These can be summarised as follows:

- the financial resources and needs the applicant, any other applicant and any beneficiary of the deceased's estate have or are likely to have in the foreseeable future;
- any obligations and responsibilities the deceased had towards any applicant or beneficiary of the estate;
- the size and nature of the net estate;
- any physical or mental disability of any applicant or beneficiary of the estate; and

- any other matter including the conduct of the applicant or any other person, which in the circumstances of the case the court may consider relevant.

5.18

These factors echo those to be taken into account by a court when making an order for financial provision on divorce as set out in Matrimonial Causes Act 1973, s 25(2). However, whereas the provision relating to conduct has been amended in the matrimonial situation to limit its scope to conduct which it would be inequitable to disregard, the 1975 Act has not. 'Relevant conduct' had been narrowly interpreted by the courts and it is submitted that this interpretation of relevant conduct may well be imputed into the workings of the 1975 Act in the future. Generally, it can be seen that the relative needs and resources of all the potential beneficiaries have to be weighed against each other and the existence of life assurance benefiting one or more of them will be of great relevance. In addition, the size of the net estate will be critical to the approach and outcome of any claim.

5.19

Additionally, s 3(2A) sets out further factors that will influence the court in determining the amount of reasonable provision for a cohabitant's maintenance. It states:

> 'Without prejudice to the generality of paragraph (g) of subsection (1) above, where an application is made under s 2 of this Act by virtue of s 1(1)(ba) of this Act, the court shall, in addition to the matters specifically mentioned in paragraphs (a) to (f) of that subsection, have regard to—(a) the age of the applicant and the length of the period during which the applicant lived as the husband or wife or the civil partner of the deceased and in the same household as the deceased; (b) the contribution made by the applicant to the welfare of the family of the deceased, including any contribution made by looking after the home or caring for the family'.

In *Thompson v Ragget* [2018] EWHC 688 (Ch), a female cohabitant who had lived with her deceased partner for 42 years but who had been expressly excluded by him from benefiting under his Will was granted one of his properties worth £225,000 (the court accepting that this property had been purchased with a view to the couple retiring to it), £160,000 for her future maintenance and care and £28,845 to renovate the property. He had left his whole estate, valued at £1,535,060, to tenants and friends. In making the order, His Honour Judge Jarman QC said that 'the real issue in this case, in my judgment, is what amounts to reasonable financial provision for Mrs Thompson's maintenance. The powers of the court to make orders to provide for such provision are set out in section 2 of the Act and are very wide. It is not in dispute that this includes provision for her accommodation and care needs.'

5.20

In *Ilott v The Blue Cross* [2017] UKSC 17, the Supreme Court considered the exercise which the court must undertake in assessing the s 3 factors in each case and noted that this section provides no guidance about the relative importance to be attached to each of the relevant criteria in order to make a value judgment on a given set of facts. The relevant date for assessing the factors is the date of the hearing not the date of death. The right to bring a claim under the Act is a personal one and it cannot therefore be continued by the applicant's personal representatives should the applicant die before the court has determined the application.

(b) Claims by children

5.21

A child of the deceased (s 1(1)(c)) and a child treated by the deceased as a child of the family (s 1(1)(d)) are eligible as of right to bring an action against the deceased's estate, claiming that reasonable financial provision has not been made for them out of the deceased's estate. The relevant criteria for assessing whether or not reasonable financial provision has been made are as set out above, but with some important distinctions. In particular, s 3(4) does not apply to children and thus no assumption of responsibility needs to be shown. The court though must have regard to the manner in which the applicant was being, or might expect to be, educated or trained. In the case of an application by a child of the family the court must also have regard to whether the deceased maintained the applicant and, if so, to the length of time for which and basis on which the deceased did so, and to the extent of the contribution made by way of maintenance, whether and, if so, to what extent the deceased assumed responsibility for the maintenance of the applicant, whether in maintaining or assuming responsibility for maintaining the applicant the deceased did so knowing that the applicant was not his own child and to the liability of any other person to maintain the applicant (s 3(3) as amended by the Inheritance ad Trustees' Powers Act 2014). Provision is however again limited to maintenance and, of course, minor children (as opposed to adult children) are likely to be treated far more generously as there is no duty to maintain an adult child. In most of the cases where adult children have succeeded, they have shown a moral obligation on the part of the deceased to provide for them (see eg *Re Pearce* [1993] 2 FCR 179 and *Re Goodchild, Pearce v Davis Pearce* [1996] 1 WLR 694), although this is not necessarily a prerequisite (see *Re Hancock (Deceased) Goodchild v Goodchild* [1993] 1 FLR 500). Indeed, in *Espinosa v Bourke* [1999] 1 FLR 747 CA, the court effectively overrode the clear wishes of the deceased to leave his estate to his student grandson on the basis that he had helped his daughter more than enough during his lifetime. He had been financially assisting his adult daughter who had previously helped care for him but later abandoned him. He had also promised his late wife that he would leave a portfolio of shares to the daughter. At the time of her father's death, she was in difficult financial circumstances, whereas the grandson (her own son) had lesser needs and the court found an obligation towards the daughter existed. Similarly, in *Gold v Curtis* [2005] WTLR 673, an adult son, who had suffered from depression and had a dependent daughter with a mental disability, obtained an order for provision from his mother's estate to augment his income and purchase capital assets, in circumstances where he had been estranged from her for some time. However, the court in *Garland v Morris* [2007] EWHC 2 (Ch), [2007] 2 FLR 528 rejected the applicant's case that there existed a moral obligation to maintain her in circumstances where she had had no contact with her father for fifteen years prior to his death and had already inherited her mother's estate, even though she was living in difficult financial circumstances.

5.22

Ilott v The Blue Cross [2017] UKSC 17 is now the leading authority on cases involving applications by adult children. In this case, an adult daughter (living on state benefits with five children) sought provision from her deceased mother's £486,000 estate, despite being estranged from her for over 25 years and being fully aware that her mother did not intend to leave her anything in her Will. The deceased had left her entire estate to three charities. The judge at first instance found that the absence of provision for the daughter was unreasonable, having considered, among other factors, the daughter's obvious financial need, the size of the estate and the unreasonable conduct of the deceased towards the daughter and awarded her £50,000 (representing capitalised maintenance). The daughter appealed and eventually when the case was brought before it, the Supreme Court upheld that order, despite Lord Hughes stating that 'some judges might legitimately have concluded that the very long and deep estrangement had meant that the deceased had no remaining obligation to make any provision for her independent adult daughter'. Their lengthy estrangement and the daughter's straitened financial circumstances were the dominant factors in this case and the Supreme Court's judgment gives a strong indication that an able-bodied adult child who is capable of living independently will need to show something more than a qualifying relationship in order to succeed, as the (lack of a) relationship between the parties may be a key factor.

(c) Orders available to the court

5.23

The court, by virtue of s 5, has power to make interim orders in favour of an applicant who is 'in immediate need of financial assistance'. This is likely to take the form of periodical payments, but a lump sum may be made if the circumstances merit it.

5.24

The final orders available to the court, which are set out in s 2, once again resemble those which can be made on divorce or dissolution and are:

- periodical payments;
- lump sum;
- transfer of property;
- settlement of property;
- acquisition of property not comprised in the estate out of property which is so comprised for transfer or settlement to or settlement on the applicant; and
- varying for the applicant's benefit the trusts on which the deceased's estate is held (whether arising under the Will or the law relating to intestacy or both).

5.25

Notwithstanding that an order in favour of a cohabitant can extend to reasonable provision for his or her maintenance only, this can still take the form of any of the orders listed above. The court can order that specific property be acquired for the benefit of a claimant. For example, a smaller home may be ordered to be purchased rather than transferring the existing home to the applicant.

5.26

In addition, under s 9, the court has a discretion to order that the deceased's severable share of a beneficial joint tenancy be treated as part of the net estate, but the court must rule on this when it is deciding the preliminary issue of whether or not reasonable financial provision had been made and not when it is making the final orders. Further this can be done only where the application is brought within the initial six-month time limit for bringing an action as discussed below. The effect of this rule is that where the deceased was a co-owner of a property his share in which would normally pass to the other co-owner by virtue of the rule of survivorship, the court can rule that the deceased's share of the property should, for the purposes of the Act, be deemed to form part of his net estate. Severance of a joint tenancy will be ordered only where it is 'just in all the circumstances of the case' and only in so far as is necessary. Thus, if some but not all of the value of that share is needed, the balance will still pass to the co-owner by right of survivorship.

(d) Defending a claim

5.27

Defending a claim will arise only where the deceased's Will benefits his or her cohabitant and/or children of their relationship but fails to provide reasonable financial provision for other eligible applicants – principally a present or former spouse or civil partner, other children of the deceased and any other adult dependants falling within s 1(1)(e), discussed above.

5.28

The terms of the Act are to the effect that a spouse or civil partner (who remains such until the day any decree absolute of divorce or dissolution order is made) is able to receive more generous provision than any other type of applicant. The test is whether reasonable provision, and not reasonable provision *for his or her maintenance*, has been made by the estate. However, all the circumstances of the case, including, it seems, the existence of any divorce or dissolution proceedings, will be taken into account, as well as the general factors set out above and contained in s 3. A spouse or civil partner may receive provision similar to that which he or she would have received on divorce or dissolution in light of the House of Lords decision in *White v White* [2000] 2 FLR 981 and the 'yardstick of equality'. In *Cunliffe v Fielden* [2005] EWCA Civ 1508, [2006] 1 FLR 746, however, it was held that although there was no reason why the *White* approach not be applied to s 2 applications, caution was necessary when considering the yardstick of equality as divorce involves two living spouses. A deceased spouse who left a widow was entitled to bequeath his estate as he pleased and his only obligation was to make reasonable financial provision for her. Depending on the value of the estate, the concept of equality may bear little relation to such provision. Any other person who is supporting the spouse will of course be relevant, as will any provision which has been made by way of life assurance, and the size of the estate.

5.29

A former spouse is in a much weaker position, as the question of financial provision between the spouses will have been decided by the court (see *Barrass v Harding and Newman* [2001] 1 FLR 138 for a recent application of the principles). Indeed many orders made on divorce specifically preclude an application under the 1975 Act.

5.30

Any children of the deceased may likewise make a claim against the estate.

5.31

Where a cohabitant beneficiary is faced with a claim, it is clearly preferable to reach agreement by negotiation. Litigation is costly and will quickly deplete the estate available for distribution. Although the general rule is that costs will normally be awarded to the successful party against the loser(s), the court has a wide discretion to make a different order (CPR 1998, r 44.2 as amended). If the applicant is successful, then his or her costs may be paid out of the estate. An unsuccessful applicant may be ordered to pay not only the costs of the defendant beneficiaries but also the costs of the personal representatives. Where an unsuccessful applicant is legally aided, any order for costs is likely to be unenforceable in any event.

(e) Procedure

5.32

An important requirement in relation to inheritance claims is that they comply with a strict time limit. Section 4 stipulates that applications must be made within six months of the date on which representation (a grant of probate or letters of administration as appropriate) with respect to the estate of the deceased was taken out, unless the court grants permission for a late application. Good reason will be needed for a late application, and an application for leave must set out the grounds for the request. However, nothing prevents the making of an application before the representation has been taken out.

5.33

These applications are governed by Civil Procedure Rules 1998 and must be issued in accordance with the 'alternative procedure' in the CPR 1998, Pt 8 (see CPR 1998, r 57.16 (1) and PD 57). Claimants must use the Part 8 procedure. Thus, the claimant must file the Part 8 claim form N208 together with any written evidence on which he or she intends to rely including an official copy of the grant of representation and of every testamentary document admitted to proof. The proceedings will be treated as being allocated to the multi-track and the defendant must acknowledge service not more than 21 days after service of the claim form on him. When the court allocates a case to the multi-track, it will give directions for the management of the case and set a timetable for the steps to be taken between the giving of directions and the trial, and/or to fix a case management conference (CPR 1998, r 29.1–29.9 as amended). The CPR 1998 Practice Direction on pre-Action Conduct (a revised version of which came into effect on 6 April 2015) lists the steps which the court will expect both parties to have taken prior to proceedings being issued. The applicant must give concise details of their claim in a letter before action. The defendant must respond within a reasonable time and the parties must then exchange sufficient information (and key documents) to enable settlement negotiations to get underway or to narrow the issues (CPR 1998, PD on Pre-Action Conduct, para 6). The court will expect the parties to have attempted to reach a settlement by way of negotiation or some form of non-court dispute resolution such as mediation. Non-compliance with the PD can have consequences in terms of costs orders (CPR 1998, r 44.2 (5)).

(i) Legal Aid and Inheritance Act claims

5.34

The Legal Aid, Sentencing and Punishment of Offenders Act 2012 permits legal aid for Inheritance Act claims, which may take the form of Legal Help, Family Help or Legal Representation in cases where there is evidence (or an allegation) of domestic (or child) abuse. An application for Legal Representation may be refused if the prospects of success or of obtaining the order sought are poor. The Legal Aid Agency must also apply the 'cost benefit' test, ie unless the likely benefits to be gained from the proceedings for the client justify the likely costs having regard to the prospects of obtaining the order sought and are such that a reasonable private paying client would be prepared to take or defend the proceedings in all the circumstances, Legal Representation will be refused. Further, the Merits Regulations stipulate that the Legal Aid Agency must have regard to the following question when dealing with all applications for Legal Representation:

> 'Is it reasonable in all the circumstances for the proceedings in respect of which funding is sought to be funded privately having regard to the financial circumstances of the client and the value of the assets in dispute?'

If so, Legal Representation may be refused.

5.35

Of particular concern is the impact of the statutory charge which has always applied to such claims. The statutory charge is the mechanism by which the costs payable out of the Legal Aid fund in respect of the proceedings under which money or property has been recovered or preserved is repayable to the fund. Unless regulations provide otherwise, the unrecovered cost of providing legal aid to the applicant (ie the legal costs incurred which are not covered by a successfully enforced order for costs) gives rise to a first charge on any property recovered or preserved by the client in any proceedings or in any compromise or settlement of any dispute, in connection with which legal aid has been granted. The Statutory Charge Manual (last updated April 2014) is available in electronic form on the Legal Aid Agency (LAA) website. Usually, but not necessarily, an order for costs will be made against the estate where a claimant is successful. However, this will affect the size of the estate available to be distributed and thus may be taken into account in evaluating the appropriate sum to be awarded. Where property which the court has ordered is to be used as a home for the claimant or their dependants is transferred, the LAA may, if satisfied that the property will provide adequate security for the sum which is the subject of the charge, agree to defer the enforcement (Civil Legal Aid (Statutory Charge) Regulations 2013, reg 22(1)(a)). The LAA will then take a legal charge over the property, and simple interest will accrue to the initial sum charged at a rate of 8% per annum from the date of registration of the charge. In addition, if a sum is recovered by a legally aided claimant under the 1975 Act which the court orders is to be used to purchase a home for the claimant or their dependants, the LAA may again, on the same conditions, agree to postpone enforcement by taking a legal charge over the property purchased. Where the LAA does agree to postponement and the claimant subsequently wishes to move to a new home, reg 22(3) gives the LAA discretion to accept a substitute charge on the new property.

5.36

The form of the court order is critical to the LAA's agreement to deferment of the statutory charge, and practitioners must ensure that it clearly states that the property transferred or to be purchased is to be used as a home by the legally aided applicant or his/her dependant(s). A suggested form of words for inclusion in an order to comply with the requirements of the regulations is:

> '... and it is certified that for the purpose of Civil Legal Aid (Statutory Charge) Regulations 2013, reg 22 the lump sum of £ has been ordered to be paid to enable the [dependant] to purchase a home for himself/herself or his/her dependants/that the property at has been preserved/recovered for the [dependant] for the use as a home for himself/herself or his/her dependants'.

5.37

The LAA will require the assisted person to agree in writing to the conditions of deferment of enforcement, but the applicant's liability to pay interest on the statutory charge sum does not depend on his/her signing a form agreeing to do so. No interest will actually have to be paid until the legal charge in favour of the LAA is redeemed, although the LAA will of course accept any repayment which the assisted person wishes to make and will deduct this from the total sum repayable. Statements of interest accrued are issued each year by the LAA.

2 Fatal accident claims

5.38

A cohabitant who can show dependence on the deceased may well be able to bring a claim under the Fatal Accidents Act 1976 (FAA 1976) against a third party who was responsible, due to a wrongful act, for the death of the partner. The act needs to be such as would have entitled the deceased to bring an action and recovered damages if death had not ensued. Thus where a cohabitant dies due to a road accident or an accident at work caused by another party's negligence, a claim will lie. A child of the deceased who was dependent on him or her at the date of the death also has a right of action under the Act.

5.39

A quite separate action brought by the personal representatives of the deceased in his or her name under the Law Reform (Miscellaneous Provisions) Act 1934 for compensation for loss incurred up to the date of death, may also benefit a cohabitant and any children who are beneficiaries under the deceased's Will. However, any damages payable are assessed quite independently of any claim under the 1976 Act, and will not be taken into account in assessing quantum in a successful Fatal Accidents Act claim.

5.40

Section 1(3) of the FAA 1976, as amended, provides that an application may be made by the following persons:

(i) the surviving spouse or civil partner and dependant children whether or not the parties have been married or were civil partners; and

(ii) cohabitants, but only if they had been living together in the same household as spouses or civil partners for at least two years before the date of death.

5.41

It should be noted that a period in which parties intended to cohabit and gradually drifted towards doing so would not be included within the two-year period required (see *Kotke v Saffarini* [2005] EWCA Civ 221, [2005] 2 FLR 517). In *Swift v Secretary of State for Justice* [2013] EWCA Civ 193, [2013] All ER (D) 155 (Mar), the claimant had cohabited with the deceased for just six months before he dies and was not entitled to compensation under the FAA 1976.

5.42

Section 3(4) of the Act goes on to provide that the fact that such an applicant has no enforceable right to financial support by the deceased as a result of their living together must be a consideration. Thus in determining the appropriate multiplier to be applied in assessing damages, the fact that either party could have determined the relationship at will, without any right to maintenance ensuing, will be taken into account and is likely to reduce awards made to cohabitants as opposed to spouses or civil partners. It is thought that the greater the degree of stability of the relationship shown, the greater the award. Any cohabitation agreement could be of great significance in such a situation.

Apart from this additional consideration, damages will be assessed in accordance with the normal principles of tort.

5.43

Cohabitants are not entitled to statutory bereavement damages (currently £12,980), which are automatically awarded to a spouse or civil partner where liability is proved under the 1976 Act. However, the Cohabitation Rights Bill 2017–19, which had its first reading in the House of Lords on 5 July 2017, if it ever becomes law, would put a cohabitant, who has lived with the deceased for a continuous period of three years or more (in the absence of there being a child when the three-year period does not apply), in the same position as a spouse or civil partner in terms of qualifying for the statutory bereavement damages.

5.44

In the meantime, some moves to improve the position of surviving cohabitants have also been made by the courts. In *K v JMP Co Ltd* [1976] QB 85, the court sought to assist a cohabitant who was the mother of the three children of the relationship and where the couple and their children had lived together as a family unit before the death of the children's father. Only the children could at that time bring a claim. However, in assessing the multiplicand, the Court of Appeal deducted a sum in respect of the deceased's expenses, but decided not to deduct a sum in respect of the applicant's expenses previously paid by the deceased, resulting in a larger sum to be paid to each of the children. Although the award went to the children, it was recognised that the children could not without their mother do certain things, such as visiting their relatives in Ireland, and provision was made for her expenses in this regard. The court was clearly keen that she should have this assistance.

5.45

This decision is not entirely redundant. There will be cases where a cohabitant has the responsibility of bringing up the child of the deceased, but cannot make a claim under the Act because they had not lived together for two years. In such a situation, it might be felt appropriate to increase provision for the children in accordance with the reasoning in *K v JMP Co Ltd* (above).

5.46

Other than in respect of statutory bereavement damages, not presently available to cohabitants, dependency is also a prerequisite of a successful claim under the Act for all categories of applicant. Any dependant child of the deceased will also have a claim under the FAA 1976, but any child who cannot prove dependency will not be eligible.

(a) Procedure and Legal Aid

5.47

Fatal Accident Act claims are currently governed by CPR 1998, Pt 16 and PD 16 which sets out what a claimant must include in the particulars of claim. Legal Aid is no longer available for claims made under the FAA 1976 as civil legal services provided in relation to personal injury or death are expressly excluded under the Legal Aid, Sentencing and Punishment of Offenders Act 2012, Sch 1, Part 2.

3 Criminal Injuries Compensation Scheme

5.48

Where a partner dies as a result of a violent crime, some cohabitants may be eligible to apply for compensation from the Criminal Injuries Compensation Authority (CICA) through the Criminal Injuries Compensation Scheme 2012. Compensation is awarded on a tariff basis with currently 20 levels of compensation in respect of physical and mental injuries and 15 levels of compensation in respect of fatal injuries, sexual and physical abuse. A table of the tariff of injuries is appended to the documents relating to the 2012 Scheme (at Annex E) and can be viewed on the CICA website at www.cica.gov.uk. The maximum award which may be made under this Scheme in relation to a fatal criminal injury is £500,000 (2012 Scheme, para 60).

5.49

A qualifying relative includes the partner of the deceased (other than a spouse or civil partner), who was living with them in the same household and had done so for a continuous period of at least two years immediately before the date of the deceased's death. It also includes a partner who would otherwise satisfy the two-year cohabitation period requirement but who did not live with the deceased because of either person's ill-health or infirmity (2012 Scheme, para 59).

5.50

A child of the deceased, including a child of the family or a dependant child, is also a qualifying claimant. All claims must be made within two years of the incident in respect of which the claim is made, although this limit may be waived if there is good reason for the delay and it is in the interests of justice to do so. The compensation payable will normally be in the form of a lump sum assessed on the tariff scale plus, where the claimant was dependent upon the deceased, and providing the deceased's only normal income was not from social security benefits, a further dependency payment based on a loss of earnings calculation will also be made (paras 67–74). Where there is only one qualifying claimant a bereavement payment of £11,000 is payable. Where there is more than one, each claimant is awarded a sum of £5,500 (para 62).

5.51

Reasonable funeral expenses are also payable and, in assessing these, account should be taken of the religious and cultural background of the victim and his family. The amount of a funeral payment is £2,500, but a payment above £2,500 may be made in respect of funeral expenses reasonably incurred, up to a further £2,500 (paras 76–77).

5.52

The scheme requires an application to be completed online at www.gov.uk/claim-compensation-criminal-injury for consideration by CICA. Claims are assessed by claims officers, reviewed by adjudicators and appeals go to the First-tier Tribunal (Criminal Injuries Compensation). Decisions are notified through the post to the applicant. However, it should be noted that there may be delays in processing compensation claims. The scheme is discussed further in the context of domestic abuse (see Chapter 7 below).

CHAPTER 6

Cohabitants and matrimonial or civil partnership proceedings

1 Introduction

6.01

It is not unusual in a cohabitation relationship for one partner to be separated, but remain married to or in a civil partnership with another person or, even where the marriage or civil partnership has been dissolved, to be involved in ongoing court proceedings relating to unresolved issues concerning arrangements for any children or financial matters. The fact of the new 'permanent' nature of the cohabitation relationship and the resources of the partner may then become relevant to a court's determination of such issues. This affects cohabitants to the extent that what is paid or received as financial provision from a previous relationship may limit or extend the financial resources available in the new cohabiting relationship.

6.02

Cohabitants may be brought into divorce proceedings by the opposite sex spouse of a cohabitant by being named as a co-respondent in the divorce petition. It is relevant to note here that with regard to a marriage between a same sex couple (and equally to civil partnerships), adultery is not one of the facts that may be relied on in order to seek its dissolution (the definition of such involving intercourse between two people of the opposite sex).

2 Cohabitants and divorce or dissolution

6.03

Cohabitants involved in divorce or dissolution proceedings will most commonly either be alleging or responding to allegations of adultery (s 1(2)(a) MCA 1973 – opposite sex couples only) or unreasonable behaviour (s 1(2)(b) MCA 1973), s 44(5)(a) CPA 2004), as the alternative is to wait until the parties have been separated/living apart for two years when divorce or dissolution will be granted on the basis of that separation providing the respondent consents to such order (s 1(2)(d) MCA 1973, s 44(5)(b) CPA 2004), or five years' separation where the respondent's consent is not required (s 1(2)(e) MCA 1973, s 44(5)(c) CPA 2004). Divorce or dissolution following desertion of a period of two years is of course still available to the party deserted (s 1(2)(c) MCA 1973, s 44(5)(d) CPA 2004), but is in practice little used.

6.04

Under the current law, cohabitation if it involves a sexual relationship with another person of the opposite sex can be cited as evidence of adultery based on inclination and opportunity sufficient to prove irretrievable breakdown of marriage under s 1(2)(a) MCA 1973. Whilst the cohabitant could be named and joined as co-respondent to the proceedings, it is not necessary to name in the petition the person with whom the spouse is alleged to have had sexual relations. Thus, a married cohabitant who is to be the respondent in the divorce proceedings may choose to agree to admit the adultery upon the basis that the petitioner will not name the co-respondent in the petition. It should be noted that, where the cohabitant is named as a co-respondent in divorce proceedings, this renders the cohabitant and their partner's spouse 'associated' for the purposes of the domestic violence legislation under s 62(3)(g) FLA 1996. In this situation alone, a cohabitant could if necessary apply for a non-molestation order against the spouse or vice versa.

3 Cohabitants and children

(a) *Child arrangements ('lives with' and 'spends time with') orders*

6.05

The existence of a cohabitant is obviously of significance in relation to disputes relating to children of one of the parties from a previous marriage or civil partnership, both in terms of the child maintenance calculation and other possible claims for financial provision by the children discussed in Chapter 9. It is also of significance in terms of the (shared) care arrangements for those children, which need to be agreed or decided by the court following divorce or dissolution. Such disputes will be resolved in accordance with the principles laid down in the Children Act 1989 (see Chapter 8), the most notable of these being that the welfare of the child is paramount (s 1(1) CA 1989).

6.06

The extent to which the new cohabitation relationship of a parent is relevant depends on the nature of the orders sought. Cohabitation may be taking place at the time of the divorce or dissolution proceedings or one or both parents may begin a cohabitation relationship some time after the arrangements for children have been agreed. This often leads to renewed hostility between the parties, making any agreed arrangements difficult to achieve or maintain and necessitating court orders or variation of existing orders to determine the appropriate arrangements (s 8 CA 1989).

6.07

Broadly, and particularly where the cohabiting parent is seeking a child arrangements ('lives with') order, the court will be most concerned to examine the suitability of the cohabitant as a parent (see for example *S v S* [1986] 1 FLR 492) as well as the stability of the cohabitation relationship (see *Stephenson v Stephenson* [1985] FLR 1140). Usually, where a welfare report is ordered (carried out by a child and family reporter under the auspices of the Child and Family Court Support Advisory and Support Service (CAFCASS) as discussed in Chapter 8 below), it will include an assessment of these matters for the court, and a cohabitant who did not want to hinder their partner's case would normally need to co-operate with this process.

6.08

Where there are disputes over where/with whom a child is to live and how much time they are to spend with each parent, the fact that one parent may be in a gay cohabitation relationship is not a green light for discrimination against that parent as had so often been the case in the past. In *G v F (contact and shared residence: applications for leave)* [1998] 2 FLR 799, a case where shared residence of a child was sought following the breakdown of a same-sex relationship, Bracewell J was clear that 'it would be entirely wrong … and unsustainable to seek in any way to reflect against the applicant by reason of the nature of her relationship with the respondent' (at p 805).

6.09

With regard to child arrangements ('spends time with') orders, there is a presumption that it is better for the child to know both parents (see *Re H (minors) (access)* [1992] 1 FLR 148 and *Re W (a minor) (contact)* [1994] 2 FLR 441) and thus, generally, the existence of a cohabitation relationship by the partner seeking such order should not of itself prevent such order being made, even where the court has concerns about the suitability of contact between the child and the parent's cohabitant. Conditions can be attached to any s 8 order (see s 11(7) CA 1989) and some form of contact (whether direct or indirect) should nearly always be possible. This point was underlined in the Court of Appeal decision of *Re O (a minor) (contact: imposition of conditions)* [1995] 2 FLR 124.

(b) Change of surname

6.10

Where a child comes to live with one parent and their cohabitant, they will not be a child of that family as there is no marriage or civil partnership between the adults. It has already been noted that such a child does not have any direct claim against the estate of their parent's cohabitant, although if dependency can be proved they may fall within the residual category of applicants under s 1(1)(e) I(PFD)A 1975. However, a child in that situation may want to change their surname to that of the cohabitant. Although any person with unfettered parental responsibility might have been thought to be able to independently change a child's name, as discussed in Chapter 2, case law has made it clear that consent or a s 13 or specific issue order needs to be obtained (see *Dawson v Wearmouth* [1999] 1 FLR 1167). Even where only one parent has parental responsibility, whilst *Re PC (change of surname)* [1997] 2 FLR 730 suggested they may act independently to change a child's name, with the other parent needing a prohibited steps or specific issue order, dicta in the House of Lords in *Dawson v Wearmouth* and the Court of Appeal in *Re W, Re A, Re B* [2001] Fam 1 have indicated that consent of the other parent or leave of the court is required before a surname can be changed, although given the wording of s 2 CA 1989, the authority for this is unclear as is the penalty for failing to obtain consent. Where a child arrangements ('lives with') order is in force, either the written consent of every person with parental responsibility is required or leave of the court must always be obtained (s 13(1) CA 1989). Where the children's names are to be changed by deed poll, the written consent of all persons with parental responsibility is required and the deed poll would be lodged at the Royal Courts of Justice. If the change is objected to and there is no 'lives with' order in force, a specific issue order should be sought (s 8 CA 1989) and the criteria for making the decision relate to the child's welfare (*Re F (child: surname)* [1994] 1 FLR 110, CA). Where a 'lives with' order is in force an application under s 13 CA 1989 must be made. In such a case, as the child's welfare was paramount, the s 1(3) checklist was a useful *aide-memoire* whereas it applies directly in s 8 applications.

6.11

In *Re B (minors) (change of surname)* [1996] 1 FLR 791 the Court of Appeal refused an application on behalf of children to change their surname to that of their stepfather, despite there being little contact with the natural father, and the teenage children's clear wishes to adopt their stepfather's surname which they had already done informally. However, in *Re S (change of surname)* [1999] 1 FLR 672, it was made clear the views of a *Gillick* competent child should be given the most careful consideration where a change of surname application was concerned. Again in *Re C (minor) (change of surname)* [1994] 1 FCR 110, the Court of Appeal accepted that to change a name which had been in informal use for a long period of time may well not be in a child's best interests. *Dawson v Wearmouth* (above) and subsequent cases have affirmed that the courts do regard change of surname by children to be an extremely important issue which will not be done lightly, and the courts lean towards retaining the status quo, even in the face of strong feelings by older children themselves, making it now extremely difficult to change a child's surname.

(c) Child support and maintenance

6.12

As discussed in Chapter 9, a cohabitant is not expected to maintain the children of his/her partner's former relationship and thus, on relationship breakdown, no maintenance will be payable in respect of these quasi-step-children, either by way of a child maintenance calculation by the Child Maintenance Service (CMS) or by way of a court order, even though their parent's partner has maintained them throughout the relationship.

6.13

At the present time, the effect of a new cohabitation relationship on the level of child support payable by a non-resident parent is dependent upon whether there are any relevant other children of that new relationship living in the same household as the non-resident parent (see Chapter 9). Where the non-resident parent is supporting a new partner, the child maintenance calculation makes no allowance for an adult dependant. If however an application is made to court for a top-up award (ie maintenance over and above the maintenance calculation), the non-resident parent would be entitled to make reference to any such financial support offered to his new partner and their household expenses.

6.14

Conversely, a new partner's income is not taken into account for the purposes of calculating the income of the non-resident parent from which the amount of the maintenance calculation is to be made, but in the case of an application for a top-up award is relevant as regards the court potentially attributing to them one half of the household expenses in order to determine whether the non-resident parent has any disposable income from which a top-up award could/should be paid.

4 Cohabitation and financial provision on divorce or dissolution

6.15

The existence of a new cohabitation relationship by one or both parties to financial provision proceedings is, of course, a significant factor when the court is deciding financial provision on divorce or dissolution. Of itself, cohabitation is not conduct which it would be inequitable to disregard (s 25(2)(g) MCA 1973, CPA 2004, Sch 5, Pt 5, para 21(2)(g)) when deciding financial remedy applications. Unlike remarriage or forming a new civil partnership, cohabitation does not have any direct effect on the court's jurisdiction to make a periodical payments (maintenance) order and is a relevant factor to be considered by the court when deciding whether or not to make lump sum and property adjustment orders, particularly given that there is no legal obligation on cohabitants to maintain each other either during or after the relationship. The court is under a duty to have regard to all the circumstances of the case (s 25(1) MCA 1973, CPA 2004, Sch 5, Pt 5, para 20), and cohabitation is undoubtedly one important circumstance to be weighed in the equation.

6.16

Where a formerly dependant spouse or civil partner is now cohabiting with another partner, that partner's resources are not directly relevant and whatever his or her current circumstances, due regard must be had, *inter alia*, to the age of the parties, the duration of the marriage or civil partnership and the contribution made to the welfare of the first family by the spouse or civil partner when making financial provision and property adjustment orders (s 25(2) MCA 1973, CPA 2004, Sch 5, Pt 5, para 21). The court has a duty to consider whether a 'clean break' can be achieved (s 25A(1) MCA 1973, CPA 2004, Sch 5, Pt 5, para 23 (2)) and, where there is cohabitation on the part of a formerly dependant spouse or civil partner, it is much more likely that a clean break will be ordered, although much may depend on the length of the marriage or civil partnership as well as the length and stability of the new relationship.

6.17

Nonetheless, the existence of a cohabitation relationship will have an indirect effect upon the financial provision to be ordered, in so far as a new partner's resources or need for support will always have an impact upon the financial position of the former spouse or civil partner involved in financial remedy proceedings. For example, where one party to proceedings is being provided with accommodation by their new partner, this may mean that the court is more likely to transfer property to the other spouse or civil partner who has care of the children of the family, given that the children's welfare is the court's first consideration (s 25(1) MCA 1973, CPA 2004, Sch 5, Pt 5, para 20). Conversely, in *Suter v Suter and Jones* [1987] Fam 111, a cohabitant living with a woman and three children from her previous marriage was expected to make a contribution to the family's housing costs and thus periodical payments payable to her by her former husband were reduced on appeal. Even unenforceable moral obligations to maintain a new cohabitant and their children may amount to a relevant circumstance and act to reduce the resources the court considers available to maintain a former spouse as in *Roberts v Roberts* [1970] P 1, although generally the needs of the former spouse and any children of the first family will not be subjugated to those of the second.

6.18

In *A v A (financial provision: variation)* [1995] 2 FCR 353 at page 359, Thorpe J summarised the principles to be applied when dealing with financial relief applications where there is a new cohabitation relationship:

> 'First, cohabitation is not to be equated with marriage. In performing its functions under the Matrimonial Causes Act 1973 (as amended) the fact of cohabitation is not to be given any decisive weight.
>
> Second, cohabitation is, however, a relevant factor in that it bears upon the financial circumstances, particularly upon the assessment of the wife's financial needs.
>
> But it seems to me above all that the court should strive to discern the realities in determining what weight to give to the factor of cohabitation, particularly since the subjective presentation of the parties often seeks to disguise or distort the realities.'

Thus, there are no hard and fast rules as to the extent to which the existence of a cohabitant will affect proceedings. In this case, the former wife's periodical payments were reduced in proportion to the contribution to the living costs her cohabitant was making or was able to make in the view of the court. Clearly, no order should be made which can only be met by a former spouse (or civil partner) from the resources of his or her cohabitant and the court should be satisfied that any order made can be met out of the party's own resources (see *B v B (periodical payments) (transitional provisions)* [1995] 1 FLR 459).

6.19

Cohabitation is of great importance where a settlement provides for payment of maintenance (or indeed other provision such as occupation of the family home) 'until remarriage, formation of a new civil partnership or cohabitation with another person' for a specified period of time. Here what exactly amounts to cohabitation is critical and the courts have looked to the reality of the situation. In *K v K (enforcement)* [2000] 1 FLR 383, such a maintenance clause had been agreed. The wife had formed a relationship with an American and they became engaged. The new partner had his own accommodation but spent several nights a week with the wife helping to run her bed and breakfast business. Evidence of this was provided by the husband's enquiry agent and formed the basis of his refusal to continue to pay maintenance to the wife. The court found that the reality was that the wife and her fiancé had been cohabiting and whilst the husband was ordered to pay the arrears, maintenance should cease. The court went on to enumerate a list of factors based on s 137(1) Social Security

Contributions and Benefits Act 1992 and other authorities which were of assistance in determining whether there was cohabitation. These were:

- *living together in the same household* – this did not mean they always had to live under the same roof, although this was the normal meaning;
- *a sharing of daily life*;
- *stability and a degree of permanence* – a passing relationship such as a holiday romance is not sufficient;
- *shared finance* – although it is not at all unusual for couples to maintain separate bank accounts they must pool their resources to some extent even if it just in the sharing of outgoings or one providing financial support for the other;
- *children*;
- *intention and motivation*; and
- *the opinion of the reasonable person with normal perceptions* (see *Kimber v Kimber* [2000] 1 FLR 383).

6.20

Thus cohabitation remains a matter of fact and may mean different things in different contexts. This case contrasts, for example, with that of *Re Watson (deceased)* [1999] 1 FLR 878 discussed in Chapter 5. However, in the context of continuing maintenance provision for a spouse or civil partner, the courts seem keen to show they are alert to avoidance tactics and cohabitants should beware of litigating on the basis of sham arrangements.

6.21

A spouse or civil partner living with a new partner is obliged to give full details of his or her partner in his Financial Statement (Form E) prepared for the court. This includes details of their income, capital and property interests.

6.22

Problems may arise where a party has (or claims to have) no knowledge of their new partner's financial position in their Form E, although that party can be ordered to file a statement (of truth) providing full details of what they do know about their partner's means. A cohabitant, whether or not a co-respondent, cannot be joined as a party for the purpose of financial remedy proceedings, but may seek to intervene and become a party. However, an order for disclosure (of information or documents) will be ordered against them only if it is relevant to the issue being tried (*S v X (intervenors)* [1991] FCR 39). Nevertheless, the Family Procedure Rules 2010 empower the district judge hearing a financial remedy application to order the disclosure and production of any document (FPR 2010, r 21.2 and PD 21A).

6.23

In addition, *Frary v Frary* [1994] 1 FCR 595 gives guidance as to the way in which the court can compel a cohabitant to produce evidence of their means in respect of an application for financial provision where their partner indicates they have no knowledge of their means. Providing the cohabitant is to be called as a witness, FPR 2010, r 21.2 permits the court to order any person to produce at an 'inspection appointment' any document necessary for the disposing fairly of the application for financial relief or the saving of costs. The leading case of *Livesey (formerly Jenkins) v Jenkins* [1985] AC 424 has clearly stated that disclosure in such cases must be full and frank to enable the court to properly exercise its discretion under s 25 MCA 1973 (and under CPA 2004, Sch 5, Pt 5, para 21) and the FPR 2010 clearly now embody this approach.

PART II

Relationship breakdown

7.00

It is on relationship breakdown that legal advice is most often sought by cohabitants. As has been noted in Chapters 1 to 6, the legal position of cohabitants on breakdown of their relationships depends to a large degree on any legally binding arrangements that have been made between them. At the present time, there is no 'divorce law equivalent' for those who have not made pre-emptive arrangements by entering into full or partial cohabitation agreements as discussed in Chapter 1 or who cannot otherwise reach agreement on breakdown. Whilst the need for change in the law in this field has been recognised by both the Law Society and Resolution (formerly, the Solicitors' Family Law Association) for many years, there is little appetite it seems from government or in Parliament generally to do something to address the oftentimes precarious position a cohabitant could be left in after relationship breakdown. The Cohabitation Rights Bill 2017 which had its first reading in the House of Lords on 5 July 2017 (if it were to become law) affords protections of a financial nature to cohabitants (being any two people whether of the same sex or the opposite sex who live together as a couple) who live together and:

(i) are each treated in law as being mother, father or parent of the same minor child;

(ii) there is in force in respect of a minor child either a joint residence order in respect of both of them or a child arrangements order stipulating arrangements by which the child is to live, spend time or have contact with them;

(iii) they are the natural parents of the child as yet unborn at the date when they ceased living together as a couple; or

(iv) they have lived together as a couple for a continuous period of three years or more.

As at the date of writing, no date has been announced for its second reading in the House of Lords and if it passes through both Houses is unlikely to become law before 2019.

Under current law the fallback position for cohabitants is the general law applicable to the area or areas of dispute. As a rule, the more comprehensive the arrangements that have been made between cohabitants, the less scope there should be for lengthy and bitter litigation. However, most cohabitants fail to make any arrangements at all. Faced with this situation, as in divorce or dissolution, the aim should be for the parties to reach agreement without having to resort to the courts, particularly in relation to the arrangements for any children. Legal aid is now only available in family proceedings where the applicant can prove an element of domestic abuse, so access to legal advice and/or to the court is a real issue. Mediation is encouraged as a means of resolving issues out of court, but, whilst mediation relies on both parties willing to co-operate and to compromise to reach a resolution that is fair and reasonable and which meets the needs and interests of any minor child, mediation can be used to pressurise a weaker party into accepting something that a court would not order. It is imperative therefore that either cohabitants are able to access legal advice before agreeing to any final arrangement in mediation or that the mediator is sufficiently trained to recognise a power imbalance that may be contributing to a more one-sided agreement and then to halt the process.

Legal advice on the appropriateness of tentative agreements reached between the parties is often sought. This can place the advisor in the position of having to indicate that the agreement is not in the client's best interests. Whilst there is a duty to explain why this view has been formed, it is also important for practitioners to explain that, despite this, bitter litigation rarely allows amicable relations between the parties in the long term. Yet no client should be allowed to agree to an arrangement which would severely prejudice his or her long-term future unless all the other options have been explained, explored and rejected. Solicitors are often criticised for tending to exacerbate the tension between parting couples. The possibility of counselling, conciliation or mediation for cohabitants on relationship breakdown may be overlooked. The availability of such services will depend on the area in which the couple live, but, particularly in relation to disputes about children, this is an avenue of help of which the client should at least be aware.

The Lord Chancellor's Department's Marriage and Relationship Support Programme, provided funding to organisations under Family Law Act 1996 s 22, which promoted the programme's aim of 'positively promoting the provision of high quality, cost effective services in the vital area of marriage and relationship support to ensure that as many couples as possible can benefit'. This programme recognised that all relationships, not just marriages and civil partnerships, are deserving of such support (notwithstanding the wording of FLA 1996, s 22), and was clearly intended to provide services to cohabitants. In December 2010 the (then) Prime Minister announced that £7.5 million a year would be available for marriage and relationship support (speech by David Cameron to Relate on Families and Relationships, 10 December 2010) over the spending review period 2011 to 2015 to meet the (then) coalition government's commitment to 'put funding for relationship support on a stable, long-term footing, and make sure that couples are given greater encouragement to use existing relationship support'. The organisations awarded national contracts were: Marriage Care; One Plus One; Tavistock Centre Couple Relationships; Relate; and Contact a Family. These organisations would be working in partnership with other voluntary sector organisations to deliver the services, including the Asian Family Counselling Service; PACE; Grandparents Association; Family Action; Fatherhood Institute; 4 Children; and Working Families.

Amicable settlement is not, however, always possible. The prime example is a case of domestic abuse. Here the only remedy available may be prompt court action. This section will explore the protections provided by the provisions of Part IV Family Law Act 1996, as well as the Domestic Violence Disclosure Scheme and the protections in the criminal law sphere including Domestic Violence Protection Notices and Orders.

Some of the main sources of advice for victims are listed below:

- Refuge: www.refuge.org.uk/
- Women's Aid: www.womensaid.org.uk/
- SafeLives: www.safelives.org.uk/
- Welsh Women's Aid: www.welshwomensaid.org.uk/
- National Centre for Domestic Violence: www.ncdv.org.uk
- Solace Women's Aid: http://solacewomensaid.org/
- Respect: http://respect.uk.net/
- Broken Rainbow: www.brokenrainbow.org.uk
- Woman's Trust: www.womanstrust.org.uk/
- Southall Black Sisters: www.southallblacksisters.org.uk/
- Action on Elder Abuse: www.elderabuse.org.uk/

The Istanbul Convention on preventing and combating violence against women and domestic violence (the Istanbul Convention) was adopted by the Council of Europe in April 2011. Its website explains what the convention (which came into force on 1 August 2014) means for individual states. Governments who have agreed to be bound by the convention have to do the following:

(i) train professionals in close contact with victims;

(ii) regularly run awareness-raising campaigns;

(iii) take steps to include issues such as gender equality and non-violent conflict resolution in interpersonal relationships in teaching material;

(iv) set up treatment programmes for perpetrators of domestic violence and for sex offenders;

(v) work closely with NGOs; and

(vi) involve the media and the private sector in eradicating gender stereotypes and promoting mutual respect.

Twenty-one EU states have ratified the convention so far. Although the UK signed the convention in 2012 it has not yet ratified it, the government stating on 14 October 2015 that 'the UK already complies with the vast majority of the articles through its comprehensive work to protect women and girls'. On 27 June 2017 the Preventing and Combating Violence Against Women and Domestic Violence Act 2017 came into force. It required the Secretary of State to lay a report before Parliament setting out the steps to be taken to enable ratification of the convention and the expected timetable for ratification, no later than 1 November 2017 (which as at the date of writing has not yet been complied with) and then to report annually thereafter on progress.

The Queen's Speech of June 2017 promised a Courts Bill which would 'end direct cross-examination of domestic violence victims by alleged perpetrators in the Family Court and allow more victims to participate in trials without having to meet their alleged assailant face to face'. As at the date of writing, this Bill has not been published and as Brexit negotiations dominate the work of the government and Parliament it may well be some time before this Bill sees the light of day (if it does at all). This protection for victims is urgently required if the courts are to properly protect and support victims of violence, who may well continue to be further victimised by their assailants.

Disputes about the children will be considered in the following chapter, and the law relating to child support, financial provision for children, and housing and property rights between cohabitants, which have all undergone significant changes since the last edition of this book, will be considered in later chapters.

Another radical overhaul affecting practitioners acting for cohabitants undergoing relationship breakdown is that of the new legal aid regime. Whilst the new rules and regulations are noted where appropriate in each of the following chapters, the overall impact of the new scheme in the context of relationship breakdown is summarised below.

Legal Aid

On 1 May 2012 the Legal Aid, Sentencing and Punishment of Offenders Act 2012 (LASPO) received Royal Assent. Under this Act, the Legal Aid Agency (LAA) was created and took over responsibility for legal aid from the LSC on 1 April 2013. The LAA is an executive agency of the Ministry of Justice. Funding is now available for only a limited number of family law issues, including, in the context of cohabitants, public law cases (eg care or supervision proceedings) regarding protection of children, private law cases (eg for a child arrangements order) where there is evidence of domestic abuse (where the client is at risk of or has suffered such abuse) or of child abuse (or genuine child protection concerns), child abduction matters, representation for child parties in private law family cases, legal advice in support of mediation and domestic violence injunction cases.

Schedule 1 to the Act sets out the levels of service for which legal aid may be provided (which are defined at regs 4–10 of the Civil Legal Aid (Procedure) Regulations 2012 as amended). Legal aid will only be available in private law family cases where a client has provided specific evidence of alleged domestic violence/abuse (including financial abuse) or child protection need. The LASPO definition of domestic violence is any incident or pattern of incidents of controlling, coercive or threatening behaviour, violence or abuse (whether psychological, physical, sexual, financial or emotional) between individuals who are associated with each other.

In order to carry out legally aided work, providers are required to have signed Standard Civil Contracts with the LAA.

The levels of service are as follows:

(1) *Legal Help* – essentially 'advice and assistance' work.

(2) *Family Help* – authorises help in relation to a family dispute including assistance in resolving that dispute through negotiation or otherwise. Whilst Family Help does not include the provision of mediation services, it does cover help and advice in support of Family Mediation. Family Help covers all services within the scope of either Legal Help or Legal Representation other than preparation for or representation at a contested final hearing or appeal. Family Help (Lower) means advice and assistance excluding the issuing of proceedings or representation in proceedings other than help in obtaining a consent order following settlement of a family dispute. Family Help (Higher) is a grant of Family Help only available in private law family cases and includes all work done following the issue of proceedings (save in respect of the obtaining of a consent order).

(3) *Family Mediation* – available only to approved mediators and authorises mediation of a family dispute including assessing whether mediation is suitable to the dispute and the parties and all the circumstances.

(4) *Help with Family Mediation* – authorises legal services to be provided in relation to ongoing or recently completed Family Mediation and also to obtain a consent order following the settlement of a dispute in such Family Mediation. Applicants for this level of legal aid provision are not required to provide evidence of domestic violence in order for their applications to be considered.

(5) *Legal Representation* – authorising (by way of a legal aid certificate) litigation and advocacy services and all such help as is usually given by a person providing representation in proceedings, including steps preliminary or incidental to proceedings and all such help as is usually given by such a person in arriving at or giving effect to a compromise to avoid or bring to an end any proceedings.

Domestic abuse cases will initially be covered under Legal Help in respect of the initial advice but if an injunction order is required a legal aid certificate (for Legal Representation) must be applied for.

The time taken to process an application for a certificate of Legal Representation may defeat the interests of justice or cause hardship and there is therefore provision for the grant of Emergency Representation in urgent circumstances without assessment of resources. However, the client must still generally provide sufficient information to enable it to be determined whether the conditions for granting Legal Representation are likely to be fulfilled and that it is in the interests of justice that the applicant should as a matter of urgency be granted Legal Representation. Emergency Representation therefore may be granted before the client has been assessed as being financially eligible under the regulations but only if in the opinion of the LAA or solicitor sufficient information has been provided to demonstrate that the client is likely to be financially eligible. Solicitors who have a contract with the LAA to undertake family law work are able to exercise devolved powers (delegated functions of the LAA) to grant a certificate of Emergency Representation (eg in the case of an urgent injunction required under Part IV Family Law Act 1996).

If the applicant has provided specific evidence of alleged domestic violence/abuse (including financial abuse) or child protection need, he or she will automatically qualify for legal aid on income grounds if in receipt of income support, income-based jobseeker's allowance, income-related employment and support allowance, universal credit or guarantee credit but would still need to satisfy the capital requirement. The maximum disposable capital for financial eligibility is £8,000. For all applications made on or after 4 April 2016 any client who has gross income of more than £2,657 per calendar month (or disposable (net) income of more than £733 per calendar month) is automatically excluded from eligibility. There is provision for a monthly income contribution in the case of annual disposable income over £3,780 however. The LAA is able to waive the upper disposal income limit of £733 per calendar month (as well as the gross income limit and disposable capital limit) in domestic abuse cases to benefit the victims of such abuse who are seeking protection from the court although the gross income cap and any contributions from disposable income if in excess of £315 per annum will still apply.

The statutory charge is the mechanism by which the costs payable out of the legal aid fund in respect of the proceedings under which money or property has been recovered or preserved is repayable to the fund ie is a first charge on any such property recovered or preserved by the client in any proceedings or in any compromise or settlement of any dispute, in connection with which legal aid had been granted (LASPO, s 25(1)). The charge will not arise in respect of the cost to the LAA of Help with Family Mediation save where this level of service was made available to the client in connection with the same proceedings or dispute in respect of which a substantive certificate (Family Help (Higher) or

Legal Representation) was granted. Equally, it does not apply to Legal Help in relation to family proceedings save as above.

The LAA can only defer enforcing the charge if the property subject to the charge is the home of the client or his dependants or, in family cases, is money to be used to buy a home for the client or his dependants (Civil Legal Aid (Statutory Charge) Regulations 2013, reg 22(1)(a)) and the charge is registered (reg 22(2)) and it is satisfied that the home would provide appropriate security for the charge (reg 22(1)(b)). Interest upon a deferred charge accrues from registration at 8% per annum (regs 25(1)(a)–(c)). It is calculated on a simple basis and applied to the lesser of either the amount of the statutory charge outstanding from time to time excluding accrued interest or (if the value of the property was lower at the time of recovery) the value of the property when it was recovered or preserved (reg 25(10)(d)).

The Statutory Charge Manual (last updated April 2014) is available in electronic form on the LAA website.

For further information in relation to the levels of service funded by the LAA, readers should consult the LAA Civil Finance Electronic Handbook available on its website and the chapter on legal aid in Butterworths' looseleaf Family Law Service which is updated quarterly and which covers the current eligibility criteria for all levels of legal aid funding and the rates of remuneration for all work undertaken under the Scheme.

CHAPTER 7

Domestic abuse and the family home

7.01

The family home can be a violent environment for some families, whether married or unmarried, homosexual or heterosexual. The Domestic Violence Disclosure Scheme (also known as 'Clare's Law') was introduced by the Crime and Security Act 2010 and after a 14-month pilot period was effective nationwide as of 8 March 2014. This scheme enables the applicant to ask the police for information where they have concerns that their partner may pose a risk to them or to any child of theirs (the 'right to ask'). If an application is made the police will carry out checks to see whether the partner has any record of abusive offences or whether there is any other information to indicate that they may be at risk from the partner and will consider sharing this information with the applicant where it is proportionate and necessary to do so (the 'right to know'). It is also possible for the family or friends of a person who it is feared is at risk to apply for information from the police. Where the police receive indirect information about a person's safety and after appropriate checks are made determine that disclosure should be made to safeguard that person they may do so. The maximum time to complete the disclosure process (for the police to decide if it is necessary to disclose information) is 35 days unless immediate protection is needed. No written copy of the disclosure is provided to the applicant. The relevant disclosure information is read out to the applicant who must then sign a form to say that they have received the information.

7.02

The fact remains though that many perpetrators of domestic abuse are not known to the police. Thus, the police checks and any disclosure (or non-disclosure) is not a guarantee of a person's safety. If the police do not provide any information on the partner the applicant should not be lulled into feeling that they are then completely safe and not at risk. Police data showed that from implementation up to 31 December 2014 a total of 4,724 applications had taken place with 1,938 disclosures made. Further, data from the 15 police forces that submitted returns from 1 January 2015 to 31 July 2015 show that a further 691 Domestic Violence Disclosure applications with 297 disclosures were made during that period (from Home Office report *Domestic Violence Disclosure Scheme (DVDs) One year on – Home Office Assessment of National Roll Out* March 2016).

7.03

In the Autumn of 2013, the government issued a new definition of 'domestic abuse' (subsequently adopted in the revised Practice Direction 12J of the Family Procedure Rules 2010 which came into force on 2 October 2017) to include 'any incident or pattern of incidents of controlling, coercive or threatening behaviour, violence or abuse between those aged 16 or over who are or have been intimate partners or family members regardless of gender or sexuality. This can encompass, but is not limited to, psychological, physical, sexual, financial, or emotional abuse. Domestic abuse also includes culturally specific forms of abuse including, but not limited to, forced marriage, honour-based violence, dowry-related abuse and transnational marriage abandonment'. Domestic abuse cases comprise 33% of all recorded assault with injury crime, making it the single largest category of violent crime (see HMIC report 'Increasingly everyone's business: A progress report on the police response to domestic abuse' issued in December 2015). Even after couples separate, violence may still occur. Depending on the effects of an assault, criminal and/or civil remedies may be available to a cohabitant victim. Reporting domestic abuse has often resulted in a somewhat half-hearted police response. In recent years, many initiatives have been taken in different parts of the country to highlight domestic violence as a crime to be taken seriously by the police and public alike.

7.04

As reported by Pat Strickland and Grahame Allen in their Briefing paper on Domestic Violence in England and Wales (Number 6337, 21 June 2017), some 7.0% of women and 4.4% of men were estimated to have experienced domestic abuse in 2015/16, equivalent to an estimated 1.2 million female and 651,000 male victims. Further, the Crown Prosecution Service (CPS) in its Violence against Women and Girls crime report 2015–2016 recorded that in 2015/16, there were 117,882 domestic violence cases referred to the CPS by the police – a fall of 4% on 2014/15, but compared to 2009/10 an increase of 29%.

7.05

The overall police response to victims of domestic abuse was found to be 'not good enough', in a report published on 27 March 2014 by HM Inspectorate of Constabulary (HMIC), following an inspection of all 43 police forces in England and Wales, and police forces were required to 'take decisive action to rectify this'. The report, 'Everyone's business: Improving the police response to domestic abuse', found that while most forces and police and crime commissioners had paid lip service to the ideal that domestic abuse was a priority for their areas, this was not being translated into an operational reality and not all police leaders were ensuring that domestic abuse was indeed a priority in their forces. Some work was undertaken to address these issues and some progress has been made, as acknowledged in the updated report from HMIC 'Increasingly everyone's business: A progress report on the police response to domestic abuse' issued in December 2015, although it concluded that there was 'much more still to be done'.

7.06

Arguments which had traditionally been cited by the police as justification for declining to bring charges against violent partners, such as an alleged propensity for victims to change their minds about pressing charges and/or a reluctance to testify against their partners, have largely been debunked and the police are better trained to offer support to victims through the possible court process. However, whilst there is no room for complacency, following the HMIC reports, all police forces should now have policies in place which give much more positive help to victims of domestic abuse, including at the very least a willingness to arrest where this is appropriate as well as support for victims. They should all have a specialist domestic abuse unit, with a significant number of specially trained officers who have an understanding of the often difficult choices facing victims of domestic abuse. Whilst many forces have carried out the necessary actions required, there is still a huge disparity between different areas of the country which effectively makes police response a postcode lottery. In the 12 months to 30 June 2016 domestic abuse arrest rates in England and Wales varied from 25% in Hampshire to 83% in the City of London (HMIC annual report on the State of Policing 2016), which whilst accepted by HMIC as 'unacceptable' is unexplained in the report, leaving it to readers to speculate about the (lack of) seriousness with which complaints of domestic abuse are still being treated.

7.07

The recorded levels of domestic abuse have generally declined over the past decade. In the year ending March 2005 there were approximately 2.7 million victims compared to just under 2 million in the year ending March 2016 (Briefing paper 6337). This statistically significant reduction of 27% has not been explained and one wonders how much this is due to victims assuming perhaps that the police force in the area in which they live would not be supportive or would not readily believe them. Thus, whilst the number of arrests may well have increased in some areas, in others the numbers have either levelled out or dropped. Of the 117,882 domestic abuse cases referred to the CPS by the police in 2015/16, a decision to charge was made in only 69.7% of such cases and of those prosecutions the number of convictions was 75,235 representing 74.5% of the prosecutions made (and 63.8% of the cases referred to the CPS) which percentage has remained fairly constant over the last decade, varying from 71.9% to 74.6% (Briefing Paper 6337). The Human Rights Act 1998 (HRA 1998) is clear that the state has a duty to protect its citizens from torture or inhuman or degrading treatment (Article 3 ECHR) and this includes prevention rather than cure (see *A v United Kingdom (human rights: punishment of child)* [1998] 2 FLR 959). It is interesting and important to note in this context that in March 2016, the Home Office published its 2016–20 strategy to end violence against women and girls, and on 17 February 2017 the Prime Minister announced 'a major programme of work leading towards bringing forward a Domestic Violence and Abuse Act' under which a Domestic Violence and Abuse Commissioner would be established, protection powers would be consolidated and aggravated sentences where abusive behaviour involves a child introduced.

7.08

It should be noted that the lack of a safe address to flee to which is unknown to the abuser will make many victims reluctant to use the criminal remedies available or even avail themselves of civil remedies for fear of reprisals. Victims of domestic abuse (and the children in their care) are accordingly a priority need category in terms of re-housing for local authorities. Unfortunately, although Part IV Family Law Act 1996 (FLA 1996) provides an improved range of civil remedies, a victim still has to choose whether to agree to testify in a police prosecution in the event of the abuser pleading not guilty, or personally to seek protection in the form of civil remedies.

1 Criminal proceedings

(a) Domestic Violence Protection Notices and Orders

7.09

Domestic Violence Protection Notices (DVPNs) and Orders (DVPOs) were brought into effect by the Crime and Security Act 2010, ss 24–27 and implemented across England and Wales from 8 March 2014. These enable the police (and magistrates) to put in place protection for victims of domestic abuse in the immediate aftermath of a domestic abuse incident. The advantage of speed is obvious. Under a DVPO, a perpetrator can be banned from returning to the home and from having contact with the victim for up to 28 days, allowing the victim time to consider their options and to get the support they need.

7.10

Before the making of a DVPO, a police officer (not below the rank of superintendent) must first issue a DVPN, where there are reasonable grounds for believing that the perpetrator has used or threatened violence towards the victim. The DVPN must contain a provision prohibiting the perpetrator from molesting (using or threatening violence, harassing or otherwise behaving in a coercive or controlling manner towards) the victim and where the parties live in the same premises may also contain provision for his or her eviction, exclusion or prohibition in relation to a specified distance from the home. The DVPN must be in writing and served personally by a police officer on the perpetrator. Following the issue of a DVPN an application must be made for a DVPO to a magistrates' court, which application must be heard no later than 48 hours after the DVPN was issued (s 27). The court may make a DVPO on a similar basis to the criteria for a DVPN, ie that the court is satisfied on a balance of probabilities that the person against whom a DVPO is to be made has been violent or has threatened violence towards the victim and that the court thinks that making a DVPO is necessary to protect the victim (s 28(2)–(3)). A DVPO must state the period for which it is to be enforced and may be enforced for no fewer than 14 days and no more than 28 days beginning with the day on which the order was made (s 28(10)–(11)).

7.11

Police data (from the Home Office report on *Domestic Violence Protection Orders – One year on* published in March 2016) shows that from implementation up to 31 December 2014 3,337 DVPNs had been authorised with 3,072 DVPOs granted by magistrates. 565 (18%) DVPOs had been breached. Data from the 17 police forces that submitted returns from January 2015 to 31 July 2015 show that a further 1,384 DVPOs were granted in this period. The Home Office is now considering holding a consultation on criminalising the breach of a DVPO. In its response to the Home Office report, Women's Aid released a press release on 8 March 2016 offering that in its view the breach of a DVPO 'must become a criminal offence' and that 'any consultation should not drastically delay victims from getting the protection they need'.

(b) Prosecution

7.12

Although not always appropriate, there may be circumstances in which both victim and perpetrator may benefit from the knowledge that domestic abuse is increasingly viewed by the police as a serious criminal offence warranting prosecution. There is no specific criminal offence of domestic violence; rather, there are a number of possible offences for which perpetrators can be prosecuted, including but not limited to murder and manslaughter, rape, assault, threatening behaviour and (non-violent but repeated or continuous) coercive or controlling behaviour, the latter offence introduced in December 2015 by the Serious Crime Act 2015, s 76 and carrying a maximum sentence of five years' imprisonment and/or a fine.

7.13

The proceedings which may be brought, whether victim and perpetrator are of the same or the opposite sex, are identical, but how effective they are usually depends on the police response, and the seriousness of the assault. The most serious incidents of domestic violence involve charges of murder or manslaughter. The Offences Against the Person Act 1861 enables prosecution for assaults occasioning actual bodily harm (at least bruising usually – s 47); grievous bodily harm (very serious harm – s 18); or wounding (some puncturing of the skin – s 20). In *R v Ireland v Burstow* [1998] AC 147, the House of Lords accepted that harassing conduct could amount to 'assault' and that 'bodily harm' was not restricted to physical harm but could include psychological injuries. Section 30 Criminal Justice Act 1988 also provides a statutory offence of common assault for which the police themselves will now often prosecute, rather than, as was their previous policy, suggesting that the victim take out a magistrates' court summons for common assault. Although the latter is still an option, it is rarely appropriate as legal aid is not available, leaving the victim to bring his or her own case.

7.14

The Serious Crime Act 2015 introduced in December 2015 a new offence of controlling or coercive behaviour in intimate or familial relationships. The behaviour complained of must have had a 'serious effect' on the victim, namely that it has caused the victim to fear violence will be used against them on 'at least two occasions' or it has had a 'substantial adverse effect on the victim's day to day activities'. The alleged perpetrator must have known that their behaviour would have a serious effect on the victim or the behaviour must have been such that he or she 'ought to have known' it would have that effect. The controlling or coercive behaviour does not relate to one single incident but to a purposeful pattern of behaviour which takes place over time in order for the perpetrator to exert power, control or coercion over the victim. Controlling behaviour is a range of acts designed to make a person subordinate and/or dependent by isolating them from sources of support (family, friends etc), exploiting their resources and capacity for personal gain, depriving them of the means for independence (eg controlling bank accounts and access to money), resistance and escape and regulating their everyday behaviour (eg not allowing them to leave the home). Coercive behaviour is a continuing act or a pattern of acts of assault, threats, humiliation and intimidation or other abuse that is used to harm, punish or frighten the victim. The offence carries a maximum sentence of five years' imprisonment and/or a fine.

7.15

There are many reasons why a cohabitant may not want his or her partner prosecuted, as where the victim is financially dependent upon their assailant, particularly if there are children. Pressure is often brought to bear on victims in these situations to withdraw the charge, although the victim, having made a statement and been summoned to give evidence, can be jailed for contempt, however frightened about his or her personal safety, if he or she does not attend court.

7.16

One advantage of calling the police and allowing the perpetrator to be charged is that it will almost certainly result in the court imposing a bail condition that the defendant must not contact the victim pending trial. This is often an effective way of keeping the violent partner at bay, allowing time to dwell on the seriousness of the situation. On the other hand, prosecution can result in a guilty plea and the matter being dealt with by the magistrates' court on the day after the incident, with nothing more than a fine being imposed, particularly if it is a first offence. This may leave the perpetrator at large, angry and vengeful, placing the partner in a vulnerable position and in need of the additional protection of the civil law. Another difficulty with bail conditions is that a victim may not be made aware that bail conditions have been changed or even that the case has been dealt with. Given that the victim is not a party to the criminal proceedings but merely a witness, victims are often not informed of developments. It also seems that in some cases the existence of bail conditions may be used to justify the refusal of legal aid for civil injunctions (see Crisell, 'Injunctions v Bail Conditions' [1995] Fam Law 85) upon the basis that this would involve the unnecessary duplication of proceedings which have the same effect at the expense of public funds. Yet the protection offered by bail conditions is only ever temporary, and is protection which is likely to be withdrawn by the court without even hearing from the victim or giving him or her notice of this. Thus, this line of argument should be fiercely resisted. However, when applying for a certificate for emergency representation (or considering the use of devolved powers to grant such a certificate) a solicitor must enquire whether the police have been informed about the assault and, if so, whether any action will be, or has been, taken. If the police have charged and placed the perpetrator on police bail, depending on the terms of such bail, emergency representation may be refused. If the police have not been informed then the victim may be asked to contact the police first, and only if the police decline to act, will a certificate be granted.

7.17

One other important development in this field is the Protection from Harassment Act 1997 (PHA1997), which offers a mixture of civil and criminal remedies and which was aimed at stalkers but applies more widely. PHA 1997, s 1(1) introduced a summary arrestable offence of harassment. This is defined in s 1 in relation to its effect upon the victim and measured against the objective standard (see s 7(2)) of whether 'a reasonable person would have realised that this behaviour would cause the alleged victim to fear the use of violence or to be harassed, alarmed or distressed'.

7.18

Section 1 states:

'(1) A person must not pursue a course of conduct—

(a) which amounts to harassment of another, and

(b) which he knows or ought to know amounts to harassment of the other.

(2) For the purposes of this section, the person whose course of conduct is in question ought to know that it amounts to harassment of another if a reasonable person in possession of the same information would think the course of conduct amounted to harassment of the other.'

7.19

Thus, it is no defence to claim that the defendant was unaware of the harassing nature of their conduct if they ought to have known. It is a defence to show, *inter alia*, that the conduct was reasonable in all the circumstances or necessary for the detection or prevention of a crime (s 1(3)). To amount to harassment, the conduct complained of will need to be shown to be aggressive, bullying or threatening (see *Saha v Imperial College of Science, Technology & Medicine* [2013] EWHC 2438 (QB), [2013] All ER (D) 54 (Aug)) and can include abusive telephone calls and harassing texts.

7.20

However, to be guilty of an offence under s 2, such conduct must have occurred on at least two occasions (s 7(3)). In *Lau v DPP* [2000] 1 FLR 799, the issue arose whether there had to be a nexus between the two incidents to amount to a 'course of conduct' under the Act and the court found that there did. Thus, the fewer the occasions and the wider they are spread, the less likely it will be that a finding of harassment can be reasonably made. In this case, only two separate incidents four months apart were proven by the prosecution, with three intervening matters (which would have assisted the claim to a course of conduct) not found to be proved to the court's satisfaction. Again, as illustrated in the case of *R v Hills* [2001] 1 FLR 580, this requirement of a course of conduct also arises in connection with the more serious offence under s 4 (discussed below). Here a conviction for two assaults some six months apart by a cohabitant on his partner of 18 months standing was quashed as, on the evidence the necessary cogent link between the two assaults had not been made out and there was therefore no course of conduct. These two cases vividly illustrate some of the pitfalls and difficulties in using the 1997 Act in domestic abuse cases, where the criminal standard of proof applies and evidence will often be no more than the word of one party against the other.

7.21

A person who is found guilty of an offence under s 1 is liable on a summary conviction to be sentenced to imprisonment for up to six months and/or to pay a fine on scale 5. Further, on conviction of a s 1 offence, an injunction restraining the conduct can be issued under s 5. Section 3 provides that an actual or apprehended breach of s 1 may be the subject of a claim in civil proceedings by the victim and damages may be awarded for among other things 'anxiety caused by the harassment'. Section 4 of the Act also creates the indictable offence of putting people in fear of violence, which is committed where such a course of conduct has occurred on at least two occasions (note *R v Hills* (above)) and where he or she knows or objectively ought to know the behaviour will put the victim in fear of violence. It carries a maximum penalty of five years' imprisonment and/or a scale 5 fine. The Protection of Freedoms Act 2012 amended the PHA 1997 and created two new offences of stalking under s 2A (pursuing a course of conduct which amounts to harassment and which also amounts to stalking) and s 4A (stalking involving fear of violence or serious alarm or distress) which came into force on 25 November 2012.The maximum prison sentence for the more serious offence (s 4A) was doubled to ten years in April 2017.

7.22

Any decision made by a victim of domestic abuse in relation to pressing charges must be an individual one, but where possible it should be one made in the fullest possible knowledge of the benefits and disadvantages of doing so at that time and in the future.

(c) Compensation for criminal injury

7.23

If a person has been injured (physically or mentally) as a result of a criminal act perpetrated upon them (or which is directly attributable to being present at and witnessing an incident or the aftermath of an incident as a result of which a loved one sustained a criminal injury) they may be entitled to claim compensation through the Criminal Injuries Compensation Authority (CICA) Scheme, which is administered by CICA (under the auspices of the Ministry of Justice) and governed by the Criminal Injuries Compensation Scheme 2012.

(d) The Criminal Injuries Compensation Authority Scheme

7.24

One advantage of using the criminal law against a violent partner is the possibility of obtaining compensation for injuries under the Criminal Injuries Compensation Scheme. Claims are assessed by claims officers, reviewed by adjudicators and appeals go to the First-tier Tribunal (Criminal Injuries Compensation). The working of the scheme is kept under review by the Secretary of State. From an advisor's point of view, the most important point to note is that applications must be made as soon as possible and in any event within two years of the injury, unless the limit is waived because it is in the interests of justice to do so.Applications for compensation can be made online at www.gov.uk/claim-compensation-criminal-injury. Compensation is awarded on a tariff basis with currently 20 levels of compensation in respect of physical and mental injuries and 15 levels of compensation in respect of fatal injuries, sexual and physical abuse. A table of the tariff of injuries is appended to the details of the scheme (at Annex E) and can be viewed on the CICA website at www.cica.gov.uk.

7.25

A claims officer may refuse compensation where the victim and the person responsible for the injuries are living in the same household as members of the same family (see paragraphs 20 and 21 of the guidance to the 2012 Scheme) and an award will not be made if the perpetrator may benefit from the award.

7.26

For a victim to qualify for compensation, it is not necessary that the perpetrator has been prosecuted or convicted. The CICA pay out awards ranging from £1,000 to £500,000, depending on the severity of the injuries.

7.27

Where a criminal compensation order or a civil award of damages has been made, then any compensation awarded under the scheme will be reduced by the sum received from that other source. If such sums are awarded after compensation has been paid under the scheme, they must be paid over to the Authority (para 85 of the 2012 Scheme).

7.28

Applications for compensation must be made within two years of the incident that gave rise to the injuries, and compensation is awarded on the basis of the tariff injuries table. The only special damages payable relate to loss of earnings and certain restricted out-of-pocket expenses (paras 50–56).

7.29

Claims are limited to those meriting a minimum award of £1,000. Thus, if a victim has suffered minor bruising and no loss of earnings, he or she may not receive any compensation, as their entitlement is to less than the minimum, after the deduction of any social security payments paid as a direct result of the injuries. The tariff injuries table at Annex E to the 2012 Scheme gives a guide to the injury threshold at which compensation begins to become payable.

7.30

Advisors should be aware of the existence of the scheme, despite the minimum level rule and will find the CICA website of assistance with any potential claim. Legal costs are not recoverable and where advice is given under the Legal Help scheme, the statutory charge applies and costs are deductible from compensation obtained. Applications should whenever possible be made online and the application process should not take any longer than 20 minutes. For those without access to online services (and those needing help with the application), Customer Service Centre advisors can be contacted on 0300 003 3601.

7.31

Criminal prosecution may serve only to exacerbate a victim's vulnerability when the partner is once again outside the confines of the criminal justice system, and compensation under the CICA scheme will not of itself remove the threat of violence. Thus additional remedies may be required. Even where the victim wishes the criminal law to be used, civil proceedings may also be appropriate. The housing situation may also need urgent consideration by the victim's legal advisor.

2 Civil remedies

7.32

Part IV FLA 1996 (with the exception of s 60) which came into force on 1 October 1997 provides a uniform code of domestic abuse remedies available, in the main, in all courts with jurisdiction in family proceedings. It has been variously amended in the years since then to widen its powers and remit and to meet contemporary social norms (eg is now gender neutral). The FLA is now the most common and perhaps (with the exception of DVPOs) the simplest method by which a victim of domestic abuse is able to obtain protection from assault, threats and molestation against a partner through non-molestation orders and occupation orders. One overlap with the criminal law remedies available to victims of violence is that following the introduction of the Domestic Violence Crime and Victims Act which came into force on 1 July 2007, breach of a non-molestation order is now dealt with by arrest by the police and criminal charges brought in the magistrates' court, rather than the use of a power of arrest and subsequent committal proceedings.

(a) Part IV Family Law Act 1996

7.33

Under Part IV of the Act the court can make two types of order:

(i) non-molestation orders (s 42); and

(ii) occupation orders (ss 33–8).

7.34

These orders are available to specified classes of applicant called 'associated' persons, defined in s 62(3), including but not limited to spouses and former spouses, civil partners and former civil partners and cohabitants and former cohabitants. By s 42(4A), the court when considering whether to make an occupation order shall also consider whether to make a non-molestation order.

7.35

All applications are made in the Family Court. The procedure is set out in FPR 2010, Part 10 and PD 10A. The application, for which there is no fee payable, is made on Form FL401 and sent to the court together with a signed (not sworn but incorporating a statement of truth) statement in support and a draft order.

(i) Non-molestation orders

7.36

The aim of such an order is to restrain a party from molesting the applicant or any relevant child. There is no definition of 'molestation' contained in the Act; a deliberate omission designed to ensure that the line of authorities dealing with such protective orders such as *Vaughan v Vaughan* [1973] 1 WLR 1159, where 'pestering', by a man who called upon his estranged wife morning and evening, at home and at work, making a thorough nuisance of himself, and *Spencer v Camacho* (1983) 4 FLR 662, where, following a series of other incidents a man rifling through his partner's handbag, were both held to amount to molestation, remain good law. Subsequently, in *C v C (non-molestation order: jurisdiction)* [1998] 1 FCR 11, the then President, Sir Stephen Brown, stated that 'molestation implies some quite deliberate conduct which is aimed at a high degree of harassment of the other party, so as to justify the intervention of the court'.

7.37

In essence, conduct amounting to both physical and mental harassment falls within the scope of the 1996 Act. However, prior to the implementation of the FLA 1996, in *Johnson v Walton* [1990] 1 FLR 350, the court took the view that in addition to the actual harassment not amounting to violence, there must also be an intent to cause distress or alarm for it to amount to molestation. It is not just violence or the threat of violence which amounts to molestation. Domestic abuse includes non-violent abuse, such as harassment and controlling behaviour, it being recognised that the psychological effects of such behaviour can be as equally damaging and upsetting as physical assault and it follows that such non-violent abuse would also amount to molestation.

7.38

Section 42(6) makes it clear that molestation of both a general or specific nature may be prohibited by an order, and advisors in drafting orders should consider both specifying particular types as behaviour from which protection is required whilst at the same time also prohibiting molestation of a more general nature, to maximise the victim's protection.

I Criteria

7.39

FLA s 42(5) provides that, in deciding whether to exercise its powers under this section and, if so, in what manner, the court shall have regard to all the circumstances including 'the need to secure the health, safety and well-being' of the applicant and any relevant child. The term 'well-being' is sufficiently wide to ensure that courts do not feel restricted to making orders only in cases where violence or threat of violence can be proven. What has become clear following *C v C (non-molestation order: jurisdiction)* [1998] 1 FLR 554 is that the motive for the conduct allegedly amounting to molestation may be relevant to whether or not the court is prepared to grant a non-molestation order. In this case the husband's application for a non-molestation order preventing his estranged wife from making revelations about him to the press was refused on the basis that her intention was not to harass him but rather to give a public airing to her side of the story. Thus, in contrast to the approach of the Protection from Harassment Act 1997 which considers the effect of the conduct upon the victim, here the respondent's actions had to amount to more than an intrusion of the applicant's privacy in order to constitute molestation, which as noted above was said must be 'some quite deliberate conduct which is aimed at a high degree of harassment of the other party' (per Sir Stephen Brown at pp 556H–557A).

7.40

The term 'relevant child' is defined in s 62(2) and extends beyond children residing with the applicant. It includes any child who lives or might reasonably be expected to live with either party to the proceedings, any child in respect of whom an order under the Adoption and Children Act 2002 or the Children Act 1989 is in question in the proceedings and any other child whose interests the court considers relevant. This is wide and might encompass a situation where, for example, a child came to stay with an applicant for a brief period whether under a child arrangements ('spends time with') order or as otherwise agreed between the parents, or was cared for during the day by an applicant, although did not reside with them.

II Who may apply?

7.41

Own motion powers

A non-molestation order (in contrast to an occupation order) may be granted by a court in any family proceedings to which the respondent is a party without an application having been made for one. Where the court considers that an order should be made for the benefit of any other party to the proceedings or any relevant child, it can of its own motion make a non-molestation order (see s 42(2)(b)). This, of course, follows the approach found in the Children Act 1989 with respect to the making of s 8 orders.

It should be noted that a non-molestation order made in other family proceedings will cease to have effect should these proceedings be withdrawn or dismissed (s 42(8)).

7.42

Eligible applicants

Freestanding applications under Part IV FLA 1996 may, of course, also be made by eligible applicants, including both same-sex and opposite-sex cohabitants and former cohabitants.

7.43

Those entitled to apply for non-molestation orders must be 'associated' with the respondent. 'Associated persons' are defined by s 62(3) to include:

- spouses and former spouses;
- civil partners and former civil partners;
- heterosexual and homosexual cohabitants and former cohabitants;
- those living or having lived in the same household otherwise than merely by reason of one of them being the other's employee, tenant, lodger or boarder;
- those falling within a defined group of close relatives, in respect of whom cohabitants are equated with spouses for the purpose of ascertaining the relationship (see s 63(1));
- those who have at any time agreed to marry or to enter into a civil partnership with each other;
- those who have or have had an intimate personal relationship with each other which is or was of significant duration (added with effect from 1 July 2007 and arguably including couples who have been 'dating' for a 'significant duration' but not 'one night stands');
- parents with a child of the relationship or a child in respect of whom they both have or have had parental responsibility; and
- those who are both parties to the same family proceedings other than proceedings brought under Part IV FLA 1996.

7.44

Furthermore, in *G v F (non-molestation order: jurisdiction)* [2000] 2 FCR 638, Wall J held that where it was not entirely clear whether or not the parties were associated, s 62(3) should not be interpreted so as to exclude borderline cases but should be given purposive construction to offer as much protection as possible to domestic violence victims. Here a couple who, for social security purposes, had represented that they had not been cohabiting but had spent several nights a week together were found by Justices at first instance not to be associated, leaving the woman without a remedy under the Act. On appeal, the Family Division found that the evidence when viewed as a whole was sufficient to support the proposition that the parties were cohabitants within the meaning of the Act as three of the 'signposts' set out in *Crake v Supplementary Benefits Commission* [1982] 1 All ER 498 were present – ie sexual relationship, living in the same household and a joint bank account.

7.45

If not considered to be 'associated persons', the victim would need to consider an application under the Protection from Harassment Act 1997.

7.46

A non-molestation order may be made 'for a specified period or until further order' (s 42 (7)). Commonly, orders made on notice are made for 12 months, although shorter periods of six or even three months are possible, having regard to how long the protection is realistically needed for. In exceptional cases, an indefinite period may be considered to be appropriate (see *Re B-J (a child) (non-molestation order: power of arrest)* [2000] 2 FCR 599, [2001] 1 All ER 235). The duration of without notice non-molestation orders should not normally exceed 14 days.

7.47

In difficult s 8 Children Act 1989 cases, where there are child arrangements issues, it might well be appropriate to make an order that would last until the child has attained the age of 16 or even 18. In the case of *Re SO* [2015] EWHC 935 (Fam), 1 April 2015, Baker J extended a non-molestation order against a father beyond the child's 18th birthday as he was satisfied that there was a continuing risk to the child.

7.48

It is worthy of note that whereas s 44 stipulates the means by which an agreement to marry or to enter into a civil partnership must be proven (the applicant must be evidenced in writing unless it can satisfy the court that there has been the gift of an engagement ring or an engagement ceremony witnessed by at least one person), there is no statutory guidance on acceptable evidence of cohabitation. There is clearly no minimum period of cohabitation or, indeed, of living in the same household required before an applicant within these categories of associated person may apply. However, should an applicant be unable to show that they are a person associated with the respondent on the grounds of cohabitation, advisors should always clarify whether they may fall within one of the other categories of associated persons set out above.

7.49

Where the behaviour complained of amounts to molestation and the association between the parties is proven, the court is still not obliged to make a non-molestation order. Thus, in the case of *Chechi v Bashir* [1999] 2 FLR 489, involving two brothers, who were therefore associated, whilst the court had jurisdiction to grant a non-molestation order even though their dispute concerned business matters, the order was refused.

7.50

Children under 16 may apply for a non-molestation or occupation order but only with leave of the court. This may be granted where the court is satisfied that the child has sufficient understanding to make the proposed order (s 43). Given that non-molestation orders may be made against close relatives, whether or not living in the same household, it is logical that children with sufficient understanding should have the same *locus standi* here as they have in respect of applications under the Children Act 1989. Applications by children for leave have to be made to the High Court pursuant to s 43 FLA 1996.

7.51

One lacuna, which may affect cohabitants, is the inability of a person to apply for a non-molestation order against their partner's former partner/spouse. The formation of new relationships often sparks vengeful acts amounting to violence or harassment against the new partner as well as the former spouse/civil partner or cohabitant. Given that they are not associated unless both are parties to the same family proceedings, such molestation would have to be addressed either through the law of tort or the criminal or civil remedies available under the Protection from Harassment Act 1997.

(ii) Occupation orders

7.52

These orders may be either declaratory or regulatory and are detailed in ss 33–41 FLA 1996. Different types of occupation orders are available depending, first, on whether or not the applicant is an 'entitled' applicant, entitled in their own right to occupy the family home, in which case a s 33 occupation order can be sought by any 'associated' person; and, secondly, ss 35 and 36 occupation orders where the respondent but not the applicant is entitled to occupy the family home, in which case the remedy is limited to former spouses/civil partners, cohabitants and former cohabitants who are 'non-entitled' applicants. There are also two residual categories of occupation order where neither party is entitled to occupy under ss 37 and 38. These are available to former spouses/civil partners and cohabitants/former cohabitants respectively as discussed below. As will be explained, different criteria must be applied by the court to different categories of applicant when determining their applications.

I Section 33 occupation orders and entitled applicants

7.53

To be able to apply for a s 33 occupation order, an applicant must be able to show two things: first, that they have an entitlement to occupy the accommodation and, secondly, that the accommodation either was or was intended to be their home jointly with a person with whom they are associated. Section 33(1) defines entitlement to occupy as either having a legal or beneficial estate or interest, or by virtue of contractual or statutory rights including 'home rights' (defined by s 30 as arising by virtue of marriage or civil partnership). Therefore, both heterosexual and gay cohabitants who are sole or joint owners, or tenants (whether contractual or statutory) in the rented sector may apply for an order against their partner or former partner regardless of their partner's legal status in relation to occupation of the home. This is because an order can be sought against any person with whom the applicant is associated within the meaning of s 62(3).

II Nature of the s 33 occupation order

7.54

Section 33(3) sets out the nature of s 33 occupation orders, which can do any of the following:

(i) enforce the applicant's entitlement to remain in occupation as against the respondent;

(ii) require the respondent to permit the applicant to enter and remain in the dwelling-house or part of it;

(iii) regulate the occupation of the dwelling-house by either or both parties;

(iv) if the respondent is entitled to occupy the home other than by virtue of home rights, prohibit, suspend or restrict the exercise by him/her of his/her rights to occupy the dwelling-house;

(v) if the respondent has home rights in respect of the dwelling-house, restrict or terminate those rights;

(vi) require the respondent to leave the dwelling-house or part of it; and

(vii) exclude the respondent from a defined area in which the dwelling-house is included.

7.55

The court therefore has great flexibility in terms of the type of declaratory and regulatory orders that can be made. It should be noted, as discussed below, that additional provisions in respect of matters such as maintenance of the property, taking care of furniture and payment of rent, mortgage or other outgoings can be included in a s 33 occupation order (see s 40 and para 7.86 below), although this is one area where the effectiveness of the FLA has proved not to be as effective as had been hoped.

III Criteria for making a s 33 occupation order

7.56

First consideration must be given to the *balance of harm test* set out at s 33(7), which states that if it appears to the court that the applicant or any relevant child is likely to suffer significant harm attributable to the behaviour of the respondent if an order is not made, then the court *shall* make the order unless:

(i) the respondent or any relevant child is likely to suffer significant harm if the order is made; and

(ii) the harm likely to be suffered by the respondent or child in that event is as great or greater than the harm likely to be suffered by the applicant or child if the order is not made.

7.57

Subject to the *balance of harm test*, s 33(6), the court, when considering whether to make an occupation order, is directed to have regard to all the circumstances including:

(i) the respective housing needs and housing resources of the parties and relevant child;

(ii) the respective financial resources of the parties;

(iii) the likely effect of any order, or of any decision by the court not to exercise its powers to make an order on the health, safety or well-being of the parties and of any relevant child; and

(iv) the conduct of the parties in relation to each other and otherwise.

7.58

The *balance of harm test* creates a presumption in favour of an order where a child or the applicant is likely to suffer significant harm without one. This can only be avoided where it can be shown that *as great or greater* harm is likely to be suffered by the respondent or child if an order is not made. The interaction of these two subsections was considered by Thorpe LJ in *Chalmers v John* [1999] 2 FCR 110, who indicated that they implied a two-tier approach.

First, a court must decide whether the applicant or a relevant child is likely to suffer significant harm attributable to the conduct of the respondent if an order is not made. If it concludes in the negative, then the making of an order is discretionary in accordance with the criteria in s 33(6). If on the other hand, it considers that significant harm is likely, only then must it make an order unless balancing likely harm to the respondent against the likely harm to the applicant under s 33(7), the likely harm to the respondent is as great or greater, in which case it reverts to being a matter of discretion for the court.

7.59

Chalmers v John has seemingly placed the harm threshold back exactly where it was under the old law, limiting both the granting of occupation orders and the application of the presumption in favour of an order in s 33(7) to 'extreme' or 'exceptional'. The shift in this direction can be seen to have been prompted at least in part by the facts in *Chalmers v John*. The parties were cohabitants of some 25 years' standing whose relationship was described as 'tempestuous'. They had two children, one of 25 and the other only seven. Despite several incidents of violence over the years in connection with which both parties had suffered minor injuries – there had been police involvement and the respondent had been prosecuted unsuccessfully – Thorpe LJ took the view that this was 'in the range of domestic violence, a slight case' (at p 396H). It was not one where the applicant and the younger child (who had by then left the family home and moved to temporary accommodation much further from the child's school) were likely to suffer significant harm if the order was not made. Thus, the court, applying the standard criteria, declined to make an occupation order in the applicant's favour, not even one regulating occupation of the home as between the parties. The fact that other matters of dispute between the parties were to be heard by the court within two months was also an influential factor, with Thorpe LJ commenting that 'as a matter of generality, it seems to me that a court should be cautious to make a definitive order at an interlocutory stage with a final hearing only six or seven weeks distant' (at pp 396–397).

7.60

The term 'significant harm' is borrowed from the CA 1989 and it was confirmed in *Chalmers v John* (at p 398) that its meaning in s 33(7), coincided with that in s 31 CA 1989 and considered by Booth J in *Humberside County Council v B* [1993] 1 FLR 257, namely harm that was 'considerable, noteworthy or important'. 'Harm' is defined in s 63(1) FLA 1996 as meaning ill-treatment or impairment of health and, in the case of a child, development. What is significant may be judged in the context of its effect on the victim and is clearly not confined to physical health. It must, however, be attributable to the respondent's conduct but does not have to be intentional conduct, nor is there any need to establish that actual physical violence has occurred (*G v G (occupation order: conduct)* [2000] 2 FLR 36, [2000] 3 FCR 53). However, once an applicant has reached this threshold of significant harm, then the occupation order must be made unless the respondent or relevant child would suffer equal or worse significant harm if the order were to be made.

7.61

In *B v B (occupation order)* [1999] 1 FLR 715, [1999] 2 FCR 251 heard after *Chalmers v John*, Butler-Sloss LJ indicated that men or women who subject their partners to domestic violence causing injury or driving them from the family home will generally be made subject to an occupation order (at p 724F–H). This case also illustrates how the balance of harm test should work in practice. Here, the parties were married and joint tenants of their council home in which they lived with the husband's six-year-old son by a previous relationship and their own baby daughter. The wife was driven to leave the home with the daughter by the husband's violence and moved to bed and breakfast accommodation, where she would have to stay until an offer of alternative accommodation was made by the council in several months' time. The husband and son remained in the home, located near the son's school. He had been advised by the council that should an occupation order be made against him, he would be considered intentionally homeless and would face either a move away from the area to only temporary accommodation, forcing the son to change schools. His only other option was the placement of his son in local authority accommodation. The Court of Appeal, overturning the occupation order made against the husband at first instance, held that whilst the trial judge had been entitled to find that the wife and baby were likely to suffer significant harm attributable to the husband's conduct if an order was not made, he had not taken sufficient account of the son's interests and thus had not correctly applied the balance of harm test:

> '... whilst in no sense underestimating the difficulties and frustrations of living with and caring for a toddler in bed and breakfast accommodation, the essential security for a child of [the baby's] age is being with her mother. Furthermore ... [the wife's] residence in bed and breakfast accommodation is likely to be temporary. For [the son] the position is much more complex. His security depends not just on being in the care of his father, but on his other day-to-day support systems, of which his home and his school are plainly the most important' (at pp 723–4 per Butler-Sloss LJ).

7.62

The reluctance to make occupation orders other than in extreme cases, where there has been physical violence, was again endorsed by Thorpe LJ in the case of *G v G (occupation order: conduct)* [2000] 3 FCR 53, [2000] 2 FLR 36, where he made clear that an occupation order could only be warranted where something over and above the normal tensions surrounding the process of relationship breakdown exists. Here he reiterated (at p 41):

> '... this was not a case in which the wife had suffered any violence at the hands of the husband. It has been said time and time again

that orders of exclusion are Draconian and only to be made in exceptional cases.'

7.63

Black LJ in *Dolan v Corby* [2011] EWCA Civ 1664 clarified that both *Chalmers v Johns* and *G v G* should not be read as saying that an occupation order can only be made where there is violence or a threat of violence. That would be 'to put a gloss on the statute which would be inappropriate'. Thorpe LJ's two-stage test was subsequently approved by the Court of Appeal in *Re L (children) (occupation order: absence of domestic violence)* [2012] EWCA Civ 721, [2012] 1 FLR 1417, in which case the court allowed the respondent's appeal against an occupation order made on the basis of a series of relatively minor incidents. The court reiterated that such a draconian order should only be made in 'exceptional circumstances'.

7.64

Overall, short of further legislation or a change of direction by the Supreme Court in future cases, it seems that little has changed in terms of the availability of occupation orders in the domestic abuse context, although advisors should seriously consider whether an applicant's situation can be improved by imposing conditions on each party's continued occupation of the home.

7.65

A possible exception may however arise where, although there is not violence as between family members, the granting of an occupation order would serve another meritorious purpose, such as promoting the interests of a child. Thus, in *S v F (occupation order)* [2000] 1 FLR 255, a case where no violence was alleged between the parties, an occupation order was granted to a father enabling him to continue to occupy the London family home with his son who wished to remain in London to complete his education and therefore did not wish to move away from London with his mother and siblings. Outside the domestic violence context at least then, occupation orders may have provided more scope for regulation of the family home than permitted by the predecessors.

7.66

The standard criteria in s 33(6)(a)–(d) are common to all occupation orders. The housing needs and resources of the parties and any affected child are obviously critical, and financial needs and resources affect the ability to secure accommodation elsewhere. The current homelessness legislation now found in Part VII Housing Act 1996, as amended by the Homelessness Act 2002, imposes a duty on local housing authorities to provide accommodation to those with priority need. In terms of how the court will exercise its discretion in non-mandatory (ie s 33(6) not s 33(7)) cases, it is probably still the case that the court is more likely to grant an occupation order excluding the respondent if the applicant can show that the respondent can easily find other accommodation with a member of his or her family, or has the means to rent other accommodation (see *Baggott v Baggott* [1986] 1 FLR 377).

7.67

To conclude, it is important to note that an occupation order would seem only to be justified if the circumstances are deemed exceptional. Such circumstances may however include non-violent behaviour (*Dolan v Corby*). It is left to the courts to identify those particular circumstances and there will undoubtedly be ongoing debate and hopefully further clarification of what behaviour would constitute 'exceptional circumstances'.

IV Duration of s 33 orders

7.68

Occupation orders under this section may be made for a specified period, or until a specified event or further order (s 33(10)). Thus, in contrast to ss 35, 36, 37 and 38, where an occupation order is limited to a maximum period of six months in the first instance, no statutory time limit has been imposed where an applicant is entitled.

V Non-entitled applicants and s 36 occupation orders

7.69

These orders may be sought by a cohabitant or former cohabitant who has no existing right to occupy the home from which (or from a part of which) he or she is seeking to exclude the other. Given that a violent situation is not a prerequisite for the making of an occupation order, it may be a useful tool for a deserted non-entitled former cohabitant who quickly needs to assert their status in relation to a third party such as a mortgagee or landlord. There seems to be no reason why orders cannot be made to safeguard the position of an applicant in this way pending final resolution of matters between the parties, and the decision in *S v F* (above) shows that occupation orders may be made to regulate occupation of the family home outside the domestic abuse context.

VI Who may apply for a s 36 order?

7.70

Applications are limited to non-entitled cohabitants and former cohabitants (defined in s 62(1)(a)) and do *not* extend to any other category of 'associated' persons. Non-entitled former spouses and civil partners may apply for a s 35 occupation order, which is subject to criteria similar to that applicable to s 33 orders including the balance of harm test where a s 35(5) occupation order is to be made (s 35(8)).

7.71

Where one cohabitant or former cohabitant has a legal or statutory right of occupation as defined by s 36(1)(a) FLA 1996 in respect of the family home and is thus entitled to occupy it, but their partner/former partner has no such right, then, provided they live or have lived together or intended to do so, in that dwelling-house, the partner without a right of occupation may apply for a s 36 occupation order as against their partner or former partner. There is no qualifying period of cohabitation required for applicants to be able to avail themselves of this remedy, but proof of cohabitation may become an issue as was the case in *G v F* (above), although here the court indicated eligibility for domestic violence remedies should be construed inclusively rather than restrictively.

7.72

Where a person claims to have an equitable interest in the home or the proceeds of sale thereof, but has no legal estate, they may be treated as having no right to occupy for the purpose of applying under s 36, without prejudice to the right of any such person to apply under s 33 if such a right to occupy does exist.

VII Nature of a s 36 occupation order

7.73

By s 36(3) and (4), depending on whether or not the applicant is in occupation, every s 36 occupation order must contain a provision either giving the applicant the right not to be evicted or excluded from the dwelling-house or part of it by the respondent and prohibiting the respondent from evicting or excluding the applicant during the period of the order, or giving the applicant the right to enter into and occupy the dwelling-house for the period specified in the order and requiring the respondent to permit the exercise of that right. Thus, for the period of the order, the occupant is given personal rights of occupation equivalent to homes rights set out in s 30(2) as against the respondent. In addition, a s 36 occupation order may by virtue of s 36(5) regulate the occupation by one or both parties, prohibit, restrict or suspend the exercise of the respondent's right to occupy, require the respondent to leave all or part of the dwelling-house and/or exclude the respondent from a defined area in which the dwelling-house is included.

7.74

In deciding whether or not to include a restriction or exclusion provision, s 36(7) directs the court to have regard to matters specified in s 36(6)(a)–(d), which are the standard criteria also found in s 33(6). These are, namely, the housing needs and resources of the parties or any relevant child, the financial needs and resources of the parties, the likely effect of any order or decision not to make an order on the health, safety or well-being of the parties and any relevant child and the conduct of the parties in relation to each other. In addition, it must have regard to the questions posed in the balance of harm test as contained in s 33(7) (para 7.56 above). However, in contrast to the position of entitled applicants and non-entitled former spouses it does *not* require the court to impose such a provision where it appears that an applicant or relevant child is likely to suffer significant harm if it is not included. This remains a matter for the court's discretion and is an example of how Part IV FLA 1996 differentiates between the remedies available to cohabitants as opposed to those available to spouses and civil partners.

7.75

Section 36(13) extends to cohabitants, former cohabitants and former spouses, in whose favour a s 36 occupation order has been made, some of the effects of home rights' protection as set out in s 30(3)–(6). This only lasts for the period of the occupation order, a maximum of six months in the first instance, extendible only once for a further maximum six-month period. The rights in this context are personal and do not operate as a charge on the respondent's estate in the same way as home rights do pursuant to s 31 and thus cannot be registered as a notice under the Land Registration Act 1925, although, of course, the applicant will be in actual occupation.

7.76

The effect of s 36(13) is perhaps most striking in relation to the applicant whose partner or former partner is a tenant as it elevates for some purposes the occupant's status to that of occupation by a spouse or civil partner. This, together with s 40 (see below), enables the occupant to make rent and mortgage payments or other outgoings without fear of them being refused on the grounds of their lack of legal status. It particularly avoids the problem of statutory tenants under the Rent Act 1977 and the Rent (Agriculture) Act 1976, meets the principal home test for HA 1985 and Part I, HA 1988 (discussed further in Chapter 10) as well as dealing with the position where occupation is under a trust. In all these cases, the non-entitled applicant's occupation under a s 36 order will be treated as if it were occupation by the entitled respondent.

7.77

Thus, whilst falling short of simply giving non-entitled cohabitants s 30 home rights for all purposes, and despite, as developed below, having made concessions to drawing sharper distinctions between a spouse/civil partner and a cohabitant, Part IV FLA 1996 has resolved many of the difficulties of non-entitled cohabitants.

VIII Criteria for making s 36 occupation orders

7.78

In addition to the common criteria set out in s 33(6)(a)–(d) and repeated in s 36(6)(a)–(d), other factors must also be taken into account under s 36 and thus the applicant arguably has a more difficult task than under s 33. Besides the standard criteria and, as discussed above, the ability of the respondent to find alternative accommodation, when considering a s 36 application, the court must, in the case of cohabitants and former cohabitants, also have regard to further matters specified in s 36(6)(e)–(i):

(e) the nature of their relationship and in particular the level of commitment to it;

(f) the length of time during which they have cohabited;

(g) whether there are or have been children of both parties or in respect of whom both have or had parental responsibility;

(h) the length of time that has elapsed since the parties ceased to live together; and

(i) the existence of any pending proceedings between the parties:

- (i) for orders for financial relief against parents under para 1(2)(d) or (e) to Sch 1 CA 1989; or
- (ii) relating to the legal or beneficial ownership of the dwelling house.

7.79

It is probably likely that the closer the relationship approximates to a marriage or civil partnership with children, the more likely it is that an application will be successful, although the degree of harm likely to be suffered by the applicant and any relevant child, which may not be a child of the relationship, must also be a powerful factor.

IX Duration of s 36 orders

7.80

Unlike s 33 occupation orders, which may be made for an indefinite period, those made under s 36 are limited to a period of six months in the first instance, with one single possible extension for further maximum period not exceeding six months (s 36(10)). The position also contrasts with orders made in favour of former spouses/civil partners under s 35, which, although limited to six months in the first instance, may be extended on one or more occasions for further maximum periods of six months at a time (s 35(10)). This disparity is yet another example of how the 1996 Act was intended to privilege protection to those who have chosen to marry or to enter into a civil partnership.

X Occupation orders where neither cohabitant is entitled to occupy – s 38 – eligible applicants

7.81

Section 38 occupation orders are appropriate where neither cohabitant (or former cohabitant) is entitled to occupy the family home by virtue of any beneficial estate or interest or contractual or statutory rights. It will therefore only apply to a small category of people, such as squatters and bare licensees. Under s 38, applications can be made by cohabitants and former cohabitants providing they live or lived together in the accommodation. It is useful to contrast s 38 orders with those available to spouses, former spouses, civil partners and former civil partners where neither is entitled to occupy the home as once again marriage or civil partnership can again be seen to be privileged. For here, only the standard criteria in s 33(6) and the balance of harm test (s 33(7)) apply. In addition, the occupation order, although initially for six months, may be extended on one or more occasion for further maximum periods of six months at a time.

XI Nature of s 38 occupation orders

7.82

Obviously, no declaration of occupation rights will be made as part of these orders. However, the court can make regulatory orders contained in s 38(3) requiring the respondent to permit the applicant to enter and remain in the home, regulating its occupation by one or both parties, requiring the respondent to leave all or part of it and/or excluding the respondent from a defined area in which it is situated.

XII Criteria for making a s 38 occupation order

7.83

Sections 38(4) and (5) apply the standard criteria to the making of an occupation order as applied to both entitled and to non-entitled cohabitants under s 33(6)(a)–(d) and s 36(6)(a)–(d) (housing and financial resources, likely effect of the order and the conduct of the parties), as discussed above. Interestingly, the additional criteria applied to cohabitants in s 36(e)–(i) (nature of the parties' relationship, whether there are children, length of time since cohabitation ceased and existence of pending proceedings under Sch 1 CA 1989) are not to be applied by the court in deciding whether to make a s 38 order, where the respondent has no property rights in the family home. However, once again, although the balance of harm test criteria must be taken into account, there is no requirement to make an order, even though the court concludes that significant harm is likely to be suffered by the applicant or relevant child. The matter rests, as in s 36 applications, in the court's discretion.

XIII Duration of s 38 orders

7.84

Section 38(6) provides for the same duration as under s 36, namely a maximum of six months in the first instance which can be extended for one further maximum period of six months.

XIV Interrelationship of different types of occupation order

7.85

It should be noted that ss 36 and 38 do not prevent cohabitant applicants from claiming an interest in property in subsequent proceedings for example under s 14 TLATA 1996 or Sch 7 FLA 1996 (s 39(4)). Furthermore, if an application is made for an occupation order under one section, but the court considers it has no power to make it under that section but does have power to make an order under one of the other sections, then it can do so (s 39(3)). Thus, in an appropriate case a s 36 occupation order can be made when a s 33 occupation order has been applied for.

XV Additional provisions – s 40

7.86

The court may make additional provision to regulate certain matters between the parties relevant to the occupation of the accommodation after the making of an occupation order. These provisions only apply for the duration of the order. However, in terms of their practical effectiveness, lacunae have been exposed by case law as discussed below.

7.87

On making an occupation order under ss 33, 35 or 36 (but not ss 37 and 38) or, it should be noted, at any time thereafter, the court may:

(a) impose on either party obligations as to repair and maintenance of the dwelling-house or the discharge of relevant rent or mortgage payments or other outgoings;

(b) order a party occupying the dwelling-house or part of it (regardless of whether or not they are entitled to occupy the accommodation in their own right) to make periodical payments in respect of the accommodation to the other party, who, but for the order would themselves be legally entitled to occupy the accommodation;

(c) grant either party possession or use of furniture or other contents of the dwelling house;

(d) order either party to take reasonable care of any furniture or other contents of the dwelling-house; and

(e) order either party to take reasonable steps to keep the dwelling house, furniture or other contents secure.

7.88

In deciding how the court should exercise its powers under this section, s 40(2) provides that the court should have regard to all the circumstances of the case including:

(a) the financial needs and financial resources of the parties; and

(b) the financial obligations which they have or are likely to have in the foreseeable future, including financial obligations to each other and any relevant child.

7.89

Advisors must therefore carefully think through exactly what their client will need to do to effectively occupy the accommodation or to be compensated for their loss of it. Enquiries must be made of clients to ascertain details of rent and mortgage payments and other outgoings. A priority must be to ensure that these payments continue to be paid either by the occupant or by the excluded partner. Where the property is rented, attention should be turned to whether housing benefit needs to be transferred or applied for. In all cases, information as to the parties' respective means and financial commitments will need to be available. Close attention should be paid to the question of maintenance and repair needs in the case of an owner-occupied property, as well as ensuring that one or both parties will meet the necessary ground rent and service charge payments where appropriate.

7.90

Thus, whilst consideration of these matters should not prevent or delay the relief required in emergency cases, in practice enforcement of s 40 orders is not possible as revealed by *Nwogbe v Nwogbe* [2000] 2 FLR 744. In this case the applicant was granted an occupation order and the respondent was consequently ordered to pay the rent, rent arrears, council tax and water rates on the former matrimonial home, which he subsequently failed to pay. The applicant therefore applied for him to be committed to prison for contempt of court. However, the Court of Appeal found that the respondent could not be committed to prison as payments under s 40 FLA 1996 did not fall within any of the exceptions to the Debtors Act 1869, which abolished imprisonment for unpaid debt. Furthermore, it did not accept that committal could be made as if it were a breach of the occupation order itself, as this would have meant an implied repeal of s 5 Debtors Act 1869. Neither could it be enforced under the Attachment of Earnings Act 1971, as it was not listed in Sch 1 to that Act. To add insult to injury, the applicant could not even enforce the order through conventional means as the payments were due to a third party rather than the applicant herself. Whereas in the case of spouses and civil partners, making a periodical payments (maintenance) order could circumvent this situation, this is of no use in the cohabitation context. This apparent flaw in the court's powers, as the Court of Appeal noted, requires legislative intervention. As things currently stand, whilst the court can undoubtedly make orders ancillary to an occupation order under s 40, this may be of little use to a cohabitant where their former partner fails to comply.

7.91

In terms of what orders the court can make, it is clear that it can make an order for periodical payments of what may be termed an 'occupation rent' to the excluded party, regardless of whether or not the occupant is entitled in their own right to occupy the property. This applies to all cohabitants occupying the subject property pursuant to a s 33, s 35 or s 36 occupation order. How this is to be calculated, is a matter that has not yet been authoritatively decided by the courts in relation to equitable accounting following separation, where both parties have a beneficial interest in an owner-occupied property (see discussion in Chapter 11). In the context of an occupation order, however, cases where such periodical payments should be ordered have proven to be the exception rather than the rule, given that beneficial entitlement will normally be ascertained later in separate proceedings if necessary and an equitable accounting exercise performed. However, orders for an occupation rent are not restricted to the dispossessed owner-occupier and may be appropriate where the family home is rented.

7.92

Where an occupant is dependent on housing benefit, although payment of the rent could be claimed following an occupation order, no extra payment of any type of benefit would be available for payment to the respondent. The excluded party could in these circumstances be relieved of the rent payments and it is submitted no further order for payment of an occupation rent would be appropriate. Given that payments must be periodical, it does not seem to be possible for the court to order a lump sum equivalent to a deposit on rented accommodation to be paid to the respondent where the parties' means permitted and such a payment appears appropriate. It should be noted here that, as discussed in Chapter 10 below, separating cohabitants may now apply for transfer of tenancy orders pursuant to s 53 and Sch 7 FLA 1996, where the family home was rented. In this context, compensation may be awarded to the cohabitant whose interest is transferred, and would be in the form of a lump sum.

7.93

Although occupation orders can offer a measure of protection to victims of domestic abuse granting them occupational status in the home for a period, they are still in essence a temporary remedy. It is therefore imperative that where an occupation order is made, that thought is given to what form the final resolution of the position between the parties is to take if there is no reconciliation. It is probable that even under s 33, where an indefinite period is a possibility, the courts will in most situations make occupation orders for a specified period of time. Although in some cases extension of orders may be obtained, this is not to be relied upon, particularly under s 36, where two six-month periods is the absolute maximum. Thus, whilst not suggesting that unnecessary pressure be put upon the occupant, it is vital that advisors ensure that a s 33 or s 36 occupant is aware of the final remedies available and that the appropriate applications are made in good time for a transfer of tenancy order or an order under s 14 TLATA 1996.

(iii) Urgent applications – without notice non-molestation and occupation orders

7.94

FPR 2010, PD 18A states that a without notice application should only be made where there is 'exceptional urgency' or where the overriding objective is best furthered by doing so. Orders made without notice to the respondent, because breaches of them may result in imprisonment, should be of limited duration and will only be appropriate if immediate protection is deemed necessary, as the respondent must be given an opportunity as soon as possible to advance his or her case in response to the application. As the President of the Family Division stressed in the most recent guidance issued by him (Practice Guidance: Family Court – Duration of ex parte (without notice) orders [2017]) on 18 January 2017, to grant injunctive relief on an ex parte (without notice) basis 'for an unlimited period is wrong in principle and that the practice of granting such orders for an unlimited time must stop'. It had been the habit of some courts not to schedule a hearing on notice (so that the respondent could be heard) but instead to make non-molestation orders for a period of 12 months which included a provision that if he or she wanted to discharge or vary the order during that period the burden was on the respondent to apply on notice with an application supported by a sworn statement. Such orders would certainly contravene this latest guidance and it is hoped are no longer being made.

7.95

Section 45 FLA 1996 states that both non-molestation and occupation orders may be made *without notice* when the court considers it is 'just and convenient to do so'. In determining whether to exercise this power, the court shall have regard to all the circumstances including:

(a) any risk of significant harm to the applicant or a relevant child if the order is not made immediately (s 45(2)(a));

(b) whether it is likely the applicant will be deterred or prevented from pursuing the application if an order is not made immediately (s 45(2)(b)); and

(c) whether there is reason to believe that the respondent is deliberately evading service and that the applicant or a relevant child will be seriously prejudiced by the delay involved in effecting substituted service (s 45(2)(c)).

7.96

'Harm' is defined in s 63(1) as follows:

(a) in relation to a person who has reached the age of 18 years, means ill-treatment or the impairment of health; and

(b) in relation to a child, means ill-treatment or impairment of health or development.

7.97

'Health' includes physical or mental health. In relation to a child, 'ill-treatment' includes sexual abuse and forms of ill-treatment which are not physical and 'development' means physical, intellectual, emotional, social or behavioural development. What would amount to 'significant' harm is not specified in relation to an adult. However, where a child's health or development is involved, s 63(2) indicates that the question of whether the harm suffered is significant should be determined by comparison with the health and development reasonably expected of a similar child. These definitions follow those found in s 31(9) and (10) CA 1989. Section 45(2)(b) covers the situation where an applicant is so terrified of the respondent that they will not proceed with the application unless they have the court's protection first. However, that is not to say that the court cannot be persuaded of other appropriate situations for the making of a without notice order. Whenever such an order is applied for, it will be important to be able to explain to the court why it is inappropriate or impossible for the application to be made on notice. It may also be possible to apply for abridgement of notice in appropriate cases. It should also be noted that the presumption in favour of a power of arrest (s 47(2)) does not apply to orders made without notice (see s 47(3)), as will be discussed more fully below.

7.98

Where *without notice* orders are made, s 45(3) provides that the respondent must be given an opportunity to make representations relating to the order as soon as just and convenient at a hearing on notice. Whilst it is certainly arguable that the making of a without notice occupation order could amount to a breach of the respondent's right under Art 6 of the European Convention on Human Rights (the right to a fair and public hearing), the limited duration of such an order (usually seven days until the return date) and the need to offer the alleged victim and any children safety and freedom from the risk of real or alleged violence would outweigh possibly any short-term inconvenience to the respondent. Further, it is usual when making without notice occupation orders for the court to also include a provision that the respondent may apply to have the order set aside on 48 hours' notice.

7.99

In *R v R (Family Court: procedural fairness)* [2014] EWFC 48, [2014] All ER (D) 138 (Dec), Mr Justice Peter Jackson offered guidance on how courts should treat without notice applications. In granting an appeal by a respondent to an order made without notice, he stated that:

'(1) The default position of a judge faced with a without notice application should always be "Why?", not "Why not?"

(2) The court should use its sweeping powers under the FLA with caution, particularly at a one-sided hearing.

(3) Extra injunctive provisions such as exclusion areas and orders prohibiting any direct communication between parties should not be routinely included in non-molestation orders. They are serious infringements of a person's freedom of action and require specific evidence to justify them.'

(iv) Powers of arrest and other methods of enforcement of non-molestation and occupation orders

7.100

A power of arrest can be attached to an occupation order, but not to a non-molestation order. This is because under s 42A(1) a person is guilty of a criminal offence if 'without reasonable excuse (he) does anything he is prohibited from doing by a non-molestation order'. Section 47(2) FLA 1996 provides that on making an occupation order, the court *shall* attach a power of arrest where 'it appears … that the respondent has used or threatened violence against the applicant or a relevant child *unless* satisfied that in all the circumstances of the case the applicant or child will be adequately protected without such a power of arrest'. Only where adequate protection without a power of arrest can be shown will the court not impose one, meaning that in most cases, a power of arrest will be attached to one or more provisions of the occupation order. This makes a compromise through undertakings doubly attractive from a respondent's point of view, and is a good reason for a vulnerable victim not to be persuaded to agree to an undertaking where an order will be granted.

7.101

The court may attach a power of arrest to one or more provisions of an occupation order made without notice if it appears that the respondent has used or threatened violence against the applicant or a relevant child and that there is a risk of significant harm to the applicant or child, attributable to the conduct of the respondent, if the power of arrest is not attached to those provisions immediately (s 47(3)). If a power of arrest is attached to certain provisions of an occupation order, a police officer may arrest without warrant a person whom he has reasonable cause for suspecting to be in breach of any such provision (s 47(6)).

7.102

If however the court has made a non-molestation order or has made an occupation order but has not attached a power of arrest to any provision of it (or has attached that power only to certain provisions of the order), the applicant is able to apply to the court which made the order to issue a warrant for the arrest of the respondent if the applicant considers that the respondent has failed to comply with (has breached) the order (s 47(8)). A warrant for the arrest of the respondent will only be issued if the court has reasonable grounds for believing the respondent has failed to comply with the order (s 47(9)). One potentially serious difficulty is that there is only a *power* and not a *duty* to arrest for breach at the discretion of the police officer. This leaves a victim who has had a power of arrest attached to an occupation order unable to use the warrant procedure where the police have declined to make an arrest, leaving committal proceedings as the only remedy. Ironically, in these circumstances, a victim with an order without a power of arrest is in a better position than a victim with a power of arrest, exercise of which has been declined by the police. The Family Court has power to remand the arrested respondent in custody or on bail where he or she cannot be dealt with immediately (see s 47(10)–(12) and Sch 2). Additionally, the court has the powers to remand for medical reports or a report under s 35 Mental Health Act 1983 (s 48).

7.103

Generally, breach of an order (or of an undertaking) is enforceable by an application to commit the respondent (to prison) under the procedure set out in FPR 2010, Pt 37 and PD 37A. However, it is hoped that if the respondent has breached a non-molestation order the police would arrest him and charge him with a s 42A(1) offence. In order to take steps under Pt 37, it is essential that the order contains a prominently displayed penal notice (a warning to the respondent that a breach of the order would be a contempt of court punishable by imprisonment, a fine or sequestration of assets) (FPR 37.9). In the case of *Re Dad* [2015] EWHC 2655 (Fam), 15 September 2015, Holman J struck out an application to commit a person for breaching an order which did not contain a properly worded penal notice prominently displayed on the face of the order.

7.104

An application for enforcement by committal is issued in the court where the original order was made. The requirements for the contents of an application to commit are set out in FPR 2010, Pt 37 (and see *Cherwayko v Cherwayko (No 2)* aka *W v H (No 2) (contempt, contents of application notice)* [2015] EWHC 2436 (Fam), 21 August 2015 (Bailii)). The need to comply precisely with procedural requirements when applying for committal combined with the court's heightened awareness of its duty to protect the contemnor's European Convention rights was underlined by the case of *Couzens v Couzens* [2001] 2 FLR 701, when the courts' failure to serve the suspended committal order in accordance with Form N79 prevented the court from activating the term of imprisonment following a further breach.

7.105

Committal proceedings are criminal charges for the purposes of Art 6 of the European Convention on Human Rights and accordingly the respondent has the right to representation. Where he is unrepresented, the judge should enquire as to why this is at the outset of the hearing and consider whether there should be an adjournment to enable him to be represented. In *Hammerton v Hammerton* [2007] EWCA Civ 248, [2007] 3 FCR 107, the Court of Appeal stressed that 'a sense of urgency often impedes the fair conduct of committal proceedings, but the important rights enshrined in Art 6 should not be sacrificed in the interests of time and costs'.

(v) Undertakings

7.106

An undertaking is a promise to the court and is as binding as a court order. Thus, undertakings remain a common method of compromise between parties, providing protection equivalent to a non-molestation order, whilst avoiding the need for an applicant to prove their case and permitting a respondent to 'save face' with no finding of molestation having been made by the court. The use of undertakings in this way has been criticised for being used to put pressure on a victim who then loses the opportunity of the best form of protection – a power of arrest.

7.107

Section 46 permits undertakings to be accepted by the court in any case where the court has power to make a non-molestation or occupation order. Section 46(2) makes it clear that no power of arrest may be attached to an undertaking, although it is enforceable in the same way as an order by means of committal proceedings (see s 46(4)). Whether the warrant procedure under s 47(8) extends to undertakings is still a moot point and has not been tested in the courts. Section 46(3) makes it clear that the court must not accept an undertaking instead of making an occupation order where a power of arrest would otherwise be attached. Note that in determining whether a power of arrest should be attached to an occupation order, the court has to form a view as to whether or not the respondent has used or threatened violence (s 47(2)). Further, s 46(3A) provides that the court must not accept an undertaking in place of making a non-molestation order where the respondent has used or threatened violence against the applicant or a relevant child and for the protection of the applicant or child it is necessary to make a non-molestation order so that any breach may be punishable under s 42A (ie as a criminal offence).

7.108

This prohibition on the acceptance of undertakings places the court in a difficult position where parties are keen to resolve the matter by means of undertakings. In principle, if on reading the statement of evidence, the court forms a *prima facie* view that either a power of arrest would be attached to an occupation order or that for the protection of the applicant or child it would be necessary to make a non-molestation order so that any breach may be punishable under s 42A, the court must proceed to hear the case and decide this issue, regardless of the wishes of the parties. Whilst fully accepting that undertakings could be used to pressurise a victim, it is questionable whether a forced hearing of the evidence can be justified on public policy grounds, and although it seems that courts are still inclined in practice to accept undertakings clear reasons have to be given as to why they are being accepted. However, it is to be regretted that Parliament has not sought to change the law to enable powers of arrest to be attached to undertakings. Where parties are keen to compromise, a consent order incorporating a power of arrest could avoid a protracted hearing, but does not of course shield the respondent from a finding that there has been violence or threat of violence.

7.109

The breach of an undertaking is enforceable by an application to commit the respondent under the procedure set out in FPR 2010, Pt 37 and PD 37A. To be enforceable, the form of undertaking must be endorsed with a notice setting out the consequences of failing to comply with it, stating that '*You may be held in contempt of court and imprisoned or fined, or your assets may be seized, if you break promises that you have given to the court*' (FPR 2010, PD 37A, para 2.1).

7.110

It should be noted that the court may decline to accept an undertaking unless the respondent/the party giving it makes a signed statement to the effect that he or she understands the terms of the undertaking and the consequences of failure to comply with it, such as '*I understand the undertaking I have given and that if I break any of my promises to the court I may be sent to prison, or fined, or my assets may be seized, for contempt of court*' (FPR 2010, PD 37A, para 2.2).

(vi) Procedure

7.111

The procedure on a non-molestation or occupation order application is set out in FPR 2010, Pt 10 and PD 10A. All applications are made in the Family Court. Applications do not have to be issued in the Family Court local to where the applicant lives, as there may well be occasions when proceedings need to be issued in a completely different geographical area in order to protect the whereabouts of a vulnerable victim.

7.112

There is a comprehensive application form (Form FL401) for both non-molestation and all types of occupation order. This should be accompanied by a signed statement (and draft order) and filed at court and served upon the respondent personally not less than two clear days before the hearing, although abridgement of this period can be ordered by the court before service (FPR 2010, 10.3(1)). It requires details of the parties, the type of relationship, any relevant children, other family proceedings, whether a without notice application is to be made and the reasons for this, the family home, any mortgage and the types of orders applied for. The same form should also be used for applicants under 16 years of age, although this will be treated as an application for leave to the High Court in the first instance and if leave is granted may, if appropriate be transferred to the Family Court. Form FL403 is used to apply for variation, extension or discharge of an order.

7.113

Where an occupation order is made on an application under s 33 or s 36, any mortgagee or landlord must be served with a copy of the order (FPR 2010, 10.6(3)). Any orders made must be served personally on the respondent (FPR 2010, 10.6(1)).

7.114

District judges as well as lay justices may hear applications under Part IV, which will be heard in chambers. Bail applications on behalf of a person arrested pursuant to an attached power of arrest may be made orally or in writing, with the details to be included in a written application set out in the rules.

7.115

It should be noted that, whilst s 60 FLA 1996 indicates that rules of court may provide for a representative to apply for an occupation or non-molestation order on behalf of the victim, this has to date not been brought into force.

7.116

Emergency legal aid will usually be appropriate where protection is sought under these provisions and may if necessary be granted by solicitors' firms either using delegated functions of or by the Legal Aid Agency via email application or over the telephone. Guidance from the Legal Aid Agency provides that letters should be written trying to prevent the behaviour complained of before injunction proceedings are issued and a legal aid certificate granted save where protection is required as a matter of urgency. In this situation it should also be considered whether an approach should be made to the police. This will often not be appropriate and may just serve to exacerbate the situation and leave the applicant without protection. Delay in bringing proceedings could prejudice the outcome of an application and this should be borne in mind by advisors.

(b) Injunctions ancillary to the Children Act 1989

7.117

Given the extended categories of 'associated persons', the broad definition of 'relevant child' and the ability of the court to make non-molestation orders of its own motion in family proceedings, Part IV FLA 1996 has largely removed the need for cohabitants or former cohabitants to seek protection from molestation or attempt to exclude another party ancillary to the CA 1989. It is to be remembered, however, that the Family Court and High Court can grant non-molestation orders ancillary to a s 8 order to protect the child and residential parent pursuant to ss 38 and 39 County Courts Act 1984 and s 37 Senior Courts Act 1981, although no power of arrest can be attached.

7.118

It should also be noted that s 52 and Sch 6 FLA 1996 amend the CA 1989, inserting new ss 38A and 44A, which enable a court making an interim care order or an emergency protection order to exclude a suspected abuser (rather than the child) from the home, leaving the allegedly abused child living in their home surroundings. In addition, the court may attach a power of arrest to such an exclusion order.

(c) Injunctions in tort actions

7.119

The only possible remedies available for those who have had a relationship but who have not lived together or entered into an agreement whether to marry or register as civil partners are those offered by the law of tort. To bring an action under the general law of torts, it must be shown that a tortious act has been committed, and the extension of the tort of nuisance to include harassment or molestation now permits actions to redress such behaviour in addition to the use of the torts of assault, battery and trespass where appropriate. A victim of violence may apply for an injunction ancillary to an action for damages in tort for assault, battery, trespass or nuisance whereby the court can restrain the other party from behaviour which amounts to assault, battery, trespass or nuisance.

7.120

Developments in the case law in this field had enabled an action to be taken in nuisance for behaviour amounting to harassment which usefully extended the applicability of this remedy beyond obvious cases of physical violence and trespass. It was found that verbal harassment not strictly amounting to a threat was actionable if it could be shown to cause the victim to suffer mental or physical illness and despite the victim having no proprietary interest in the property at which the offending persistent telephone calls were being made (see *Khorasandjian v Bush* [1993] 3 All ER 669, CA and *Burnett v George* [1992] 1 FLR 525, CA). However, in *Hunter v Canary Wharf Ltd, Hunter v London Docklands Development Corpn* [1997] 2 All ER 426, the House of Lords overruled *Khorasandjian v Bush* in so far as it held that a mere licensee could sue in private nuisance. Despite Lord Cooke delivering a dissenting judgment on the point, saying that for him occupation of the property as a home was an acceptable criterion for entitlement to sue in private nuisance and one which was consistent with international standards, it seems that the usefulness of this remedy in the family context has been greatly reduced for those unable to use the domestic violence legislation, leaving the Protection from Harassment Act 1997 as the best avenue to explore, despite the attendant difficulties of having to prove a 'course of conduct' as discussed above.

7.121

The procedure for applying for protection in this way involves an application on Claim Form N1 including details of the claim/matter complained of and a statement of truth out of the appropriate High Court or county court for the district where the claimant or defendant resides. An injunction can be applied for without a claim for damages or other relief by virtue of s 38 County Court Act 1984. Such free-standing injunction applications are governed by the Civil Procedure Rules 1998. The Civil Claim Form N1 is supported by an N16A injunction application in the county court. An injunction may be granted if the other party behaves in an unconscionable manner or threatens to do so, or if an order is necessary to protect a person from the invasion of a legal or equitable right.

7.122

Applications may be made without notice on affidavit, and, unlike hearing under Part IV FLA 1996 or the CA 1989, the matter will be heard in open court, not in chambers. Two days' notice is otherwise required for an injunction application. It is not clear whether an exclusion order can be made other than where there is an action for trespass, and no power of arrest can be attached to these injunctions. Breach of an injunction will again be punishable as contempt and in such a situation, committal proceedings can be issued and pursued and a warrant of arrest can be granted also in respect of a breach.

7.123

Another consideration is the possibility of civil proceedings under the Protection from Harassment Act 1997. Section 3 provides that an actual or apprehended breach of s 1 harassment may be the subject of a claim in civil proceedings by the victim, and damages may be awarded for among other things 'anxiety caused by the harassment'. A breach of this statutory tort of harassment provides a civil remedy regardless of whether or not the individuals concerned are 'associated', and makes a claim for damages available. The county court and High Court when hearing a civil action also have power to grant injunctions to restrain the harassment. This civil remedy is a welcome addition to the limited remedies available for harassment under the law of nuisance following developments in the case law in *Khorasandjian v Bush; Hunter v Canary Wharf Ltd; Hunter v London Docklands Development Corpn* and *Burris v Azadani* [1996] 1 FLR 266, CA. Breach of the civil injunction requires an application for a warrant before an arrest can be made and thus for cohabitants and former cohabitants able to seek a s 42 FLA 1996 non-molestation injunction with power or arrest attached, it is an inferior remedy where a non-molestation injunction can effectively target the behaviour complained of.

3 Emergency accommodation

7.124

Often the most urgent need of a victim of domestic violence is a safe place to live, either permanently or temporarily, until court orders affording some protection against violence can be obtained. Many victims are reluctant to go and stay with relatives or friends, as these are likely to be the violent partner's first port of call on discovering that they have fled the home. There is now a fairly wide network of women's refuges (and a growing number of safe houses for male victims of domestic abuse) offering temporary accommodation and the local Women's Aid will provide details of possible refuges. However, such accommodation, whilst safe, often leaves a great deal to be desired and can only ever be temporary. However, there is provision for victims of domestic abuse to obtain permanent rehousing under the section on Homelessness at Part VII Housing Act 1996. Local housing authorities are now under a duty to provide the statutory homeless with permanent accommodation (s 193(3) HA 1996 as amended by the Homelessness Act 2002, s 6, which abolished the minimum period (of two years) for which a local authority was subject to a duty to rehouse).

7.125

Applicants must show that they are eligible for assistance and not excluded by being an asylum seeker or a person from abroad subject to immigration control (see ss 183(2), 185 and 186). This is in addition to having to show they are homeless or threatened with homelessness (s 175), that such homelessness is unintentional (see s 191) and that they are in priority need (s 189). A local authority must make enquiries under s 184 to see whether a duty is owed to secure accommodation. Where there is an apparent priority need, there is a duty to provide accommodation pending their enquiries (s 188). A victim of domestic abuse in need of urgent accommodation, regardless of whether or not they are the tenant or owner of accommodation, may still be homeless within the meaning of the Act.

7.126

Section 177(1) specifically indicates that a person is homeless if they have accommodation which it is not reasonable for them to occupy because it is 'probable' that this will lead to domestic violence or other violence against them or a person who might reasonably be expected to reside with them ('other violence' added by s 10(1)(a) of the Homelessness Act 2002). In determining whether it would be reasonable for the person to continue to occupy accommodation regard may be had to the general circumstances prevailing in relation to housing in the area (s 177(2)). In addition, s 175(2) treats a person as homeless if they have accommodation but cannot secure entry to it, although this provision under the 1985 legislation offered in practice nothing more than short-term temporary accommodation as authorities required a person to use their legal remedies to re-enter or be found intentionally homeless.

7.127

Domestic violence is defined in s 171(1A) as violence or threats of violence likely to be carried out made by a person with whom the applicant is 'associated' which is given the same meaning as in Part IV FLA 1996. Thus, a person who would succeed in getting a non-molestation order due to harassment not amounting to violence or threats of violence would not be assisted by this provision, which effectively requires the applicant's physical safety to be in jeopardy, although the violence need not have occurred within the home. As with re-entry, local authorities have in the past expected victims of domestic abuse to use their legal remedies and apply for non-molestation and occupation orders, saying that failure to do so will result in a finding of intentional homelessness. Whilst there may be situations where an authority may reasonably require an applicant to use their domestic violence remedies (as in *R v Eastleigh Borough Council, ex p Evans* (1984) 17 HLR 515), such as where they have an interest in the property from which they have fled and the court would be likely to make an occupation order in their favour, fleeing from domestic abuse is now readily accepted as establishing 'priority need'. The current Department for

Communities and Local Government Homelessness Code of Guidance for Local Authorities published 24 July 2006 acknowledges that injunctions will not necessarily deter people and applicants should not be found intentionally homeless if they have not pursued domestic abuse remedies. In such cases, whilst housing authorities may wish to inform applicants of the option of seeking an injunction, they should make clear that there is no obligation on the applicant to do so. Where applicants wish to pursue this option, it is advisable that they obtain independent advice as an injunction may be ill-advised in some circumstances. Housing authorities should recognise that injunctions ordering a person not to molest, or enter the home of, an applicant may not be effective in deterring perpetrators from carrying out further violence or incursions, and applicants may not have confidence in their effectiveness. Consequently, applicants should not be expected to return home on the strength of an injunction. To ensure applicants who have experienced actual or threatened violence get the support they need, authorities should inform them of appropriate organisations in the area such as agencies offering counselling and support as well as specialist advice (para 8.23).

7.128

Applicants should not be pressured into taking out injunctive orders and should not necessarily be asked to return to their home, having obtained such orders. The guidance offers that 'where there would be a probability of violence if the applicant continued to occupy his or her present accommodation, the housing authority must treat the applicant as homeless and should not expect him or her to remain in, or return to, the accommodation. In all cases involving violence the safety of the applicant and his or her household should be the primary consideration at all stages of decision making as to whether or not the applicant remains in their own home' (para 8.24). Unfortunately, although authorities must have regard to the Code of Guidance, it does not have the force of law. However, advisors should attempt to resist such pressure upon their clients, and particularly where injunctions have been breached in the past or where the violence is so serious that a further attack should not be risked or where, perhaps, it can be shown that an injunction with a power of arrest attached will be no deterrent. Nonetheless, providing priority need can be established, emergency accommodation should be available pursuant to s 188 where there has been or is likely to be actual or threatened violence.

7.129

Victims of domestic violence are arguably always in priority need in their own right on account of being vulnerable within the meaning of s 189(1)(c) as a result of a 'special reason' and s 177(1). However, an applicant can also establish priority need under s 189 if they are pregnant; have dependent children residing with them or who might reasonably reside with them; or are vulnerable as a result of old age, mental illness or handicap or physical disability or other special reason, or if such a person might reasonably reside with the applicant.

7.130

Given that the homelessness legislation now provides a direct route into permanent accommodation, applicants should no longer be forced to pursue a remedy in relation to the former family home in any event. In the case of a sole tenant or joint tenant of a property governed by the Housing Act 1985 (secure tenancy) or who has secured an assured tenancy which is not an assured shorthold tenancy and which is granted by a private registered provider of social housing, by the Regulator of Social Housing or by a housing trust which is a charity, the Secure Tenancies (Victims of Domestic Abuse) Bill 2017–2019 would impose upon a local housing authority an obligation to grant old-style secure tenancies (discussed at 10.73 ff) in cases of domestic abuse suffered by the tenant (or a member of that person's household). This Bill was started in the House of Lords and on 27 March 2018 passed the committee stage in the House of Commons. The Bill will next be considered by the House of Commons at Report Stage, although no date as yet has been scheduled for this and if passed is unlikely to become law until (or after) 2019.

7.131

It is likely that the degree of violence will have a great bearing on the authority's approach to a victim who has interest in former accommodation. Even where the hurdles set out above are successfully overcome, the applicant may be referred to another authority with which he or she has a local connection pursuant to s 198. Advisors should be aware that where the applicant, or a person reasonably expected to reside with the applicant, runs the risk of domestic violence in that other district, no referral should be made (s 198(2A)).

7.132

Applicants must be advised in writing of the local authority's decision and the reasons for the decision where a duty to secure accommodation is denied pursuant to s 184(3) of the Act. The letter must also inform the applicant of their right to request a review under s 202 within 21 days of notification of the decision (s 202(1A)(3)). This right to review is a prerequisite to the right of appeal to the county court under s 204 on a point of law. On appeal the court can confirm, quash or, significantly, vary the decision of the local authority giving the county court slightly wider powers than those available to the High Court on judicial review. It is still the decision letter which will form the basis for the appeal, subject to the review procedure having been unsuccessfully pursued. Advisors should ensure that they request copies of the information on the local authority's file to which the applicant or advisor is entitled and from which the strength of the review or legal challenge can be assessed.

7.133

Another option where a violent partner and the victim are joint tenants of public sector rented accommodation is for the victim to give notice to quit the accommodation, as notice by one joint tenant is valid to terminate the tenancy, even though the other joint tenant does not know and would not wish the tenancy to be terminated. This was established by the House of Lords in *Hammersmith and Fulham London Borough Council v Monk* [1992] 1 AC 478. Normally this action may render the notice giver intentionally homeless but it is a device used where the local authority agrees to it in consideration of their providing alternative accommodation in their area. This device, which is likely to be available only to local authority, or possibly housing association tenants will be discussed further in Chapter 10, where permanent housing solutions for cohabitants will be considered. However, it should be noted here that this approach of collusion between a social landlord and domestic violence victim is not always straightforward, although its efficacy was further endorsed by the House of Lords in *Harrow London Borough Council v Johnstone* [1997] 1 FLR 887. Grounds for possession are also available in the independent housing sector, inserted by s 145 HA 1996 in relation to secure tenancies and s 149 HA 1996 in relation to assured tenancies where the landlord is a registered social landlord or housing trust can be used. This enables the landlord to gain possession where one partner has left the accommodation because of violence or threats of violence made by the other towards them or towards a member of their family living with them. Thus, the landlord can recover the accommodation from the violent partner.

CHAPTER 8

The status of children on relationship breakdown: resolving disputes under the Children Act 1989

1 Introduction

8.01

When a relationship breaks down, any children of the relationship all too frequently become a focus for the dispute between their parents. Both parties often seek legal advice as regards their respective positions in relation to the children. The CA 1989 established a statutory code available to the courts to resolve issues relating to children on relationship breakdown, regardless of the marital status of the parents.

8.02

It is generally accepted, barring child safety concerns, that children benefit from continuing relationships with both parents after the relationship between the parents breaks down. This thinking is now embedded in the amended principle set out in s 1(2A) Children Act 1989. Largely gone is the notion that it is better for the children to maintain a loveless potentially emotionally damaging relationship than to separate. The importance of enabling a child to maintain a relationship with a parent was reiterated recently by the Court of Appeal in *Re S* [2015] EWCA Civ 689, [2016] 2 FLR 217, stressing the importance of 'allowing a child to continue to have a relationship with her absent parent'. Since the last edition of this book, residence and contact orders under s 8 CA 1989 have been replaced by child arrangements orders (by the Children and Families Act 2014), which are defined as orders 'regulating arrangements relating to …. (a) with whom a child is to live, spend time or otherwise have contact, and (b) when a child is to live, spend time or otherwise have contact with any person'.

8.03

Parents are encouraged to attempt to resolve the arrangements for their children themselves whenever possible. Sometimes the intervention of lawyers can make a bad situation worse if the focus is not on the welfare of the children (the question to ask being 'What is in the best interests of the children?' as opposed to 'How can I use the children to hurt him/her or to cause him/her the most upset?')'. In *Re O (a child) (contact: withdrawal of application)* [2003] EWHC 3031 (Fam), [2004] 1 FLR 1258, Wall J reminded that (1) contact cases are best resolved outside the court system, working best where parents respect each other and are able to co-operate, and (2) the court process is stressful, slow and adversarial and tends to entrench parental attitudes rather than encourage change.

8.04

Mediation has long been promoted both by the courts and the Legal Aid Agency (although funding for children cases has now largely been withdrawn save in cases involving an element of domestic or child abuse) as well as the Law Society and Resolution (formerly, the Solicitors' Family Law Association (SFLA)) in their codes of conduct. Legal aid remains available however for mediation for those who are financially eligible. Parenting courses are also widely available (including such courses as self-explanatory as 'Parenting after Parting' and the 'Separated Parents Information Programme') in the hope that disputes involving arrangements for children can be kept out of the court arena. It should be noted that where parents have been engaged in the process of family therapy and one of them refuses to continue with it, whilst the court has no power to order the parent to re-engage in it, the court can draw adverse inferences against the parent for continued refusal (see *Re S (unco-operative mother)* [2004] EWCA Civ 597, [2004] 2 FLR 710). It is now much better recognised that unmarried cohabiting parents have similar needs and concerns to married parents, with the welfare of the children in either style of family being uppermost for all involved. All parents are encouraged to agree a Parenting Plan if they can – see www.cafcass.gov.uk/grown-ups/parenting-plan.aspx.

8.05

Thus, whether or not a client is eligible for legal aid, advisors of unmarried parents in dispute about their children's future arrangements on relationship breakdown should, in the first place (except where there are concerns about violence within the relationship), suggest a mediation appointment to see whether differences can be resolved by reaching an out-of-court agreement. Where appropriate, this can be translated into a consent order in court proceedings. Legal Aid funding of private law family disputes (ie not care proceedings) will only be available where a client has provided specific evidence of alleged domestic violence/abuse (including financial abuse) or child protection need. The Legal Aid, Sentencing and Punishment of Offenders

Act 2012 definition of domestic violence is any incident or pattern of incidents of controlling, coercive or threatening behaviour, violence or abuse (whether psychological, physical, sexual, financial or emotional) between individuals who are associated with each other. In cases where one parent is eligible for legal aid mediation is rarely if ever promoted or encouraged.

8.06

Both (but not exclusively) the National Family Mediation and the Family Mediation Council offer information about and guidance on mediation and its benefits. The Ministry of Justice on its website also provides an easy how-to guide for parents considering using mediation as a means of resolving their particular child-related dispute.

8.07

When relationships break down, the key issues to be decided in connection with the children are with whom they will primarily live and how much time (if any) they will spend with the other parent – a child arrangements order under s 8 CA 1989. Section 8 also provides for prohibited steps orders and specific issue orders to be made where the context requires in such disputes.

8.08

Whereas all married parents are automatically endowed with parental responsibility in respect of their children, only mothers, not fathers, have this status automatically conferred on the birth of a child where the parents are unmarried (see Chapter 2). Thus, unless a s 4 parental responsibility order or agreement has been made before the parents' relationship breaks down, fathers may at this juncture seek to acquire parental responsibility and this will be considered below.

8.09

First, however, the general principles of the Act which to a large extent govern the way in which disputes between parents relating to their children are decided, will be considered.

2 General principles – s 1 CA 1989

8.10

The Foreword to *An Introduction to the Children Act 1989* (HMSO) refers to the Act as 'the most comprehensive piece of legislation which parliament has ever enacted about children. It draws together and simplifies existing legislation to produce a more practical and consistent code. It integrates the law relating to private individuals with the responsibilities of public authorities, in particular local authority social services departments, towards children. In so doing the Act strikes a balance between family autonomy and the protection of children.' Section1(1) states that 'when a court determines any question with respect to (a) the upbringing of a child or (b) the administration of a child's property or the application of any income arising from it, the child's welfare shall be the court's paramount consideration'.

8.11

Prior to the implementation of the Human Rights Act 1998 (HRA 1998), there was some concern as to whether the welfare principle conflicted with the right to private and family life in Article 8 of the European Convention on Human Rights. Whilst the rights of children are protected by the Convention, so are the rights of the adults in the family and these require careful balancing where there is a dispute between family members. Was legislation, which clearly prioritised the rights of children, therefore incompatible with the Convention? In *Scott v United Kingdom* [2000] 1 FLR 958, the European Court of Human Rights concluded that it was not. Here the making of a freeing order and the dismissal of an alcoholic mother's application for increased contact with her child was not a breach of Article 8 on the basis that Article 8 was not an absolute right and is qualified by Article 8(2) which permits interference on certain grounds. Article 8 states:

> '1. Everyone has the right to respect for his private and family life, his home and his correspondence.
>
> 2 There shall be no interference by a public authority with the exercise of this right except such as is in accordance with the law and is necessary in a democratic society in the interests of national security, public safety or the economic well-being of the country, for the prevention of disorder or crime, for the protection of health or morals, or for the protection of the rights and freedoms of others.'

8.12

Thus the balancing of the rights of family members fell within the state's margin of appreciation and here the welfare principle could be justified 'for the protection of the rights and freedoms of others'. Therefore, whilst in principle each family member's rights start with equal protection, this has to be measured in each case against the justifications for interference with those rights, including the need to protect the rights of others.

8.13

In addition to the welfare principle, the 1989 Act introduced a welfare checklist (s 1(3)), a statutory principle of no delay (s 1(2)) and, perhaps most radical of all, a presumption that the courts would make no order unless it could be shown that the order would bring some positive advantage to the child (s 1(5)). These will each be considered in turn as they provide the background against which all disputes relating to children on parental relationship breakdown are decided.

3 Parental responsibility on relationship breakdown

8.14

Parental responsibility is defined in s 3(1) as 'all the rights, duties, powers, responsibilities and authority which by law a parent of a child has in relation to a child and his or her property'. It is given automatically on the birth of a child, jointly to both parents where they are married to each other, but only to the mother where they are unmarried, save that the unmarried father can acquire parental responsibility if (since 1 December 2003 by s 111 of the Children and Adoption Act 2002) he is registered as the child's father. The circumstances in which the father may be registered or, where his name was not originally entered in the register, re-registered, as the child's father are (a) at the joint request of the mother and father, in which case both must sign the register or (b) at the request of either the mother or the father, on the production of statutory declarations of paternity and the mother's acknowledgement of it.

8.15

Thus, unless he has been registered or, where his name was not originally entered in the register, re-registered, as the child's father (as above) or has already been granted a s 4 parental responsibility order or entered into a parental responsibility agreement with the mother (see Chapter 2), a father may seek to acquire parental responsibility after the parents' relationship has broken down, in addition to resolving the obvious issues with regard to with whom the child should live. Where an unmarried father obtains a child arrangements order under which the child lives with him following breakdown of the relationship, the court must make a s 4 order giving him parental responsibility (s 12(1)), and this cannot be brought to an end whilst the child arrangements order remains in force (s 12(4)).

8.16

Perhaps surprisingly, despite the s 1(5) no order presumption, the courts have for the most part been ready and willing to grant parental responsibility orders wherever the father is seeking to have contact with the child. One reason for this approach can be found by comparing the position of married parents with unmarried parents. Following breakdown of the relationship, where both parents have 'parental responsibility' arising out of marriage, they retain it, even though a child arrangements ('lives with') order is made in favour of one parent alone.

8.17

In the case of married parents, parental responsibility cannot be withdrawn from either parent, although the making of child arrangements, specific issue or prohibited steps orders can restrict it. In the case of unmarried parents, this is also true of the mother. Thus even where an unmarried father becomes the sole resident parent and a s 4 order is accordingly also made, the mother will retain parental responsibility, which cannot, by virtue of s 2(9), be surrendered or transferred. However, as the unmarried father can acquire parental responsibility only by virtue of s 4, his parental responsibility can, subject to s 12(4), be terminated in accordance with s 4(3), upon the application of himself or of any other person who has parental responsibility for the child or, with leave of the court, on the application of the child. It should also be stressed that s 2(8) states that the fact that a person has parental responsibility for a child shall not entitle them to act in any way which would be incompatible with any order made under the Act. Thus, although a non-resident parent may retain parental responsibility and thus may approach the child's school, or consent to medical treatment, it does not entitle him or her to take the child to live with him or her where there is a child arrangements ('lives with') order in favour of the child's other parent.

(a) Summary of options for unmarried parents

8.18

The options with regard to parental responsibility on relationship breakdown, although almost always linked to arrangements generally for the child, are as follows.

(i) Where a father does not have parental responsibility on relationship breakdown

8.19

The parties can make their own arrangements, without seeking a formal court order or making a parental responsibility agreement. This leaves an unmarried father in a vulnerable position, as only the mother has parental responsibility and he has no legally recognised status *vis-à-vis* his child. This could present difficulties with third parties even if there are no problems with the child's mother. From the father's point of view, this is the least favourable option, and one, it is suggested, which is inappropriate where the parents have cohabited and undertaken joint parenting for any length of time. It does, however, leave the mother in a position of theoretical complete control unless and until such time as the father makes applications for parental responsibility or a child arrangements order.

8.20

The parties can enter into a parental responsibility agreement and make their own arrangements, without seeking to formalise these in a court order. If the arrangements break down, s 8 orders will have to be sought at that stage. Alternatively, a consent order could be sought, but the court could refuse to make it on the basis of the s 1(5) no order presumption if arrangements have been made and are working well, as discussed above. In *Re X (minors) (parental responsibility agreement)* [2000] 1 FLR 517, the Court of Appeal confirmed that the parents' ability to enter into a parental responsibility agreement was an important part of their right to respect for private and family life under Article 8 of the European Convention on Human Rights. Thus even where the child was in care and the local authority objected to the father having parental responsibility for the child, the mother could not be prevented from entering into the agreement under s 4 CA 1989, and, in contrast to a parental responsibility order, the welfare principle is not applicable in the case of a parental responsibility agreement.

8.21

The parties can agree neither arrangements nor the issue of parental responsibility and thus the only option is for the father to apply for a s 8 order and, if he wishes, a parental responsibility order. The court could make a parental responsibility order in any event and must do so if a child arrangements ('lives with') order is made in favour of the father (s 12(1)). This cannot be brought to an end whilst the order is in force (s 12(4)). Where a father applies for a child arrangements ('spends time with') order and parental responsibility, the recent trend in the courts, as indicated below, is that the father should almost always be granted the status of parental responsibility despite objections by the mother, although in *Re H (parental responsibility)* [1998] 1 FLR 855, the Court of Appeal stated that this does not amount to a presumption in favour of granting parental responsibility. There is some evidence from research that the dropping of applications for parental responsibility orders were being used as a bargaining tool in negotiations relating to contact (see Butler *et al*, *The Children Act 1989 and the Unmarried Father* (1993) 5 JCL 157 and [1993] Fam Law 90). An alternative is for a mother to cross-apply for a child arrangements ('lives with') order, even though there is no dispute about with whom the child is to live, to ensure that s 2(8) will prevent any inconsistent use of the father's parental responsibility. However, the no order presumption will have to be overcome by showing that this would provide the child with a positive benefit. Whether the resident parent's peace of mind would supply this is questionable, although if the child itself were expressing a desire to have its permanent home settled by the court, this would presumably be sufficient.

(ii) Where a father has previously acquired parental responsibility

8.22

Both parents retain parental responsibility and no further orders are made, with all arrangements being made between the parents by agreement. This places the parents in the same position as most married parents, and it may be that an agreement has been reached following successful mediation. A consent order could be sought to formalise the agreed arrangements, but the court could refuse to make it on the basis of the s 1(5) no order presumption if arrangements have been made and are working well, as discussed above. A deed of separation could be used to formally record the arrangements. Alternatively, should arrangements break down, appropriate s 8 orders can be sought at this later time.

8.23

Both parents retain parental responsibility but subject to child arrangements orders. Where there is a dispute as to the arrangements for the children at the time of the relationship breakdown, this is the most likely scenario. In the normal course of events, even though an unmarried father's parental responsibility is capable of being terminated by the court (s 4(3)), it is highly unusual for this to happen. The no order presumption (s 1(5)) predicates against it and it would have to be shown that such a step was required in the interests of the child. In *Re P (terminating parental responsibility)* [1995] 1 FLR 1048, FD, it was stated that there was a presumption that parental responsibility would continue. However, in *Re D (a child)* [2014] EWCA Civ 315, it was found that there is no presumption as to the continuance of parental responsibility. It is the welfare of the child that creates the presumption, not the parenthood of the unmarried father. It should be noted that if a 'spends time with' order only is in issue, the court may feel it inappropriate to make a 'lives with' order in respect of the other parent in view of s 1(5). If the resident parent or a child feels insecure, given the other parent's parental responsibility, it could be argued that a 'lives with' order would be in the child's interests, given the resultant restrictions of s 2(8) on the exercise of parental responsibility.

8.24

Mother retains parental responsibility but father's parental responsibility is terminated by order of the court. This is unlikely to happen unless the father has shown complete disregard to the child's welfare. In *Re P (terminating parental responsibility)* (above), where the father, unbeknown to the mother, had seriously injured the child, it was confirmed that the welfare principle (s 1(1)) applied to an application to terminate parental responsibility and that the same tests of attachment and commitment between father and child as applied on an application for parental responsibility were to be used to assess an application to terminate it. It was useful to consider whether the court would have granted parental responsibility, if the father did not already have it.

(b) The case law

8.25

Even after the implementation of s 111 of the Adoption and Children Act 2002, there are still fathers who do not jointly register the birth and thus do not automatically acquire parental responsibility in this way. Thus the ability to enter into a parental responsibility agreement and to apply for a parental responsibility order remain important, but increasingly less so.

8.26

The Court of Appeal has made clear that it considers parental responsibility to be a status which does not interfere with the day-to-day care of a child and is, accordingly, a status which should normally be granted to a father who has shown commitment and attachment to his child. Where there has been cohabitation by a child's parents, this will normally be straightforward, as in the absence of matters which would prejudice the child's welfare, a father will usually have done enough. In *Re S (a minor) (parental responsibility)* [1995] 3 FCR 225, CA, Ward LJ said that the essence of granting a parental responsibility order was the grant of status. He indicated that it was wrong to concentrate on an applicant's rights and powers and said it was the status given to a father by fatherhood that should be concentrated upon. It has been suggested that parental responsibility 'reflects the everyday reality of being a parent' and taking the necessary decisions for the child's welfare (see *R v E and F (female parents; known father)* [2010] EWHC 417). In *Re H-B (contact)* [2015] EWCA Civ 389, Munby P offered his view of parental responsibility as 'a fundamentally important reflection of the realities of the human condition, of the very essence of the relationship of parent and child … First and foremost, and even more importantly, parental responsibility involves duties owed by each parent to the child.'

8.27

In *Re H (minors) (illegitimate children: father: parental rights) (No 2)* [1991] 1 FLR 214, it was held, pre-CA 1989, that a father whose children were in care and about to be placed for adoption should be granted an old-style parental rights order, providing the court was satisfied as to the degree of commitment which the father had shown towards the children, the degree of attachment between father and children and the reasons for the father applying for the order.

8.28

This has become the accepted test approved by the Court of Appeal many times since the coming into force of the CA 1989 in the context of parental responsibility orders (see eg *Re G (a minor) (parental responsibility order)* [1994] 1 FLR 504, CA). In *Re C and V (minors) (parental responsibility and contact)* [1998]

1 FLR 392, a father of a child with special medical needs, which only the mother had been trained to meet, was refused contact but granted the status of parental responsibility to reflect his commitment.

8.29

Further guidance was given in *Re P (a minor) (parental responsibility order)* [1994] 1 FLR 578, where it was held that the fact that parents cannot co-operate is not a reason for refusing a parental responsibility order, for the effect of s 2(8) is to prevent a person with an order interfering with the day-to-day management of a child's life where the child lives elsewhere. Thus a mother's objection is not a reason to refuse an order, although in light of s 2(8) it would be a reason for seeking s 8 orders to carefully regulate other matters. Furthermore, although financial commitment to the child may be a factor, and in *Re S (a minor) (parental responsibility)* [1995] 2 FLR 648, Butler-Sloss LJ stated that a father showing real commitment ought to cement it by sharing the burdens as well as the pleasure of looking after a child, in *Re H (a minor) (parental responsibility order: maintenance)* [1996] 1 FLR 867, the Court of Appeal made it clear that the court should not refuse to make a parental responsibility order as a means of coercing a father to pay maintenance. The thrust of these cases is that nearly all unmarried fathers will obtain parental responsibility if they want it, and this gives credence to the argument that all parents should get parental responsibility for their children regardless of their marital status.

8.30

The Court of Appeal has confirmed that there is no presumption in favour of a father being granted parental responsibility (*Re H (parental responsibility)* [1998] 1 FLR 855). Clearly the welfare principle applies to any application for a parental responsibility order, and will be refused where a father's misconduct shows a lack of commitment to the child. In *Re H (parental responsibility)* [1998] 1 FLR 855, the Court of Appeal refused to grant an order to a father who had deliberately harmed his son and in *Re P (parental responsibility: change of name)* [1997] 2 FLR 722, a father who had been imprisoned on numerous occasions as a result of his criminal activities had thereby demonstrated a lack of commitment to his child. Account may also be taken of the father's criminal conduct, including his failure to accept it and its effect on the child in refusing to grant a father parental responsibility for his child (see *Re G (domestic violence: direct contact)* [2000] 2 FLR 865). The motive for applying for parental responsibility may also be relevant. In *Re P (parental responsibility)* [1998] 2 FLR 96, it was indicated that an order should be refused where the father's reasons for applying were demonstrably wrong, improper or inappropriate, such as to interfere with and possibly undermine the mother's care for the child (see also *Re M (handicapped child: parental responsibility)* [2001] 2 FLR 342) and where s 8 orders were not likely to prove an effective barrier. Such motives and the ineffectual nature of s 8 orders will not, however, always be easy to prove.

8.31

A parental responsibility order can be an important means of an unmarried father obtaining *locus standi* in other proceedings. In *Re H (a minor) (parental responsibility)* [1993] 1 FLR 484 a court granted an order to a father whose child had moved to Scotland and whose stepfather now intended to adopt, in order to protect his position in these proceedings.

8.32

In *Re E (a minor) (parental responsibility blood test)* [1995] 1 FLR 392 where a father, whom the mother feared might remove the child from the jurisdiction, had enjoyed frequent contact but was refused staying contact, the Court of Appeal stated that the approach to any application for a parental responsibility order by a father who had shown the degree of attachment and commitment to a child as this father was that *prima facie* an order would be for the welfare of the child. There would have to be cogent evidence that the child's welfare would be adversely affected for the order to be refused. In *Re T (parental responsibility: contact)* [1993] 2 FLR 450, CA, it was held that where there had been intense hostility by the father towards the mother, showing her hatred and serious violence and showing no regard for the child's welfare (going so far as to fail to return the young child after contact for nine days), the court was right to refuse, *inter alia*, a parental responsibility order.

(c) Other issues

8.33

It seems important that, on relationship breakdown, fathers are made aware of the potential significance of not acquiring parental responsibility. For example, they will not be automatically entitled to notice of certain types of proceedings, such as discharge of care order proceedings unless they have lived with the child for a period of at least three years, s 8 proceedings. This in itself may in some cases raise human rights issues under Articles 8 and 14 of the European Convention, were a child to be adopted rather than placed with a potentially committed father, as almost happened in *Re O (a minor) (custody: adoption)* [1992] 1 FLR 77. In other circumstances, their status as a parent of the child may require that they be given notice. This is the case with emergency protection orders (s 44(1)), care orders (s 31), child assessment orders (s 43(1)) and applications for appointment of a child's guardian (s 5(1)). From a mother's point of view, a parental responsibility order made on breakdown may give rise to feelings of insecurity, although her position is no less secure than that of any married mother, *vis-à-vis* her children on divorce. In practice, a father who is likely to abuse the arrangements agreed or decided upon by the court is likely to do so regardless of whether or not parental responsibility is granted. Abuse, which blatantly disregards the welfare of the child, may well be sufficient to found an application to terminate parental responsibility, as discussed above.

8.34

The issue of disputed parentage may arise in relation to both parental responsibility and s 8 applications as well as in the context of child support. The Child Support, Pensions and Social Security Act 2000 introduced, with effect from April 2001, a mechanism for obtaining a declaration of parentage in all contexts. Section 55A FLA 1986 enables a person to apply for a declaration of parentage ie a declaration as to whether or not a person named in the application is or was the parent of another person so named. Anyone with a sufficient personal interest may bring an application for a declaration of parentage. Where a child is concerned the court has power to refuse to hear the application if it considers this is not in the child's best interests and no subsequent application can then be made without leave (ss 55A(5) and (6) FLA 1986). Section 23 FLA 1986 (as amended by the Child Support, Pensions and Social Security Act 2000, s 82) permits bodily samples other than blood (such as semen, saliva and hair roots) to be taken to resolve parentage disputes including DNA testing. Further, s 21(3) Family Law Reform Act 1969, enables the court to consent to a bodily sample being taken from a child under the age of 16 for such test where it believes it to be in the child's best interests, where the resident parent refuses to do so. If the person with primary care (in the Act 'care and control') does give consent, the child can be tested without his consent. However, in *Re D (paternity)* [2006] EWHC 3545 (Fam), [2007] 2 FLR 26, Hedley J, found the 11-year-old boy to be a troubled and angry person who was strongly opposed to the application for blood tests but that he understood the issues involved, and decided that it was not in the boy's best interests to compel provision by the boy of a blood sample for testing.

8.35

Thus, it is no longer necessary for the court to draw inferences from either party's refusal to consent. The welfare test has always applied to such applications (see *O v L (blood tests)* [1995] 2 FLR 930, CA) and it has been said that every child has the right to know the truth about their parentage (see *Re H a minor (blood tests: parental rights)* [1997] Fam Law 89, CA in which the Court of Appeal invoked the support of the UN Convention on the Rights of the Child, Article 7(1) that every child has the right to know the truth of his identity unless disclosure is clearly contrary to his best interests). So, in *Re T (paternity: ordering blood tests)* [2001] Fam Law 738 where the mother and her husband were unable to have children and the mother had had sexual relationships with four other men with a view to becoming pregnant and a child was born in 1994, one of whom subsequently claimed to be the father, DNA tests were ordered to establish who was indeed the father. Here, where the child had the right to respect for his private and family life in the sense of knowing his true identity, it conflicted with a competing right to respect for a private and family life within the stability of his mother's social family unit. Nonetheless, where as here the disputed parentage was in the public domain and there was a risk of the child learning of it, certainty of parentage was in the child's best interests even when balanced against the rights of the mother and husband, whose relationship was thought stable enough to withstand the testing. It was also stated that the child's interests in knowing his identity carried the most weight and any interference with the mother and husband's rights under Article 8 was proportionate to the legitimate aim of providing the child with the knowledge of his true roots.

4 The welfare of the child

(a) The welfare principle

8.36

Section 1(1) CA 1989 states that the child's welfare shall be the court's 'paramount consideration' when determining any question regarding the upbringing of the child or the administration of a child's property. 'Upbringing', however, it should be noted, is defined as including the care of the child, but not its maintenance (s 105(1)).

8.37

Although, in applying the welfare principle, the court will in practice ask itself 'What is best for the child?', the CA 1989 has not expressly made the child's welfare the sole consideration. Nevertheless, in reality, any other factor, including the wishes of the parent(s), is relevant only in so far as it helps the court to determine what is in the best interests of the child. With effect from 22 October 2014, the CA 1989 now contains a *presumption of involvement* of a parent in their child's life, s 1(2A), 1(2B) and 1(6) providing that a court is to presume, unless the contrary is shown, that involvement (whether direct or indirect) by the parent in the child's life in a way that does not put the child at risk of suffering harm will further the child's welfare.

8.38

Importantly, the welfare of the child is *not* the court's paramount consideration, although it is important, on an application under s 10(9) for leave to apply for a child arrangements order, as otherwise some of the matters in that subsection would be otiose (see *Re A and W (minors) (residence order leave to apply)* [1992] 2 FLR 154 and *Re C (residence: child's application for leave)* [1995] 1 FLR 927, CA). By analogy, this must also be the case in relation to all applications for leave to apply for or any of the other s 8 orders.

8.39

However, in *Oxfordshire County Council v M* [1994] 1 FLR 175, the Court of Appeal held that under the 1989 Act and in wardship where the child's interests are paramount, legal professional privilege attaching to medical reports has to yield to that overriding principle. As a matter of practice, any leave granted for medical reports to be obtained is usually upon condition that the report is disclosed to all parties, forcing practitioners to make a tactical decision as to its likely impact on their client's case. Clients need to be carefully advised as to the advantages and disadvantages of obtaining this kind of evidence.

8.40

Issues have arisen in the public law arena as to how to resolve situations where the welfare of one child conflicts with that of another, an issue that could equally arise in the private law sphere. In *Birmingham City Council v H (No 3)* [1994] 1 FLR 224, where both mother and baby were children, the House of Lords (now, the Supreme Court) established the principle that it was the best interests of the child who was the subject of the application which should prevail ie that the paramountcy principle applied to him and that it was his upbringing and not that of his mother which was in issue. However, in *Re F (a minor) (contact: child in care)* [1994] 2 FCR 1354, where a child in care sought contact with siblings not in care and who were opposed to contact, the Court of Appeal held that in respect of an application under s 34 (for contact between the child in care and another person), the child in care's welfare was paramount, although a contact order could not in practice bind the siblings. Yet, on a s 8 application by the child in care for contact with siblings, it was the siblings' welfare which was paramount. In *Re T and E (proceedings: conflicting interests)* [1995] 1 FLR 581, it was agreed that where applications involved different welfare tests, then the welfare of the child subject to the 1989 Act prevailed due to the paramountcy principle. In *Re S a minor (contact: application by sibling)* [1998] 2 FLR 897, where an application for contact was brought by an adopted child for contact with her birth sister who had also been adopted, it was made clear that it is the welfare of the child who is the subject of the application, here the birth sister and not the applicant, which will be paramount. Where all other things were equal however, and a conflict of welfare demands arises, the test is to provide the situation of least detriment to all the children.

8.41

In Re S (children) (permission) [2011] EWCA Civ 454, [2011] 2 FLR 678, the Court of Appeal emphasised that, when a court is asked to consider the (possibly competing) welfare interests of siblings, the case of each requires careful and separate consideration pursuant to CA 1989, s 1. An individual welfare assessment is required in respect of each child and, where there is a conflict between the interests of each child, the court must then balance the welfare of one against that of the other(s) in coming to its decision.

(b) The welfare checklist

8.42

Section 1(3) states:

> 'In the circumstances mentioned in subsection (4), a court shall have regard in particular to—
>
> (a) the ascertainable wishes and feelings of the child concerned (considered in the light of his age and understanding);
>
> (b) his physical, emotional and educational needs;
>
> (c) the likely effect on him of any change in his circumstances;
>
> (d) his age, sex, background and any characteristics of his that the court considers relevant;
>
> (e) any harm which he has suffered or is at risk of suffering;
>
> (f) how capable each of his parents, and any other person in relation to whom the court considers the question to be relevant, is of meeting his needs; and
>
> (g) the range of powers available to the court under this Act in the proceedings in question.'

8.43

This welfare checklist is essentially a set of priorities to which the court must have particular regard; but this is confined by s 1(4) to two specific situations. It applies first where the court is deciding whether to make, vary or discharge a s 8 order and this is opposed by any party to the proceedings. Thus, if the parties are agreed and the application is unopposed, the court does not have to apply the checklist, and, subject to the welfare principle and the no order presumption contained in s 1(5) (discussed below), the court cannot reject agreements made between parties on the basis of the checklist considerations alone. The wishes and feelings of a child, not a party to the proceedings would not, for example, therefore normally be an issue in a consent application. Nonetheless, although the court does not have to have regard to it in other situations, given it is for the most part a restatement of matters which courts have traditionally considered in the context of the welfare principle, matters contained in the checklist may well be taken into account when applying s 1(1). Indeed, it has been described by the Court of Appeal as 'a useful *aide memoire*' (see *Re B (minors) (change of surname)* [1996] 1 FLR 791). The other context in which the checklist is mandatorily applied is where the court is considering whether to make a care or supervision order under Part IV of the Act. Here, agreement cannot oust the court's power to intervene and apply the checklist. Yet, care and supervision orders can be made only on application to the court by a local authority or other authorised person such as the NSPCC. Section 37 enables the court to order an investigation of the child's circumstances by the local authority where it feels it may be appropriate for a care or supervision order to be made, but the court has lost its power to make a care or supervision order of its own motion in family proceedings where it is troubled by the unsatisfactory nature of the arrangements proposed by the parents. Although an application can be made for a care or supervision order, either as an end in itself or in other family proceedings (s 31), the court's loss of power to intervene in this way is a sign of the shift made in the 1989 Act towards leaving responsibility for children much more with their parents and free from state interference.

8.44

From the point of view of cohabitants on relationship breakdown, the checklist is likely to be of most significance in relation to s 8 applications where the parties cannot agree arrangements for the children following breakdown. The weight given to these individual factors is still a matter for the discretion of the individual court.

8.45

A body of case law has grown up around the matters specified in the checklist and now provides useful indicators of how courts are likely to view the issues raised.

(i) Ascertainable wishes and feelings

8.46

Although this heads the list that is not to say that any greater weight is to be given to these than to any of the other checklist considerations (*Re W (a minor) (medical treatment: court's jurisdiction)* [1993] 1 FLR 1, CA). It is, however, the matter which best illustrates a departure from the approach under the old law towards a more child-centred approach. The fact that the wishes must be ascertainable and must be considered in the light of the child's age and understanding, indicate that the maturity of the child is critical to the weight which will be given by the court to these factors. In *Re P (a minor) (education)* [1992] 1 FLR 316, the Court of Appeal held that it was the court's duty to take the wishes and views of older children into account, especially if they were sensible, mature and intelligent. Nonetheless, the wishes of younger children may be ascertainable through indirect means, such as observation by a children and family reporter of behaviour with the adults involved. The maturity of the child must also be assessed in the context of the issue which was to be decided. Thus in *Re E (a minor)* [1993] 1 FLR 386, a 15-year-old Jehovah's witness who wished to refuse a blood transfusion in the knowledge that he might die, was nonetheless adjudged by the court not to be able to fully appreciate the implications of his decision, despite being found to be mature enough to make decisions about his own welfare generally. This underlines the fact that although regard must be had to wishes and feelings where the child is sufficiently mature, that is not to say that they are paramount where these conflict with their own welfare. In *Re P (wardship: care and control)* [1992] 2 FCR 681, Butler-Sloss LJ made the principle clear:

> '[I]n all family cases it is the duty of the court to listen to the children, ascertain their wishes and feelings and then make decisions about their future, having regard to but not constricted by those wishes.'

8.47

Some illustrations in context are useful. In *Re F (minors) (denial of contact)* [1993] 2 FLR 677, the Court of Appeal found that great weight was correctly given to the views of brothers aged 12 and 9 who did not want to have contact with their transsexual father. In cases where leave is sought to remove a child permanently from the jurisdiction, the wishes and feelings have often been critical. In *M v M (minors) (jurisdiction)* [1993] Fam Law 396, the Court of Appeal found that a trial judge who granted leave to a mother to take two articulate children to Israel against their wishes was wrong and had failed to sufficiently consider the wishes and feelings of the children and the views of the welfare officer. Again, in *M v A (wardship: removal from jurisdiction)* [1993] 2 FLR 715, a mother, with whom the children had their principal home (although their care was shared with their father), was refused leave to take two boys aged 12 and 9 permanently to Canada in view of their wish to remain in England with their father despite finding that they loved both homes.

8.48

A change of approach has been taken by the Court of Appeal in relation to the weight to be given to children's views on a change of surname. In *Re F (child surname)*, CA, it was confirmed that this was an important issue not to be taken lightly and to be decided in accordance with the child's welfare; and in *Re B (minors) (change of surname)* [1996] 1 FLR 791, it was held that although the wishes and feelings of adolescent children usually prevail in issues of residence or contact, this did not extend to a formal change of surname from that of their father to stepfather. It should be noted that this application was treated as an application under s 13 CA 1989 given the existence of an old-style custody order and not as a s 8 application for a specific issue order. The court was not therefore specifically directed to the checklist, although the court described it as a useful *aide memoire*.

8.49

How the court ascertains children's views may vary, although the usual course would be through a Cafcass officer/Family Court Adviser's report. Whether it is appropriate for the judge to see the child personally in private remains a matter of discretion for individual judges, although increasingly the argument is being made that the child should be heard from directly, given their right to a fair hearing reinforced by the HRA 1998 (Article 6). It follows that not only would this assist the judge but also that to allow the child's voice to be heard directly falls within the court's overriding objective 'of enabling the court to deal with cases justly, having regard to any welfare issues involved' (FPR 2010, 1.1). In April 2010, the Family Justice Council produced 'Guidelines for Judges Meeting Children who are subject to family Proceedings' [2010] 2 FLR 1872, the purpose of which was 'to encourage judges to enable children to feel more involved and connected with proceedings in which important decisions are made in their lives and to give them an opportunity to satisfy themselves that the judge has understood their wishes and feelings and to understand the nature of the judge's task'. The timing of any meeting between the judge and the child is crucial in this regard and the Court of Appeal in *Re A (children: meeting with children: contamination of proceedings)* [2012] EWCA Civ 185, [2012] 1 FCR 600, [2012] 2 FLR 369, where the trial judge had met with one of the children after evidence had been closed but before judgment was given, criticised the judge's timing of the meeting, Thorpe LJ saying that 'to give the child the impression that his mind was still open and that he was susceptible to influence, was to give completely the wrong impression'. Although a child may have a right to be heard (by the judge), he does not have a right to give evidence (*Re P-S* [2013] EWCA Civ 223, [2-013] 2 FCR 299) as the meeting is not for the purpose of gathering evidence (per Moore-Bick LJ in *KP (a child) (abduction: judge meeting child: conduct of interview)* [2014] EWCA Civ 554, [2014] 2 FCR 545 'the meeting is primarily for the benefit of the child, rather than for the benefit of the forensic process by providing additional evidence to the judge'). There are cases in which children are themselves represented in order to avoid potential breach of Article 6 of the European Convention on Human Rights which a court, as a public body, has a duty to prevent under the 1998 Act. If leave is granted, then children of sufficient understanding may become parties to proceedings (s 10(8)), and in private law proceedings, it is for the court to decide whether they may be made a party to the proceedings whether directly (FPR 2010, 16.2 and see FPR 2010, PD16A) or through a Children's Guardian (FPR 2010, 16.3 and 16.4 and FPR PD 16A para 7) or represented through a Litigation Friend (FPR 2010, 16.5) or whether, in the case of older children, they may instruct a solicitor directly (FPR 2010, 16.6). In *Re S (a minor) (independent representation)* [1993] 2 FLR 437, the Court of Appeal held that, save in a relatively straightforward matter or in the case of an older child, the court would be unlikely to grant leave unless the child proposed to be legally represented. In the leading authority prior to the introduction of the FPR 2010, the Court of Appeal allowed the appeal of three brothers then aged 13, 15 and 17 against the trial judge's refusal to allow them to be separately represented in respect of the application of their mother for residence. It held that 'if direct participation would pose an obvious risk of harm to the child arising out of the nature of the continuing proceedings and, if the child is incapable of comprehending that risk, then the judge is entitled to find that sufficient understanding has not been demonstrated. But judges have to be equally alive to the risk of emotional harm that might arise from denying the child knowledge of and participation in the continuing proceedings (see *Mahon v Mahon* [2005] EWCA Civ 634, [2005] 2 FLR 1011 at paras [29]–[36]).

(ii) The child's physical, emotional and educational needs, the ability to meet them, the risk of harm and the effect of change

8.50

Many of the checklist factors are matters which in the context of the arrangements on relationship breakdown, overlap and may be more or less influential depending on the nature of the order sought. Advisors need to assess their client's proposals for a child in this overall context. They need then to compare them with the proposals of any other party to the proceedings in order to present their client's proposals as the arrangements most likely to promote the child's welfare.

8.51

In terms of a child's physical needs, unless a child has particular medical or special needs (in which case the availability of appropriate facilities to meet these within reach of each parent's proposed home will be a very significant factor), the major issue is likely to be the accommodation which a resident parent can offer. That is not to say that the parent who can offer the most materially is at an advantage, as often the court is in a position to equalise the effects of such imbalance through maintenance and transfer of property orders or settlements under Sch 1 CA 1989 (see Chapters 9 to 11). However, a parent with unsatisfactory or undetermined accommodation is at a disadvantage as compared with one whose arrangements are clear and satisfactory. Stability in terms of the home will always be an important factor and the arrangements proposed for the child's education, particularly if these involve a move to a new school will be examined. The effect of any change in the child's circumstances is another factor to which the court is directed to have particular regard (s 1(3)(c)) and thus any change that is proposed by a parent needs to be as positive as possible for the child. However, the quality of day-to-day care available probably carries most weight, which is a matter which links in with the question of how capable each of the parents is in meeting the child's needs (s 1(3)(f)). Continuity of care has always been considered an important factor and there is a tendency for courts to want to retain the *status quo* if possible. Thus, all other things being equal, the parent who has the children immediately after relationship breakdown places themselves in a position of advantage, particularly if a long time elapses before the matter is heard (see eg *Re A (a minor) (custody)* [1991] 2 FLR 394). That said, the length of time that a child has been living with one parent does not create a presumption in favour of the child living with that parent (see *Re E-R (a child)* [2015] EWCA Civ 405, [2016] 1 FLR 521).

Whilst courts are extremely reluctant to split up brothers and sisters (see eg *Re P (custody of children) (split custody order)* [1991] 1 FLR 337), the fact that there may be regular contact between all the children and the parents could mitigate the problem of the children growing up in separate households (see *Re B (T) (a minor) (residence order)* [1995] 2 FCR 240, CA; *Re O (children) (residence)* [2003] EWCA Civ 1915).

8.52

In terms of the child's emotional needs, the closeness of the relationship that each parent has with the child and the ties between a child and his or her brothers and sisters will be powerful factors. The ability of the resident parent to meet the child's needs, including the need to have contact with the other parent, can be critical to the decision as to which parent should be the resident parent (see *Re A (a minor) (custody)* [1991] 2 FLR 394 per Butler-Sloss LJ at p 400). More recently, in *Re D (minors) (family appeals)* [1995] 1 FCR 301, the Court of Appeal refused to interfere in the decision of the lower court to place young children with a working father as it was not plainly wrong, given, it seems, the mother's underestimation of the importance of a father to the children, whereas the father had a proper recognition of the importance of a mother.

8.53

Where one parent is working and the other not, this can prove to be an advantage to the parent able to offer full-time care. However, if for example, the children are used to going to a nursery or childminder and are happy there, a change from this routine to remaining at home with one parent may not be viewed so positively.

8.54

Finally, the important factor of whether a child has suffered or is at risk of suffering harm (s 1(3)(e)) has been deliberately widely drawn to ensure that it is capable of encompassing both physical and emotional 'harm'. This must be judged in the context of the individual child and the history of the family. Where there has been domestic violence directed by one parent at the other parent (usually but not always the mother) but not the child, the child's right to know both parents overrode in most cases, in the court's view, any negative impact the mother's fear would have on the child. However, the Court of Appeal has indicated that family courts need to have a heightened awareness of the existence of and consequences to children of exposure to domestic violence between their parents and experts' reports on the issue will be critical (see *L, V, M, H (contact: domestic violence)* [2001] FAM 260).

8.55

Clearly, findings of abuse, whether physical, sexual, psychological or emotional, by a parent will weigh heavily against that parent, but conduct that is uninhibited or indiscreet needs careful examination before a court should reach the conclusion that it is potentially abusive and harmful. Whether a matter is likely to cause harm is not always obvious. In *Re W (residence order)* [1999] 1 FLR 869, the trial judge had taken the view that the mother and her new partner's lack of inhibitions towards nudity in front of the children would be harmful to them. However, the Court of Appeal held that there was no clear evidence that this behaviour would be harmful and thus should not have been taken into account.

(iii) Age, sex, background and other relevant characteristics

8.56

It is now well established that there is no principle that (a) a child should reside with the parent of the same sex or that (b) a young child should reside with their mother in preference to the father *(see Re A (a minor) (custody)* [1991] 2 FLR 394, CA; *Re S (a minor) (custody)* [1991] 2 FLR 388; *and Re A (children: 1959 UN Declaration)* [1998] 1 FLR 354, CA), although in *Re W (a minor) (residence order)* [1992] 2 FLR 332, CA, Lord Donaldson held that there was a rebuttable presumption that the interests of a baby (in that case just four weeks old) were best served by being with the mother.

8.57

A child's background and other relevant characteristics obviously encompass religious upbringing and cultural differences between parents which may be lost once the family splits up. However, these characteristics may carry little weight if the child has little or no perception of them (see *Re P (Section 91 (14) guidelines) (residence and religious heritage)* [1999] 2 FLR 573, CA). The range of orders available to the court should enable exposure to valuable features of a child's life to be preserved on relationship breakdown. A specific issue order can determine the child's religious education following breakdown and conditions on child arrangements orders could ensure contact with parents of different religions during important religious festivals or cultural events. Similarly, particular interests, which have always been undertaken with the non-resident parent, can be preserved by attaching conditions to a child arrangements order, if this is necessary to ensure any such activities continue.

(iv) Range of powers available to the court

8.58

This factor draws attention to the fact that the court may make various orders under the CA 1989 in 'family proceedings' of its own motion, regardless of whether there is an application for such an order before the court. Thus, it may make a s 8 order in any 'family proceedings' (see s 8(3)) in which a question arises with respect to the welfare of the child if it considers it right to do so (s 10(1)(b)). Furthermore, the court has various options if it is concerned about the arrangements and making no order at all (s 1(5)) does not resolve the situation.

8.59

Section 7 does give the court power, of its own motion, when considering any question with respect to a child under the Act, to seek welfare reports from a Cafcass officer (or Family Court Adviser) or a local authority on specified matters relating to the welfare of the child. It has been underlined that the ordering of a report where the court has taken into account the relevant factors such as delay, is a matter for the court's discretion. It is highly unlikely to be 'plainly wrong' and reversed on appeal (*Re W (welfare reports)* [1995] 2 FLR 142). Thus, if a court was dissatisfied about the agreed arrangements in respect of which s 8 orders were being sought by the child's parents, the court has power to order a report with a view, if appropriate, to the local authority's then applying for a care or supervision order. Alternatively, as will be discussed below, the court can in exceptional circumstances make a 'family assistance order' pursuant to s 16 of the Act, requiring a Cafcass officer (or Family Court Adviser) or local authority officer to advise, assist or befriend any person named in the order providing the adult parties agree. Finally, as mentioned above, where they feel a care or supervision order may be appropriate, the court can order a s 37 investigation by the local authority. This factor has gained particular prominence since the decision in *Re B (care proceedings: appeal)* [2013] UKSC 33, [2013] 2 FLR 1075 and subsequent cases which have emphasised the need for judges (particularly in public law cases/care proceedings) to conduct a comparative welfare analysis of all of the realistic possible outcomes for the child. In *Re K (children) (contact: interim care order)* [2014] EWCA Civ 1195, Ryder LJ confirmed that 'in a private law case where the issue is the removal of a child from the care of one parent or the denial of a relationship with a parent by the cessation of contact, nothing less than an analysis of this kind will do. The balance sheet approach of benefits and detriments is equally applicable to the welfare analysis of options in (*these cases*)'.

(c) The principle of no delay

8.60

Section 1(2) requires the court to have regard to the general principle that delay in determining a question relating to the upbringing of a child is likely to prejudice the welfare of the child. Section 11 goes on to direct that in s 8 proceedings a timetable must be drawn up by the court to determine the matter without delay and to give directions to ensure adherence to the timetable as far as possible and there is a similar provision in respect of care and supervision proceedings in s 32. The practical procedures are now contained in r 12.13 FPR 2010, bolstered by FPR Practice Direction PD 12B – Child

Arrangements Programme. In relation to s 8 cases, see *Re G and B (disclosure: protocol)* [2010] EWHC 2630 (Fam), [2011] 1 FLR 1089, in which the court reminded practitioners, Cafcass and the lower courts of the programme and the clear structure that should be followed in private law cases. The European Court of Human Rights has held that delay may amount to a breach of Article 6(1) of the European Convention on Human Rights (right to a fair trial) eg as delay in determining where and with whom a child is to live may decide the issue by tipping the balance in favour of the status quo (see *EO and VP v Slovakia (Application No 56193/00 and 57581/00)* [2004] 2 FCR 242 and *Deak v Romania and United Kingdom* [2008] 2 FLR 994).

8.61

FPR 2010, rr 16.33(4) and 16.38(3) require Cafcass to assist the court in avoiding delay. It is though the *court* that is to have regard to the principle of avoiding delay. Where proceedings have been initiated and the court has fixed a timetable and a party then deliberately fails to comply with it, the application of s 1(2) may well justify a decision of the court not to adjourn the proceedings even if the party is consequently unable to put their case as to the substantive issues (see *Re SW (a minor) (care proceedings)* [1993] 2 FLR 609; *H v Cambridgeshire County Council* [1996] 2 FLR 566). If the party is able to either give instructions or to present his case himself and has been thus far able to take part in the proceedings and if the adjournment would be damaging to the relationship between the other party and the child, the court would be entitled to refuse the adjournment (*Blunkett v Quinn* [2004] EWHC 2816 (Fam)] [2005] 1 FLR 648). However, where on the facts the only reasonable way of ensuring a fair trial would be to grant a short adjournment, this could be agreed (see *Re M (children)* [2009] EWCA Civ 1216, [2010] 1 FLR 1089).

8.62

However, although the court may be reluctant to allow departure from the prescribed timetable on the one hand, where there is good reason for delay which might actually promote the child's welfare, practitioners should not be deterred from applying for further time. In *C v Solihull Metropolitan Borough Council* [1993] 1 FLR 290, it was stated that, whilst delay is normally inimical, a planned purposeful delay may well be beneficial to the welfare of the child. In *Re B (a minor) (contact: interim order)* [1994] 2 FLR 269, the Court of Appeal held that delay occasioned purposively by the court welfare officer (now, Cafcass officer) supervising trial basis contact does not offend the no delay principle and should have been allowed by justices. Further problems may arise where the Cafcass officer who has made a report is unable to attend the date fixed for hearing. The court must then decide whether his attendance is necessary and whether the harmful effects of delay outweigh the benefit to be gained from his attendance. In *Re CB (access: attendance of court welfare officer)* [1995] 1 FLR 622 and *Re C (Section 8 order: court welfare officer)* [1995] 1 FLR 617, the Court of Appeal found that although it is desirable that a court welfare officer should be present if either party so wishes, a court was nonetheless entitled to hear a case in their absence upon the basis of the no delay principle, but should not depart from the recommendation in the report without having heard their oral evidence. In all cases, the court will have to balance whether the child's interests are best served by proceeding on the basis of incomplete evidence or by yet further delay.

(d) The no order presumption

8.63

Section 1(5) states that 'where a court is considering whether or not to make one or more orders under this Act with respect to a child, it shall not make the order or any of the orders unless it considers that doing so would be better for the child than making no order at all'. However, as discussed below, it is now quite clearly established that this presumption will not routinely prevent a court from making a parental responsibility order where a father has shown appropriate commitment to the child (where there would seem to be a presumption that a parental responsibility order should be made providing there is no evidence that it would adversely affect the child's welfare (*Re G (a minor) (parental responsibility order)* [1994] 1 FLR 504, CA; *Re E (a minor) (parental responsibility: blood tests)* [1995] 1 FLR 392, CA; *Re H (parental responsibility: maintenance)* [1996] 1 FLR 867; *Re P (parental responsibility)* [1997] 2 FLR 722, CA), nor be used to refuse a child arrangements ('spends time with') order (formerly, a contact order) under s 8 (see *Re R (a minor)* [1993] 2 FLR 762).

8.64

One practical problem, which the no order presumption embodies, is that of the agreement of arrangements for a child which all parties wish to have formalised by way of consent order. Such orders not only give effect to what has already been agreed by the parents, but may confer status including parental responsibility on the unmarried father where there is no parental responsibility agreement or order. If the father has not yet acquired parental responsibility or secured a child arrangements order providing for contact with his child, he will effectively have no legal right to see his child, and conversely, the child has no legal tie with that parent. Furthermore, a father who does not have parental responsibility and intends to care for the child or even enjoy substantial contact following relationship breakdown will have no proof that, for example, he is entitled to make decisions about medical treatment on behalf of the child or meet the child from school even if the child's mother has verbally delegated parental responsibility for these purposes. Accordingly, there are very good practical reasons for an order to be made. In *B v B (a minor) (residence order)* [1992] 2 FLR 327, the Court of Appeal recognised this in the context of a grandparent carer without parental responsibility, who was encountering difficulties in making arrangements for the child with the Education Authority. Although in the absence of an issue upon which the court's intervention was necessary, the court would usually decline to make the order even though the order was sought by consent, where the child's carer did not have parental responsibility, a residence order (now, child arrangements 'lives with' order) would be better for the child than making no order at all.

8.65

Thus, whilst in general, a positive benefit to the child must be shown in order to rebut the no order presumption, this may in practice be easier in the unmarried as opposed to the married context. It should perhaps also be said that the practical application of s 1(5) in relation to consent orders may vary from court to court.

5 Section 8 orders

8.66

Section 8 CA 1989 sets out the orders that can be made with respect to children in family proceedings and these are known as s 8 orders. Child arrangements orders direct with whom a child is to live and with whom a child is to spend time or otherwise have contact. In addition, s 8 provides for prohibited steps and specific issue orders, which may be used to control where appropriate and necessary, the steps which can and cannot be taken by a parent in relation to a child following breakdown of the parents' relationship.

8.67

On breakdown of an unmarried relationship where there are children, in order to clarify any arrangements and ensure they are as far as possible acknowledged in law and enforceable, it may still be necessary for the parents to seek s 8 orders, although those seeking public funding/legal aid will only be able to do so should they be able to provide evidence of domestic (or child) abuse. Thus, in most cases now appearing before the court, the parents are either self-representing or supported by solicitors for whose fees they are personally liable. Parents are encouraged therefore to attempt to resolve issues out of court, whether through mediation or other forms of alternative dispute resolution. This section defines the orders that can be made with respect to children in 'family proceedings', which, by virtue of subs 3, means wardship proceedings and proceedings under Parts I, II and IV of the 1989 Act; the Matrimonial Causes Act 1973; Schedules 5 and 6 to the Civil Partnership Act 2004; the Adoption and Children Act 2002; the Domestic Proceedings and Magistrates' Court Act 1978; Part III of the Matrimonial and Family Proceedings Act 1984, proceedings under s 54 Human Fertilisation and Embryology Act 2008 (HFEA 2008) and Part IV and 4A of the Family Law Act 1996 (FLA 1996).

8.68

In applications under Pt IV FLA 1996 where there are children of the relationship, in addition to granting injunctions and declaring rights of occupation, the court can of its own motion make orders under s 8 if a question arises with respect to the welfare of a child and the court considers the order should be made, even if there has been no application (s 10(1)(b)).

8.69

Section 8 orders are defined as follows by s 8(1):

> '"*a Child arrangements order*" means an order directing with whom a child is to live and with whom a child is to spend time or otherwise have contact;
>
> "*a prohibited steps order*" means an order that no step which could be taken by a parent in meeting his parental responsibility for a child, and which is of a kind specified in the order, shall be taken by any person without the consent of the court; and
>
> "*a specific issue order*" means an order giving directions for the purpose of determining a specific question which has arisen, or which may arise, in connection with any aspect of parental responsibility for a child.'

(a) Applicants

8.70

Applications for s 8 orders are not restricted to parents. In addition to any parent or guardian of the child, any step-parent who by virtue of s 4A has parental responsibility for the child and any person who is named in an existing child arrangements order as a person with whom the child is to live may apply as of right for any s 8 order (s 10(4). A further group may apply as of right just for child arrangements orders (s 10(5)) including as follows:

> 'Any party to a marriage or civil partnership in respect of which the child is a child of the family;
>
> Any person with whom the child has lived for three out of the past five years, providing that period of time has not ended more than three months prior to making the application; and
>
> Any person who has the consent of either each of the persons named in a child arrangements order as a person with whom the child is to live

> or of each of the persons having parental responsibility for the child, or, where the child is in care, the consent of the relevant local authority.
>
> A relative of a child is entitled to apply for a 'lives with' order if the child has lived with him for a period of at least one year immediately preceding the application (CA 1989, s 10(5B).'

8.71

Any person not included in these categories, including the child him/herself, providing the court considers he or she has sufficient understanding, may also apply with the court's leave (s 10(8)). How courts and solicitors should judge a child's understanding is a difficult issue (see *Re CT) (a minor) (wardship: representation)* (above)), and one already raised in the context of a child's wishes and feelings (see para 8.49). In line with the *Gillick* principle (see *Gillick v West Norfolk and Wisbech Area Health Authority* [1986] 1 FLR 224) the older a child, the more significant their wish to take proceedings becomes. However, in *Re S (a minor) (independent representation)* [1993] 2 FLR 437, the Master of the Rolls made it clear that age is not the only indicator of understanding. He observed:

> 'Children have different levels of understanding at the same age. And understanding is not absolute. It has to be assessed relative to the issues in the case.' (At p 444H)

8.72

Where, by virtue of the HFEA 2008, the biological father is not to be treated as the legal father, he has no right to apply for a s 8 order and will have to seek the leave of the court to make an application (see *Re G; Re Z (children: sperm donors: leave to apply for Children Act orders)* [2013] EWHC 134 (Fam)).

8.73

The paramountcy principle in s 1(1) CA 1989 does not apply to applications for leave, and thus considerations other than the child's welfare may hold sway in granting or refusing applications for leave (see *Re H (residence order: child's application for leave)* [2000] 1 FLR 780). On such applications the court will, in addition to deciding whether the child is mature enough to bring the application, also consider whether the matter is sufficiently serious to justify a court hearing and/or whether it ought rather to be resolved by the family themselves. In *Re SC (a minor) (leave to seek section 8 orders)* [1994] 1 FLR 96, a 14-year-old wanted to go abroad on holiday with her friend's family and also wanted to go and live with them. The issue of the holiday was not considered sufficiently serious to warrant court intervention and her wish to move in with another family was felt to be something which the family ought to resolve rather than the court. The court must also judge the likely success of the application for leave, and the fact that the proposed application is not hopeless is a factor in favour of granting leave. However, if the issues the child's application raises are already being raised by one of the adult parties, then it seems this is likely to be a reason to refuse the application (see *Re H (residence order: child's application for leave)* [2000] 1 FLR 780).

8.74

Whilst the child's welfare is not paramount in such applications, leave was refused where it was thought not to be in the child's interest to hear the evidence of his bitter and hostile parents *(Re C (residence: child's application for leave)* [1996] 1 FCR 461. The implications of the HRA 1998 on the need for children to have a voice in court proceedings has led to an increase in the number of cases where children are separately represented and to a greater number of leave applications being granted to children to bring s 8 applications in their own right. This was acknowledged by the Court of Appeal in *Re A (a child) (contact: separate representation)* (2001) *The Times*, 28 February where it was said that children who needed someone to orchestrate the investigation of the case on their behalf may need party status and legal representation. How the court ascertains children's views may vary, although the usual course would be through a Cafcass officer/ Family Court Adviser's report under s 7 CA 1989. This is discussed at para 8.49 above. In cases where there is a significant foreign element, or where the child has been refused leave to instruct a solicitor direct under FPR 2010 16.6 but continues to wish to do so, it might be appropriate to grant party status to a child.

8.75

Section 8 orders can be sought or made by the court of its own motion in any family proceedings (s 10(1)), as defined above, or where there are no family proceedings, on the application of any person who is entitled to apply for a s 8 order or who has been granted leave to do so (s 10(2)). These provisions are subject to s 9, which prevents a court making a s 8 order, other than a child arrangements ('lives with') order, with respect to a child who is in the care of a local authority; prevents a local authority from applying for a child arrangements order; and prevents such an order being made in favour of an authority. Normally, a person seeking to remove a child from care would apply to discharge the care order pursuant to s 39. However, an unmarried father without parental responsibility is not eligible to make such an application. Thus his only course would be to apply for a s 8 child arrangements ('lives with') order, for, once such an order is made in relation to a child who is in care, this automatically discharges the care order (s 91(1)).

(b) Child arrangements ('lives with') orders

8.76

Such orders are used to settle where and with whom a child should live, usually, but not exclusively, on the breakdown of a child's parents' relationship. As has been seen above, although in the context of the unmarried family it is likely to be the child's parents who will be the parties to the proceedings and who will be seeking the order, applications for s 8 orders are open to a wide range of people. Where parents agree the arrangements, the court does not have to, but may have regard to the checklist set out in s 1(3). However, where the court feels there is cause for concern, welfare reports or a s 37 investigation can be ordered, or a family assistance order made under s 16. This power should not be exercised unless the court is satisfied that the circumstances are exceptional. The effect of such an order is discussed below (see para 8.88).

8.77

Although these orders must be judged in accordance with the welfare principle, the checklist and the no order presumption, other relevant circumstances including financial considerations may be looked at. In *Re R (residence: financial considerations)* [1995] 2 FLR 612, the Court of Appeal held that a judge who ordered that a three-year-old child should live with her father during the week and her mother most weekends was entitled to look at the case realistically in the round and anticipate the likely effect of the mother giving up work and drawing state benefits. As noted above, where all other things are equal, a parent's attitude to contact with the other parent may be influential in deciding who should become the primary carer, given the importance of maintaining contact with both parents (see *Re D (minors) (appeal)* (above)).

(i) Child arrangements orders, parental responsibility and s 1(5)

8.78

As indicated in the section on parental responsibility above, the approach of the courts and indeed the parents themselves may vary according to whether the father has already acquired parental responsibility. That is not to say that in s 8 applications the presence or absence of parental responsibility is more influential than the nature of a child's relationship with their father or his actual commitment to the child, but rather that the options available to the court in terms of the orders they may make may be viewed differently. The 1989 Act leaves parental responsibility with both married parents after the making of a child arrangements order. Where an unmarried father becomes the resident parent on breakdown, s 12(1) directs that the court shall also make a s 4 order giving him parental responsibility. As the court cannot take away a mother's parental responsibility, both parents will in this situation have parental responsibility for the child subject to the s 8 orders. Where a s 4 order or agreement has been made granting the father parental responsibility, it is open to the mother (or, with leave, the child) to apply to discharge the s 4 order on breakdown. However, as discussed above the presumption is that it will be retained (see *Re P (terminating parental responsibility)* (above)). Any person who is not a parent but in whose favour a child arrangements ('lives with') order is made, is automatically given parental responsibility while the order remains in force by virtue of s 12(2). However, their parental responsibility is limited to the extent that they are specifically denied power to consent or refuse to consent to adoption, and cannot appoint a guardian for the child (s 12(3)). Where the court makes a child arrangement ('lives with') order in favour of a woman who is a parent of a child by virtue of HFEA 2008, s 43 it must, if that woman would not otherwise have parental responsibility for the child, also make an order giving her that parental responsibility (CA 1989, s 12(1A)).

(ii) Shared care

8.79

A court may under s 8 make a child arrangements ('lives with) order in favour of two or more persons who do not live together (see *Re K (shared residence order)* [2008] EWCA Civ 526).

8.80

It is not necessary for the parents to have exactly the same amount of time with the child for it to be in the child's best interests for each parent to have a 'lives with' order. In *Re P (children) (shared residence order)* [2005] EWCA Civ 1639, [2006] 2 FLR 347, Wall LJ stressed that 'such an order emphasises the fact that both parents are equal in the eyes of the law, and that they have equal duties and responsibilities as parents. The order can have the additional advantage of conveying the court's message that neither parent is in control and that the court expects parents to co-operate with each other for the benefit of their children'.

8.81

Orders determining that it would be in a child's best interests for each parent to have a 'lives with' order are becoming increasingly popular with the courts, recognising in appropriate cases the relationships between the child and his parents and the reality of the shared care arrangements already in place or sought, although it is still safe to say that they remain very much the exception rather than the rule. There is no presumption in favour of making such orders, but where a child is spending equal amounts of time with each parent, such an order will usually be the starting point for the judge (see *Re M (residence order)* [2008] EWCA Civ 66, [2008] 1 FLR 1087).

8.82

These orders are not limited to cases where the parents are on good terms and are not limited to exceptional cases (see *Re D (children) (shared residence orders)* [2001] 1 FLR 495, CA). In this case the Court of Appeal confirmed a shared residence order where the arrangements had broken down. They also indicated that contrary to earlier case law, it is not necessary to show that exceptional circumstances exist before a shared residence order may be granted, neither is it probably necessary to show a positive benefit to the child. However, the order must be in the interests of the child in accordance with s 1 CA 1989. They went on to say that while guidance from the Court of Appeal should be valuable to courts of first instance, they were still free to make the right decision in the interests of the children on the individual facts of each case. Here the children, over a number of years, had divided their time between their parents' homes, despite a high level of animosity between the parents. When the arrangements broke down the father applied for a shared residence order which was granted notwithstanding the hostility between the parties and with a view to attempt to lessen the animosity and help them co-operate better over the arrangements.

8.83

If such an order is to be refused on the grounds that it would be misused by one of the parents (for example in order to interfere in the other's life or to undermine the other), that conclusion should be supported by clear reasoning (see *Re P (children) (shared residence order)* [2005] EWCA Civ 1639, [2005] 2 FLR 347).

8.84

Where both parents have parental responsibility, there is arguably no need for both parents to have a 'lives with' order, even where the children are effectively sharing their time between the two homes.

8.85

Another possible use of a joint 'lives with' order is to enable parental responsibility to be given to a cohabitant who is not the natural parent of the child, but who has treated the child as a child of the family and wishes to continue to play a role on breakdown. In *Re H (shared residence: parental responsibility)* [1996] 3 FCR 321, the Court of Appeal stated that where there were circumstances which justified a shared residence order, then the fact that this would also confer parental responsibility on the 'step'-father was an additional ground for making the order. However, in *Re WB (minors) (residence orders)* [1995] 2 FLR 1023, Thorpe J held that a shared residence order would only be appropriate if the shared regime was most likely to promote the interests of the child. It was not appropriate where the sole purpose was to vest full parental responsibility on the stepfather, when in reality the child lived with the mother and had contact with the father. It should be noted though that CA 1989, s 4A provides for parental responsibility to be acquired by a step-parent, whether by order of the court or with the agreement of the parent(s) with parental responsibility. Where a female same-sex couple have children born into the relationship as a result of AID or other fertility treatment, on breakdown of that relationship child arrangements orders may be sought in order to create a legal relationship between the child and the non-resident partner, although under CA 1989, s 4ZA the second female parent can acquire parental responsibility by order of the court or under the terms of a parental responsibility agreement entered into with the child's mother. Although CA 1989, s 4ZA was only inserted into the Act on 6 April 2009 by the HFEA 2008, in *G v F (contact and shared residence)* [1998] 2 FLR 799 the practical parenting problems which arose on the breakdown of a same-sex relationship were dealt with sympathetically by the court which granted leave to apply for a shared residence (now, child arrangements 'lives with' orders in favour of more than one person) order to the 'social' parent.

8.86

The effect of granting each parent a 'lives with' order is that each parent will have or will acquire parental responsibility but cannot exercise it in a way that is incompatible with any conditions of that order or indeed any other orders made under the 1989 Act (s 2(8)). It should also be noted that such order specifically gives the right to remove the child from local authority accommodation under s 20 of the 1989 Act.

(iii) Without notice s 8 orders

8.87

The normal route to any form of 'lives with' order is an application on notice. This is underlined by the requirements of Article 6 of the European Convention on Human Rights, which guarantees a fair and public hearing and implies that there should be 'equality of arms' as between the parties. However, s 8 orders may be made without notice in emergency proceedings and under the inherent jurisdiction of the High Court (FPR 2010 r 12.16). If an order is made without notice, it is essential that the full application is before the court as soon as possible (see *Re J (children: ex parte orders)* [1997] 1 FLR 606 and *ND v KP* [2011] 2 FLR 662). The court should consider *inter alia* how significant such an order might be, eg will a without notice interim 'lives with' order cause the child's schooling (or other aspects of the status quo) to change?

(iv) Effects of a child arrangements ('lives with') order

8.88

Should a child's parents resume cohabitation for a continuous period exceeding six months, then any child arrangements order directing that the child 'lives with' one of them will lapse (CA 1989, s 11(5)). When a 'lives with' order is in force, no person may cause the child to become known by a different surname, or remove the child from the UK, without either the written consent of every person who has parental responsibility for the child, or leave of the court (s 13(1)). However, a parent named in a child arrangements order as being the parent with whom the child is to live may take the child out of the UK for a period of up to one month (s 13(2)) without consent or leave; and the court may grant leave for other proposed visits out of the UK, either generally or for specified periods or places, when making the order (s 13(3)). Opposition to holidays abroad by one parent (usually the non-resident parent) normally arises where it is feared that the children will not be returned to the jurisdiction.

8.89

However, in *Re S (leave to remove from jurisdiction: securing return from holiday)* [2001] 2 FLR 498 it was made clear that to prevent such a trip a parent must satisfy the court that there was a real risk of the children not being returned, which the father had not done in this case. Nevertheless, the court took the view that there was a need to safeguard the children's interests and their human rights by ensuring they would be returned from their proposed holiday to visit relatives in India, a country which is not a party to the abduction Conventions. The children were therefore made wards of court and the mother was required to provide the father with copies of the return airline tickets and only apply for tourist visas which she could not seek to extend; neither could she apply for Indian passports for the children. The orders were then served on the Indian High Commission and the Foreign and Commonwealth Office.

8.90

The requirements of s 13 apply to children of unmarried, as well as married, parents. Whilst holidays abroad for a period of up to one month where the child is to travel with the parent who has the 'lives with' order are possible, advisors might give thought to whether a blanket consent for all foreign trips of any length should be sought at the time the order is being made to prevent either having to get the permission of the other parent to travel or the prospect of an application from the other parent to prevent such.

8.91

Separate issues arise where, following separation, the resident parent wishes to take the child permanently out of the jurisdiction which is not permitted without leave of the court where a child arrangements ('lives with') order has been made. The removal of a child from the UK without the requisite permission or order is likely to amount to child abduction (see *Re W (minors) (abduction: father's rights), Re B (minors) (abduction; father's rights)* [1999] Fam 1, [1998] 2 FLR 146).

8.92

Removal cases are complex and particularly post-Human Rights Act, the courts must be seen to be balancing and protecting the right to family life of all family members. If the court were for example to elevate the weight it attaches to the reasonable proposals of the primary carer into a legal presumption (that leave would in those circumstances be granted unless the court concluded that it would be incompatible with the welfare of the child) this could amount to a breach of the respondent's rights not only under Article 8 (right to respect for family and private life), but also his rights under Article 6 (right to a fair trial) (see *Payne v Payne* [2001] EWCA Civ 166, [2001] 1 FLR 1052 and *K v K (relocation: shared care arrangement)* [2011] EWCA Civ 793, [2011] Fam Law 1078). In *Re A (permission to remove child from jurisdiction: human rights)* [2000] 2 FLR 225, a mother who wished to take up a new life in New York, where she believed she would be able to better pursue her musical career, was granted leave to take her 10-month-old child with her. The Court of Appeal confirmed the order despite the father's opposition and claim that it would breach Article 8 rights of both himself and his daughter in that they would effectively be denied contact with each other. It made clear that the Convention rights of the father and child had to be balanced against the mother's conflicting Article 8 right to private life and that the careful and conscientious balancing of these rights by the judge at first instance could not be challenged on Convention grounds in the Court of Appeal as this had been carried out in a way that was 'beyond attack'. The mother's wish to move away was reasonable. She did however give undertakings to litigate any issue relating to contact in the English courts, return the child to England at least twice a year and allow additional contact if she were in England in addition to facilitating e-mail and postal contact.

8.93

In another Court of Appeal decision, *Re C (leave to remove from jurisdiction)* [2000] 2 FLR 457, a mother was refused leave to remove her six-year-old from the jurisdiction to go and live in Singapore, the home of her new husband, who wished to practise medicine there. The trial judge had found that the mother's reasonable plans to go abroad were outweighed by the fact that a permanent move would severely limit the child's contact with her father, despite the effect this would have on the new family who would be separated. The Court of Appeal (with Thorpe LJ dissenting) felt it was not entitled to interfere with the decision of the judge who had heard all the evidence at first hand and had properly applied the law. The dissenting opinion of Thorpe LJ took the view that the risk of emotional harm to the child consequent upon the break-up of her new family unit had not been given proper weight.

8.94

In *Payne,* the Court of Appeal made it clear that there was no presumption in favour of the resident parent created by s 13(1)(b) CA 1989. Yet the reasonable proposals of the parent with a 'lives with' order wishing to live abroad will carry some weight. Such proposals must be carefully scrutinised and it must be clear that the motivation to relocate is genuine and not one intended primarily to terminate the child's contact with the other parent. All the considerations must be viewed in relation to the paramountcy principle (CA 1989, s 1(1)), which as the Court of Appeal reminded in *Re F (a child) (permission to relocate)* [2012] EWCA Civ 1364, [2013] 1 FLR 645 is the only principle to be applied when determining a relocation case. The effect upon the possible new family and the child is very important as is the effect of the denial of contact and the opportunity to continue contact notwithstanding the move may be critical, but the welfare of the child has to be the governing principle. It should also be noted that relocation by a parent within the UK may also be subject to challenge but the court will only in exceptional cases make a child arrangements ('lives with') order specifying where in the UK the applicant must live (see *Re H (residence order: relocation)* [2001] *The Times*, 29 August, discussed at para 8.115; *Re L (a child) (internal relocation: shared residence order)* [2009] EWCA Civ 20, [2009] 1 FCR 584).

8.95

Another aspect of these applications is the operation of the no order presumption. In *Re X and Y (leave to remove from jurisdiction: no order principle)* [2001] 2 FLR 118, heard just before *Payne,* this issue was considered in a case concerning cohabitants, where the mother wished to return to live near her family abroad. Here leave was granted and it was made clear that the court has to apply the welfare principle alongside the no order presumption having regard to the s 1(3) checklist.

8.96

In terms of the powers available to the courts to punish non-compliance with a 'lives with' order, since December 2008, CA 1989, ss 11J–11N (as inserted by the Children and Adoption Act 2006) provide for the making and monitoring of enforcement orders. An enforcement order imposes an 'unpaid work requirement' of between 40 and 200 hours on a person, where a child arrangements order has been made and the court is satisfied beyond a reasonable doubt that the person has failed to comply with it.

(c) Child arrangements ('spends time with') orders

8.97

Before 22 April 2014, a contact order required the parent (or other person) with whom the child was living to permit the child to visit or stay or otherwise have contact with the person named in the order. Contact orders have been replaced by child arrangements ('spends time with') orders, which regulate with whom and when a child is to spend time or otherwise have contact with any person. Although such orders will not be made automatically on relationship breakdown where both parents have parental responsibility, the Court of Appeal, in a decision that is still good law, made it clear that this does not entitle a parent to take a child away from their settled home or to refuse to return a child after a contact visit (see *Re B (minors) (residence order)* [1992] 3 All ER 867; *Re H (a minor) (interim custody)* [1991] 2 FLR 411). In practice, therefore, a non-resident parent with parental responsibility should be advised that the courts are likely to view such abuse of parental responsibility as tantamount to 'snatching', whatever their technical position in law.

8.98

Whilst the child is with a parent under the terms of a 'spends time with' order, if that parent does not also have parental responsibility, the parent may nevertheless do what is reasonable to promote or safeguard the welfare of the child (s 3(5)); a parent with parental responsibility may not do anything that is inconsistent with any child arrangements or other order under the Act (s 2(8)).

(i) The right of the child

8.99

The received wisdom of the old law that contact is the right of the child (a right which is underlined in the United Nations Convention on the Rights of the Child), rather than the right of the parent has been made clear in a number of cases (see eg *Re R (a minor) (contact)* [1993] 2 FLR 762). In *Re D (a minor) (contact: mother's hostility)* [1993] 2 FLR 1, Balcombe LJ stated at p 3:

> 'One starts with the premise that it is the child's right to know both its parents but there may be cases … where there are cogent reasons why the child should be denied that opportunity.'

8.100

Decisions in respect of applications for 'contact' are governed by the paramountcy principle. However, it is nearly always in the interests of children that they should have a continuing relationship with both parents (see *Re P (supervision)* [1996] 2 FLR 314 CA). Whilst there has not been a reversal of this position, there is an increased willingness by the court to take the effect of 'contact' on the resident parent into account particularly where there has been domestic violence (see *L, V, M, H (contact: domestic violence)* [2001] FAM 260, discussed further below and *Re T (a child: one parent killed by other parent)* [2012] Fam Law 125). Whereas previously mothers who objected to 'contact' were automatically seen as the villains and were castigated as 'implacably hostile', the courts are now encouraged to consider the validity of such hostility and perhaps require a positive change in the violent partner's behaviour prior to granting 'contact'. Whether or not it is in the child's interests to spend time or otherwise have contact with a parent has to be judged in accordance with the welfare principle and checklist where the application is opposed.

(ii) Implacable hostility to contact between child and a parent

8.101

Much case law has developed with regard to how the courts should deal with applications where the resident parent is hostile to 'contact'. Fear of violence is often the reason given by a mother who is alleged to be 'implacably hostile' to 'contact' but this term is used to cover a range of situations, as observed by Wilson LJ in *Re P (contact: discretion)* [1998] 2 FLR 696 (at 703), who said that 'it seems to me that a mother's hostility towards contact can arise in three different situations. The first is where there are no rational grounds for it. In such a case the court will be extremely slow to decline to order contact and will do so only if satisfied that an order in the teeth of the mother's hostility would create a serious risk of emotional harm for the child. The second is where the mother advances grounds for her hostility which the court regards as sufficiently potent to displace the presumption that contact is in the child's best interests. In that case the mother's hostility as such becomes largely irrelevant: what are relevant are its underlying grounds, which the court adopts. The third is where the mother advances sound arguments for the displacement of the presumption but where there are also sound arguments which run the other way. In such a situation, so it seems to me, the mother's hostility to contact can of itself be of importance, occasionally of determinative importance, provided, as always, that what is measured is its effect upon the child'.

8.102

In fact, following *Re L (contact: domestic violence); Re V (contact: domestic violence); Re M (contact: domestic violence); Re H (contact: domestic violence)* [2001] Fam 260 the Court of Appeal laid great store by the need to pay heed to expert evidence on the effect of contact with a violent parent on the resident parent victim and arguably such a principle may extend beyond cases involving violence where the deterioration of the resident parent's health and well-being will impact negatively upon the child.

8.103

This decision involved four appeals heard together in each of which the father had been violent to the child's mother and had been refused contact with their child at first instance. The Court of Appeal held that there was no presumption against contact where domestic violence was alleged or proved, but violence was one highly material factor which the court must consider in the balancing exercise required by the application of the welfare principle and the welfare checklist in s 1(1) and (3) CA 1989. It went on to say that in appropriate circumstances, it could offset the 'assumption' in favour of contact with the non-resident parent. Thus, there is some evidence of downgrading of the child's right to contact from a presumption to a lesser assumption. Furthermore, it made clear that courts needed to have a heightened awareness of the effect on children of being exposed to domestic violence by one parent against the other and allegations ought to be investigated and findings of fact made before the contact application is heard. Where interim contact is sought, the court should give particular consideration to the likely risk of harm if contact is granted or refused, and take steps to ensure the risk of harm is minimised and the safety of the child and the residential parent secured before, during and after contact. On hearing a contact application where there are such allegations, the court should consider the conduct of the parties towards each other and the child; the effect of contact on the child and the resident parent, and the motivation of the parent seeking contact.

8.104

Whilst domestic violence is not an absolute bar to 'contact', the court must be aware of the consequences for children of such domestic violence (see FPR 2010 PD 12J: Child Arrangements and Contact Order: Domestic Violence and Harm; FPR 2010 r 12B). In *Re V (a child)* [2015] EWCA Civ 274, [2015] 2 FLR 1472, McFarlane LJ reminded practitioners that 'the court must ascertain at the earliest opportunity whether domestic violence or abuse is raised as an issue of risk of harm to the child which is likely to be relevant to any decision of the court relating to the welfare of the child, and specifically on the making of any child arrangements order'.

8.105

The ability of the offending parent to recognise his past conduct, to be aware of the need to change and to make genuine efforts to do so is likely to be an important consideration. Recent cases have all reasserted that contact between a parent and child is a fundamental element of family life and is almost always in the interests of the child and should be terminated only in exceptional circumstances, where there are cogent reasons for doing so and where there is no alternative ie if it will be detrimental to the child's welfare (see *Re C (a child) (suspension of contact)* [2011] EWCA Civ 521, [2011] 2 FLR 912; *Q v Q* [2015] EWCA Civ 991, [2016] 2 FLR 287; *Re K (children) (contact: failure to consider alternative means)* [2016] EWCA Civ 99, [2016] Fam Law 440).

8.106

Another important issue is how the no order presumption in s 1(5) affects the willingness of the courts to make orders where the resident parent is implacably hostile to 'contact'. In *Re H (a minor) (parental responsibility)* [1993] 1 FLR 484, CA, and in *Re B (contact: stepfather's opposition)* [1997] 2 FLR 579, CA it was stated that it was not necessary to show positive benefit for the child before making a contact order, although in these cases the stepfather's threat to leave the mother and effectively abandon the child should a contact order be made, in fact forced the court not to make the contact order it would otherwise have made.

8.107

Overall, implacable hostility places advisors of both parties in difficult positions. However, whilst the courts' old certainty that contact is always in a child's best interests has gone, it is accepted that wherever possible continuing contact between a child and his parents after the parents' separation should be encouraged and supported, unless there is a good reason not to do so. Obviously, the father's behaviour towards the child and the mother and the effect on the child of such behaviour are likely to be critical. The marital status of the parents should not affect the court's decision and in practice this is largely the case.

(iii) Enforcement of child arrangements orders

8.108

In terms of the powers available to the courts to punish non-compliance with 'spends time with' orders, since December 2008, CA 1989, ss 11J–11N (as inserted by the Children and Adoption Act 2006) provide for the making and monitoring of enforcement orders. An enforcement order imposes an 'unpaid work requirement' of between 40 and 200 hours on a person, where a child arrangements order has been made and the court is satisfied beyond a reasonable doubt that the person has failed to comply with it. The application of the criminal standard of proof is consistent with the individual's Article 6 right to a fair trial in view of the unpaid work requirement sanction. The court will not make an enforcement order if it is satisfied (on the balance of probabilities) that the person who is alleged to have failed to comply with the child arrangements order had a reasonable excuse for doing so. As the Act is silent as to what constitutes 'a reasonable excuse', it has fallen to the courts to offer guidance in this regard. In *Re L-W (children) (contact: committal)* [2010] EWCA Civ 1253, [2011] 1 FCR 78, Munby LJ suggested that 'a typical case might be where a child suddenly falls ill and the defendant, reasonably in the circumstances, takes the child to the doctor rather than going to contact'.

8.109

The court must be satisfied that the making of an enforcement order is necessary to secure that person's compliance with the child arrangements order and that the likely effect of the proposed order is proportionate to the seriousness of the breach of the order. An enforcement order may be suspended by the court to give the person time to comply with the child arrangements order. If made, a Cafcass officer will be asked to monitor or to arrange the monitoring of the person's compliance with the unpaid work requirement imposed by the order and then to report to the court. Note that in making an enforcement order, the court is required by CA 1989, s 11L(7) to take into account the welfare of the child who is the subject of the child arrangements order, but not to make it the paramount consideration (as it is not being asked to determine a question with regard to the child's upbringing).

(iv) Interim orders

8.110

The court has power to make interim child arrangements orders pursuant to s 11(3) CA 1989. Guidance was offered in *Re D (contact: interim orders)* [1995] 1 FLR 495, which confirmed that caution should prevail where there are unresolved issues. This was reaffirmed by the need to be wary of granting interim contact in domestic violence cases and the need to ensure protection for mother and child as noted in *Re M (interim contact: domestic violence)* [2000] 2 FLR 377 and *Re L (contact: domestic violence); Re V (contact: domestic violence); Re M (contact: domestic violence); Re H (contact: domestic violence)* discussed above. Where the principle of 'contact' has been accepted, then an interim 'spends time with' order is likely to be appropriate. Where the principle of 'contact' is not agreed, then the welfare test must be applied and any interim order should not be made, unless the court has already had sufficient information to conclude that an interim order providing for the child to spend time or otherwise have contact with the applicant parent is in the child's interests. Normally, this would only arise after hearing oral evidence and having received a safeguarding letter or report from Cafcass suggesting that there are no concerns about the 'contact' proposed.

(v) Dismissing applications for a child arrangements order

8.111

A child's opposition to 'contact' may lead to an application being dismissed or no order being made. In *Re C (contact: no order for contact)* [2000] Fam Law 699, it was accepted that a child was terrified of his father and this justified an order prohibiting even indirect contact. Where a child is mature enough to make her own decisions, it has been accepted that there is little the law can do to force compliance with court orders defining 'contact' very specifically and thus a 'no order' may be appropriate (see eg *M v M (defined contact application)* [1998] 2 FLR 244). In circumstances in which the child is stating that they do not wish to have contact with a parent, the court must balance the harm of not having a relationship with that parent with the harm caused by forcing a child against their will. In *Re J-M (contact proceedings: balance of harm)* [2014] EWCA Civ 434, [2015] 1 FLR 838, the Court of Appeal upheld the lower court's decision to set aside an order for direct contact (and to substitute an order permitting indirect contact only) on the basis that to force the child to have contact against his expressed wishes would cause him harm.

8.112

When deciding such cases, the court must make it clear whether it is dismissing the application or making no order (*D v D (application for contact)* [1994] 1 FCR 694). If the court is to accept that there should be no order for contact due to disturbance to the mother and child, there should be direct evidence of the nature and extent of such a disturbance (see *Re S* [2015] EWCA Civ 689).

8.113

Even when courts feel that 'contact' is not appropriate, applications to dismiss contact should only be made where there are truly exceptional circumstances. CA 1989, s 91(14) provides that 'on disposing of any application for an order under this Act, the court may (whether or not it makes any other order in response to the application) order that no application for an order under this Act of any specified kind may be made with respect to the child concerned by any person named in the order without leave of the court'. In *Re F (minors) (contact: restraint order)* [1995] 1 FLR 956, Waite LJ stated that a s 91(14) order is 'principally appropriate where there is a real fear that children may become distressed or have their stability disturbed through the vexatious, ill-judged or obsessive pursuit by a party of the litigious process.' Thorpe LJ in *Re C (litigant in person: s 91(14) order)* [2009] EWCA Civ 674 cautioned that the 'making of these orders should always be exceptional and careful consideration in every case should be given to the duration of the order to see that by unnecessary extension it did not prejudice rights of access to the court'.

(vi) Other issues

8.114

Child arrangements ('spends time with') orders will not of course be made in relation to parents both of whom have secured 'lives with' orders in respect of their child, whose care is being shared between them. As with 'lives with' orders, 'spends time with' orders cease to have effect if the child's parents live together for a period of more than six months. Clients should be advised that if a reconciliation takes place, the whole procedure for securing child arrangements orders will have to be gone through again should the reconciliation last for more than six months but prove not to be permanent.

(d) Conditions on child arrangements orders

8.115

Section 11(7) permits the court to both give directions on how a child arrangements order is to be carried into effect and also to impose conditions which must be complied with by specified persons (s 11(7)(b)). This needs also to be considered in the light of s 10(5) which provides that specific issue and prohibited steps orders should not be made with a view to achieving a result which could be achieved by making a child arrangements order. Case law has developed which has shed some light on the sort of conditions that can legitimately be imposed and the inter-relationship of the four different s 8 orders. In an exceptional case where the welfare of the child demanded such an approach, a condition could be attached to a child arrangements order to prevent the resident parent's relocation to another part of the UK with the child where the proposed change of residence would consequently so reduce contact between the child and the non-resident parent as to be harmful to the child's welfare (see *Re H (children) (residence order: condition)* [2001] EWCA Civ 1338, [2001] 2 FLR 1277; *B v B (residence: condition limiting geographic area)* [2004] 2 FLR 979). It should be noted though that the Court of Appeal in *Re G (contact)* [2006] EWCA Civ 1507, [2007] 1 FLR 1663 held that an order requiring the child to attend a school which was 40 miles away from where he and his mother lived imposed a completely unrealistic condition on the residence *('lives with')* order made in the mother's favour. There is no power to impose conditions which effectively order parents to have contact with each other (*Croydon London Borough Council v A* [1992] 2 FLR 341), but conversely it may be appropriate to impose a condition designed to keep the parents apart and so minimise the risk of confrontation between them eg arrangements for third party handover of children.

8.116

Where a court is considering making an order providing for indirect contact between the child and his parent, it can include in the child arrangements order wide conditions aimed at effectively ensuring and facilitating that contact (see *Re D (children)* [2016] EWCA Civ 89, [2016] 1 FCR 545). In *Re M (a minor) (contact: conditions)* [1994] 1 FLR 272, FD, the court considered it appropriate to grant an unmarried father serving a prison sentence contact by post with his two-and-a half-year-old child, despite the child not really knowing his father, the father's violence towards the mother and his imprisonment for robbery, burglary and theft. With regard to the imposition of conditions, Wall J felt that whilst there was possibly jurisdiction to order the mother to implement contact by reading the letters to a child who could not read provided the mother agreed, an order compelling the mother to read the contents of any letter could not stand and had to be subject to a right of censorship. The view was taken that the court could not by virtue of s 11(7) order the mother to write progress reports, as this would effectively order contact between the parents. It was felt that indirect contact should be carefully drawn to define the number of letters and phone calls.

8.117

In *Re O (contact: imposition of conditions)* [1995] 2 FLR 124, however, the Court of Appeal examined the ambit of s 11(7). At first instance the judge made an order for indirect contact requiring the mother to send photographs of the child every three months, copies of all nursery reports, information about serious illness and to accept delivery of cards and presents for the child through the post, to read and show the child any communication and give him any presents. The mother appealed upon the basis that the court did not have jurisdiction to make such an order, relying on the dicta in *Re M (a minor) (contact: conditions)* (above). However, her appeal failed and the court took the opportunity to set out the principles involved:

- as contact was usually in the child's interests, indirect contact should be ordered where direct contact was not appropriate, so that the child could grow up knowing the absent parent. The court did have powers to enforce contact;
- s 11(7) gives the court a wide discretion which is not subject to limitation and it did not accept propositions based upon *Re M (a minor) (contact: conditions)* (above) that the court could not impose positive obligations such as reading letters to the child or providing transport or travel costs for direct contact. It was reasonable to require the mother to read the letters and this should not be subject to any right of censorship;
- the court should not automatically define the indirect contact by prescribing a number of letters to be sent; and
- the court has ample power to compel one parent to send photographs, school and medical reports in order to promote meaningful contact between father and child and in a proper case could compel the mother to write reports.

8.118

CA 1989, ss 11A–11G (as inserted into the Act by s 1 of the Children and Adoption Act 2006) give power to the courts to make activity directions and activity conditions aimed at promoting and strengthening the relationships between a child and his parents when considering the making or varying of a child arrangements order. An activity direction or condition requires an individual who is a party to the proceedings concerned to take part in an activity that would, in the court's opinion, help to establish, maintain or improve the involvement in the life of the child concerned of (a) that individual, or (b) another individual who is a party to the proceedings. There does not have to be a dispute regarding the child arrangements for an activity condition to be made, but the court can only make an activity direction if 'there is a dispute as regards the provision about the matter that the court is considering whether to make in the proceedings'.

8.119

By ss 11A(5) and 11C(5), the activities that may be required to be undertaken include, in particular:

(a) programmes, classes and counselling or guidance sessions of a kind that may assist a person as regards establishing, maintaining or improving involvement in a child's life or which may, by addressing a person's violent behaviour, enable or facilitate involvement in a child's life (ie 'contact'); and

(b) sessions in which information or advice is given as regards making or operating arrangements for involvement in a child's life, including making arrangements by means of mediation.

An activity direction or condition cannot be used however to require a person to take part in mediation or to undergo medical or psychiatric examination, assessment or treatment.

8.120

Whenever a court makes or varies a child arrangements order, it must attach a 'warning notice', warning the parents of consequences of failing to comply with that order, which may be an enforcement order as discussed above (under s 11J), a financial compensation order (under s 11O) or the use of the court's existing sanctions for contempt (including committal to prison) (see *Re A (a child) (intractable contact dispute)* [2013] EWCA Civ 1104, [2013] 3 FCR 257).

(e) Prohibited steps orders, specific issue orders and wardship

8.121

The two remaining s 8 orders are defined as follows:

> '"*a prohibited steps order*" means an order that no step which could be taken by a parent in meeting his parental responsibility for a child, and which is of a kind specified in the order, shall be taken by any person without the consent of the court;
>
> "*a specific issue order*" means an order giving directions for the purpose of determining a specific question which has arisen, or which may arise, in connection with any aspect of parental responsibility for a child.'

8.122

One of the aims in introducing these orders was, according to the Law Commission, to incorporate into the statutory code the most valuable features of the wardship jurisdiction (see Law Com No 172, 4.20). The definitions of the two orders allow the court to give negative and positive directions to any person in relation to the exercise of aspects of parental responsibility. Thus it can prohibit a person without parental responsibility from doing any act which could be done by a person with parental responsibility. For example, an unmarried father without parental responsibility could, it seems, be prevented from contacting the child's school even though, strictly, this is an act that only a parent with parental responsibility should do. Wardship, however, has not been abolished but recourse to wardship has been considerably reduced although it remains available for use by individuals, in contrast to local authorities whose use of the inherent jurisdiction has been severely curtailed.

8.123

In wardship, parental responsibility is vested in the court, so that no important step can be taken in relation to the child without leave of the court. Although there is no general embargo as in wardship, by using these two orders the court can define matters upon which it wishes to be consulted before action is taken. This can be achieved by imposing a prohibited steps order and/or giving directions on any matter in dispute by means of a specific issue order.

8.124

Although neither of these orders should be imposed with a view to achieving a result which could be obtained by making a child arrangements order (s 9(5)(a)), they may be made where no such order is being sought. A prohibited steps order could be made preventing the child being taken out of the UK in a case where no child arrangements order has been made regulating with whom the child is to live and therefore the automatic restrictions imposed by s 13 do not apply (see *SH v MM and RM (prohibited steps order; abduction)* [2011] EWHC 3314 (Fam), [2012] 1 FLR 837). A specific issue order could be made in relation to the appropriate schooling or religious education for a child where there is no agreement between the parents (see *Re P (parental dispute: judicial determination)* [2001] EWCA Civ 1627, [2003] 1 FLR 286). These orders can also be made supplemental to child arrangements orders and can be applied for not only by parents but by any other person eligible to apply for a s 8 order pursuant to s 10(2), although they may need leave of the court to make the application.

8.125

Section 11(7) enables the court to impose conditions when making a s 8 order on, *inter alia*, any person who is named in the order as a person with whom the child concerned is to live, spend time or otherwise have contact, any parent or person with parental responsibility, and to 'make such incidental, supplemental or consequential provision as the court thinks fit'. It is difficult to think of a wider discretion for attaching conditions, and where a child arrangements order is being made, almost any result desired by the making of a prohibited steps or specific issue order, could probably also be achieved by attaching conditions to the child arrangements order and thus separate orders need not be made – in line with s 9(5). These orders are therefore most likely to be sought other than in the context of relationship breakdown, or possibly where disputes arise some time after breakdown, when the child arrangements issues have already been resolved. Case law has now shed some light on both the ambit of the orders and when it is inappropriate to make them.

8.126

In *Nottinghamshire County Council v P* [1994] FAM 18, the Court of Appeal confirmed that an application for a prohibited steps order by a local authority that a father should vacate the household and have no contact save under local authority supervision could not be made as it contravened s 9(5) and was in fact seeking disguised residence and no contact orders. In *Re H (prohibited steps order)* [1995] 1 FLR 638, the local authority sought to prevent the mother's cohabitant, who was not a party to the proceedings but whom they now suspected of abusing children, from having contact with them. The Court of Appeal held that a prohibited steps order against the mother, preventing her allowing the cohabitant contact, amounted to a 'no contact' order and offended s 9(5). However, it took the view that a prohibited steps order be made against the cohabitant even though he was not a party to the proceedings, provided he was given liberty to apply (s 11(7)(d)).

8.127

A prohibited steps order cannot be used to prevent contact between parents, as it does not relate to parental responsibility (*Croydon London Borough Council v A* [1992] 2 FLR 341). Similarly, it cannot be used to restrain one parent from assaulting another (*M v M (residence order: ancillary jurisdiction)* [1994] Fam Law 440), or to oust one parent from the family home eg to prohibit a married father spending time with his child by staying overnight at the matrimonial home (see *D v D (ouster order)* [1996] 2 FCR 496, *CA; Re K (a child) (contact: ouster injunction)* [2011] EWCA Civ 1075, [2012] 1 FCR 89).

8.128

In *Re B (minors) (residence orders)* [1992] 3 All ER 867, it was held that a specific issue order requiring the return of a child after a 'snatch' was inappropriate in view of s 9(5) as the same result could be achieved by a residence order with appropriate directions and conditions attached pursuant to s 11(7). In *Re HG (specific issue) (sterilisation)* [1993] 1 FLR 587, it was confirmed that provided there was a question to be answered, there did not have to be a dispute between the parties before a specific issue order could be made.

8.129

Like a prohibited steps order, a specific issue order may be made on its own or together with a child arrangements order. Its scope is broad. A specific issue order may be made to determine whether a child should attend a local state school or a private school (see *Re A (specific issue order: parental dispute)* [2001] 1 FLR 121, *CA; M v M (specific issue: choice of school)* [2005] EWHC 2769 (Fam),

[2005] 1 FLR 251); whether a child should attend a school in England or abroad (see *M v H (a child) (educational welfare)* [2008] EWHC 324 (Fam), [2008] 1 FLR 1400); or what his surname should be (see *G v A (children: surname)* [1995] 2 FCR 223n, *Re T (change of surname)* [1998] 2 FLR 620, CA, *Re C (change of surname)* [1998] 2 FLR 656, CA). In *Re C (a child) (HIV test)* [2001] Fam 48, the Court of Appeal endorsed a specific issue order requiring a baby to undergo an HIV test against her parents' wishes.

8.130

The court can again make these orders of its own volition in any 'family proceedings' (s 10(1)). Section 100(2) essentially prohibits the court using the wardship jurisdiction for the purpose of placing a child in the care or under the supervision of a local authority, or in relation to a child already in care. Neither can it be used to confer on a local authority power to determine any question relating to parental responsibility for a child. Thus specific issue and prohibited steps orders cannot be used to circumvent the deliberate restriction of a local authority's powers in this regard. It should also be noted that no local authority may seek to invoke the wardship jurisdiction without leave of the court (s 100(3)), ensuring that authorities are largely confined to the powers specified in Parts III and IV of the Act relating to care proceedings and emergency protection of children – matters outside the scope of this book.

8.131

Where a child is not in care, however, wardship remains an option both for parents and non-parents in relation to specific matters concerning the child's upbringing. The prohibitive cost does not make this an easy option, but one advantage where a non-parent is seeking the assistance of the court is that no application for leave will be required in order to ward the child. As regards matters between parents themselves, s 8 orders may be applied for without leave, and in most cases, there need be no thought of wardship proceedings. It should be noted, however, that even though there is no restriction on wardship proceedings being issued by private individuals, and that this offers a uniquely speedy form of protection which may be of particular importance in child abduction situations, wardship proceedings should not be allowed to continue where the statutory framework provided by the CA 1989 is just as effective. In *Re T (a minor) (child representation)* [1994] Fam 49, it was held that, where possible, application should be made under CA 1989 rather than in wardship. The court may under its inherent jurisdiction, in addition to all of the orders available to it in family proceedings including s 8 orders, make a wide range of injunctions for the child's protection, including orders to restrain publicity, prevent an undesirable association, to protect abducted children and to order the return of children to and from another jurisdiction (see FPR 2010 PD 12D para 1.2 and *Re B (a child) (removal from jurisdiction: removal of family's passports as coercive measure)* [2014] EWCA 843, [2015] 1 FCR, *sub nom Re B (a child: evidence: passport order)* [2015] 1 FLR 871).

8.132

In practice, therefore, it seems that the wardship probably has greatest value when dealing with child abduction, although other situations where the court's overall control could have advantages include the management of a child's property in the event of their parents' death. A useful discussion of the use of wardship and the court's wider inherent jurisdiction can be found in White *et al, The Children Act in Practice*, 2nd edition, 1995, Butterworths, pp 267–283.

(f) Duration of s 8 orders

8.133

As noted above, interim s 8 orders may be made as the Act states that where the court has power to make such an order it may do so regardless of the fact that it is not in a position finally to dispose of the proceedings (s 11(3)). Thus an order can be made until the date of the next hearing or a specified event (see also s 11(7)(c)).

8.134

It has also been seen that child arrangements orders cease upon the child's parents resuming cohabitation for a continuous period of more than six months (s 11(6)). Section 9(6) provides that no court shall make a s 8 order (other than a child arrangements ('lives with') order) which will continue to be effective after the child is 16 unless it is satisfied that the circumstances are exceptional. Thus normally s 8 orders will be expressed to continue until the child attains the age of 16. After this, the *Gillick* principle, that young people of this age are well able to make up their own minds on these issues, comes into play under the Act. Section 9(7) goes on to say that no s 8 order, other than one varying or discharging an existing order shall be made in relation to a child who is already 16 unless the court is satisfied that the circumstances are exceptional. It is thought that exceptional circumstances would certainly include a child who is mentally handicapped, for example. Similarly, where unorthodox medical treatment with potentially serious repercussions is being considered for or by a 17-year-old, it may still be appropriate to make a specific issue order.

8.135

Where a s 8 order does continue in respect of a child beyond the age of 16, it shall then cease on the child's reaching the age of 18 (s 91(11)). If a care order is made in respect of a child, this automatically discharges any s 8 orders relating to the child (s 91(2)).

(g) Directions and conditions

8.136

In proceedings where the question of making a s 8 order arises, the court must draw up a timetable with a view to determining the question, and give appropriate directions to ensure adherence to that timetable (s 11(1)). Rules of court specify appropriate periods for particular steps. The court may give directions of its own motion or on written (or oral if urgent) request subject to certain procedural requirements (FPR 2010 Part 12). As noted above, the court is given very wide discretion, when making s 8 orders to impose conditions on any parent or person with parental responsibility or with whom the child lives (see s 11(7)). The wide ambit of this provision has been confirmed by the courts in *Re B (a minor) (residence order)* [1992] Fam 162, CA and *Re O (contact) (imposition of conditions)* (above). Further, as discussed above, ss 11A–11G provide for the making of activity directions and activity conditions.

6 Appointment of guardians, parental responsibility and child arrangements ('lives with') orders

8.137

The interrelation of parental responsibility and child arrangements orders has already been canvassed both in this chapter (see paras 8.78 ff) and in Chapter 2. It should be noted that, once a child arrangements order has been made, where the non-resident parent retains parental responsibility, this does not postpone the effectiveness of the appointment by the resident parent of a testamentary guardian in the event of death (s 5(7)). However, the guardian would have parental responsibility jointly with the surviving non-resident parent. Any appointment of a testamentary guardian by a parent where the surviving parent has parental responsibility and no child arrangements ('lives with') order has been made, or where a no child arrangements ('lives with') order has been made in favour of the deceased parent and the surviving parent jointly, will not take effect until after the death of the surviving parent.

7 Family assistance orders

8.138

CA 1989, s 16 gives the court power in any family proceedings, where the court has power to make a s 8 order and regardless of whether or not it does make such an order, to make a family assistance order requiring a Cafcass officer or local authority officer to advise, assist and (where appropriate) befriend any person named in the order. Such orders can be made only where the court is satisfied that the circumstances are exceptional and where every party named in the order, other than the child, consents.

8.139

Such orders may require a person named in the order to keep the officer informed of the address of any person named in the order and to allow them to visit. An order will last for a maximum of 12 months. It enables the officer to refer to the court the question of a variation or discharge of a subsisting s 8 order (s 16(6)). For the officer's powers and duties, see FPR 2010, 16.38 and Practice Direction 16A, Part 8. If the order is to be in force at the same time as a child arrangements ('spends time with') order in respect of the child, the order may direct the officer concerned to give advice and assistance as regards establishing, improving and maintaining contact with such of the persons named in the order as may be specified (s 16(4A)).

8.140

It is perhaps surprising that the consent of older children is not required before such an order is made, but to assist the court, before making a family assistance order, the (oral or written) opinion of the appropriate officer about whether it would be in the best interests of the child for such order to be made, and if so, how the order could operate and for what period must be sought. Advisors should be aware that clients do not have to consent to these orders, although it may be that the consequence of refusing to consent will be for welfare reports to be ordered if this has not already been done and the appropriate local authority applying for a supervision or care order pursuant to s 31, following a direction from the court to investigate the child's circumstances pursuant to its power under s 27.

8.141

Before making an order, the court must give any person whom it proposes to be named in the order an opportunity to comment upon the opinion given by the officer (see Practice Direction: Family Assistance Orders: Consultation [2007] 2 FLR 626). In practice, family assistance orders have been little used. They cannot be misused, so as to provide an indirect way of providing someone to accompany a child to visit his father in prison (*S v P (contact application: family assistance order)* [1997] 2 FCR 185, but one was appropriate to assist a child and her grandparents, with whom it was decided the child should reside, to establish a new life together (*Re U (application to free for adoption)* [1993] 2 FLR 992). They can also be a good means of involving the local authority in the supervision of contact (see *Leeds City Council v C* [1993] 1 FLR 269). One important difficulty with the order, however, came to light in *Re C (a minor) (family assistance order)* [1996] 1 FLR 424, FD. Here the court was in effect unable to compel a local authority to comply with a family assistance order where they claimed they had inadequate resources so to do. A local authority officer can only be appointed if the local authority agrees or the child lives or will live within the local authority's area (s 16(7)).

8 Welfare reports

8.142

CA 1989, s 7 gives the court power of its own motion, and at its absolute discretion (see *Re W (welfare reports: appeals)* [1995] 2 FLR 142, CA) when considering any question with respect to a child under the Act, to seek welfare reports from a Cafcass officer or a local authority on specified matters relating to the welfare of the child (see FPR 2010, r 12.6(d)). In *Re K (contact: psychiatric report)* [1996] 1 FCR 474, CA, it was held that the court had no power to order a local authority to instruct a child psychiatrist to provide a report under s 7(1)(b)(ii) and parties should either have been invited jointly to instruct such an expert or RSC Order 40 had to be invoked.

8.143

On referral the courts are asked to specify the areas of concern to be reported on and the reasons for requiring a report. Reports are usually ordered to be filed with the court and copies served on (the solicitors for) the parents within eight weeks or so. There are occasions when more time is required and also when a report is required more urgently by the court. Cafcass officers are set targets by the Ministry of Justice with regard to the timing and filing of reports. For 2015/16, the target for the completion and filing of s 7 reports by the agreed date was 97%. Cafcass achieved 98.8%.

9 Jurisdiction and procedure

8.144

By virtue of s 92 of the Act, the Family Court and High Court have concurrent jurisdiction in proceedings under the Act.

8.145

The procedure applicable in relation to Children Act proceedings in both courts is now almost uniform, but the majority of family proceedings are now heard in the Family Court (which since April 2014 has brought together into one single court structure the family jurisdiction of the county court and magistrates' courts). Where both the Family Court and High Court have jurisdiction, the proceedings must be commenced in the Family Court (unless there are related proceedings in the High Court or any rule, enactment or practice direction otherwise requires or the court otherwise directs) (FPR 2010, r 5.4).

8.146

Cases in the Family Court can be allocated to judges of the High Court (sitting in the Family Court), circuit judges, district judges and lay justices (aka magistrates) – see the Family Court (Composition and Distribution of Business) Rules 2014, SI 2014/840.

8.147

The FPR 2010 provide for the transfer of proceedings between the High Court and Family Court (r 29.17), for the movement of cases in the Family Court between different areas (r 29.18) and for the allocation of cases to different levels of judge in the Family Court (r 29.19).

8.148

Proceedings are issued by completing the appropriate form. Where there are no family proceedings in existence, then applications for free-standing s 8 orders and parental responsibility orders are all made on Form C100. Where there are existing family proceedings, then the application is on Form C2. In the unmarried context, unless another party has already issued proceedings, or a separate issue has arisen within ongoing proceedings, then the first application will be made on Form C100. There is now only one form per family, although in addition to the court giving a court reference number to the case. Form C1 is also used where leave to apply is required unless another party has already issued proceedings in respect of the child.

8.149

No supporting statement is necessary as the application form requires fairly detailed information about the applicant, the child, the child's family and the respondent. Service on the respondent, giving notice of the hearing (provided by the court on Form C6), is required as specified in the rules and is now effected in all cases by the applicant, not by the court. It should be noted that in urgent cases applications for all s 8 orders may now be made *without notice* (FPR 2010, r 12.16 and see *Re G* [1993] 1 FLR 910; *Re P* [1993] 1 FLR 915). Within 48 hours of the without notice order being made, the applicant is required to serve a copy of the application and of the order on each respondent (r 12.16(4) and (5)).

8.150

Any further evidence can be filed in the form of a statement which is signed and dated by the maker and contains a declaration by him or her that the contents of the statement are believed to be true and that it is understood that the statement may be placed before the court. The respondent must file an acknowledgement of service to the application, within the period specified by the rules, on the appropriate form where there is one. In the case of s 8 proceedings, the period is 14 days of service and the appropriate form is Form C7. An answer may (but need not now) be filed by the respondent and must be served at least two clear days prior to the hearing date.

8.151

The initial court hearing in respect of the s 8 application is the First Hearing Dispute Resolution Appointment (FHDRA) at which a timetable for the case will be set (CA 1989, s 11(1)) and consideration will be given to any necessary directions including for a welfare report (FPR 2010 PD 12B, para 14.13). Save in urgent cases, when the FHDRA should take place within four weeks, it will ordinarily be listed during the fifth week after issue (FPR PD 12B, para 14.1). Initial child protection/safety checks and inquiries are made by Cafcass prior to the FHDRA by which date it is required to file with the court and to send to each party/parent a safeguarding letter setting out the results of the initial checks (FPR 2010 PD 12B, para 13.1).

8.152

Where a person requires leave to apply for an order under the Act, a written request setting out the reasons for the application should be made to the court, and a draft of the appropriate substantive application form, with sufficient copies for service, should be filed. The court then considers whether or not to grant leave immediately; if so, the applicant is notified and the matter proceeds. If the court cannot grant leave immediately, it must fix a date for the hearing of the application and notify the applicant and other appropriate persons.

10 Appeals

8.153

It is well established that the appeal courts will not interfere with the decisions of the court of first instance unless the reasoning can be shown to be plainly wrong (see *G v G (minors) (custody appeal)* [1985] FLR 894, HL). An appeal against a decision of the court may lie to the Family Court, the High Court or the Court of Appeal depending on the level of judicial decision maker. FPR 2010 PD 30A confirms that an appeal from a family bench (of two or three magistrates or lay justices), justices clerk, deputy district judge and district judge (including of the Central Family Court) is to a Circuit Judge; from a district judge of the High Court to a High Court Judge; from a Circuit Judge to a High Court Judge; and from a High Court Judge to the Court of Appeal.

8.154

Permission to appeal is required (FPR 2010, r 30.3(1)). Note that in the case *Re W; Re A; Re B (change of name)* [2001] FAM 1 the Court of Appeal held that the test to be applied by the appellate court in children cases should be in accordance with the principles established in the case of *G v G (minors) (custody appeal)* [1985] FLR 894.

8.155

Notice of Appeal must be filed and served within 21 days of the decision, or such other time ordered by the judge (FPR 2010, r 30.4(2)) and served not later than seven days after filing (FPR 2010, r 30.4(4)).

CHAPTER 9

Financial provision for children

1 Introduction

9.01

Financial Provision for children continues to be dominated by the child support legislation which was fundamentally amended yet again by the Child Maintenance and Other Payments Act 2008 and the subsequent Child Support Maintenance Calculation Regulations 2012 (MC Regulations 2012). Since 25 November 2013, the Child Maintenance Service (CMS) is the sole statutory body dealing with new child maintenance cases, as the Child Support Agency (CSA) is due to formally close in 2018 as cases decided by it either come to an end or are phased into the CMS. Thus, in this chapter, the focus is on the powers and functions of the CMS but will also include relevant provisions relating to the CSA in respect of cases still covered under it.

9.02

The aim of the Child Support Act 1991 (CSA 1991) was to take over entirely from the courts the role of assessing, collecting and enforcing maintenance payments for children. It was intended to ensure that as many as possible of the non-resident parents who were not paying maintenance or making any other provision for their children would under the terms of this Act be made to contribute towards the upkeep of their children, especially where those children and their carers were being supported by the state through the benefits system. Thus, the CSA 1991, with its formulaic approach to the assessment of maintenance for children ousts the court's jurisdiction in most cases where the parent with care has applied for a maintenance calculation.

9.03

The current provisions for financial relief for children in unmarried families, other than child support maintenance, are to be found in s 15 and Schedule 1 CA 1989 and will be discussed in greater detail later in this chapter. Schedule 1 is not restricted to financial relief for children on the breakdown of unmarried relationships. However, given the continuation of the relevant provisions of the MCA 1973, in particular enabling orders for financial relief for children of married families to be made under more generous criteria, the schedule is mostly used by unmarried parents and is certainly of great importance to them, as it provides the only means for them to obtain final orders for financial provision for their children.

9.04

Before the advent of the Child Support Acts, it was possible to deal with the issues of child maintenance and other financial provision for children as a global package which the court could assess using its powers under Sch 1 CA 1989. However, now, whilst the issue of child maintenance is, in most cases, outside the jurisdiction of the court, it remains negotiable as between the parties. Thus, the starting point where periodical maintenance for children of unmarried parents is sought must be to determine, first, whether the CMS has jurisdiction; and, secondly, what issues, if any, lie to be determined by the courts under Sch 1 CA 1989. In the unmarried context, where all the applications for financial provision can only be for the benefit of the child, the division of child maintenance from other forms of financial provision makes the process of settling issues between the parties particularly fragmented and cumbersome. Although it is possible for parents to reach either voluntary agreements about child maintenance, it is not possible to agree to oust the jurisdiction of the CSA 1991.

Preliminary issue

Does the CMS or the court have jurisdiction?

9.05

A child support calculation is bound to have consequences for any other financial provision being sought for a child on relationship breakdown under Sch 1 CA 1989 and this calculation will often be the advisor's starting point.

9.06

The CMS has jurisdiction to undertake a maintenance calculation where the parent with care of the child, the non-resident parent and the child are all habitually resident in the UK. It should be noted that where the non-resident parent is habitually resident overseas but is a member of the Diplomatic or Overseas Civil Services, Armed Forces or the employee of a company registered in the UK the CMS still retains jurisdiction.

9.07

Section 8(3) CSA 1991 makes clear that where the CMS has jurisdiction, the general powers of the courts to make child maintenance orders are suspended, although they retain a residual jurisdiction in some circumstances.

9.08

Broadly the court retains its powers to make orders in relation to financial provision for children where:

(i) either or both parents habitually reside abroad (save as at 9.06 above);

(ii) maintenance over and above the maintenance calculation is required by the parent with care (ie 'top-up' cases) (CSA 1991, s 8(6));

(iii) the children aged 18 or over are receiving education or training or where there are special circumstances (eg the child is disabled) (CSA 1991, ss 8(7) and 8(8));

(iv) a school fees order is sought;

(v) a lump sum, transfer or settlement of property or secured periodical payments is sought.

2 Child Maintenance

9.09

The powers of the CMS derive from s 83 CSA 1991. Before making an application to the CMS the parent with care must first contact Child Maintenance Options (see guidance at www.cmoptions.org; at the time of writing its contact numbers were 0800 0835 130 and 0800 988 0988). CSA 1991, s 2 provides that in making a determination/maintenance calculation the CMS must have regard to the welfare of any child likely to be affected by the decision. The obligation under this 'welfare of the child' principle is to 'have regard' rather than to give priority or paramount consideration to the child's welfare (see *R v Secretary of State for Social Security, ex p Biggin* [1995] 1 FLR 851 in which case it was held that welfare is not paramount or even particularly significant). It is not just the subject child whose welfare is to be considered. Regard must also be had to the effect of a decision on the children of the non-resident parent in a different family (see *R (on the application of Joplin) v Child Maintenance and Enforcement Commission* [2010] EWHC 1623 Civ, [2010] 2 FLR 1510 and *Brookes v DWP* [2010] EWCA Civ 420, [2010] 3 FCR 262 although in both these cases the welfare of the children in the non-resident parent's household was held to be subsidiary to the need to enforce child maintenance liabilities).

9.10

The CSA 1991 introduced a new vocabulary into the world of child maintenance. The Act applies only to 'qualifying' children; the qualification being that one or both parents are non-resident parents. A child is defined as being under 16, or aged between 16 and 20 if in full time non-advanced education or training (CSA 1991, s 55(1) and MC Regulations 2012, reg 76). A child is a 'qualifying child' if, in relation to that child, one or both parents are non-resident parents (CSA 1991, s 3(1) and see *Child Maintenance Enforcement Commission v NC* [2009] UKUT 106 (AAC), [2010] 2 FLR 1812). A 'non-resident parent' is one who does not live in the same household with the child, where the child has his or her home with the parent with care. The parent with care provides the day-to-day care for the child. Child maintenance, calculated in accordance with the child support legislation, must be paid by the child's non-resident parent(s) in respect of their qualifying child or children, and this is the only recognised way of discharging their duty to maintain their child (CSA 1991, s 1(2)). A 'relevant other child' is a child in the household of the non-resident parent (CSA 1991, Sch 1, para 10C as amended).

(a) Making an application

9.11

As at the date of writing, application forms for a maintenance calculation could be obtained from Child Maintenance Options (which can be contacted on 0800 0835 130 and an adviser will give a reference number and explain how to apply if that is the decision ultimately made). An application for a maintenance calculation is deemed to be made on the date on which it is received provided it complied with any requirements as to form (MC Regulations 2012, reg 9) and (if applicable) the application fee is paid.

(b) Maintenance calculation

9.12

Unless it decides not to make a calculation the CMS will decide whether any child maintenance is payable and if so how much (CSA 1991, s 11(2)). The amount is calculated by reference to the non-resident parent's gross income, with the primary evidence of such gross income being sought directly from HMRC (MC Regulations 2012, regs 35 and 36), although a non-resident parent in receipt of income support may be treated as having no assessable income (CSA 1991, s 11(6), Sch 1). A maintenance calculation continues until a child support officer sets it aside, reviews it, cancels it or decides that it should cease to have effect or on the death of either parent, the death or adoption of any qualifying child or where the parents (as in the parent with care and the non-resident parent) live together for a continuous period of six months (CSA 1991, Sch 1 para 16(1)). An accidental error in any decision can be corrected at any time by a child support officer and notice given to the applicant/parent with care and the paying party/the non-resident parent (MC Regulations 2012, reg 27 A).

9.13

If the gross (pre-tax) income of the non-resident parent (the paying party) exceeds £156,000 per annum the applicant is entitled to apply to the court for a top-up (CSA 1991, s 8(6)). The court in that instance must be satisfied that the circumstances of the case make it appropriate for there to be additional maintenance paid. Previously excluded sources of income (eg from the Territorial Army) are now included and students previously exempt from paying child maintenance are now liable. Pension contributions continue to be deducted in the calculation of income.

9.14

The main difference in the calculation of child maintenance by the CSA and CMS is that the CSA would calculate the maintenance payable as a percentage of the non-resident parent's NET weekly income as follows:

(i) 15% for one qualifying child;

(ii) 20% for two qualifying children; and

(iii) 25% for three or more qualifying children.

9.15

Where the non-resident parent had one or more relevant other children (ie he/she had one or more children who lived in his/her household as their main home) the following percentage reduction applied to the non-resident parent's *net* weekly income before the percentage calculation for the qualifying children was carried out:

(i) 15% for one qualifying child;

(ii) 20% for two qualifying children; and

(iii) 25% for three or more qualifying children.

9.16

The CMS calculates maintenance on the *gross* income of the non-resident parent as follows:

(i) 12% for one qualifying child;

(ii) 16% for two qualifying children; and

(iii) 19% for three or more qualifying children,

with a tapered additional sum payable where the non-resident parent's income exceeds £800 per week of the following corresponding percentages of such income over £800 per week (9%, 12% and 15%).

9.17

Where the non-resident parent has other children resident in his/her household then the gross weekly income is reduced prior to the appropriate percentage calculation being made by the following amounts:

(i) 11% where there is one relevant other child;

(ii) 14% where there are two relevant other children; and

(iii) 16% where there are three or more relevant other children.

9.18

Under both CMS and CSA where the qualifying child or children spend nights with the non-resident parent then a decrease in maintenance payable will apply. If a child has overnight stays with the non-resident parent one or two nights per week the reduction in maintenance payable is one-seventh; if a child spends more than two nights but less than three nights per week the reduction is two-sevenths. Over three nights per week but less than one-seventh nights per annum the reduction is three-sevenths and more than one-seventh nights per annum the reduction is one half (MC Regulations 2012, Regulations 46 and 47). Where care is shared equally between the parents no child support maintenance is payable (MC Regulations 2012, Regulation 50).

(c) Default maintenance calculations

9.19

Default maintenance calculations are imposed where there is insufficient data to undertake a maintenance calculation and are prescribed as being £39 per week where there is one qualifying child, £51 per week where there are two qualifying children and £64 per week where there are three or more qualifying children (MC Regulations 2012, reg 49).

(d) Flat rate and reduced rate maintenance

9.20

Non-resident parents in receipt of welfare benefits (or gross income of less than £100 per week) pay a flat rate of £7 per week (MC Regulations 2012, reg 44 and CSA 1991, Sch 1, Part 1, para 4). Reduced rate maintenance is payable where a parent's gross weekly income is between £100 to £200, being the flat rate of £7 together with an uplift calculated by reference to a table within the MC Regulations 2012 (reg 43).

(e) Who can apply for a child maintenance calculation?

9.21

CSA 1991, s 4 permits either the non-resident parent or the parent with care (but not the child) to voluntarily apply for a maintenance calculation in respect of a child. If an application is made the CMS is obliged to carry out a maintenance calculation. A s 4 application can be withdrawn at any time before the calculation is made.

(f) The effective date

9.22

The date on which the maintenance calculation becomes effective is the date on which written notification of the application was sent to the non-resident parent (MC Regulations 2012, regs 11 and 12).

(g) Revisions

9.23

Any decision by the CMS in respect of a maintenance calculation may be revised (CSA 1991, s 16(1A)), the parent requesting the review having to do so within 30 days of the date of the letter informing him or her of the decision or such longer time as may be permitted and must tell the CMS why the decision should be reviewed (MC Regulations 2012, regs 14 and 15). There is scope to revise a decision on grounds of non- or under disclosure, official error or a relevant paternity decision (MC Regulations 2012, reg 14). Any decision to revise the maintenance calculation will be deemed to have effect from the date on which the original decision was to take effect (CSA 1991, s 16(3)).

(h) Supersessions

9.24

An alternative route to change a calculation exists by way of supersession of the decision (MC Regulations 2012, regs 17–18). Supersession is the method to deal with changes in circumstances that have arisen after a calculation has been made. The earlier decision can be superseded by the CMS of its own initiative or further to an application made by either the parent with care or the non-resident parent.

(i) Reviews

9.25

An annual review takes place by reference to updated income information from HMRC/Inland Revenue (MC Regulations 2012, reg 19) but if there is a change in circumstances during the year it is subject to a 25% tolerance (ie the change in the maintenance calculation will need to be at least 25%) for any alterations to be made (MC Regulations 2012, reg 23).

(j) Variations

9.26

Either parent is able to apply to the CMS to make a variation to the maintenance calculation to take account of the following special expenses (see CSA 1991, Sch 4B, para 2(2)):

(i) contact costs including any present and reasonably foreseeable future costs of travel and accommodation incurred or to be incurred in respect of such contact by the non-resident parent with his child and the costs of another person accompanying either the non-resident parent or child to such contact and whose presence is considered to be necessary (MC Regulations 2012, reg 63);

(ii) costs necessarily incurred by the non-resident parent due to the long-term illness or disability of a relevant other child (MC Regulations 2012, reg 64);

(iii) the repayment of debts incurred before the parents separated incurred for the joint benefit of both parents or of the child (apart from where the non-resident parent has retained the asset in relation to which that debt was incurred or if it is a gambling debt, a fine, a credit card debt or business debt or other such borrowing) (MC Regulations 2012, reg 65);

(iv) the maintenance element of boarding school fees (although the maximum amount by which the non-resident parent's income could be reduced to take account of such payments is 50% of his net weekly income) (MC Regulations 2012, reg 66); and

(v) payments in respect of certain mortgages, loans or insurance policies made directly in relation to a home where the parent with care and the child still live if the non-resident parent retains no interest in that home (or endowment policy) (MC Regulations 2012, reg 67).

9.27

To be taken into account for the purposes of para 2(2) of Schedule 4B to the 1991 Act the expenses so incurred must be equal or exceed £10 per week.

9.28

Unearned income of the non-resident parent equal to or exceeding £2,500 per annum will be taken into account by the CMS when considering a variation to the maintenance calculation. Unearned income will include (rental) income from property, interest on savings and dividends (MC Regulations 2012, reg 69).

9.29

If the non-resident parent is assessed as paying a nil or flat rate but the CMS is satisfied that there is additional income of £100 or more per week available to or received by the non-resident parent a variation of the maintenance calculation can also then be made (MC Regulations 2012, reg 70).

9.30

If the non-resident parent deliberately diverts his income to another person or persons or opts to receive benefits in kind in lieu of income, the whole of the amount by which the CMS is satisfied that the non-resident parent has reduced his income by will be taken into account in respect of the assessment of his gross income (ie will be added back) and in these circumstances a variation to the maintenance calculation may be likely (MC Regulations 2012, reg 71). Where the making by the non-resident parent of excessive payments of pension contributions is alleged to be a deliberate diversion of income, anecdotally it appears that the CMS will tolerate up to about 20% of gross income being paid to pension contributions before considering an 'add back'.

(k) Investigative powers of the CMS

9.31

In order to make a maintenance calculation, the CMS will need to gather information about the means of the non-resident parent and by regulations, principally, the Child Support Information Regulations 2008, it has been given far-reaching powers to assist it in the collecting of the necessary information, including access to information held by the DWP, local authorities and the Inland Revenue for the purpose of tracing and assessing the means of non-resident parents, and ascertaining their habitual residence. Other information that can be required and which the provider is under a duty to disclose varies as between the different informants (reg 3 for the applicant and reg 4 for other persons including the employer or former employer of either parent or carer, and officers of the court where there has been a maintenance order made in respect of the child). Information relating to a paternity dispute may be obtained from a relevant court. A person is guilty of an offence if, following a request for information, he makes a statement or representation which he knows to be false or provides, or knowingly causes or allows to be provided, a document or other information which he knows to be false (CSA 1991, s 14A(1)). On conviction, the person will be liable to a fine and the principal sanction in respect of the non-resident parent is the possibility of a default maintenance calculation.

9.32

Furthermore, s 15 gives inspectors wide powers to enter specified premises and to question people over 18, including employers. They may enter specified premises other than a dwelling house at reasonable times and may question the employer, employees or an occupier of the premises who must furnish the inspector with all information and documents 'as the inspector may reasonably require'. A person does not have to disclose information that may incriminate him/her or his/her spouse or civil partner (CSA 1991, s 15(7)).

9.33

However, it is a criminal offence to intentionally delay or obstruct an inspector or refuse or neglect without reasonable excuse to answer questions or furnish information when required to do so (CSA 1991, s 15(9)). For example, an employer must not hinder or impede or in any other way prevent the inspector from interviewing the non-resident parent/employee.

9.34

These powers do little to address the practical difficulties traditionally faced by the courts in extracting information from the self-employed, although the wider powers of search now extend to premises which are not exclusively residential and where it is believed a non-resident parent carries on a trade, business or profession or where it is believed that information is held about the non-resident parent's trade, business or profession (CSA 1991, s 15(4A)). Nonetheless, it seems that this category of non-resident parent remains problematic for the CMS.

(l) Enforcement

9.35

After the maintenance calculation has been made, a non-resident parent will be instructed how to make the payments, eg by standing order (see s 29). The CMS is empowered to make a 'deduction from earnings order', directed to the liable person's employer instructing him to make deductions from earnings and to pay them directly to the CMS. This order is made by the CMS and not by the court under CSA 1991, s 31. This order can be made before any arrears of payments have accrued (CSA 1991, s 31(3)). The first 60% of the paying parents' income is protected.

9.36

Where a payment has been missed the CMS may (having considered the child's welfare) by CSA 991, s 33 apply to a magistrates' court for a liability order against the liable person if it is considered that a deduction from earnings order has been ineffective or would be inappropriate (eg if the non-resident parent is self-employed) (see *Law v Inostroza Ahumuda* [2010] EWCA Civ 1149, [2011] 1 FLR 708). The magistrates have no power to question the maintenance calculation but are able to determine whether the non-resident parent is liable to pay it at all (see *Farley v Secretary of State for Work & Pensions (1)* [2005] EWCA Civ 778, [2005] 3 FCR 327). Liability orders can be enforced in the same way as county court judgments by way of a third-party debt order or charging order.

9.37

The ultimate sanction for non-payment of maintenance is committal to prison for a maximum of six weeks or disqualification from driving for a maximum period of two years (CSA 1991, ss 39A, 40 and 40B), but only if the court is of the opinion that there has been wilful or culpable neglect on the part of the liable person (CSA 1991, s 40(3), (7)). The disqualification order can be suspended or it can be used to prevent the obtaining of a licence where none is held but in either case must be revoked when the outstanding maintenance is paid in full. If payment has not been made by the end of the disqualification period, a further period can be imposed.

(m) Charging and fees

9.38

Since 11 August 2014, by virtue of the Child Support Fees Regulations 2014, fees are payable to the CMS for collecting and paying out child maintenance as follows:

(i) an application fee of £20 which can be exempted if the applicant is under 19 or is a victim of domestic violence (regs 3 and 4);

(ii) parents with care will be charged 4% (by way of deduction from the child support maintenance due) to use the collection service (regs 7 and 8);

(iii) non-resident parents will be charged a 20% fee for having maintenance paid through the collection service (although this payment may be deducted from the payments made through the collection service) (regs 7 and 8); and

(iv) fees will apply in respect of enforcement of the maintenance calculation – £50 where a deduction from earnings order/request or regular deduction order is made, £200 where a lump sum deduction order is made and £300 where a liability order is made (reg 10).

(n) *Maintenance agreements or family-based arrangements*

9.39

It is not necessary to contact either the CMS or indeed the court in order to make a voluntary maintenance agreement (CSA 1991, s 9(1)). Family-based arrangements are child maintenance agreements which parents have agreed between themselves. CSA 1991, s 9(2) defines such agreements as 'any agreement for the making, or for securing the making, of periodical payments by way of maintenance to or for the benefit of any child'. The CSA 1991 has always encouraged parents to make agreements about maintenance for their children and the Child Maintenance and Other Payments Act 2008, s 2 reiterated and enforced this statutory objective to 'encourage and support the making and keeping by parents of appropriate voluntary maintenance arrangements for their children'.

9.40

A family-based arrangement may be a quick confidential and cost-efficient method of resolving child maintenance issues enabling flexibility if circumstances change. However, there are obvious risks to the parent with care as a voluntary agreement is not of itself enforceable although it may be capable of being converted into a court order (CSA 1991, s 8(5)). The Children Act 1989, Sch 1, paras 10–11 permits the court to vary or alter the terms of a maintenance agreement made between parents of a child.

9.41

A template for a family-based arrangement which was at the date of writing available from child maintenance options at www.cmoptions.org.

3 Orders for financial provision under Sch 1 CA 1989

9.42

All forms of financial provision for children of unmarried parents other than child maintenance (save for cases that fall outside the jurisdiction of the CMS) are contained in Sch 1 CA 1989.

9.43

All paragraph numbers cited in this section refer to Sch 1 CA 1989. Paragraph 1(2) lists the orders available as follows:

'(a) an order requiring either or both parents of a child—

(i) to make to the applicant for the benefit of the child; or

(ii) to make to the child himself, such periodical payments, for such term, as may be specified in the order;

(b) an order requiring either or both parents of a child—

(i) to secure to the applicant for the benefit of the child; or

(ii) to secure to the child himself, such periodical payments, for such term, as may be specified in the order;

(c) an order requiring either or both parents of a child—

(i) to pay to the applicant for the benefit of the child; or

(ii) to pay to the child himself, such lump sum as may be so specified;

(d) an order requiring a settlement to be made for the benefit of the child, and to the satisfaction of the court, of property—

(i) to which either parent is entitled (either in possession or reversion); and

(ii) which is specified in the order;

(e) an order requiring either or both parents of a child—

(i) to transfer to the applicant for the benefit of the child; or

(ii) to transfer to the child himself, such property to which the parent is entitled (either in possession or reversion) as may be specified in the order.'

9.44

In addition, para 2 of the Schedule provides for applications to be made by a person over 18 for periodical payments or a lump sum order, providing the applicant's parents are not living together in the same household and the applicant did not have the benefit of a periodical payments order in force when he or she reached the age of 16. Surprisingly, no specific reference is made excluding those children who have the benefit of a child maintenance calculation made by CMS at the age of 16 (see s 2(6)), although it would seem unlikely that an application for periodical payments in such circumstances would prove successful, as in any event the calculation will expire after the child's 16th birthday or his 19th birthday if in full-time secondary education. Orders in respect of children over the age of 18 would be appropriate only where the child is or will be undergoing education or training, or where there are other special circumstances which justify the making of an order.

9.45

Paragraph 6 permits the variation or discharge, including the temporary suspension, of an order for secured or unsecured periodical payments. Whilst interim periodical payments orders (and any appropriate directions which the court thinks fit) may be made pursuant to para 9, such orders will only be made where the CMS have no jurisdiction, or where there is substantial wealth, clearly justifying 'top-up' maintenance. On variation or discharge of an order under paras 1 or 2, the court has power at that stage to capitalise the periodical payments and to order the paying parent to pay a lump sum (para 5(3)).

9.46

Subject to s 8(3) CSA 1991, orders for periodical payments can be made for any appropriate amount as decided by the court having taken into account the matters set out in para 4. These factors (see para 9.59) must be considered in relation to any application made under paras 1 and 2 and are also referred to in relation to applications for variation and discharge. In practice, periodical payments will only be made where the CMS does not have jurisdiction or where the court's supplemental jurisdiction may be called upon pursuant to s 8(6)–(8) CSA 1991. Holman J in *Dickson v Rennie* [2014] EWHC 4306 (Fam) held that the court's power to order top-up maintenance is only available where the CMS has assessed that the payer's income exceeds the maximum maintenance assessment of £3,000 gross per week. Accordingly, where top-up maintenance is applied for under s 8(6), the applicant will first have to show that there has been a child maintenance calculation and that the paying parent's annual income exceeds £104,000 net (CSA cases) or £156,000 gross (CMS cases) (see CSA 1991, s 8(6)(b) and CA 1989, Sch 1, para 10(3) as amended and para 9.66). They then have to satisfy the court that it is appropriate in all the circumstances for further maintenance to be paid by the non-resident parent. The dominating factors here would be the needs of the child and the means of the parents as compared with the size of the assessment. The court would then have to decide the additional sum to be paid in accordance with the criteria set out in para 4 CA 1989 (discussed below). It should be noted that the court has the power (under para 1(1)) to order secured periodical payments.

9.47

Section 8(7) enables the court to award additional educational expenses (ie to make school fees orders), regardless of whether there is a child maintenance calculation in existence or not, for a child of 18 or under for the sole purpose of meeting the cost of the education or training being undertaken at an 'educational establishment'. This is not limited to school fees and would cover all other expenses directly attributable to the education or training. Nor is it restricted to 'recognised educational establishments'. The criteria in para 4 would then be applied to the application. Section 8(8) provides that where a child is disabled (defined in s 8(9)), additional periodical payments may be ordered to meet some or all the expenses directly attributable to the disability. Again, a child maintenance calculation is not a pre-requisite, and the para 4 criteria would be applied where a periodical payments order for this purpose was made or secured under para 1(2)(a) or (b). As noted in *C v F (disabled child: maintenance orders)* [1998] 2 FLR 1 such an order can, unlike a child support maintenance calculation, extend beyond the child's 19th birthday.

9.48

Lump sum orders under paras 1 and 2 may be made in consideration of liabilities or expenses reasonably incurred before the making of the order in connection with the birth or in maintaining the child (para 5(1)). Thus if a court feels a lump sum should be made in respect of a child's future needs under para 1(2)(c), and in addition accepts that expenses have been incurred in maintaining the child prior to the application, this sum may be added to the former. This situation is most likely to arise where the parties have not been cohabiting and thus such earlier expenses have not been shared or met by the paying parent. In *Phillips v Peace* [1996] 2 FLR 230, a lump sum of some £24,500 was ordered to be paid by the father in respect of such expenses and to furnish a home for the child. In *V v V (child maintenance)* [2001] 2 FLR 799, the Court of Appeal ordered lump sums of £21,000 and £29,000 for two children whose father would not agree to the level of periodic maintenance the court felt appropriate by means of a written agreement order. In *J v C (child: financial provision)* [1999] 1 FLR 152, the child's parents separated when the mother was pregnant. Some two years later the father won over a million pounds on the national lottery. The mother's application for a substantial lump sum to enable the child to be brought up in a manner which reflected the father's new-found wealth, including living in a four-bedroomed house and a car in which the child could be driven around, was granted by Hale J. There is no restriction on what can be applied for eg for funds to buy a car to take the child to school or to transport them to activities, to buy a musical instrument for the child or even to invest to pay for future school fees (see *Tracey v Tracey* [2006] EWCA Civ 734, [2006] 2 FCR 481). There is no limit on the number of lump sum applications that can be made before the child attains the age of 18 (CA 1989, Sch 1, para 1(5)) and thus where circumstances change a further application is now possible in appropriate circumstances.

9.49

The court can also order the lump sum to be paid by instalments, and has power to vary such an order, to change the number of instalments or the amount payable in respect of any instalment and also the date on which any instalment is payable. The total amount of the lump sum cannot be varied (see sub-paras 5(5) and (6)).

9.50

Whilst the court will not make an order for the outright transfer or settlement of a property on a child (see *Lilford v Glynn* [1979] 1 All ER 441, [1979] Fam Law 81, CA), orders under Sch 1 can be expressed to remain in force for the benefit of the child until the child is 17 or completes full time (tertiary) education (usually limited to first degree level) whichever is the later (see *T v S* [1994] 1 FCR 743).

9.51

Settlement of property may require specialist advice, including advice on the tax implications, which is outside the scope of this book, although the possibility of settlement of the family home will be considered. Broadly, the same considerations apply as for children of married parents in divorce proceedings, subject to some significant differences apparent in the drafting of Sch 1 discussed below. Settlements will generally be appropriate where there are substantial assets available for the benefit of the child. Only one application for a settlement or transfer of property order may be made against the same person in respect of the same child (CA 1989, Sch 1, para 1(5)(b)).

9.52

However, where property which was the family home is owned solely by one parent who is not to be the resident parent following breakdown, settlement of the property for the benefit of a child until the age of 18 or some other appropriate event, rather than transfer of the property to the resident parent for the benefit of the child which could lead to persons other than the child and the resident parent benefiting, is likely to be more appropriate. Settlements, on unmarried relationship breakdown where there is no duty to make provision for the resident parent, may be more frequently used in relation to families of less substantial means to ensure that the child is adequately housed during his minority whilst preserving the interest of the non-resident parent to be realised at some future date. This may also be appropriate where both parents have contributed to the purchase of the home and both have legal and/or equitable interests in the property, but it is not possible to achieve a clean break.

9.53

Such case law as there is certainly favours settlements rather than outright transfers of property for the benefit of the child. In *A v A (financial provision)* [1994] 1 FLR 657, FD the father was enormously wealthy and a property had been bought as a home for the mother and child in the name of an offshore company. However, the mother's application for outright transfer to her of the property for the benefit of the child was rejected and a settlement of the home for the benefit of the child on trust to terminate six months after she reached 18 or finished her full-time tertiary education was ordered instead. In *T v S (financial provision for children)* [1994] 2 FLR 883, FD a sum was ordered to be used to buy a small property to provide a home for the five children of former cohabitants and at first instance this was to be held on trust until the youngest child reached 21 and thereafter to be divided equally between the children. On appeal, the court varied the terms of the trust to secure the reversion for the father, as it was not appropriate either for the children to benefit as adults, or for the mother to be the recipient of an indirect windfall. Thus, at the end of the term, the property (or the relevant portion of it) is returned to the respondent unless special circumstances apply and as referred to above extreme wealth is not such a circumstance (see *T v T* [2007] EWHC 883 (Fam)). Disability or other special needs might be.

9.54

The above-mentioned decisions make it clear that settlements of property which revert to the non-resident parent once the child reaches financial independence are the proper form of provision even in cases involving substantial assets. The same applies where a sum of money is settled on trust to provide housing for a child. Thus, in *J v C (child: financial provision)* (above), a case which usefully reviews all the authorities, it was ordered that £70,000 of the father's lottery winnings should be settled on trust to provide a house for the child, her mother and her two half-sisters to live in until the child reached 21 or six months after the end of her full-time education, whichever was the later. The property was to revert thereafter to the father, but subject to an option for the mother to buy at the open market price. Such a settlement offered some protection to the mother by allowing the trust to endure until the child reached 21, rather than just 18 and also provided an option to buy at the end of this period, although if she were unable to find the open market price at that stage, she would have to return to a humbler abode.

9.55

The court has power to order the transfer of *any* property to which the parents are entitled, to either the applicant, who will usually be the other parent, for the benefit of the child; or to the child him/herself. 'Property' includes both real and personal property and the court can order, for example, the transfer of stocks and shares. The transfer of property provision may therefore conceivably be used where there is an unresolved dispute relating to personal property vested jointly in the parents (such as shares or even a building society or bank account) which the court can order should be transferred to the resident parent for the benefit of the child.

9.56

Another potential use of Sch 1 transfer of property orders is in applications for a transfer of a rented tenancy. In *K v K (minors: property transfer)* [1992] 2 FLR 220, the Court of Appeal held that a transfer of property order for the benefit of a child pursuant to para 1(2)(e) was not limited to cases where a financial benefit was to be conferred on the child. Accordingly, a secure tenancy could be transferred in this way, although the court remitted the matter back to the county court for consideration of the implications of the father's lost potential 'right to buy' discount. However, this remedy has been rather overtaken by the arguably superior transfer of tenancy order available to cohabitants on relationship breakdown introduced by s 53 and Sch 7 Family Law Act 1996, although itself subject to practical difficulties in some circumstances as discussed in Chapter 10.

9.57

Orders may be made against any legal parent of the child (para 1(2)). This includes a step-parent where one of the natural parents of a child is or was married to each other (para 16(2)).

9.58

As discussed, the court has enormous power and discretion to make both maintenance (in specific circumstances) and capital orders for the benefit of the child, but as no part of the financial provision afforded by the order is to provide any direct benefit and separate benefit for the resident parent (eg enabling her to make savings out of periodical payments or to retain the unused balance of any lump sum payment made for school fees or expenses) such orders can leave the resident parent at a huge financial disadvantage. In *Re P (a child) (financial provision)* [2003] 2 FLR 865, Thorpe LJ took the opportunity to make some key observations that all those advising parties in this area would do well to keep in mind. When considering income provision, he made clear that '... a more generous approach to the calculation of the mother's allowance is not only permissible but also realistic' and although 'there can be no slack to enable the recipient to fund a pension or an endowment policy or put money away for a rainy day' the mother should have 'control of a budget that reflects her position and the position of the father, both social and financial'.

Whether as Parliament reviews the law relating to unmarried co-habitants this will be addressed remains to be seen.

4 Criteria for making orders under Sch 1 CA 1989

9.59

CA 1989, Sch 1, para 4(1) lists the matters to which the court must give consideration when making, varying or discharging orders for financial provision for a child, prefaced by the indication that the court shall have regard to all the circumstances of the case. These considerations can be summarised as follows:

(i) the income, earning capacity, property and other financial resources which each parent has or is likely to have in the foreseeable future;

(ii) the financial needs, obligations and responsibilities which each parent has or is likely to have in the foreseeable future;

(iii) the financial needs of the child;

(iv) the income, earning capacity (if any), property and other financial resources of the child;

(v) any physical or mental disability of the child;

(vi) the manner in which the child was being, or was expected to be, educated or trained.

9.60

Where it is envisaged that an order is to be made against a non-parent (which means a step-parent in this context (see para 16(2)), then additional considerations apply (see para 4(2)). However, this is unlikely to affect the unmarried family directly, as marriage is the mechanism by which an adult becomes a stepparent.

9.61

The criteria can be seen to owe a great deal to s 25 MCA 1973, although important distinctions remain. First, para 4 does not require the welfare of the child to be the 'first consideration' as is specifically stated in s 25 MCA 1973. Although the court must take the child's welfare into account as a part of 'all the circumstances of the case', this is not the first consideration, simply one of the factors to be taken into account. The general welfare principle does not apply to applications for financial provision as they do not concern the upbringing of the child (s 105(1) and see also *B v B (transfer of tenancy)* [1994] Fam Law 250). When considering the child's welfare, in *Re P (a child) (financial provision)* [2003] 2 FLR 865, Thorpe LJ commented that 'welfare must be not just "one of the relevant circumstances" but, in the generality of cases, a constant influence on the discretionary outcome.' '*All the circumstances*' includes the standard of living enjoyed by the child prior to his parents' separation (see *Re MM* [2014] EWCA Civ 276) and conduct that it would be inequitable to disregard (see *O v P (No 2) (Sch 1 Application: Stay: Forum Non Conveniens)* [2014] EWHC 2255, [2015] 2 FLR 77 in which case the father was convicted of incitement to murder the mother).

9.62

Thus it is open to the court to give greater priority to, say, a father's difficult financial position than to the benefit to the child of remaining in a home which happens to be a property owned solely by the father. There is clearly scope for orders to be less generous than those made on divorce, partly of course because the court will not usually be dealing with a maintenance application for the resident parent, as there is no provision for the maintenance of cohabitants by each other. However, in *A v A* (above), Ward J stated at page 659H:

> 'A purposive interpretation of the Act leads to the conclusion that the claims of children whose parents are unmarried should be dealt with in similar manner to the claims of children where the parents are or were married. I remain of that view, notwithstanding the fact that there are some differences between the Matrimonial Causes Act 1973 and Schedule 1 Children Act 1989.'

9.63

This factor could in some circumstances benefit a child, as it will leave the departing parent with more disposable income than if he or she also had a duty to maintain the former partner. In any event, the financial position of the wealthy non-resident parent is likely to be very influential in terms of the award made. In *H v P (illegitimate child: capital provision)* [1993] Fam Law 515 (Wandsworth County Court), it was stated that the child was entitled to be brought up in circumstances which had some sort of relationship with the father's resources. In *A v A* (above), where the father was immensely wealthy, the court felt that the fact that the father had been paying large sums in maintenance 'set some standard'. Again, in *J v C (child: financial provision)* [1999] 1 FLR 152, Hale J concluded that the child's standard of living should reflect that of her millionaire father. The generosity of approach envisaged by the Court of Appeal in *Re P* (above) has been taken up by subsequent judges. Singer J in *F v G (child: financial provision)* [2005] 1 FLR 261 was faced with a young child, a working applicant mother and a wealthy respondent father. In keeping with *Re P* he awarded generous provision, both as to capital and income.

9.64

Another distinction is that any future earning capacity the court feels either parent could reasonably be expected to take steps to acquire is not expressed to be a factor, in contrast with the MCA provisions. However, the financial needs and resources that either party is likely to have in the foreseeable future are express and fundamental criteria. It is significant that the resident parent's financial needs, as well as those of the child, form part of the express criteria. Obviously, care of the child will affect a resident parent's earning capacity, which raises the question of whether financial provision made under the Sch 1 could contain an element for the resident parent.

9.65

It is now accepted that a child's financial needs include a need to be cared for by a person who is, generally and financially, in a position to provide that care, enabling the resident parent's needs to be taken into account (see *Re P* (above), *A v A (a minor)* [1995] 1 FLR 657 and *Haroutunian v Jennings* (1977) 1 FLR 62, FD). The words 'for the benefit of the child' are given wide meaning (see *Re S (Child: Financial Provision)* [2004] EWCA Civ 1685, [2005] 2 FLR 94 and *M-T v M-T* [2006] EWHC 2494 (Fam), [2007] 2 FLR 925). Thus, maintenance for a child could properly include a proper sum towards the services rendered by the mother to that child (a *carer's allowance*). Likewise, providing a home for a child will inevitably and necessarily involve providing a home for the primary carer/resident parent and any half-siblings of the child. Thus, in *A v A*, whilst it was thought that this approach may be restricted to the unusual facts of this case where the father led a precarious life and his residence outside the jurisdiction would prevent a claim under the I(PFD) Act 1975 in the event of his death, this attitude was echoed in case of *J v C* (above), although perhaps the fortuitous way in which the previously penniless father had won his fortune may have influenced the outcome. Hale J's judgment marked a turning point in the way in which the courts dealt with capital applications under Sch 1 CA 1989 and applied the relevant criteria. It was made clear that the circumstances surrounding the child's birth and the poor quality of the parents' relationship (where the parties had never cohabited and the father had denied paternity which was subsequently confirmed) were not matters of great weight in this context. The child's welfare, whilst not paramount or the first consideration under Sch 1, must be one of the relevant circumstances to be taken into account when assessing whether and how to order financial provision. Where the father, as here, had sufficient resources for all of his children, the provision for this child should not be reduced because the mothers of his other children had not sought to make any claim on their behalf. Importantly, the concept of reasonable requirements was said to be as appropriate to considering the financial needs of a child as it would be in the case of a spouse. Such requirements clearly included the need for a carer and in turn the carer's needs (which here included the need to accommodate her other children) must be taken into account. Another important point made was that the fact that the father acquired his assets after relationship breakdown, was irrelevant and the child was entitled to be brought up in circumstances bearing some sort of relationship with the father's current resources. So lottery winners, beware!

9.66

Nonetheless, the lack of willingness by the courts to capitalise the contribution towards services rendered by the mother, combined with child maintenance considerations and the jurisdiction of the CMS, means that it will only be in cases where the absent parent is very wealthy, as in *A v A* (above) and *J v C* (above), that an element included in maintenance to recognise the carer's financial needs and services rendered will be visible. The child maintenance calculation itself does currently contain an element reflecting the carer's costs and thus thinking is consistent in this respect at least. The lack of any statutory direction to achieve a 'clean break'-style settlement and the inability of the courts to make any express adjustment between the adult parties under the same legislation, in contrast to the position in the matrimonial context, makes it highly unlikely that the approach taken by the courts in Sch 1 cases to date will change in the absence of new legislation. In fact, post-*White v White* [2000] 2 FLR 981, the gulf between the settlements of the married as opposed to the cohabiting on relationship breakdown has widened.

5 Applicants and venue

9.67

Either parent or a guardian of a child, or any person in whose favour a child arrangements ('lives with') order has been granted may apply for the financial provision set out in Sch 1, para 1 of the CA 1989. This is subject, of course, to the child maintenance legislation in the case of periodical payments, as discussed above. FPR 2010, 9.11 enables those entitled to apply for 'lives with' orders and the child himself, with permission, to apply for a financial remedy under Sch 1. An application is made on Form A1 to either the Family Court (although lay justices are not permitted to hear Sch 1 cases) or the High Court. FPR 2010, r 3 and PD 3A requires the applicant before making an application to attend a Mediation Information and Assessment Meeting (MIAM), subject to exceptions.

9.68

In addition, when making, varying or discharging a 'lives with' order, the court may exercise any of its powers under Sch 1, even though no application has been made for financial provision for the child (Sch 1, para 1(6)) and thus the court can decide to look at the financial needs of the child at this stage of its own motion. The impact of this provision has been lessened since the CMS (subject to exceptions) assumed jurisdiction for child maintenance issues, although it is still possible for the court to order a lump sum. However, if the court is minded to do this it must ensure that it indicates its intention to the parties and has adequate findings of fact upon which to properly consider the criteria in para 4 to the Schedule (see *Re C* [1994] 2 FCR 1122, FD).

9.69

As was noted above, para 2 permits a person over 18 whose parents are not living together in the same household to apply for periodical payments and a lump sum order in special circumstances. The time limits and criteria for making such an application are discussed below.

9.70

Where it is known at the outset that a small lump sum only can be obtained, then an application to the Family Court will be most appropriate. Consideration should also be given to whether any other relief, such as an occupation order under the Part IV Family Law Act 1996, is to be sought which might also make the Family Court the most appropriate forum.

9.71

Where either or both parents own a property and where there are contemplated concurrent proceedings relating to a dispute between the parents under s 14 of the Trusts of Land and Appointment of Trustees Act 1996 (TLATA 1996), it may be advantageous for both sets of proceedings to be consolidated. This might also be appropriate where there is an application under s 53 and Sch 7 FLA 1996 for a transfer of tenancy order. Consolidation enables the issues relating to the respective interests in the property and the financial provision appropriate for the child to be looked at in the round. This is the nearest unmarried parents can come to having their own financial situation and those of their children dealt with in the same manner as divorcing parents.

6 Time for applying and duration of orders

9.72

The court may exercise its powers to make any of the orders under the schedule at any time whilst the child is under the age of 18, although normally an order for periodical payments, whether or not secured, will not be made to extend beyond the child's 17th birthday. An extension beyond this is possible if it appears to the court that the child will continue beyond that time in full-time education or training (whether or not in gainful employment), or there are other special circumstances, such as a physical or mental handicap. Generally, though, there are no specific time limits in which an application for financial provision for the benefit of the child must be made, providing it is made before the child becomes of age.

9.73

In para 2 there is provision for separate applications for periodical payments and/or lump sum orders by persons over 18 who remain in full-time education or training for a trade, profession or vocation, or where there are other special circumstances. However, this applies only where a periodical payments order (although not it seems a child maintenance calculation), had not been in force immediately before the child reached the age of 16. This provision seems to apply where parents separate after the child is 18 or where for some reason there has not been a previous order. If it is known that a child is likely to require the order to continue, the child's parent can apply at any time before the child's 18th birthday for the order to be extended until his or her education or training is completed. On the other hand, where there was an order in force when the child reached 16 and which subsequently ceased, if the child later decides to return to full-time education or training after the age of 18, it is not possible for the 18-year-old then to apply under para 2 for further periodical maintenance. However, if such a decision is taken, or other special circumstances arise after the order has ceased but before the child's 18th birthday, an application may be made by the child to revive the order pursuant to para 6(5).

9.74

The court has power to make interim orders for periodical payments (para 9) in relation to any application under either para 1 or 2, and this order can be backdated to the date of the application. It can be an order on such terms and for such period as the court thinks fit. It will of course cease on the final disposition of the application.

9.75

Only one order can be made in relation to settlement or transfer of property to or for the benefit of the child. However, the number of applications for periodical payments, secured periodical payments and lump sum orders is not limited. All orders for periodical payments may be varied or discharged upon the application of the payer or the recipient (para 1(4)) and there is also provision for temporary suspension (para 6(2)). Once the child has reached 16, the child, as well as the parents, can apply for variation (para 6(4)).

9.76

An application for financial provision under the Schedule can be made by either parent irrespective of whether the parents are living together at the time of the application. However, an order for periodical maintenance payments, whether secured or unsecured, made in favour of a parent for the benefit of a child, ceases to have effect if the child's parents live together for a period longer than six months (para 3(4)).

9.77

In contrast, an order payable directly to a child does not cease to be payable in this situation and so, it is possible for an order to be made and to continue, despite the fact that the child's parents are cohabiting. All periodical maintenance payments are now treated as tax free in the hands of the recipient, but there is no tax relief for an unmarried parent making maintenance payments. It is not possible for Children's Tax Credit to be claimed by more than one parent in relation to a child where the care of the child is shared as discussed in Chapter 4.

9.78

Unsecured periodical payments made pursuant to para 1(2)(a) or 2(2)(a) cease automatically on the death of the paying party, notwithstanding anything in the order. Herein lies one of the advantages of secured periodical payments, but a child (and now also a cohabitant of two years' standing) would of course have the right to apply for provision pursuant to the Inheritance (Provision for Family and Dependants) Act 1975 as discussed in Chapter 5. Although secured periodical payments do not cease on death, it is open to the personal representatives of the deceased paying party to apply for variation or discharge, having regard to the same criteria as apply on making the order and the change in circumstances resulting from the death of the parent. Such an application must be made within six months of the taking out of a grant of probate or letters of administration, although leave may be given for a late application (para 7).

7 Alteration of maintenance agreements

9.79

Where parents have made a maintenance agreement in writing, which makes financial provision for a child, Sch 1, para 10 provides that the court has power to vary the agreement if it is satisfied either that it should be varied in the light of changed circumstances, or that the agreement does not contain proper financial arrangements for the child. As discussed above, the CSA 1991 and 1995 may render a maintenance agreement ineffective, particularly where the resident parent is in receipt of welfare benefits. It is also possible to have a written agreement approved by the court under the CSA 1991, s 8(5) and if that can be agreed the benefit to the resident parent is certainty and enforceability (see *K v H (child maintenance)* [1993] 2 FLR 61 and *Drake v Strout* [2003] EWCA Civ 176, [2003] All ER (D) 268 (Jan)).

8 Enforcement of orders and preserving assets

9.80

Broadly, orders are enforceable in the same way as the equivalent financial orders made in matrimonial proceedings.

9.81

However, one important distinction is the absence of any provision equivalent to s 37 MCA 1973, enabling one party to restrain the other party from disposing of assets in order to defeat the financial claim or to set aside dispositions made with this intent. Where this situation arises, there is the procedural problem of ascertaining which judges of which court have jurisdiction to make interlocutory orders of this nature. It would seem that a High Court judge could be asked to exercise the inherent jurisdiction of the court to make an interlocutory order of this nature. Furthermore, in *Re W (injunction: jurisdiction)* noted at [1995] Fam Law 713, His Honour Judge Pugsley hearing an appeal from a district judge, held that there was jurisdiction under Sch 1 CA 1989 to issue an interlocutory injunction preventing a father dealing with money he had recently inherited. He found that reg 3(1) County Courts Remedies Regulations 1991, when read subject to reg 3(3), did provide authority. This was upon the basis that such an injunction could be made within family proceedings within the meaning of Matrimonial and Family Proceedings Act 1984, which, in the High Court is assigned exclusively to the Family Division, and CA 1989 proceedings were so assigned. His conclusion that this was the position was reinforced by his reading of *Rayden* at paras 2.10 and 28.9. For a comprehensive but pre-*Re W* discussion of these issues see Amos 'Financial Injunctive Relief under the 1989 Act' [1994] Fam Law 445. Although the County Court Remedies Regulations 1991 have since been revoked by the County Court Remedies Regulations 2014, FPR 2010, r 20.2 and FPR 2010 PD 20A offer guidance as to how and in what circumstances an order to preserve assets could be made.

9.82

Finally, it should be noted here that there is no equivalent to s 24A MCA 1973 by means of which the court can order the sale of property in order to satisfy orders for secured periodical payments, lump sum orders, settlements or transfer of property orders made under Sch 1.

9 Procedure

9.83

Applications for financial provision for a child under Sch 1 CA 1989 are governed by FPR 2010 Part 9. Forms A1 needs to be completed by the applicant, including information relating to the applicant, the child, the child's parents, any other relevant proceedings or written agreements and the child's financial needs and resources. The first appointment will be scheduled not less than 12 weeks and not more than 16 weeks after the date of the filing of the application, at which hearing matters such as discovery and the attendance of the parties at the hearing will be dealt with in accordance with the court rules. The applicant or an officer of the court will serve a copy of the application on the respondent and the court officer will (if service of the application and notice are not to be effected by the applicant on the respondent) give notice of the first appointment to both the applicant and respondent within four days of the filing of the application (FPR 2010, r 9.12). Financial information is provided to the court and exchanged by way of Form E1 not less than 35 days before the first appointment (FPR 2010, r 9.14).

10 Legal aid and the statutory charge

9.84

An applicant may only be able to apply for legal aid from the Legal Aid Agency if able both to provide evidence of domestic (or child) abuse and to satisfy the financial eligibility criteria, A client will automatically qualify for legal aid on income grounds if in receipt of income support, income-based jobseeker's allowance, income-related employment and support allowance, universal credit and guarantee credit only. The maximum disposable capital for financial eligibility is £8,000. For all applications made on or after 4 April 2016 any client who has gross income of more than £2,657 per calendar month (or disposable (net) income of more than £733 per calendar month) is automatically excluded from eligibility. Thus, the number of cases before the court where either one or both parties is legally aided has steadily declined.

9.85

If the above requirements are satisfied, it would be rare for legal aid to be refused on grounds of merit, given the significance of the orders for those concerned. Although the child may apply for legal aid in his or her own right, the resources of the relevant adult(s) will be treated as the child's unless it appears inequitable in all the circumstances to do so (eg where there is a possible conflict of interest between the parent and child), there is no real advantage (and considerable disadvantage) in doing so.

9.86

The statutory charge will apply to any property 'recovered or preserved' in the proceedings for which legal aid was granted in respect of the costs incurred. Any person applying for public funding must be advised in writing by his or her solicitor of the effects of the statutory charge. Regulation 5 of the Civil Legal Aid (Statutory Charge) Regulations 2013 lists which property is exempt from the charge. It does not apply to periodical maintenance payments but it does apply to lump sum payments. By the Civil Legal Aid (Statutory Charge) Regulations 2013, SI 2013/503, reg 22(1)(a), the Legal Aid Agency can defer enforcing the charge if the property subject to the charge is the home of the client or his dependants or, in family cases, is money to be used to buy a home for the client or his dependants and the charge is registered, and it is satisfied that the home would provide appropriate security for the charge. Interest upon a deferred charge accrues from registration at 8% per annum. This is so regardless of whether the order is made under Sch 1 CA 1989 or s 14 TLATA 1996, providing the court order stipulates that the intention of the order is to provide a home. In particular, the decision in *Parkes v Legal Aid Board* [1996] 4 All ER 271, CA makes it clear that the charge applies to property where the sale is successfully deferred, even though the respective interests in the property are not in dispute. The right to exclusive possession (with a child) over a long period of years constituted property which had been preserved within the meaning of the then s 16(6) Legal Aid Act 1988 and thus the statutory charge applied. This is still good law.

9.87

Indeed, the advantage of property being settled on the child is that it may avoid the statutory charge. Although the child, who is the assisted party, has preserved the right of occupation, there is no beneficial interest in the child's favour to which the charge can attach and so the home escapes the charge. Nonetheless, this would not succeed in avoiding the charge if the parents are also disputing their respective beneficial interests in proceedings under s 14 TLATA 1996 where one or other of them is legally aided. Here the charge will attach to the preserved publicly funded partner's share to the extent of their legal costs but where this is used as a home, it may now be postponed as indicated above.

9.88

The orders that can be made in relation to the family home on relationship breakdown, pursuant to paras 1(2)(d) and (e) Sch 1, will be considered in Chapters 10 and 11.

CHAPTER 10

The family home on relationship breakdown: rented property

1 Introduction

10.01

On relationship breakdown jointly owned or shared property commonly becomes a focus for dispute, and it is at this time that many cohabitants belatedly regret not having made advance provision for such an eventuality. The family home, whether rented or purchased, is often both the couple's most valuable asset and the place where one or both of them wish to continue to live. Other jointly acquired property may also become an issue when parties are separating.

10.02

This chapter will attempt to identify and clarify the legal issues to be addressed in relation to rented homes; Chapter 11 concentrates on owner-occupied property. In Chapter 3, the various types of tenure of a family home were discussed. On breakdown, the first issue is to identify the tenure and consequent legal rights. Any advice to cohabitants on their housing position following breakdown is governed by the legal implications of their arrangements during cohabitation. Although the transfer of tenancy provisions in the FLA 1996 have enhanced the remedies available on cohabitation breakdown, the distinctions between sole and joint tenancies, the history of the tenancy, the options exercised by cohabitants who have jointly purchased a property, the homelessness legislation and proposed reforms discussed in Chapters 3 and 7, are also still all relevant.

10.03

It is always wise to consider the possibility of mediation before litigation and this and other forms of alternative dispute resolution are actively encouraged. There are now many agencies offering professional mediation in relation to property disputes on relationship breakdown. Particularly in relation to property disputes, the cost of legal proceedings and, where appropriate, the effect of the

Legal Aid Agency's statutory charge, must be at the forefront of a practitioner's mind and makes the possibility of compromise an important avenue to explore. It can indeed be one which a client may literally not be able to afford to ignore, although the statutory charge will not apply to rented accommodation which is recovered or preserved (see *Curling v Law Society* [1985] 1 All ER 705).

10.04

Until the implementation of Part IV Family Law Act 1996 in October 1997, the court did not always have power to intervene to resolve disputes between cohabitants relating to their rented family home. This was because Sch 1 Matrimonial Homes Act 1983 (MHA 1983) only applied to married couples and transfer of property orders under Sch 1 CA 1989 were only available where there were children of the relationship. Sch 7 FLA 1996 provides a discretionary family law remedy on relationship breakdown for all cohabitants whose family home was rented in the name of one or both of them. Unlike the remedy contained in Sch 1 CA 1989, it is available in respect of all types of tenancy and regardless of whether or not there are children of the relationship, providing cohabitants without children a remedy in respect of rented accommodation. As will be explored further below, there are specified matters to which the court in exercising its discretion must have regard (para 5 of Sch 7). The court also has power to award compensation to the transferring partner (para 10). A cohabitant may often now have the choice of whether to apply for a Sch 1 CA 1989 transfer of property order for the benefit of the child(ren) of the relationship or to apply for a transfer of tenancy order pursuant to Sch 7 FLA 1996. The appropriateness and relative advantages and disadvantages of these alternative procedures will be considered further below.

10.05

The provision of a family law remedy for cohabitants with regard to the rented family home arguably places them in a position of advantage as compared with those cohabitants whose family home has been purchased by one or both of them. This group, whilst not left in a position of stalemate, are not distinguished from other co-owners in dispute and, as discussed in the next chapter, family law considerations do not specifically apply to determining their shares of the family home. This matter is, however, currently still under review by the Law Commission.

10.06

It should be noted that it is always open to cohabitants to agree which of them should remain in the rented property and in many instances this is the parent with care of any children of the family (or other children). It may be possible for the tenancy (where the terms of the tenancy, or statutory rights, permit this – ie secure tenancies and some assured tenancies) to be assigned to the remaining partner. An assignment must be made by way of a formal deed. If assignment is not permitted, it may be possible to negotiate a new tenancy with the landlord.

2 Transfer of tenancy orders – Sch 7 FLA 1996

10.07

Although the focus of this text is on cohabitants, it should be noted here that this Schedule has affected the court's powers to transfer tenancies between spouses and civil partners too. It has introduced statutory criteria in accordance with which the court's discretion must be exercised, as well as a new power to order compensation. The power to transfer a tenancy in a case involving spouses or civil partners arises whenever the court has power to make a property adjustment order under the Matrimonial Causes Act 1973 (ss 23A and 24) or the Civil Partnership Act 2004 (Sch 5, Pt 2, paras 6–9). The criteria applied in this context differ to some extent from those applicable to cohabitants on relationship breakdown.

(a) Tenancies affected

10.08

On relationship breakdown, 'relevant tenancies' may be transferred under Sch 7 and these are comprehensively defined in para 1 as including:

(a) protected and statutory tenancies within the meaning of the Rent Act 1977;

(b) statutory tenancies within the meaning of the Rent (Agriculture) Act 1976;

(c) secure tenancies within the meaning of s 79 Housing Act 1985;

(d) assured tenancies and assured agricultural occupancies within the meaning of Pt I Housing Act 1988. (This also includes assured shorthold tenancies as these are a form of assured tenancy (s 20(1) HA 1988) and statutory periodic tenancies arising after the expiry of a fixed-term assured or assured shorthold, which are deemed to be assured tenancies); and

(e) introductory tenancies within the meaning of Chapter I of Part V Housing Act 1996.

10.09

Thus, it can be seen that most rented family homes in the private, independent and public rented sectors can potentially be transferred on relationship breakdown. However, only tenancies by virtue of which one or both partners of the cohabitation relationship are 'entitled to occupy a dwelling-house' fall within the provision. Thus, at least one of a couple must be a tenant, but significantly the Court of Appeal have held in *Gay v Sheeran* [1999] 2 FLR 519 that a transfer of tenancy is *not* available to a cohabitant of a joint tenant who holds the home jointly with a third party. Here, Mr Sheeran and his original partner were granted a joint tenancy of a flat. When their relationship broke down his partner moved out and Ms Gay, his new partner moved in. However, a new joint tenancy was never granted, although the council were aware of the new position which was reflected in their council tax records. When their relationship subsequently broke down, Mr Sheeran moved out and Ms Gay continued to live in the home. The council, on discovering she was now the sole occupant of the flat, served her with notice to quit. Ms Gay successfully at first instance applied for an order under Sch 7 transferring Mr Sheeran's interest in the flat to her. The council's appeal to the Circuit Judge was granted, as was Ms Gay's application for an occupation order under Part IV of the 1996 Act. Both parties then appealed to the Court of Appeal who decided that the power to make an occupation order had been properly used and was distinct from that of making a transfer of tenancy order. It was found that, in order to make a transfer of tenancy order under Sch 7, the wording of para 3(1) required Mr Sheeran to have entitlement to occupy either at the time of the application or of the order. It was not sufficient to have had such entitlement at the point at which the relationship broke down, although the provisions did not require the application to be made in any specified period after cohabitation ceased. Given Mr Sheeran's abandonment of the tenancy of the home, it was no longer a secure tenancy (s 81 Housing Act 1985), thus it was not a tenancy capable of transfer under the Schedule.

10.10

This is also a problem when a sole tenant abandons their cohabitant. Thus, the only way of keeping the secure tenancy alive and capable of transfer in such a situation would be to immediately apply for an occupation order under s 36 FLA 1996 as, if granted, it allows the occupation of the non-tenant cohabitant to satisfy the 1985 Act occupancy condition of the secure tenancy. However, the Court of Appeal also made it clear that, whilst the statutory language of s 53 and Sch 7 FLA 1996 makes it apt to cover both the transfer by a sole tenant to their non-tenant cohabitant or by a joint tenant to their joint tenant, it is not appropriate to cover the transfer by a cohabitant who is a joint tenant with a third party to their non-tenant cohabiting party as that third party's interest in the tenancy cannot legitimately be transferred to create a joint tenancy between, as here, two strangers.

10.11

This decision is something of a body blow to these provisions as they affect cohabitants, although the finding would seem to apply equally to applications by non-tenant spouses or civil partners where the tenancy of the home was held jointly by the other spouse/civil partner and a third party. It has rightly been criticised for the interpretation given to the wording of paragraph 3 of the Schedule, requiring entitlement to be judged not at the point of breakdown but at the point of the application to or order by the court, by which time former partners (who are specifically entitled to use the provisions) would frequently be long gone from the home (see eg Coll, *'Gay v Sheeran: a Just result in the Circumstances'* [2000] Fam Law 355). It is respectfully submitted that this interpretation is not compatible with what happens on relationship breakdown and is another example of the technical nature of the law which regulates disputes between cohabitants.

10.12

Given the increasing incidence of 'serial relationships' such as described in *Gay v Sheeran*, this decision underlines the need for couples to co-operate and to put matters in order on relationship breakdown if the home is to be preserved for either of them. If advice is sought, then where there is a sole tenancy and willingness to permit the non-tenant to remain, no-one should be advised to move out unless an occupation order can be obtained. Even then, whilst a s 36 occupation order, if granted, will, in essence, preserve a sole tenancy, it may not be granted in a case where the order is only needed to resolve the longer term housing rights rather than as an end in itself. As Gibson LJ indicated in *Gay v Sheeran*, the goal of a transfer order should be 'a further purpose' of the occupation order. Where it is the sole purpose it risks not fulfilling the criteria under s 36(6)–(8) and may well not be granted.

10.13

Returning to the ambit of Sch 7, the term tenancy expressly includes sub-tenancies. However, a right of occupation by virtue of something other than a specified tenancy, such as a genuine licence to occupy premises (see *AG Securities v Vaughan* [1990] 1 AC 417), would not be subject to these provisions. Consideration should therefore be given to the type of tenancy involved prior to the making of any application for a transfer of tenancy. In practice, such applications may only be worthwhile where the tenancy involves some level of security of tenure (ie secure or assured tenancies in social housing) or has added benefits such as a right to buy (see *Kasseer v Kasseer* [2013] EWCA Civ 722). It should be borne in mind that an assured shorthold tenancy with a private landlord, which can be brought to an end by the landlord with a limited amount of notice and without grounds for possession, may not warrant the costs involved in an application to the court to transfer the tenancy from one cohabitant to the other.

(b) When can a Part II order be made?

10.14

The orders for transferring different types of tenancy are contained in Part II of Sch 7 and are known as 'Part II orders'. It should first be noted that transfer is only possible of a tenancy of the family home in which cohabitants they cohabited (Sch 7, Pt I, para 4(b)). If the parties never moved into the accommodation or never lived there together, it is not possible to use this provision. Given that in respect of spouses and civil partners, a transfer of tenancy order is limited exclusively to the present or former family home (para 4(a) and (aa)), thus theoretically, at least, permitting the transfer of more than one tenancy under the Schedule, the question is posed whether a tenancy of a rented second home could be transferred under the Schedule. The provision is not, in relation to cohabitants, specifically limited to a couple's principal home and it is arguable that a couple could live together in more than one property.

10.15

Secondly, the court's power to transfer the tenancy in the case of cohabitants/former cohabitants only arises *after* cohabitation has ceased. This is not to say that the parties will necessarily need to have separate addresses before an application is made, and indeed where the transfer of a sole tenancy is sought, this is likely following *Gay v Sheeran* (above) to prove fatal to the application unless a s 36 occupation order has been obtained in the non-tenant's favour. However, they will have to show that they are no longer 'cohabiting'. Despite its significance, 'cohabitation' goes undefined in the Act and thus its cessation, and indeed the requisite prior cohabitation, may in some circumstances be difficult to judge or to prove. What, for example, is the status of a couple whose work commitments require one of them to live and work away from home for a substantial part of the week? Are they living together as cohabitants or not? Most likely though in that scenario they would be deemed to be cohabiting. Such a common-sense view was taken in *Re Watson (deceased)* [1999] 1 FLR 878 (see Chapter 5) in the context of an application under the Inheritance (Provision for Families and Dependants) Act 1975 context which contains similar wording. With regard to cessation of cohabitation, although there is no statutory requirement of separate households, it may well be enough to establish that the relationship is at an end and a decision has been made to separate/to cease living together.

10.16

Thirdly, it must also be noted that it is only possible for the order to be made if the tenancy is in existence at the date of the application for a transfer (*Lewis v Lewis* [1985] AC 828). This may pose problems where the tenancy concerned is either vested in the sole name of the respondent or is a joint periodic assured or secure tenancy, as notice to quit by one joint tenant will validly determine the tenancy (*Hammersmith and Fulham London Borough Council v Monk* [1992] 1 AC 478, confirmed by the Supreme Court in *Sims v Dacorum Borough Council (Secretary of State for Communities and Local Government, interested party)* [2014] UKSC 63, [2015] 1 All ER 834). Given the serious consequences of no tenancy being available for transfer, where it is feared that such action is a possibility, an application to transfer the tenancy should in all cases immediately be made and served on both the respondent and the landlord. In the case of a sole statutory tenancy under Rent Act 1977 or Rent (Agriculture) Act 1976, an occupation order pursuant to s 36(3)–(4) FLA 1996 (discussed in Chapter 7) to preserve the statutory tenancy must also be applied for by the non-tenant cohabitant. In the case of any other type of tenancy, an injunction pursuant to the Family Proceedings Rules, 2010 r 8.34 (which expressly incorporates r 20.4 empowering an injunction to be granted) restraining notice to quit being given in order to preserve the tenancy which is the subject of the dispute should be urgently considered. The injunction, which must relate to the preservation of the tenancy, should immediately be served upon the landlord (see *Bater v Greenwich London Borough Council* [1999] 2 FLR 993), although following the House of Lords decision in *Harrow London Borough Council v Johnstone* [1997] 1 All ER 929, it is still not clear whether or not a notice to quit served in breach of such an injunction is valid (see Arden, 'From Greenwich to Harrow: A Trip Down Memory Lane' [1997] 1 JHL 3 for a discussion of this). The decision in this case, reversing that of the Court of Appeal, seems to indicate that a notice to quit served by an excluded tenant when, known to the landlord, an occupation order was in force, will be valid unless a *Mareva*-style injunction requiring co-operation in preserving the tenancy is also obtained. The Law Commission has recommended that a notice should terminate only the interest of the party giving it and should not terminate the whole tenancy (Law Com no 297 (2006) at paras 2.44–2.46).

10.17

If court proceedings are to be commenced in respect of a tenancy in joint names, an undertaking should be sought from the other cohabitant that no notice to terminate the tenancy will be given prior to the court's adjudication. In the absence of an undertaking, an injunction (as discussed above) should be sought. In *Bater v Greenwich London Borough Council* [1999] 3 FCR 254, Thorpe LJ offered that 'in any situation where the unilateral act of one is capable in law of destroying the interests of both, the joint tenant who would be prejudiced by the service of a notice to terminate should wisely seek from the other an undertaking not to do so prior to the court's adjudication. The resulting letter of undertaking can then be served upon the landlord. In the absence of a letter of undertaking, then an application can be made to the court for an injunction and the resulting order can be served upon the landlord'.

10.18

Another gap in the provisions relating to cohabitants arose in the case of *Gay v Sheeran* [1999] 2 FLR 519. Here, where the court was unable to transfer a secure tenancy to the cohabitant of a tenant who had held the tenant jointly with a third party and which had been abandoned by both joint tenants, an occupation order may be the only way to preserve the position of the cohabitant who wishes to remain in the home. Finally, in contrast to the position of former spouses and civil partners who have remarried or entered into a new civil partnership (Sch 7, Pt 3, para 13), it should be noted that there is no bar on applications being made by former cohabitants who have married or entered into a civil partnership or who have embarked upon another cohabitation relationship.

(c) Criteria for making orders

10.19

Schedule 7, para 5 sets out the matters to which the court must have regard in considering making an offer. It directs the court to have regard to all the circumstances of the case including:

(a) the circumstances in which the tenancy was granted to, or acquired by the cohabitant(s);

(b) the matters relevant to the making of occupation orders as set out in s 33(6)(a), (b) and (c);

(c) the suitability of the parties as tenants.

All relevant circumstances can include the parties' conduct (see *Lake v Lake* [2006] EWCA Civ 1250, [2007] 1 FLR 427).

10.20

In the case of 'entitled' cohabitants (where the applicant has an interest in the property ie is a joint tenant), s 33(6)(a)–(c) FLA 1996 provides that the court shall have regard to the following:

- the housing needs and resources of the parties and any children;
- the financial resources of the parties; and
- the likely effect of the order or of no order on the health, safety and well being of the parties or any relevant child.

10.21

Accordingly, in *Guerroudi v Rymarczyk* [2015] EWCA Civ 743, [2015] All ER (D) 152 (Jul), [2016], [2015] Fam Law 1194, the decisive factor was each party's prospects of being able to re-house. A cohabitant was successful in obtaining a transfer of a secure council tenancy in her favour, on the basis that she would have great difficulty securing affordable alternative accommodation.

10.22

In the case of 'non-entitled' cohabitants, the further matters set out in s 36(6)(e)–(h) must additionally be considered, namely:

- the nature of the relationship and the lack of commitment to marriage;
- the length of time they have cohabited;
- whether there are or have been any children for whom both parties have parental responsibility; and
- the length of time since the parties ceased living together.

10.23

Whilst the circumstances surrounding the grant of the tenancy will normally be very influential, the presence of children of the relationship may be very significant, despite the fact that, unlike a transfer of property application under Sch 1 CA 1989, the aim of the transfer is not directly to benefit children of the relationship. Particularly where the original purpose of the tenancy was to provide a home for the parties and their children, the party with whom the children are to live may well be at an advantage even though the tenancy is not vested in their name. Generally speaking, however, the provision can be seen to be aimed at finding equity between the adult parties. Non-entitled cohabitants do, however, start from a position of disadvantage on any application for a transfer of tenancy order; and the shorter the period of cohabitation the more necessary it will be to establish greater need or vulnerability for an application to stand any chance of success. It is not uncommon for one cohabitant to have given up their secure accommodation in order to begin a cohabitation relationship and it should be noted that this is not a factor to which the court is specifically directed. Thus, the court's attention needs to be drawn to such a situation as one of the general circumstances of the case and any inducements or promises made to cement the cohabitation relationship in this way could be influential evidence.

(d) Effect of order

10.24

The nature of the orders in respect of different types of tenancy (including in respect of introductory tenancies) is set out in Part II to Schedule 7.

10.25

In the case of protected, secure or assured tenancies, as well as assured agricultural occupancies and introductory tenancies, the court may by order direct that the respondent's estate or interest in the tenancy of the dwelling-house together with any rights attaching to it vest in the applicant without any further assurance (para 7(1)). Any obligations or liabilities under any covenants relating to the property arising after the date of the transfer are not enforceable against the respondent. Where the transferor cohabitant was a successor pursuant to the terms of the Housing Acts 1985 or 1988, then the transferee cohabitant is deemed to be that successor as of the date of the transfer, and effectively steps into the shoes of their former partner for these purposes.

10.26

With regard to statutory tenancies under the Rent Act 1977 and Rent (Agriculture) Act 1976, paras 8 and 9 provide that where an order is made, the court directs that the transferor is not entitled to occupy the family home from a specified date and that, from that time, the transferee cohabitant is deemed to be the statutory tenant. The transferee will acquire exactly the same status as their former partner and no succession of the statutory tenancy is deemed to have taken place for the purposes of determining further succession rights (see eg paras 5–7 Sch 1 RA 1977).

10.27

On making a Part II order, the court also has power to adjust liabilities and obligations in respect of the dwelling-house arising prior to transfer as between the parties and order that one party indemnify the other in respect of these (para 11). Thus, existing rent arrears could be apportioned, or an order could be made indemnifying one partner for rent they had paid but which was the responsibility of the other. Thus, advisors need to consider carefully what ancillary orders might be appropriate when an application is made. This power to make orders under para 11 are a separate and additional issue to the question of compensation under para 10, which will now be considered.

(e) Compensation orders

10.28

The sole object of a compensation order (under para 10) is to compensate the transferor for the loss of the tenancy. Given that it has been decided that the loss of the right to buy may be taken into account on application for transfer of property orders under Sch 1 CA 1989 (see *K v K* [1992] 2 FLR 220, [1992] 1 WLR 530), this is likely to figure in the calculation of any compensation order made in respect of a secure tenancy. The Law Commission did not foresee compensation orders being made routinely, but did express the view that even where the tenancy had no real market value, it may be appropriate to grant compensation for provision of a deposit for a tenancy in the private sector or removal expenses (Law Com No 207, para 6.10). The courts however have not been prepared to adopt such an approach, as the financial resources of the transferee cohabitant may make such an order inappropriate or unenforceable in many situations and this factor is often the determining one.

10.29

The court has power to make a compensation order payable by the transferee to the transferor cohabitant, wherever a Part II order is made. In exercising its discretion, para 10(4) provides that the court shall have regard to all the circumstances of the case including:

- the financial loss that would otherwise be suffered by the transferor as a result of the order;
- the financial needs and resources of the parties; and

- the financial obligations which the parties have, or are likely to have in the foreseeable future, including financial obligations to each other and to any relevant child.

10.30

The degree of long-term security of tenure (or lack thereof) offered by the tenancy is not a specific factor.

10.31

Paragraph 10(2) permits the court to defer payment of the compensation until a specified date or event, and also to allow payment of compensation by instalments. This power may be exercised by the court either on making the order or on the application of one of the parties 'at any time before the sum whose payment is required by the order is paid in full' (para 10(3)(a)). The court also has power to vary the order up to this point in time (para 10(3)(b)). It therefore seems that an application for both variation of the original order and for delayed payment can be made after the date on which the payment has fallen due and, on applications made at this time, there is no presumption against delayed payment. However, there is a presumption against delayed payment, when an application is made at the time of making the compensation order. Here, deferred payment or payment by instalments may not be ordered by the court unless it appears that immediate payment of the sum required by the order would cause greater financial hardship to the transferee than that which would be caused to the transferor by delayed payment (para 10(5)). One situation where a deferred compensation order would certainly seem to be appropriate would be with regard to an order for the loss of the 'right to buy' the property.

3 Transfer of tenancy order (Sch 7 FLA 1996) or transfer of property order (Sch 1 para 1(2)(e) CA 1989)?

10.32

The most obvious advantage of Sch 7 FLA 1996 is that it provides a remedy for cohabitants where there are no children of the relationship, providing the home is not vested in the joint names of just one cohabitant and a third party. Schedule 1 CA 1989 does not even provide a remedy where children of one of the parties but not of the relationship have lived in the property with them (see *J v J (minors) (property transfer)* [1993] 2 FLR 56, [1993] 1 FCR 471, [1993] Fam Law 461, FD). However, where there are children of a cohabitation relationship, there may be a choice between these two remedies. Having weighed the advantages and disadvantages of these alternatives, it seems quite clear that the 1996 Act overcomes the many practical difficulties which exist in relation to Sch 1 property transfer orders, although other practical difficulties have arisen in relation to Sch 7 itself as identified in *Gay v Sheeran*. Given that the two remedies continue to co-exist, it is useful to make an assessment of the respective merits and difficulties pertaining to each of them.

(a) *Situations where Sch 1 CA 1989 property transfer order might be used in respect of a tenancy*

10.33

As will be considered below, the two classical difficulties that have arisen with regard to tenancy transfers under Sch 1 CA 1989 are, first, whether the tenancy in question is 'property' and, if so, whether it is capable of being transferred, given that the Sch 1 order is not expressed to take effect 'without further assurance' and requires a deed of assignment. These issues aside, the other important factor to consider is the difference in the criteria to which the court are referred when making the order. Unlike the provisions in the MCA 1973, the CA 1989 remedy, although only available for the benefit of a child of the relationship, does not make the child the 'first' consideration and the welfare principle contained in s 1(1) CA 1989 does not apply to issues of financial provision. The criteria under Sch 1 contained in para 4 have been discussed in Chapter 9 and broadly comprise the income, earning capacity, needs, obligations and responsibilities of the parents; the financial needs and resources if any of the child; any disability of the child; and the manner in which the child was intended to be educated or trained. In addition, all the circumstances of the case must be considered, although the court is not specifically directed to consider the duration or nature of the relationship, or the conduct of either party. The difference between the two sets of criteria contained in the 1989 and 1996 Acts do not immediately lead to any particular category of applicant being favoured more by one remedy than the other. The housing needs and resources of and the likely effect of an order on the 'health, safety and well being' of any relevant child as well as the adults are also specific concerns of the 1996 Act. Difficulties with the assignability of some types of tenancy (discussed below) aside, it is perhaps possible that a more child-centred approach will prevail under the 1989 Act, to the extent that non-entitled applicants with children may in time be better advised to use the 1989 Act remedy.

10.34

Apart from this possible difference in judicial approach, there still may be situations where a Sch 1 property transfer order is the only order available to transfer a tenancy on relationship breakdown of former cohabitants. Where there are children of the relationship, but the parents have not lived together in the accommodation to which the tenancy refers, then the 1996 Act remedy is not available. Thus, if the tenancy relates to a second home in which the parties have not lived together, or if parties have never moved into the accommodation together, or lived in it in separate households, a 1989 Act transfer of property order is likely to be the only possible remedy.

10.35

Although it is not thought that the courts are likely to make such an order, the 1989 Act remedy, unlike the 1996 provisions, provides the possibility of a transfer of the tenancy to a child under 18.

10.36

Finally, where the tenancy is assignable, or there is landlord co-operation with regard to assignment, a Sch 1 order does avoid the making of a compensation order as between the parties. However, the wording of the Sch 7 provisions in the 1996 Act enable the court to make orders of its own motion. Thus, if the court were persuaded by the respondent, or took the view itself that a transfer of tenancy order under Part II of Sch 7 rather than a property transfer order under the 1989 Act was appropriate, the court could decide to deal with the matter in this way. Once the Part II order has been made, then the question of compensation arises. Thus this method of attempting to avoid the issue of compensation is far from fool proof.

(b) Positive features of Sch 7 FLA 1996 as compared with Sch 1 CA 1989

10.37

Schedule 7 orders apply to all types of tenancy including statutory tenancies under the Rent Act 1977 and Rent (Agriculture) Act 1976 and, furthermore, the transfer of the tenancy takes place by virtue of the court order 'without further assurance'. Thus, the assignability of the tenancy is irrelevant to the application. In contrast, a problem which exists with Sch 1 property transfer orders is that whilst, with the exception of these statutory tenancies, most tenancies would be regarded as 'property' (see *K v K* (above) and *Hale v Hale* [1975] 2 All ER 1090, CA), such that a deed of assignment is required to effect any transfer, as the order to transfer is not expressed to take place 'without further assurance'. Thus, assignability of the tenancy and/or landlord co-operation is critical to giving effect to the order to transfer under Sch 1 CA 1989. Indeed, a court may be disinclined to grant a transfer of property order under Sch 1 in respect of a non-assignable tenancy where the landlord has not consented to the transfer in view of the risk that the transfer would be ineffective and all the parties concerned, including the children, would be rendered homeless. Given that there is an implied covenant against assignment in respect of all assured and assured shorthold tenancies unless expressly overridden; that Rent Act and Rent (Agriculture) Act statutory tenancies are not assignable; and that even secure tenancies are not strictly assignable as between cohabitants without landlord co-operation where a cohabitant has not lived with the tenant for 12 months (see s 91 HA 1985), the safest course of action is to use the 1996 Act remedy. However, this does then open up the possibility of an application for a compensation order which does not appear in the 1989 Act and were the 1989 Act provisions to be amended to enable transfers of tenancies to take place without further assurance then this amended remedy could be seen to be a more advantageous route if avoidance of a compensation order was an important factor. Nonetheless, this remains subject to the court's ability to decide the matter under Sch 7 of its own motion and is consequently a strategy where success cannot be guaranteed. Once transferred under Sch 1, however, the issue of compensation becomes closed.

10.38

Although the criteria relating to the two orders are different, with the 1989 Act criteria being more child centred (see 10.33 above and Chapter 9) and also requiring the order only be made for the benefit of a child, there does not seem to be any particular advantage to be gained from a non-tenant cohabitant seeking an order under the 1989 Act as opposed to the 1996 Act, unless the 1996 Act remedy were to be interpreted in such a way that property rights hold sway over the needs of the children. If this were to happen, then a resurgence of the use of the more specifically child-centred 1989 Act remedy for all its practical difficulties may take place. Given that Part VII Housing Act 1996 (as amended by the Homelessness Act 2002) has reformed the law relating to homelessness and the requirement of local authorities to provide re-housing for those in priority need, the consequences of preferring the property interests of the original tenant over the housing needs of the children in such applications are very serious, and probably, therefore, unlikely.

4 Procedure

10.39

Applications for transfer of tenancies under both the 1996 and 1989 Acts may be made in the High Court of Family Court. In contrast to the divorce/dissolution context, where currently decree nisi or a conditional order must be obtained before a property transfer application can be made, there is no reason to delay an application under either Act on the breakdown of a cohabitation relationship.

(a) 1996 Act applications (see Family Proceedings Rules 2010, rr 8.29–8.34)

10.40

In relation to the 1996 Act application, notice must be served upon the landlord (Sch 7, para 14(1)). The landlord has a right to be heard in all cases, although the court may make an order notwithstanding the landlord's objections. It should be borne in mind that whilst an application for transfer of a tenancy on relationship breakdown under Sch 7 cannot provide a ground for possession, it may provoke notice to quit being given by a landlord where no grounds are needed in the case of an assured shorthold tenancy. Advisors should therefore consider whether an application for an occupation order may be more appropriate in this situation, certainly in the first instance, as this could be undertaken without the need to serve the proceedings on the landlord. On the other hand, where a landlord agrees to the transfer, their written consent should be produced to the court on or before the hearing of any application or consent order.

10.41

Advisors should beware of suggesting consent orders where help in relation to rehousing is to be sought by the transferor cohabitant. Intentional homelessness remains a bar to the rehousing duties currently found in Part VII Housing Act 1996 (HA 1996). Where agreement is reached in such a situation, it is vital that the order is made by the court, albeit at an unopposed hearing. Indeed, before advising a transferor cohabitant to sign a consent order, it is likely to be negligent not to have advised them that in doing so they are effectively rendering themselves intentionally homeless, unless they already have other 'settled' accommodation. Where there is a finding of intentional homelessness, but that the applicant has a priority need, a local authority will not owe any duty to secure permanent accommodation for the applicant, but 'shall secure that accommodation is available for his occupation for such period as they consider will give him a reasonable opportunity of securing accommodation for his occupation and provide him with (or secure that he is provided with) advice and assistance in any attempts he may make to secure that accommodation becomes available for his occupation' (HA 1996, s 190(2)). If the applicant is considered not to have a priority need, the duty is just to 'provide him with (or secure that he is provided with) advice and assistance in any attempts he may make to secure that accommodation becomes available for his occupation' (HA 1996, s 190(3)). A person is intentionally homeless if he or she deliberately does or fails to do anything which leads them to cease to occupy accommodation which is available and reasonable for them to occupy (HA 1996, s 191(1)) (see Chapter 3).

(b) Sch 1 CA 1989 applications

10.42

Applications for transfer of property orders can be made in the High Court or Family Court, by completing the appropriate form (C1). Any additional evidence should be in the form of a dated and signed statement containing the appropriate declaration as to the maker's belief in its truth.

10.43

Although there is no requirement in the 1989 Act to seek the landlord's consent, where it will not prejudice the applicant and where there is an absolute or qualified covenant against assignment, the landlord's consent, subject to the court order being made, should be sought.

(c) Timing and preservation of the tenancy

10.44

As noted above, whichever application is being made, a problem arises where a respondent is a sole tenant (statutory, secure or assured) and has left the home. For as soon as the tenant cohabitant leaves and is no longer occupying the accommodation as his or her residence, the security of tenure falls and the tenancy ceases to exist. However, as noted above, it is enough for the tenancy to have been in existence at the time of the application rather than at the hearing date. In the House of Lords decision in *Lewis v Lewis* [1985] 2 All ER 449, it was held that the court had jurisdiction to transfer a statutory tenancy which was subsisting at the date of the application under the MHA 1983, despite its having been determined before the date of the hearing. This reasoning was followed by the Court of Appeal in the case of a secure tenancy in *Thompson v Elmbridge Borough Council* [1987] 1 WLR 1425. There is no reason why this cannot be extended to applications for property transfer orders between cohabitants for the benefit of a child and has been confirmed to be the case with respect to applications under Sch 7 FLA 1996 in *Gay v Sheeran* (above). It is clear that an application for a transfer of property order or transfer of tenancy order as appropriate in this situation must be lodged without delay to protect the remaining cohabitant's position and that a s 36 occupation order is the only other possibility where the sole tenant has abandoned the home.

10.45

In addition, where it is feared that a joint or sole tenant respondent may intend to determine the tenancy by notice to quit, which would leave the court without any property capable of transfer and the applicant homeless, a *without notice* application for an order restraining the service of a notice to quit by the respondent pending the hearing should be urgently considered, and, where granted, served promptly upon the respondent and landlord (see FPR 2010, rr 8.34, 20.4). For once the tenancy is determined, there can be no possibility of preserving the home. The possibility (or need in the case of a statutory tenancy) for an occupation order by a non-entitled cohabitant should also be urgently considered. Where it is not possible to preserve the tenancy, the applicant would be homeless, and in no way intentionally homeless. If they were also in priority need, for example because they had children residing with them the local housing authority would be obliged to secure accommodation in accordance with the provisions of Part VII HA 1996, as amended by the Homelessness Act 2002, s 6, which abolished the minimum period (of two years) for which a local authority was subject to a duty to rehouse (see Chapter 3). It is only a valid notice to quit by one joint tenant that will act to terminate the tenancy as illustrated in *Hounslow London Borough Council v Pilling* (1993) 25 HLR 305. Here a cohabitant joint tenant who had been the victim of domestic violence gave notice to quit her joint tenancy 'with immediate effect' at the request of the council who were to rehouse her. The Court of Appeal held that this did not operate to surrender the tenancy as it both failed to give the requisite contractual notice which the council could not waive in the absence of the concurrence of both tenants and also offended s 5 Protection from Eviction Act 1977.

10.46

Where one joint tenant does unilaterally give notice to quit on a periodic joint tenancy it was thought arguable that this amounted to a breach of trust towards the other tenant, for which the latter may be entitled to be compensated. However, in *Hammersmith and Fulham London Borough Council v Monk* (above), Lord Browne-Wilkinson doubted that this was the case and indicated that, even if it were, it did not invalidate the notice to quit. In *Crawley Borough Council v Ure* (1995) 27 HLR 524, the Court of Appeal rejected that such action in relation to a periodic secure tenancy could constitute a breach of trust due to lack of consultation with the other tenant pursuant to s 26(3) LPA 1925. This position, coupled with the reduced duties towards the homeless, makes it imperative that applications for transfer of tenancy orders are made without delay in all cases where there is jurisdiction.

10.47

Desertion by a sole tenant cohabitant who does not give the landlord notice may cause an insuperable problem pending the hearing of a transfer of tenancy application unless an occupation order is sought pursuant to s 36 FLA 1996 which, by virtue of s 36(13), extends the 'home rights' contained in s 30(3)–(6) to cohabitants and entitles the deserted cohabitant to make payment of rent and occupy as if they were their tenant partner for the period of the occupation order, which is a maximum of six months in the first instance and may be renewed for one further maximum period of six months only. Without this, the remaining partner has no right to pay the rent to the landlord, nor any occupation rights. Furthermore, if residence is a requirement of the continued subsistence of the tenancy, no application can be made under Sch 1 CA 1989 or Sch 7 FLA 1996. Attention is drawn to the need to resolve the substantive application under Sch 7 FLA 1996 or Sch 1 CA 1989 within the period for which the court granted the occupation order.

(d) Enforcement of orders for compensation

10.48

Compensation orders are not subject to any special enforcement procedure and thus may only be enforced in the same way as any other debt. They are not 'maintenance' and thus cannot be enforced by judgment summons (see Sch 8 Administration of Justice Act 1970).

5 Limits to the FLA 1996 provisions

10.49

Gay v Sheeran (see above) demonstrates how Sch 7 is unable to preserve a non-tenant cohabitant's home where the tenancy was originally granted to the other cohabitant jointly with a third party. It is also of little use where the tenancy is abandoned by a sole tenant cohabitant who may at best obtain a s 36 occupation order, no matter how long he or she may have lived in the home. For even if they can reach agreement as to what should happen to the family home on relationship breakdown, they may not be able to implement the agreement; and where there is no agreement, there may be no mechanism for resolving the dispute.

6 Joint tenancies – the general position

10.50

Any form of joint tenancy gives each joint tenant the right to occupy the accommodation, and renders each jointly and severally liable to pay the rent regardless of whether or not in occupation. These factors raise obvious problems on breakdown of a relationship, even where there is broad agreement as to who should remain in the home. One partner will wish to remain in occupation without the other partner exercising the right to occupy, and the departing partner will not want to remain liable to the landlord for the rent in the event of non-payment by the former partner.

10.51

Overcoming these problems may depend on the assignability of the tenancy. Where the joint tenancy permits assignment, there is little difficulty if the parties agree a solution. Where there is agreement, but the tenancy cannot be assigned, perhaps the best protection that can be achieved is for the parties to enter into a deed of indemnity. The remaining partner will agree to indemnify the departing partner against any liability in respect of the rent, the departing partner agreeing in turn not to exercise his or her rights of occupation.

In this way, the landlord does not have to know that one partner has left and the remaining partner remains a tenant. However, notwithstanding the indemnity, the departing partner will still be liable to the landlord for the rent in the event of non-payment. Also, it is not clear whether the courts would uphold an agreement to suspend legal rights of occupation. As shall be seen, where there is no agreement, one joint tenant may unilaterally terminate a periodic tenancy regardless of whether or not the former partner wishes to remain, with varying effects on the remaining partner.

7 Rent Act tenancies

(a) Joint contractual tenancies (excluding protected shortholds)

10.52

Where the parties agree who should continue to occupy the home, the situation is relatively simple. If there is no covenant against assignment or where there is a qualified covenant but the landlord consents, (and consent should not be unreasonably withheld – s 19 Landlord and Tenant Act 1927), the departing partner can assign his or her interest in the joint tenancy to the former partner, who will then become the sole contractual tenant. Assignment should be in writing, in the form of a deed, witnessed in the normal way to comply with s 52 LPA 1925.

10.53

Where assignment is not possible and there is a periodic tenancy, the departing partner can serve notice to quit on the landlord. Providing the notice is in the form required by the agreement and complies with s 5 Protection from Eviction Act 1977, giving a minimum of four weeks' notice in writing, it operates to determine the contractual tenancy in accordance with the decision in *Hammersmith and Fulham London Borough Council v Monk* (above) unless the tenancy agreement expressly provides otherwise. However, in contrast to the periodic secure or periodic assured tenant's position, it does not operate to terminate the remaining partner's right of occupation. Instead the latter becomes the statutory tenant of the premises, providing he or she continues to occupy the home as his/her only or principal residence (see *Lloyd v Sadler* [1978] 2 All ER 529). At the same time, the notice determines the departing partner's liability to pay the rent and, of course, the right to occupy. The remaining partner will only be the statutory, and not the contractual, tenant of the premises, which can have certain disadvantages.

10.54

A fixed-term tenancy cannot be surrendered by one joint tenant alone, but only by all the joint tenants acting together (*Leek and Moorlands Building*

Society v Clark [1952] 2 All ER 492, CA) and thus effective assignment to the remaining joint tenant is dependent upon the terms of the tenancy permitting assignment.

10.55

Where the parties do not agree, or where the departing partner has deserted the remaining partner, there are various options. Where one partner has left the premises, the remaining periodic joint tenant can himself or herself give notice to quit to the landlord and providing he/she then continues in occupation of the home, the remaining partner becomes the sole statutory tenant of the premises. By this action the departing partner loses the right to occupy and liability to pay rent, but the remaining partner unfortunately thereby gives the landlord a discretionary ground for possession under Case 5 of Sch 15, Part I Rent Act 1977. The landlord would have to prove not only that the remaining partner gave notice to quit, but also that it is reasonable to make a possession order (s 98(1)). Given that Rent Act tenancies are generally unattractive to landlords, they may be keen to attempt to obtain possession in such a situation and advisors must warn of the possible consequences of a tenant's notice.

(b) Joint statutory tenancies

10.56

In this situation, where there is agreement as to who should remain, no problem arises. Both joint statutory tenants have occupation rights, but once the departing tenant ceases to occupy the premises as his or her residence and abandons any intention to return, then that person ceases to be a statutory tenant and ceases to have rights of occupation (see s 2(1)(a) Rent Act 1977). A notification by either tenant to the landlord that one but not both of them has ceased to reside in the premises should ensure that the liability of the departing partner to pay rent ceases, and falls solely on the remaining partner, who becomes the sole statutory tenant of the home and whose occupation rights are unaffected.

10.57

However, should both joint statutory tenants wish to remain in occupation, then no mechanism exists to resolve the dispute, other than the possibility of an occupation order pursuant to s 33 FLA 1996.

(c) Sole contractual Rent Act tenancies

10.58

Whether a non-tenant cohabitant, whom the parties agree should stay, can lawfully remain in occupation depends on the terms of the tenancy agreement.

There is no difficulty where the tenancy agreement does not contain a covenant against assignment, as a deed of assignment in the proper form will be effective to transfer the tenancy. An oral tenancy where no notice to quit has been served will remain contractual and will therefore usually be assignable.

10.59

Where there is a covenant against assignment, even if the sole tenant wishes his or her former partner to remain in occupation, this may not be possible. If the tenant, after departure, having made a *de facto* assignment of the tenancy, were to continue to pay the rent to the landlord, this would constitute breach of the tenancy agreement and give the landlord grounds for possession. However, if the landlord, with knowledge of the facts, continues to accept the rent, then it is arguable that he has waived the breach and accepted the cohabitant as a new tenant although after 15 January 1989 the new tenancy will be assured, not Rent Act protected. If at any point the landlord serves notice to quit, then, unless it can be argued that a new tenancy has been granted, on expiry, the contractual tenancy comes to an end. A statutory tenancy arises only if the tenant occupies the home as his/her only or principal residence or can show they have not relinquished possession despite a temporary absence and there is a definite intention to return. The longer the tenant is away, the less likely it is that such an argument will be convincing.

10.60

Once there is a statutory rather than a contractual tenancy, neither the absent tenant nor the non-tenant partner remaining in the property has a defence to possession proceedings. If a landlord is approached for consent to a new tenancy, the likely outcome is at best an offer of an assured shorthold tenancy, which will give security for a minimum six months, but is thereafter determinable by the landlord without need for grounds for possession other than the expiry of the initial fixed term and compliance with the statutory procedures.

10.61

Where there is a dispute between the parties, if the cohabitant who is the sole tenant wishes to remain, then their former partner has no right to remain and can be forced to leave by means of possession proceedings, as they are no more than a licensee with no occupation rights once these have been revoked.

(d) Sole statutory tenancies

10.62

Statutory tenancies are a personal right and cannot be assigned unless the landlord consents and is a party to the deed of assignment (see para 13, Sch 1

Rent Act 1977). Given the protection and rent restriction which a Rent Act tenancy affords, the landlord's consent is most unlikely to be forthcoming.

8 Tenancies governed by the Housing Act 1988

10.63

Assured tenancies are found most commonly in the independent sector and will be granted mainly by housing associations. Although they can be granted in the private sector, most private sector landlords prefer assured shorthold tenancies which afford tenants very little security, although during the initial fixed-term period are treated as fixed-term assured tenancies with regard to assignability. Schedule 2 HA 1996 makes all tenancies granted on or after 1997 assured shorthold unless the landlord expressly states it as assured.

(a) Joint assured tenancies

10.64

On breakdown, the joint tenants each retain the right to occupy, and remain jointly and severally liable to pay rent.

10.65

In the case of a fixed-term tenancy, assignment is permitted where the terms of the tenancy agreement do not prohibit it. Thus, if there is agreement between the cohabitants and assignment is possible, the situation is simple. All that is required is a deed of assignment in proper form.

10.66

However, in the case of periodic tenancies, regardless of whether they are periodic from the outset or are statutory periodic tenancies which arise on expiry of the fixed term, a covenant against assignment without the landlord's express consent is implied by s 15 Housing Act 1988 (HA 1988) (unless, in the case of an expressly periodic tenancy, the agreement provides otherwise, or a premium is payable on the grant or renewal of the tenancy). The statutory proviso that consent cannot unreasonably be withheld is specifically excluded. Thus, in direct contrast to the Rent Act position, an oral periodic assured tenancy where nothing at all is said about assignment is unassignable without the landlord's express consent. This is also the case with statutory periodic tenancies arising after the expiry of the fixed term, even though the original fixed-term tenancy permitted assignment. The only way to achieve certainty is therefore to obtain the landlord's consent. Whether or not this is forthcoming is entirely within the landlord's discretion.

10.67

Again, in contrast to the Rent Act position, a notice to quit given by one of two joint tenants will bind all, and thus bring a periodic assured tenancy to an end (*Hammersmith and Fulham London Borough Council v Monk* (above)). No statutory tenancy arises by operation of law as in the Rent Act situation, and accordingly the landlord will be entitled to possession. However, it seems that a notice to quit by one joint tenant will not operate to determine a fixed-term assured tenancy (see s 5(2)(b) and s 45(2) HA 1988 which, read together, confirm the common law rule that it requires all the joint tenants to determine the fixed-term tenancy).

10.68

Where one cohabitant deserts a joint tenant partner, the tenancy remains an assured joint tenancy, as s 1(1)(b) HA 1988 requires that just one of the joint tenants occupies the premises as his only or principal home to qualify for protection. A landlord may agree to accept a notice to quit from the deserted joint tenant and to grant him or her a new sole assured tenancy. Given that otherwise the remaining joint tenant continues to be vulnerable to their former partner determining the tenancy without their knowledge, this is a possibility worth exploring.

(b) Sole assured tenancies

10.69

Assignability of a sole assured tenancy depends on the landlord's express consent, and where the non-tenant wishes to remain in occupation, the landlord must be approached.

10.70

Residence by the tenant is required to continue security. Thus, once the sole tenant leaves, the protection afforded by the Act falls, as the tenant's leaving must amount to a 'surrender or other action' by the tenant which brings the tenancy to an end (s 5(2)(b) HA 1988). The landlord, on discovery of the situation, can obtain possession. Alternatively, the landlord may be prepared to grant the remaining partner a new tenancy, quite possibly, in the private sector, at an increased rent.

10.71

Once a notice to quit is served by the tenant, then again the tenancy is surrendered and there can be no defence to possession proceedings. Acceptance of rent from the remaining partner, who has no right to pay the rent may constitute evidence that a new tenancy has been granted, which in turn may assist the remaining partner's position.

(c) *Assured shorthold*

10.72

Assured shortholds are the most popular form of private sector tenancy, as on the expiry of the initial fixed term of a minimum of six months, a landlord can obtain possession (having given no less than six months' notice in writing of such) and needs no ground for possession (see ss 19A and 21 HA 1988). In this situation, other than the protection afforded for the initial fixed term, neither the tenant nor a non-tenant wishing to remain has any security of tenure, although a departing tenant remains liable for the rent. Only an indemnity to pay the rent and any legal costs incurred by the departing tenant as a result of the partner's continued occupation can assist the position between the parties, but there is no protection from ultimate eviction by the landlord.

9 Secure tenancies

10.73

A local authority tenant will usually have a periodic secure tenancy, now governed by the Housing Act 1985. Housing association tenancies granted before 15 January 1989 will also be secure tenancies, but those granted after this date will be assured tenancies and are subject to the provisions of HA 1988 as described above.

(a) *Joint secure tenancies*

10.74

As with all other types of joint tenancy, secure joint tenancies confer rights of occupation and liability to pay the rent on both joint tenants. Again, security of tenure is preserved if just one of the joint tenants occupies the premises as his or her residence. Thus, where a joint tenant is deserted, he or she continues to have security and the right to remain.

10.75

However, where a partner who has left the accommodation, serves a notice to quit upon the local authority, it will terminate the periodic tenancy even though the partner wishes to remain: *Hammersmith and Fulham London Borough Council v Monk* (above). Thus, a deserted joint tenant partner is in a vulnerable position. A remaining partner, having obtained the local authority's promise subsequently to grant a new tenancy, can himself or herself give notice to quit, but again the new tenancy is purely at the discretion of the landlord.

10.76

The only other option is to persuade the outgoing partner or the landlord to agree to an assignment or new tenancy before a notice is served. Advisors should be aware of the remaining partner's vulnerability and take preventative action where possible. It is thought that an injunction restraining the deserting partner from determining the tenancy may be possible. Alternatively, a s 33-occupation order excluding the deserting partner and allowing the remaining partner to enter and remain in the premises may have the desired effect, but problems of service on the deserting partner may arise. Arguably, if the local authority were given notice of the occupation or restraining order, this may persuade it to grant a new tenancy if a notice to quit were served in breach of either order. Once the notice has been served, all that can be done is to ask the council to grant the remaining partner a new tenancy – again a matter entirely within its discretion. Ironically, a cohabitant who would be entitled to succeed to the tenancy on death may have no right to remain in the property if deserted.

10.77

Where there is agreement, it had been thought that a secure tenancy could be assigned to the remaining joint tenant cohabitant regardless of whether or not they were capable of being a statutory successor. Section 91(3)(c) HA 1985 permits assignments to a person who would have succeeded to the tenancy on death, which, by operation of law, although not by inclusion in the list of statutory successors, includes a joint tenant, and security of tenure would be retained. This would then count as one succession on death (as discussed in Chapter 3). However, a secure joint tenancy cannot be assigned by one joint tenant to the other where the other would not be a statutory successor. Assignment is only possible where the assignee joint tenant also falls within the statutory list of qualified successors set out in s 113 which defines 'members of the family' who are permitted to succeed under s 87. In *Burton v Camden London Borough Council* [2000] 2 WLR 427 the House of Lords found (by a majority, with Millett LJ dissenting) that a deed of release by one joint tenant in favour of her friend, the other joint tenant who had moved elsewhere amounted to an assignment of the tenancy. This was held to be ineffective where the remaining joint tenant could not have succeeded to the tenancy as a member of the tenant's family, even though she would succeed as a surviving joint tenant on death. An assignment of this nature can be achieved as between cohabitants, or in other cases where the local authority agrees. In *Burton*, the local authority was not willing to agree to the arrangement as it would have left a single person occupying three-bedroomed accommodation; a drain on resources to which the House of Lords appeared sympathetic. Both parties would need to notify the local authority, who may have a form for the purpose, although there is no reason why the assignment should not be achieved by means of a deed executed in accordance with s 52 LPA 1925 as long as any agreement by the local authority is annexed.

(b) Sole secure tenancies

10.78

Sole secure tenancies can be assigned between cohabitants by agreement, where permitted by the terms of the tenancy, but security of tenure will be retained only if, immediately before the assignment, the remaining partner could have succeeded to the tenancy on the death of the outgoing tenant partner (HA 1985, s 91(3)(c)).

10.79

As discussed in Chapter 3 in the context of succession to tenancies on death, a cohabitant comes within the definition of 'a member of the tenant's family'. In *Peabody Donation Fund Governors v Higgins* [1983] 1 WLR 1091, it was held that such an assignment was permissible even though the tenancy agreement contained an absolute covenant against assignment.

10.80

CHECKLIST FOR DISPUTES CONCERNING THE RENTED FAMILY HOME

- Identify the tenant or tenants and the nature of the tenancy (secure, assured, assured shorthold, contractual or statutory Rent Act protected), asking for and examining any relevant documentation, such as written tenancy agreement, correspondence, notices served, rent book.
- Urgently consider whether an occupation order is appropriate where there is a sole tenancy or joint periodic tenancy which could be determined by the other partner or where there is a statutory tenancy which will cease to exist if not occupied by the tenant.
- Urgently consider whether, where in addition to or instead of an occupation order, other steps should be taken to preserve the tenancy pending hearing of transfer of tenancy application such as obtaining an undertaking from the other party not to terminate the tenancy or perhaps an injunction pursuant to FPR 2010, rr. 8.34 and 20.4, restraining notice to quit being served.
- Where application for tenancy transfer is to be made/resisted under Sch 7 FLA 1996, take full statement of all relevant matters specified, including a history of the tenancy and of the cohabitation relationship, details of any relevant children, the relative suitability of the parties as tenants, their relative housing and financial needs and resources.
- Consider whether ancillary orders under para 11 to Sch 7 adjusting liabilities and obligations, eg in respect of rent arrears, are appropriate.
- Consider whether compensation could be sought or payable.
- Ensure applications and orders are served on landlord where appropriate.

CHAPTER 11

The family home on relationship breakdown: owner-occupied property and other arrangements

1 Introduction

11.01

In contrast to the position of cohabitants in relation to the rented family home, where legislation (albeit imperfect) has been enacted, the legal position on relationship breakdown of cohabitants whose family home has been purchased by one or both of them remains (as it has done for what seems like decades now) under scrutiny by the Law Commission, which published a paper as long ago as 2007 on 'Cohabitation: The Financial Consequences of a Relationship Breakdown' (Law Com No 307). Whilst the need for change in the law in this field has been recognised by both the Law Society and Resolution (formerly, the Solicitors' Family Law Association) for many years, there is little appetite it seems from government or in Parliament generally to do something to address the oftentimes precarious position a cohabitant could be left in after relationship breakdown. The Cohabitation Rights Bill 2017 which had its first reading in the House of Lords on 5 July 2017 (if it were to become law) affords protections of a financial nature to cohabitants (being any two people whether of the same sex or the opposite sex who live together as a couple) who live together and:

(i) are each treated in law as being mother, father or parent of the same minor child;

(ii) there is in force in respect of a minor child either a joint residence order in respect of both of them or a child arrangements order stipulating arrangements by which the child is to live, spend time or have contact with them;

(iii) they are the natural parents of the child as yet unborn at the date when they ceased living together as a couple; or

(iv) they have lived together as a couple for a continuous period of three years or more.

As at the date of writing, no date has been announced for its second reading in the House of Lords and if it passes through both Houses is unlikely to become law before 2019.

11.02

There have, however, been significant reforms to the law of property as well as developments in the case law which affect how the courts deal with disputes relating to the owner-occupied family home arising between cohabitants on relationship breakdown. The Trusts of Land and Appointment of Trustees Act 1996 (TLATA 1996), which came into force on 1 January 1997, provided a new conveyancing regime for co-owners, who were given new powers as trustees (ss 6 and 7) and rights of occupation (s 12).

11.03

TLATA 1996, s 14 gives the court wider powers than to order or not order sale of a property. Any trustee or beneficiary under a trust of land or any secured creditor of a beneficiary may apply to the court under s 14 for any such order as the court thinks fit relating to the exercise by the trustees of any of their functions or for a declaration as to the nature or extent of a person's interest in the property subject to the trust. This obviously gives the court a broader range of options for resolving disputes. Section 15 directs the court to statutory criteria relevant to determining applications which include the welfare of any child occupying the property.

11.04

As noted above, any trustee or beneficiary under a trust of land or any secured creditor of a beneficiary may apply to the court under s 14 for any such order as the court thinks fit relating to the exercise by the trustees of any of their functions or declaring the nature or extent of a person's interest in the property subject to the trust. Thus, where the extent of a cohabitant's beneficial interest is in dispute, either because they are not a legal owner or because no express trust was declared at the point of acquisition, this is the mechanism for ascertaining it. It is possible to apply for an order for sale, where this cannot be agreed, or for an order preventing sale or exercise of other powers by trustees. In addition, orders that a beneficiary occupying the property pay an occupation rent to a beneficiary out of occupation are within the court's powers. In making orders under s 14 (other than where the application is made by a trustee in bankruptcy, which is governed by s 335A Insolvency Act 1986), the court must have regard to the matters set out in s 15, which may be summarised as:

- the intentions of the person who created the trust;
- the purposes for which the property subject to the trust is held;

- the welfare of any minor who occupies or might reasonably be expected to occupy the property as their home; and
- the interests of any secured creditor of any beneficiary.

11.05

It is, however, clear from the wording of the section that this list is not exhaustive and other relevant factors may be taken into account where appropriate. These criteria are particularly helpful in the family law context. Furthermore, the specified criteria which include the intentions of those creating the trust and the original purpose of the trust, which may often be to provide a family home, as well as an express direction to consider the welfare of any minor child who resides or may in the future reside in the property, arguably provide greater opportunity for a family law based approach to prevail.

11.06

Although the statutory basis for resolving disputes was changed with the introduction of TLATA, the determination of beneficial ownership of property is still governed by the law of trusts. Thus, although the court may have greater discretion as to what remedy to offer, and can, for example, postpone sale and instead order that an excluded co-owner be paid an occupation rent by an occupying co-owner, determination of their respective beneficial interests is still governed by the doctrines of express, implied, constructive and resulting trusts. The law in this area remains governed largely by case law. In relation to claims for declarations of shared beneficial ownership of the property there are two decisions of the most senior court. The first is the House of Lords decision in *Stack v Dowden* [2007] UKHL 17, [2007] 2 All ER 99, [2007] 2 FCR 280, [2007] 1 FLR 1858 which reviews the applicable principles substantially and the second is the decision of the Supreme Court in the case of *Jones v Kernott* [2011] UKSC 53, [2011] 3 FCR 495, both of which will be discussed below.

11.07

Thus, if there is a cohabitation contract in the form of a deed, dealing with beneficial ownership of the home and the division of property on breakdown, the courts will probably give effect to it, as discussed in Chapter 1. If there is a declaration of trust, either in the transfer document (TR1) or in a separate document executed as a deed, setting out the beneficial interests, the courts will, in the absence of fraud or mistake, treat this as conclusive. With the possible exception of cases where there are children of the relationship, there will be little reason for the parties to go to court, as their interests will have been clearly defined. As home ownership continues to be an attractive option, financial considerations make it expedient for cohabiting couples to pool their resources and buy jointly; and legal advisors have a critical role to play in establishing at the outset a couple's intentions when they purchase the property and ensuring that the title deeds clearly reflect this. Not to do so is clearly negligent (see *Walker v Hall* [1984]

FLR 126, *Springette v Defoe* and *Taylor* [1992] 2 FLR 388). Whilst it is difficult for couples and their legal advisors to foresee every eventuality, it is perfectly possible for declarations of trust to establish beneficial interests contingent upon the size of future contributions to a mortgage, as well as to reflect unequal contributions to the capital deposit, requiring only arithmetical calculations to be made on breakdown to realise each party's share. Cohabitation contracts can also set out proposed agreements for the division of property on separation, and for the effect on the beneficial interests in the property of temporary inability of either party to contribute to the mortgage due.

11.08

Where there is a declaration of trust or binding agreement relating to the beneficial ownership of the home, this does not of course prevent an application being made, where there are children, for a transfer of property order for the benefit of a child under para 1(2)(e), Sch 1 CA 1989. The jurisdiction of the court to order transfer of property cannot be ousted, but the property capable of transfer can at least be made readily identifiable by virtue of an express agreement between the parties and will save the court having to establish the interests for itself.

11.09

Where there is no conclusive express declaration of trust or cohabitation agreement relating to the cohabitants' beneficial interests, the rights of the respective parties on breakdown depend in the first instance on the legal and equitable ownership of the family home as established by the title documents. However, these are subject to any resulting or constructive trusts, or claim to equitable proprietary estoppel, which a court deems to have been created by the parties in relation to the property. Thus where the parties have lived in a property of which the legal and equitable estate is on the face of it vested in the sole name of one of them, this is not necessarily conclusive. Conversely, unequal contributions to a property vested in joint names of the parties without further declaration as to their respective interests, may lead to a conclusive presumption that the property is beneficially owned in equal shares, although the most recent case law moves away from this position as discussed below. The rights of third parties, particularly mortgagees, are also likely to be significant on breakdown and steps to be taken in this regard must also be considered. The co-operation of the mortgagee is, of course, critical where there is a negative equity situation and a sale is sought.

11.10

The principles to be applied in determining beneficial property interests were summarised by Mostyn J in *Bhurra v Bhurra* [2014] EWHC 727, [2014] All ER (D) 213 (Mar) as follows:

'(i) If there is an express declaration of beneficial interests then that is, almost invariably, the end of the matter. Such an expressed declaration could only be displaced if it has been procured by fraudulent conduct.

(ii) If there is no express agreement about the beneficial interests then there is likely to be (at least) a tacit understanding. This is hardly surprising as one would expect that when people enter into what may very well be the most important economic transaction in their lives – buying a home – they would have a pretty clear understanding of who owned what share of it. In determining whether there was such a tacit understanding and if so what it was the court will look at all the evidence holistically and will examine the whole course of the parties' conduct in relation to the property.

(iii) In the rare case where the evidence does not reveal a tacit understanding about ownership the court can reach for the presumptions. An obvious presumption is that beneficial ownership is the same as legal title.

(iv) Another is the presumption of the resulting trust.

(v) A further presumption is the presumption of advancement but this can be regarded as being on its deathbed given that it is abolished by Section 199 Equality Act 2010 (which is awaiting implementation).

(vi) Presumptions are only presumptions!

(vii) Actual facts are those which suggest that a result steered by a presumption is unfair. In *Jones v Kernott* the Justices accepted that where a tacit agreement could not be found by a process of inference the court could input to the parties a fair agreement which they never in fact made but which they should "be taken" as having made.'

11.11

However, the first task on breakdown is to establish the legal ownership of the family home. Secondly, any steps necessary to protect the client's interest in that property should be identified.

2 Establishing legal ownership

11.12

Most clients are aware of the details of ownership of the family home, but this is not always the case. An official copy of the register of title can be obtained from HM Land Registry at www.gov.uk/search-property-information-land-registry for (at the date of writing) just £3 to discover the registered proprietor (and details of any mortgages or any restrictions on the title). The Land Registration Act 2002 effectively did away with unregistered land, by requiring all property transactions to be registered. In 2013, however, because registration of title was never made compulsory *per se*, 13 per cent of land in England and Wales remained unregistered. As any remaining unregistered land is sold on, registration would automatically be triggered. The annual report of HM Land Registry for 2015 to 2016 reported that there were close to 24.5 million registered titles.

11.13

If the mortgagee is known, it can be approached for details of ownership, but a Land Registry search should always be the first step, as neither the title number nor the name of the mortgagee is necessary in order to make a search for the relevant property information. It is usually a good idea to inform the mortgagee of a dispute between co-owners and to obtain its undertaking to give notice to the legal adviser before issuing any possession proceedings if there are mortgage arrears. Where the property is leasehold, enquiries should be made about any arrears of ground rent or service charges, and advice must be given in relation to the risk of forfeiture for non-payment.

11.14

The next stage will depend on whether or not the client cohabitant is a legal owner. Joint owners will be jointly and severally liable for payment of mortgage instalments and of ground rent and service charge due under a jointly owned lease, and it may be possible to claim state benefits (see Chapter 4) to cover these payments where the estranged co-owner is failing to do so. The property cannot be sold without the co-owner's consent or an order from the court. Beneficial joint tenants may also need to sever the joint tenancy, and another urgent enquiry will relate to the need to revise any Will that has been made.

11.15

Where the title documents reveal that the client's partner is the sole legal owner of the home, the client does not have the automatic protection of home rights: rights of occupation of the family home afforded to spouses and civil partners under s 30 FLA 1996. If this is the case, thought should be given to whether an occupation order under s 36 FLA 1996 should be applied for. This will, if granted, give a personal right of occupation and not one which may be protected by registration.

11.16

If in actual occupation of the home, the absent partner is unlikely to be able to sell the property without the occupying partner's agreement. In the case of registered land, the occupying partner will have an overriding interest, which will bind a purchaser, but this cannot be protected by placing a notice or restriction on the register. However, it is for a purchaser to make enquiries of overriding interests (see *William & Glyn's Bank v Boland* (Chapter 3 above)). The Land Registration Act 2002 preserved actual occupation as an overriding interest but abolished cautions, replacing these with a system of consensual and non-consensual notices, one of which must be served on the registered proprietor.

11.17

Currently, in the very limited cases of unregistered land, a person in actual occupation is in a more precarious situation, as it is not possible to register any land charge protecting occupation, yet only a purchaser with actual or constructive knowledge of the occupation will be bound. In *Caunce v Caunce* [1969] 1 WLR 286, occupation itself did not fix a purchaser with constructive notice of a wife's occupation and it seems that this would extend to other occupants. Actual occupation has been interpreted quite broadly. In *Kingsnorth Finance Ltd v Tizard* [1986] 1 WLR 783, a wife who no longer slept at the matrimonial home but attended every day to look after the children and had left many of her belongings there was held to be in actual occupation. In *Abbey National Building Society v Cann* [1991] 1 AC 56 at page 93, it was stated that what amounted to occupation was a question of fact but that the concept involved 'some degree of permanence and continuity'. Whilst actual occupation remains an overriding interest, it will not bind a purchaser unless the occupation is apparent on reasonable inspection of the property. Thus it will be in the interests of the proprietor to hide the existence of their cohabitant's actual occupation of the property and place non-owner cohabitants in a weakened position, although any interest they subsequently can be shown to have in the property would still be enforceable as against the proprietor who will normally then be in receipt of the proceeds of sale.

11.18

However, the cohabitant will have no claim against the home unless he or she can show some form of equitable interest under a resulting or constructive trust or due to the equitable doctrine of proprietary estoppel. Where a beneficial interest under a trust, including a resulting or constructive trust, can be shown, then s 12 TLATA 1996 gives a right of occupation. Thus, although s 13 TLATA 1996 gives trustees the right to restrict occupation by a beneficiary, these powers may not be exercised to oust any beneficiary already in occupation by virtue of s 12 or otherwise. Therefore, where an informal trust has arisen between cohabitants in relation to the family home occupied by them both, the non-owning cohabitant will have both a right of occupation and protection from being excluded by use of the s 13 power. Where a property lends itself to physical partition the trustees have power under s 13 in an appropriate case to restrict a beneficiary's entitlement to occupy one part of the building and to exclude or restrict the other's entitlement to occupy the other part (*Rodway v Landy* [2001] EWCA Civ 471, [2001] Ch 703). This may be of benefit to cohabitants with children who remain on fairly good terms who could (with planning permission) convert a house into two self-contained flats as a cheaper/more cost-effective option than selling the property and purchasing two with the resulting stamp duty and other associated costs of sale and purchase to take into account.

In practice, where there is a beneficial interest of a party who is no longer in actual occupation and the land is unregistered, it is usually advisable to issue proceedings under s 41 Trustee Act 1925 for the appointment of another trustee if the legal owner refuses to do so. Proceedings under s 14 TLATA 1996 can follow where appropriate.

11.19

Some case law has developed since the introduction of the 1996 Act which appears to limit the availability of a 'family home defence' against creditors seeking to repossess. The fact that a person has an overriding interest as a person in actual occupation under the Land Registration Act 2002, Sch 3, para 2 will not prevent an order for sale being made within the discretion of the court under Section 14 – see *Bank of Baroda v Dhillon* [1998] 1 FCR 489, [1998] 1 FLR 524, CA and *Pritchard Englefield (a Firm) v Steinberg* [2004] EWHC 1908 (Ch). In *Bank of Ireland Home Mortgages Ltd v Bell* [2001] 2 All ER (Comm) 920, CA noted at [2001] Fam Law 714, the Court of Appeal considered the impact of the statutory criteria in s 15 of the 1996 Act. Here, it was held that the trial judge, who had refused to order the sale of the home, had failed to give due weight to the creditor's interest, had erred in referring to the property as a 'family home' when the husband's departure had put an end to the purpose for which the property had been purchased. Furthermore, he had given undue weight to the occupation of a son who was almost 18 and the poor health of the wife. However, in *Mortgage Corporation v Shaire* [2000] 1 FLR 973, it was acknowledged that s 15 had changed the law and allows the court greater flexibility as to how to exercise its discretion on an application for sale. In *Bank of Scotland v Hussain & Qutub* [2010] EWHC 2812 (Ch), it was further held that a bank was entitled to possession of a property despite the existence of an overriding interest in circumstances where the occupier could be taken to have authorised the bank's charge. Whereas under the old law, there was no distinction between cases where the sale was sought by the trustee in bankruptcy and those where a mortgagee or chargee wished to sell, with the wishes of those wanting sale prevailing, s 15(4) indicated that a different approach applied in bankruptcy cases.

11.20

Whenever s 14 proceedings are issued, a notice or restriction should immediately be registered against the title to the property; this will give any purchaser actual notice of the non-owner's clam to have a beneficial interest in the property, achieving indirectly that which cannot be done directly. Any prospective purchaser on notice of the claim is unlikely to complete the purchase at least until the proceedings have been concluded.

3 Joint legal ownership

11.21

Joint owners must hold a property as joint tenants of the legal estate, but as either joint tenants or tenants in common in equity. Normally, the transfer document (TR1) contains a declaration of the beneficial interests. A declaration may be made subsequently or in a separate document providing it complies with the requirements of s 53 LPA 1925. In the absence of fraud or mistake, an express declaration by joint legal owners as to their respective beneficial interests in the property will be conclusive (see *Pettitt v Pettitt* [1970] AC 777; *Goodman v Gallant* [1986] 1 All ER 311). Normally, the beneficial interests will crystallise on purchase of the property in accordance with the express declaration and notwithstanding the actual contributions to the purchase price and can be altered only by proof of a subsequent express declaration or agreement. As indicated earlier, however, it is possible for a declaration to specifically provide that the parties' respective interests will crystallise at a later date and be calculated in accordance with stated criteria.

11.22

Despite the court's wider powers under s 14 in the context of co-ownership disputes between cohabitants or former cohabitants, the court's role is likely to involve determining the respective beneficial interests of the parties in the home where these have not been clearly expressed or are subject to challenge. It must then decide, in accordance with the statutory criteria contained in s 15 (above), whether the home should be sold or prevented from being sold and the conditions upon which any order should be executed.

11.23

The starting point will be how the property is expressed to be held in the title documents. Where there is an express declaration (which may be in writing or oral (see *Lloyds Bank plc v Rosset* [1991] 1 AC 107, HL)), the position is relatively straightforward. Where there is no declaration, the joint legal ownership will usually raise a strong presumption that the parties were each intended to be beneficially entitled, unless the property was put into joint names by mistake or for a completely different purpose. Where it is clear that both co-owners are beneficially entitled, but the extent and nature of their respective interests is uncertain, the court will look at all the evidence available, including evidence of their intentions, to determine the nature and extent of the respective beneficial interests, before making a declaration under s 14 TLATA 1996. In so doing, the same principles will be applied as in the situation where the legal estate is vested in one person but the beneficial interests are shared as discussed below. These principles were usefully summarised by Neuberger J in the case of *Mortgage Corpn v Shaire* [2000] 1 FLR 973, where the beneficial ownership of cohabitants who were the registered joint proprietors of a home who had failed to make any declaration as to their respective beneficial interests fell to be determined.

4 Joint tenants in equity

11.24

A declaration that co-owners hold property as beneficial joint tenants has the effect of attributing to each of them an identical interest in the whole of the land until the joint tenancy is severed. If the property is sold, that interest is transferred to the proceeds of sale and each joint owner will take one half. Severance of the joint tenancy can be effected by either joint tenant giving written notice to the other pursuant to s 36(2) LPA 1925 and they will then hold as beneficial tenants in common in equal shares, notwithstanding their actual contributions to the property, unless the original declaration specified that unequal shares would arise on severance (*Goodman v Gallant*, above). When consulted on breakdown, the effect of severance of the joint tenancy must be explored and explained immediately. Severance will usually be appropriate, as the right of survivorship will cease to apply, which will accord with the wishes of most (but not all) clients. It should be noted that acting in a way inconsistent with a joint tenancy may also sever it without notice being served, as in *Ahmed v Kendrick* [1988] 2 FLR 22, which involved the unilateral sale of the property; and *Re Draper's Conveyance, Niham v Porter* [1969] 1 Ch 486, where the issuing of proceedings under s 30 LPA 1925 (the precursor to s 14 TLATA) was deemed to be sufficient.

11.25

Another important effect of a beneficial joint tenancy is the right of survivorship whereby on the death of one joint tenant, the deceased's share of the property passes automatically to the surviving joint tenant. This contrasts with the position of beneficial tenants in common where the interest of the joint owner passes with his or her estate and not necessarily to the co-owner. Practitioners should make sure that clear advice is given concerning the implications of a beneficial joint tenancy at the outset. It is certainly arguable that, in the cohabitation context, it is almost never appropriate for co-owners to create an equitable joint tenancy without providing for the shares that are to arise on severance or at least the mechanism by which such shares are to be calculated. Where clear instructions are given to create an equitable joint tenancy, the practitioner must ensure that both clients understand that this will result in them sharing the equity equally, however much their situation and contributions change. This advice is best given in writing to each of the co-owners and consideration should be given as to whether they should be separately advised.

11.26

Thus, cohabitants who have purchased as beneficial joint tenants where there is an express declaration are entitled to the net proceeds of sale in equal shares. Difficulties arise where there is no express declaration trust, as in *Jones v Kernott*, in which case Lady Hale and Lord Walker in their joint statement identified the following core principles 'applicable in a case such as this where a family home is bought in the joint names of a cohabiting couple who are both responsible for any mortgage but without any express declaration of their beneficial interests:

(1) The starting point is that equity follows the law and they are joint tenants both in law and in equity.

(2) That presumption can be displaced by showing:

  (a) that the parties had a different common intention at the time when they acquired the house; or

  (b) that they later formed the common intention that their respective shares would change.

(3) Their common intention is to be deduced objectively from their conduct.

(4) In those cases where it is clear either (a) that the parties did not intend joint tenancy at the outset or (b) had changed their original intention but it is not possible to ascertain by direct evidence or inference what their actual intention was as to the shares in which they would own the property 'the answer is that each is entitled to that share which the court considers fair having regard to the whole course of dealing between them in relation to their property' per Chadwick LJ in *Oxley v Hiscock* [2004] 2 FCR 295, [2004] 3 All ER 703.

(5) Each case will turn on its own facts. Financial contributions are relevant but there are many other factors which may enable the court to decide what shares were either intended (as in case 3 above) or fair (as in case 4).'

5 Tenants in common in equity

11.27

Although the legal estate must be held by co-owners as joint tenants, the beneficial interests may be held as tenants in common. The effect of this is that the co-owners each have a specified share in the equity, usually determined at the date of purchase. Such share does not pass automatically to the co-owner on death, but instead devolves to the beneficiaries of the estate. Thus, if a co-owner who holds as tenant in common wishes to leave his or her share of the home to his/her cohabitant on death, it is necessary to make a Will to that effect, as the cohabitant would not benefit on intestacy.

11.28

A tenancy in common is particularly appropriate where there have been unequal contributions to the purchase price and where the joint owners wish to preserve their interests in the property in unequal shares, although a tenancy in common can, if required, specify that the shares are held equally. A situation where parties must be advised particularly carefully about a declaration of trust and the quantification of their beneficial interest is where a property is purchased under the 'right to buy' scheme. In the cohabitation context, it is common to find one partner's contribution to be capital mainly in the form of a substantial discount awarded by virtue of their having been a local authority tenant for some years, and the other co-owner's contribution taking the form of some or all of the mortgageable income. This was the situation in *Springette v Defoe* [1992] 2 FLR 388, where solicitors were roundly criticised by the Court of Appeal for having transferred the property to the couple jointly without even having taken any instructions in relation to their beneficial interests, let alone having advised them to make a declaration of trust. This is undoubtedly a breach of a solicitor's professional duty to their client. In this case the court used resulting trust principles to establish the parties' respective interests in the property in accordance with their capital and mortgage contributions. Furthermore, a solicitor who, in a transfer, declares a beneficial tenancy in common but does not go on to specify the shares is negligent (*Walker v Hall* [1984] FLR 126, [1984] Fam Law 21). Once a declaration as to the beneficial interests has been made, it is again conclusive, in the absence of fraud, mistake or a subsequent express agreement.

11.29

Thus, if cohabitants on purchase declare that they hold the property beneficially as tenants in common in shares of three quarters to one quarter, on breakdown of the relationship when the property is sold, the net proceeds of sale will be divided in these proportions. If, before breakdown of the relationship, one partner has paid for or undertaken improvements to the property, in the absence of express agreement to the contrary, this does not alter the beneficial interests in the property and the proceeds of sale will still be divided according to the original ratio, although such improvement works may well represent an act to the claimant's detriment that enables him or her to make a claim that there was an express agreement, arrangement or understanding that s/he should have a beneficial interest in the property. The focus is upon the common intention of the parties and the courts have wide discretion to re-calculate a party's share in light of such works (see eg *Oxley v Hiscock* [2004] EWCA Civ 546, [2004] 3 All ER 703, [2004] 2 FCR 295, [2004] 2 FLR 295). It is therefore necessary to advise joint purchasers to consider making a fresh declaration of trust if future contributions render their original agreement unfair. Alternatively a clause could, and arguably should, be inserted in the original declaration providing for this and other contingencies such as revised contributions to any joint mortgage.

6 Sole legal ownership

11.30

Where a property is purchased in the sole name of one partner during the currency of the relationship, or where one partner moves into a property which was purchased by the other previously, on breakdown of the relationship, the non-owner partner is in a vulnerable position. It is in this area that the most difficulty on the breakdown of relationships between cohabitants arises, and it is here that the non-owner partner must rely on the law of trusts or the doctrine of proprietary estoppel if s/he is to establish any equitable interest in the home. In the case of *Thompson v Hurst* [2012] EWCA Civ 1752, a case decided after *Jones v Kernott*, Etherton LJ offered that 'in the case of a transfer into the name of only one of the cohabiting parties the starting point is quite different from the joint legal owner case. In the case of joint legal ownership the property is necessarily held on trust and the only question is as to the size of the respective beneficial interests of the parties. In the case of a single legal owner where there is no express declaration of trust the claimant has first to establish some sort of implied trust, normally what is now termed a common intention constructive trust … The claimant must show that it was intended that he or she was to have a beneficial interest at all. That can only be achieved by evidence of the parties' actual intentions, express or inferred, objectively ascertained. If such evidence does show a common intention to share beneficial ownership, but does not show what shares were intended, then each of them is to have that share which the court considers fair having regard to the whole of dealing in relation to the property.' See also the sole name cases of *Chapman v Jaune* [2012] EWCA Civ 476 and *Graham-York v York* [2015] EWCA Civ 72.

11.31

No rights of occupation accrue to a non-owner cohabitant unless they can either establish a beneficial interest under an express trust or more usually a resulting, implied or constructive trust as recognised by s 53(2) LPA 1925, in which case s 12 TLATA 1996 grants them occupation rights; or alternatively rights of occupation may be granted, under Part IV FLA 1996, if they obtain a s 36 occupation order. If granted, the latter would obviously afford them protection from exclusion for up to six months in the first instance and could be renewed only once for a further six-month period maximum. This option should be considered in all cases where exclusion is a possibility, as the FLA 1996 remedy is not premised upon the need for a violent situation to exist before such an order is made and it may offer a vital emergency remedy pending collation of evidence needed for s 14 TLATA 1996 proceedings. Particularly where prevention from exclusion alone is sought, the nature of the cohabitation relationship has been fairly long-term and stable and particularly where there are children, it seems likely that the courts will be prepared to preserve occupation of the family home in this way, pending final resolution of other issues between the parties. Where s 14 TLATA 1996 proceedings are to be issued with a view to establishing a beneficial interest in the property, and there is strong *prima facie* evidence of the existence of a resulting or constructive trust, it may be possible to secure occupation for the non-legal owner cohabitant by obtaining an interlocutory order or an undertaking from the legal owner cohabitant preventing them excluding their partner or former partner. The strategy adopted will depend on the quality of the evidence to hand, the nature of the cohabitation relationship and the existence of any relevant children, the availability of legal aid for either course of action where appropriate and consideration of the effects of the statutory charge.

11.32

In terms of establishing beneficial ownership, there must either be an express trust or evidence sufficient to convince the court that a resulting or implied/ common intention constructive trust has been created.

7 Fraud or mistake

11.33

An express declaration as to the beneficial ownership is conclusive in the absence of fraud or mistake (or undue influence) – see *Pankhania v Chandegra* [2012] EWCA Civ 1438, [2013] 3 FCR 16 and *Davis v Jackson* [2017] EWHC 698 (Ch), [2017] Fam Law 722). If it was induced by fraud, it will be set aside. If it was entered into as a result of a mistake in that it fails to reflect the parties' common intentions, rectification may be sought, although this will not be granted where it would prejudice a bona fide purchaser for value who was not on notice of the mistake. In *City of London Building Society v Flegg* [1988] AC 54, HL, it was held that an express declaration by purchasers that they held as beneficial joint tenants was not conclusive where their parents had contributed to the purchase price with the intention that they should retain a beneficial interest.

8 Express, resulting and constructive trusts

11.34

As Baroness Hale summed up, in *Stack v Dowden*:

> 'just as the starting point where there is sole legal ownership is sole beneficial ownership, the starting point where there is joint legal ownership is joint beneficial ownership. The onus is upon the person seeking to show that the beneficial ownership is different from the legal ownership. So, in sole ownership cases it is upon the non-owner to show that he has any interest at all. In joint ownership cases, it is

> upon the joint owner who claims to have other than a joint beneficial interest … The burden will therefore be on the person seeking to show that the parties did intend their beneficial interests to be different from their legal interests and in what way. This is not a task to be lightly embarked upon. In family disputes, strong feelings are aroused when couples split up. These often lead the parties, honestly but mistakenly, to reinterpret the past in self-exculpatory or vengeful terms … The search is to ascertain the parties' shared intentions actual inferred or imputed with respect of the property in light of their whole course of conduct in relation to it.'

11.35

The general points arising from the decision in *Stack v Dowden* are:

(a) The law should be simple and accessible.

(b) The principles to be applied are the same whether the couple are married or not.

(c) If there is an express declaration of trust, it is binding.

(d) *Oxley v Hiscock* a decision of the Court of Appeal which related to property where the legal title is in the sole name of one party was rightly decided.

(e) The law has been uncertain about the extent to which and the basis upon which a court may infer a common intention to share the beneficial interest.

(a) Express trusts

11.36

An express declaration as to the beneficial ownership is conclusive in the absence of fraud or mistake (or undue influence. If a property is purchased in joint names and the TR1 sets out the respective beneficial interests, that will usually be conclusive and any claim for a greater share is likely to fail. If on purchasing a property in which the sole legal owner is to live with his or her partner, or on a partner moving into a property solely owned by the other, the sole legal owner makes a valid express declaration of trust that he or she holds the property beneficially for himself or herself and for their partner, then the parties' respective shares on breakdown of the relationship will be determined in accordance with that express declaration, which will be conclusive as has already been discussed in the context of joint legal owners. For the declaration to be valid, it must conform to the requirements of s 53(1)(b) LPA 1925, but any written agreement will be evidence of the parties' intentions at the date of acquisition and may be of great significance where a party is attempting to show a common intention as to the beneficial ownership of the property.

(b) Resulting and implied/common intention constructive trusts

11.37

In contrast to express trusts, these trusts arise without being evidenced in writing. It is important to note that there are two important stages in ascertaining the effects of both resulting and constructive trusts. First, the court has to establish through the finding of a common intention (actual, inferred or imputed) that a non-legal owner does have a beneficial interest; and secondly, it must go on to quantify that interest. In *Jones v Kernott*, the Supreme Court considered that the order of analysis must be:

(i) Do the documents of title declare the beneficial interests in the property? If so, that declaration will be conclusive in the absence of a compelling claim to the contrary;

(ii) If not, what was the express common intention of the parties? If unable to determine this

(iii) What was their inferred common intention (ie an actual agreement to be inferred from the parties' conduct)? But, if this cannot be deduced – see *Barnes v Phillips* [2015] EWCA Civ 1056)

(iv) What is the imputed common intention of the parties (ie the intention that reasonable and just people would have formulated had they thought about it at the time)?

11.38

Traditionally a resulting trust gives effect to the parties' presumed common intention at the date the property was acquired. It will arise where a non-legal owner contributes in money or money's worth to the purchase of the property which will be held on trust in shares relative to their contributions. Equity presumes that where two parties contribute to the purchase that they intend to share the property beneficially in proportion to their contributions, although such a presumption can be rebutted by proof that the contribution was intended as a loan, a gift or rent.

11.39

In *Sekhon v Alissa* [1989] 2 FLR 94, Ch D, the presumption of a resulting trust had not been rebutted where a mother had contributed £22,500 to her daughter's purchase of a house as there was no evidence that it was intended as a gift or a loan. Another example is *Richards v Dove* [1974] 1 All ER 888, Ch D, where a woman's contribution to a deposit was held to have been intended as a loan.

11.40

Where the contribution has been made in money, and providing resulting trust principles are applied to quantification, and not constructive trust principles based on an actual or imputed common intention to share the property in different proportions to those derived from the monetary contributions, the valuation of the respective shares is relatively simple. However, the problem of quantification where there are disproportionate contributions to the capital and mortgage with which a purchase was effected, may also feature here.

11.41

Further difficulties arise where it is alleged that the contribution was made in money's worth rather than money. Prior to the Supreme Court in *Jones v Kernott* approving the decision in *Oxley v Hiscock*, the courts routinely blurred the distinction between resulting and constructive trusts in that in some cases actual physical work by a non-owner partner which had improved the property was held to give rise to a resulting trust, whilst in others it had been considered only as conduct relevant to establishing whether or not the requisite intention for a constructive trust was present.

11.42

Given the very broad principles that apply to the establishment of a constructive trust following the decision in *Stack v Dowden*, it will be increasingly rare for the courts to find that there is a resulting trust but no common intention sufficient for there to be a constructive trust. Constructive trusts (like resulting trusts) depend on a common intention. In the case of *Drake v Whipp* [1996] 1 FLR 826 at 830 Gibson LJ confirmed that 'all that is required for the creation of a constructive trust is that there should be a common intention that the party who is not the legal owner should have a beneficial interest and that that party should act to his or her detriment in reliance thereon'. Thus, a constructive trust depends on the existence of a common intention (either express inferred or, since *Stack v Dowden*, imputed) that the claimant should have a beneficial interest.

11.43

In *Jones v Kernott*, Lady Hale and Lord Walker in their joint judgement said at paragraph 25 thereof that:

> 'the time has come to make it clear, in line with *Stack v Dowden*, that in the case of the purchase of a house or flat in joint names for joint occupation by a married or unmarried couple, where both are responsible for any mortgage, there is no presumption of a resulting trust arising from their having contributed to the deposit (or indeed the rest of the purchase) in unequal shares. The presumption is that the parties intended a joint tenancy both in law and in equity.

But that presumption can of course be rebutted by evidence of a contrary intention, which may more readily be shown where the parties did not share their financial resources.'

9 Quantification of shares on breakdown

11.44

Whether co-owners hold the home as joint tenants or tenants in common in equity, once the appropriate share due to each has been established, an arithmetical calculation is necessary to translate this into the correct share of the proceeds of sale. It may well be that on breakdown the property is not actually sold, but rather one co-owner buys the former partner and co-owner's share, but the principles remain the same. Whether or not the property is sold, it is still necessary to establish the correct method of quantifying the share in cash terms. Where there is no mortgage, the calculation is often simple. The net proceeds of sale are the sale price, less the costs incidental to the sale such as estate agents' fees and legal costs. The balance is then divided in accordance with the established shares of the equity. Alternatively, it is possible to divide the gross proceeds of sale between the co-owners in the agreed ratio, each paying towards the incidental costs in the same proportions out of their share of the proceeds of sale. In fact the same figure will be arrived at, but as a matter of practice, the net proceeds of sale are usually taken as the total equity available for distribution and the courts have tended to follow this method.

11.45

Where there is an express intention prima facie the court will declare the parties have the shares in the property that they intended (*Gissing v Gissing*). In the case of *Cheese v Thomas* [1994] 1 All ER 35, [1995] 1 FCR 162, [1994] 1 FLR 118 the Court of Appeal had to decide how the loss that arose on the sale of a property should be apportioned between the parties that had contributed to its purchase. It was decided that the loss should be borne in the proportions in which the parties had contributed to its purchase. The issue was extensively examined in the case of *Oxley v Hiscock*, re-examined by the House of Lords in *Stack v Dowden* and reaffirmed by Lady Hale and Lord Walker in *Jones v Kernott* who, in their joint judgment, said in respect of the quantification of shares that 'in those cases where it is clear either (a) that the parties did not intend joint tenancy at the outset, or (b) had changed their original intention, but it is not possible to ascertain by direct evidence or by inference what their actual intention was as to the shares in which they would own the property, *the answer is that each is entitled to that share which the court considers fair having regard to the whole course of dealings between them in relation to the property*' (the words in italics borrowed from Chadwick LJ in *Oxley v Hiscock*).

11.46

Where the court infers or imputes a common intention, it has a wide discretion when deciding upon the extent of the parties' shares. Each case though will turn on its own facts. Financial contributions are relevant but there may be many other factors which would enable the court to decide what shares were either intended or fair. Bank statements may provide useful evidence as to the parties' respective contributions at the time of purchase (although it should be noted that when determining beneficial interests in a property the exercise for the court is one of overall assessment of the parties' assumed intentions as to beneficial ownership and not a strict mathematical exercise founded only on the financial contributions to capital at the outset – *Sandhu v Sandhu* [2016] EWCA Civ 1050). Contributions to any home improvements and the parties' financial arrangements during their relationship including the maintenance of children are also to be considered. In *Barnes v Phillips* [2015] EWCA Civ 1056, [2016] 2 FLR 1292, [2015] All ER (D) 206 (Oct) in which sums spent after separation on the mortgage and maintenance of the jointly owned property by the cohabitant who remained in occupation were relevant in the determination of the parties' intentions, in addition it was held that 'in principle it should be open to a court to take account of financial contributions to the maintenance of children (or lack of them) as part of the financial history of the parties save in circumstances where it is clear that to do so would result in double liability'. Thus, the court is not restricted to looking at the original purpose for which the property subject to the trust is held. A subsequent purpose may also be taken into account.

11.47

Where, as in *Oxley v Hiscock*, the property is in the sole name of one of the cohabitants, 'the claimant had first to surmount the hurdle of showing that she had any beneficial interest at all before showing exactly what that interest was. The first can readily be inferred from the fact that each party had made some kind of financial contribution towards the purchase' (per Baroness Hale in *Stack v Dowden* at para 61); the second question to be answered in cases of this nature is *what is the extent of the parties' beneficial interests in the property?* Again, in many cases, 'the answer will be provided by evidence of what they said and did at the time of the acquisition. But, in a case where there is no evidence of discussion between them as to the amount of the share which each was to have – and even in a case where the evidence is that there was no discussion on that point – the question still requires an answer … The answer is that each is entitled to that share which the courts considers fair having regard to the whole course of dealing between them in relation to the property. And, in that context, *the whole course of dealing between them in relation to the property* includes the arrangements which they make from time to time in order to meet the outgoings (for example, mortgage contributions, council tax and utilities, repairs, insurance and housekeeping) which have to be met if they are to live in the property as their home' (per Chadwick LJ in *Oxley v Hiscock* at para 69 and quoted by Baroness Hale and Lord Walker in *Stack v Dowden*).

11.48

It is now well established that the appropriate date for valuation of parties' shares in property in the absence of express contrary agreement as to the date of valuation should be the date of the sale of the property or realisation of the shares (see *Gordon v Douce* [1983] 2 All ER 228).

11.49

What happens where one cohabitant is solely responsible for discharging the monthly mortgage payments on the property that is owned beneficially by both parties? What happens when one of them leaves and the other remains in occupation enjoying sole use of the property? Should an occupational rent be paid? These issues used to be decided upon under the umbrella of the equitable principle of equitable accounting. However, they now fall squarely within the provisions of TLATA, ss 12–15. In *Stack v Dowden*, Ms Dowden remained in occupation of the property prior to its sale and the trial judge ordered her to compensate Mr Stack for the rent he had paid on another property following his departure. This was reversed by the Court of Appeal whose decision was upheld by the House of Lords, effectively changing the approach that should be adopted to equitable accounting by reference to TLATA. Baroness Hale confirmed that:

> 's 12(1) gives the beneficiary entitled to the interest in the land the right to occupy the land if the purpose of the trust is to make the land available for his occupation. Thus, both these parties have the right of occupation. Section 13(1) gives trustees the power to exclude or restrict that entitlement but under s 13(2) this power must be exercised reasonably. The trustees also have power under s 13(3) to impose conditions upon the occupier. These include under s 13(5) paying any outgoings or expenses in respect of the land and under s 13(6) paying compensation to a person whose right to occupy has been excluded or restricted. Under s 14(2)(a) both trustees or beneficiaries can apply to the court for an order relating to the exercise of these functions.'

Since then, in the case of *Akhtar v Hussain* [2012] EWCA Civ 1762 it was held that the judge had erred in not allowing a 50% discount in relation to occupational rent where the person in occupation of the property was a half owner of the property.

11.50

Where a property is jointly owned and it is charged to secure the debts of only one of the joint owners the other joint owner is entitled to have that secured indebtedness discharged out of the debtor's interest in the property (in the absence of a contrary intention) – the 'equity of exoneration' (see *Re Pittortou* [1985] 1 All ER 285, [1985] 1 WLR 58).

10 Proprietary estoppel

11.51

Another principle under which beneficial interests can be established by non-legal owners is that of proprietary estoppel. The crucial distinction between this doctrine and that of the constructive trust has been identified by Hayton ('Equitable Rights of Cohabitees' (1990) 54 *The Conveyancer* 370). He asserts that the common intention constructive trust requires a bilateral understanding or agreement that if the non-owner acts in a particular and detrimental way, they will obtain a fair share in the family home. The case of *Cobbe v Yeoman's Row Management Ltd* [2008] UKHL 55, [2008] 4 All ER 713 (a commercial case decided in the House of Lords) had seemed to virtually extinguish the doctrine of proprietary estoppel but the following year the House of Lords in the case of *Thorner v Major* [2009] UKHL 18, [2009] 3 FCR 123 quickly resurrected it. To succeed in a claim for proprietary estoppel, however, there need be only unilateral conduct by the legal owner which leads the partner to believe that he or she has an equitable interest in the home. Should that partner subsequently act to his or her detriment in reliance upon that conduct, it then becomes unconscionable for the legal owner to insist upon total ownership of the property. The court then intervenes to prevent the unconscionable conduct affecting the non-owner detrimentally. It will not necessarily perfect the gift, but rather decide what is the minimum equity to do justice. The non-owner will not necessarily obtain a realisable interest in the proceeds of sale of the property however.

11.52

Accordingly, in the case of *Suggitt v Suggitt and another* [2012] EWCA Civ 1140 Arden LJ summarised the requirements of proprietary estoppel as follows:

> 'As is well known, there are four requirements for proprietary estoppel. There must be an assurance, reliance and detriment. In addition, the relief granted by the court must be the minimum necessary to satisfy the equity.'

11.53

The doctrine is of greatest use where it is not clear whether or not the non-owner would have done the detrimental acts relied upon in the absence of a common intention that a beneficial interest had been acquired, rather than for other reasons, such as mutual love and affection, not specifically referable to the house. In contrast to the constructive trust approach, the doctrine of proprietary estoppel does not require the detrimental acts to be specifically referable in this way, although reliance on the inducement must be shown. However, once there is evidence of an inducement and some detrimental act, the burden then falls on the legal owner to show that the non-owner did not do the act in reliance upon the inducement.

11.54

Proprietary estoppel has an obvious importance when the focus is on events after purchase of the property or a non-owner is introduced to it. As in all equitable claims it may be argued where appropriate that the claim should be rejected on the grounds of delay (or laches) (see *Lester & Hardy v Woodgate & Woodgate* [2010] EWCA Civ 199).

11.55

In the case of *Thorner v Major*, in which a man claimed against the estate of his deceased cousin in relation to a farm that the deceased cousin had owned and upon which the claimant had worked for many years, Lord Walker stressed that the doctrine of proprietary estoppel is based on three main elements:

(i) a representation or assurance made to the claimant;

(ii) reliance on it by the claimant; and

(iii) detriment to the claimant in consequence of his (reasonable) reliance.

Finding for the claimant, the House of Lords held that the assurances must be clear enough and viewed in context and in this particular case 'where a very taciturn farmer given to indirect statements made remarks obliquely referring to his intention with regard to his farm after his death' (per Lord Neuberger) the claimant 'who had years of experience in interpreting what he said and did (formed) a reasonable view that (the defendant) was giving him an assurance that he was to inherit the farm and that he could rely on it' (per Lord Rodger). It would be sufficient for the claimant to show that he did rely on the assurance.

11.56

On the issue of reliance Lord Scott in *Thorner v Major* stated that 'if it is reasonable for a representee to whom representations have been made to take the representations at their face value and rely on them it would not in general be open to the representor to say that he or she had not intended the representee to rely on them'.

11.57

With regard to the relief sought and whether it is 'out of all proportion to the detriment suffered', in *Suggitt v Suggitt and another*, Arden LJ said that the court must 'do justice to the claimant given the assurances he had been given and his acting to his detriment'. He continued to say that '(this) does not mean that there has to be a relationship of proportionality between the level of detriment and the relief awarded … If the expectations are extravagant or *out of all proportion to the detriment which the claimant has suffered* the court can and should recognise that the claimant's equity should be satisfied in another and generally more limited way.'

11.58

Advising a potential claimant seeking a share or greater share of their family home, practitioners should ask the claimant to provide as much evidence as s/he can of any detrimental reliance by him or her in response to an assurance by their former cohabitant where there may be a claim for a constructive trust or proprietary estoppel. Examples of detrimental reliance include:

(i) unpaid or low-paid work done by the claimant (*Thorner v Major*; *Suggitt v Suggitt*);

(ii) regular financial contributions by the claimant (eg a payment by a cohabitant of £500 a month which the respondent had told her was 'towards the house' in relation to the property in his sole name – *Liden v Burton* [2016] EWCA Civ 275, [2017] 1 FLR 310, [2016] Fam Law 687); and

(iii) the loss of an opportunity as a result of reliance on an assurance (eg failure to apply for financial remedies as in the case of *Stallion v Albert Stallion Holdings (GB) Ltd* [2009] EWHC 1950 (Ch), [2010] Fam Law 349 or foregoing a claim for possession as in *Ely v Robson* [2016] EWCA Civ 774, [2017] 1 FLR 1704, [2016] Fam Law 1221, in which case a claimant was estopped from asserting a 50% beneficial interest in a property in her former cohabitant's sole name where there was evidence of an oral agreement between them that she would have a 20% interest coupled with evidence that he had relied on that agreement to his detriment over the following years by foregoing his claim for possession.

11 The leading cases

(i) Stack v Dowden

11.59

Mr Stack and Ms Dowden met as teenagers and began living together in their mid-20s in 1983. They had four children together but never married. For a while, they lived at a property in London, which had been purchased by Ms Dowden and in respect of which she alone discharged the mortgage repayments and all of the household bills as she had a regular income unlike

Mr Stack who was a self-employed builder with no regular income stream. In 1993 they purchased in their joint names a property in Chatsworth Road London NW2 for £190,000. £128,813 came from Ms Dowden's Halifax account (which held the proceeds of sale of her previous property), with the balance provided by way of a Barclay's mortgage in their joint names. They separated in 2002 and Chatsworth Road was eventually sold in November 2005 for £746,245. By the time of the sale Mr Stack had paid £27,000 towards the reduction of the mortgage capital whilst Ms Dowden had repaid £38,345. However, Mr Stack had paid the mortgage interest and the premiums on the joint endowment policy which together totalled £33,747. Ms Dowden paid the utility bills as she had done in respect of the property that had been in her sole name. In all other respects the parties kept their finances entirely separate.

11.60

The issue before the court was that the initial transfer of the property at Chatsworth Road to Ms Dowden and Mr Stack did not contain an explicit declaration of their respective beneficial interests in the property which was to become their home. Further, there had been no discussion at the time of purchase as to their respective shares in the property. The transfer deed simply contained a declaration by them that the survivor of them was entitled to give a valid receipt for capital money. The judge at first instance decided that there had been a common intention of the parties to share the beneficial ownership of the property in equal shares. He based this finding at least in part on the general notion of there having been a partnership between them.

11.61

Ms Dowden appealed that decision and the Court of Appeal allowed her appeal on the following grounds:

(i) The valid receipt clause in the transfer was not an express agreement that the parties' beneficial shares in the property would be equal.

(ii) The clause did not demonstrate a common intention that the shares were equal unless it could be shown that both parties were aware of its full meaning at the time of the purchase, which was not the case.

(iii) It was clear that both parties intended to have an interest in the property but there was no evidence of any agreement or discussion between them as to the quantum of those shares.

(iv) The court therefore sought to infer a common intention given the parties' relevant conduct. In this particular case the fact that Ms Dowden had contributed a much larger part of the purchase price was highly significant.

The Court of Appeal awarded Ms Dowden 65% of the proceeds of sale with 35% going to Mr Stack.

11.62

Mr Stack appealed to the House of Lords which unanimously dismissed his appeal, finding that the parties' beneficial shares in the property should reflect their financial contributions towards it. There was no express declaration of trust. The property was in joint names and therefore it was for Ms Dowden to show that the common intention was that they should hold the property other than as beneficial joint tenants. She could in the view of the Lords easily do so as a result of their unequal contributions to the property, the court able to impute a common intention that she should be entitled to a larger share of the sale proceeds.

(ii) Jones v Kernott

11.63

Ms Jones and Mr Kernott met in 1980. They went on to have two children together, born in 1984 and 1986. In 1985 they purchased 39 Badger Hall Avenue Thundersley Essex in their joint names for £30,000 with a deposit of £6,000 paid exclusively from the proceeds of sale of Ms Jones' previous (mobile) home. The transfer deed contained no express declaration of trust/no declaration as to how the relevant trust in the property was to be held. The mortgage repayments and the expenses in respect of the upkeep on the house were shared between them. In 1986 they took out a joint loan of £2,000 to build an extension, although Mr Kernott did some of the work himself. Their relationship came to an end in 1993 when Mr Kernott moved out of the property. Ms Jones remained at the property with the children, taking on all of the outgoings in respect of it. She also bore the expense of providing for their children. In 1995 the property was put on the market for sale but did not sell. Also, following their separation the parties cashed in a jointly owned life insurance policy dividing the proceeds between them. Using his share, in 1996 Mr Kernott bought his own house in Benfleet Essex. Over the years the value of the former family home increased and in 2006 Mr Kernott indicated that he wished to claim his 50% share in it. In response, Ms Jones in 2007 applied to the court for a declaration that she owned the entire beneficial interest in the property. By 2008, the property was valued at £245,000.

11.64

Ms Jones accepted that at the time of separation there would not have been sufficient evidence to rebut the assumption that each party had an equal share in the property. However, she argues that, in the 14 and a half years since separation there was evidence that their common intention had changed. Mr Kernott had ceased to make contributions towards the running of the house and had made only very limited contributions towards the support of their children. Furthermore, it was mostly during that latter period that the value of the house had increased. At first instance, the judge held that their common intention had indeed changed. In reliance upon the decision of the House of Lords in *Stack v Dowden* he held that once the initial presumption of joint beneficial ownership is displaced and there is no further clear evidence as to the division of shares in the property it falls upon the court to infer or impute an intention of the parties as to the division of the property that they as reasonable and fair people would have intended. He decided therefore that Mr Kernott had a 10% beneficial interest.

11.65

Mr Kernott appealed to the High Court who dismissed his appeal. His appeal to the Court of Appeal however succeeded with the Court then declaring that the beneficial interests were equal. Ms Jones appealed to the Supreme Court which restored the declarations made by the judge at first instance, the court confirming that 'where the intention as to division of the property cannot be inferred each is entitled to that share which the court considers to be fair. In considering the question of what is fair the court shall have regard to whole course of dealing between the parties' (per Lord Kerr).

12 The application process under s 14 TLATA 1996

11.66

As well as ordering or refusing a sale the court may under s 14 TLATA make an order preventing a sale and may also relieve the trustees of any obligation to obtain the consent of or consult with any person in connection with the exercise of any of its functions. It does not have any discretion to adjust beneficial interests according to the statutory checklist contained in s 15. Beneficial interests are to be determined and declared according to the established principles of trust law (discussed above). The application under s 14 may be made by any person who is a trustee of land or who has an interest in property subject to a trust of land. An application may therefore be made not only by trustees and beneficiaries but also for example by a secured creditor beneficiary with the benefit of a charging order as a person with an interest in the trust property. This includes a judgment creditor with a charging order over the home (see *Close Invoice Finance Ltd v Pile and another* [2008] EWHC 1580 (Ch), [2009] 1 FLR 873) or a mortgagee (see *Edwards v Edwards* [2010] EWHC 652 (Ch), [2010] All ER (D) 172 (Jun)). An application may also be made under s 14 in relation to a trust of proceeds of land (TLATA, s 17(2)).

11.67

Section 15 contains a statutory checklist of matters to which the court must have regard in determining an application for fraud under s 14. Under s 15(1) the matters to which the court must have regard in making its order include

(a) the intentions of the person or persons who created the trust; (b) the purposes for which the property subject to the trust is held; (c) the welfare of any minor who occupies or might reasonably be expected to occupy the property as its home; and (d) the interests of any secured creditor or any beneficiary. Under s 15(2) the court must also have regard to the circumstances and wishes of each of the beneficiaries who would otherwise be entitled to occupy the property.

11.68

Section 14 does not give the court the power to order or direct that one beneficiary under a trust of land sell or transfer their beneficial interest to another beneficiary. The extent of the court's powers to make specific orders relating to the sale of beneficiaries' interests under a trust of land pursuant to s 14(2) was considered by the Court of Appeal in *Bagum v Hafiz* [2015] EWCA Civ 801, [2016] 2 FLR 337, [2015] All ER (D) 249 (Jul).

11.69

Applications under TLATA fall outside the definition of 'family proceedings' and accordingly are governed by CPR 1998. The CPR Practice Direction on Pre-Action Conduct (a revised version of which came into effect on 6 April 2015) is applicable. The Practice Direction requires the parties to consider whether negotiation or some other form of alternative dispute resolution (ADR) might enable them to settle their dispute without commencing formal court proceedings. Additionally, the court may require the parties to provide evidence that ADR has been considered (CPR 98 Practice Direction on Pre-Action Conduct, paras 8–11). The court will expect the parties to have exchanged information prior to commencement of proceedings but only to an extent which is reasonable and proportionate with a view to identifying, narrowing or resolving the issues between them (CPR 1998 PD on Pre-Action Conduct, paras 3–5). The letter before action from the claimant should include details of the basis of the claim, a summary of the facts relied on, what the claimant wants from the defendant and an explanation of how any financial loss has been calculated. Key documents relevant to the issues in dispute should also be disclosed (para 6). The defendant should respond to the letter before action within a reasonable time (14 days in a straightforward case and no more than three months in a very complex one). The defendant should indicate whether the claim is accepted and if not the reasons why giving an indication of which facts and parts of the claim are disputed. Details too of any counter claim should be provided. The defendant is also obliged to provide key documents relevant to the issues in dispute (para 6).

11.70

Proceedings may be commenced in either the High Court or the county court, using the procedure under CPR Part 8 where the claimant seeks a court's decision on 'a question which is unlikely to involve a substantial dispute of facts' eg where a joint owner seeks an order for sale but the beneficial interests in the property are not in dispute (Form N208) or under Part 7 where there is likely to be a substantial dispute of facts (Form N1). The acknowledgement of service should be filed within 14 days of service of the claim form whether the claim is made under Part 7 or Part 8 (CPR 1998, 8.3 in Part 8 claims and CPR 1998, 10.3 in Part 7 claims). No defence is required to be filed in a Part 8 claim as the defendant responds to the claim in his acknowledgement of service Form N210 (CPR 1998, 8.9, PD 8A para 5.2). In a Part 7 claim the defendant may either file his defence with his acknowledgement of service or file and serve his defence separately within a further 14 days (CPR 1998, 15.4).

11.71

Where a defendant files a defence in a Part 7 claim the court will make a provisional decision as to whether to allocate the case to the fast track or the multitrack and will send a notice to all parties requiring completion of the directions questionnaire (CPR 1998, 26.3(1)). The questionnaire must be filed by both parties within 28 days of service (CPR 1998, 26.3(6)). Cases are allocated to the fast track if the court considers that the trial is likely to last no longer than one day and that the number of persons giving oral expert evidence will be within prescribed limits, ie one expert per party in relation to any expert field and expert evidence in two expert fields (CPR 1998, 26.6(5)). In a Part 8 claim the case is treated as allocated to the multitrack and so Part 26 does not apply.

11.72

Thereafter a case management conference (CMC) may be listed for the court to give directions. In addition to draft directions the parties must in advance of the CMC submit costs budgets in Form H, estimates of costs for proposed expert evidence (CPR 1998, 35.4(2)) and a disclosure report in Form N263 (CPR 1998, 31.5). The parties are under an obligation to discuss and seek to agree a proposal for disclosure not less than seven days before the CMC. If at the CMC matters cannot be agreed the court will give directions for the progress of the case including the listing of a final hearing. Application may also be made for an injunction to prevent the disposal of property pending the hearing under s 14.

11.73

With regard to costs, the general rule is that the unsuccessful party will be ordered to pay the costs of the successful party but the court has wide discretion to make a different order eg as a result of the conduct of one of the parties. In *Walsh v Singh (Costs)* [2011] EWCA Civ 80, [2011] 2 FLR 599 the Court of Appeal upheld an order that there should be no order for costs against the claimant despite the fact that she failed to beat the defendant's Part 36 offer to settle. The court at first instance had taken into account the fact that the defendant's various counter claims had failed and the defendant's 'disgraceful behaviour' which included giving untruthful evidence, attempting to portray the claimant as mentally unstable and relying on material obtained by the use of spyware on a laptop which the claimant was using.

11.74

Consideration should always be given by practitioners to making an early Part 36 offer in order to give the client maximum protection on costs and to attempt to achieve an early settlement. A Part 36 Notice of Offer to Settle can be made in Form N242A and can be made at any time including before proceedings are commenced.

13 Alternative occupation rights

11.75

A non-owner cohabitant will at the very least have a bare licence to occupy the home of the partner. However, such a licence amounts to little more than permission to occupy the home, and is determinable upon reasonable notice. On breakdown of the relationship, the licence will usually be revoked, and in the absence of any defence to possession proceedings by virtue of any of the matters discussed in this chapter, the licensee will have to leave. However, in some cases, even if it is not possible to establish a beneficial interest or use the doctrine of proprietary estoppel, it may be possible to show an alternative right of occupation.

(a) Contractual licences

11.76

Although it is usually not possible for a cohabitant to show that he or she was the tenant of the partner, there have been cases where a contractual licence to occupy has been established. If the licensee has given up some existing right or suffered some other detriment to go and live with the owner, this may constitute consideration and thus give him/her a contractual licence eg to remain in occupation at the property for life or while s/he needs the property to care for children of the relationship – see *Tanner v Tanner* [1975] 1 WLR 1346. Here, the woman gave up her rent-controlled flat and moved into a property owned by the father of her two children, although the parties never cohabited. The Court of Appeal held that giving up her flat and looking after the children amounted to good consideration for an inferred contractual licence that she should be allowed to occupy the property until the children left school. However, this remedy has not been liked by the courts in the reported cases since. In *Coombes v Smith*, discussed above in relation to proprietary estoppel, the court specifically rejected the argument that a licence had been created in not dissimilar circumstances, in that the woman's acts of leaving her husband and moving into the property did not amount to sufficient consideration.

(b) Licence by estoppel

11.77

Where the legal owner induces in the partner a belief that he or she has a right to long-term occupation of the property rather than a beneficial interest in it, then a licence by estoppel rather than proprietary estoppel will arise, whereby the court will hold that the legal owner is estopped from denying that right of occupation. This argument succeeded in *Greasley v Cooke* [1980] 3 All ER 710, [1980] 1 WLR 1306 where the woman who had originally come to live with the man as his housekeeper but subsequently lived with him as his wife had been led to believe, following breakdown of the relationship, that she could continue to live in the property for as long as she wished. As the successors in title were unable to prove that she had not acted to her detriment in reliance on the inducement, and had indeed continued to care for a member of the family who was ill without any payment, the court took the view that they were estopped from denying that she had such a right of occupation. Licence by estoppel can arise also where the owner (who is not one of the cohabitants) behaves in such a way as to lead the claimant to believe that s/he has a right to long-term occupation. In *Matharu v Matharu* [1994] 3 FCR 216, [1994] 2 FLR 597, CA, the man who owned the property encouraged his son's partner to believe that the house belonged to the son, but after the son's death he sought possession on the basis of the property's true ownership. The court however held that the partner had a licence to occupy the house for her life or such shorter period as she wanted.

(c) Occupation pursuant to a life interest in possession

11.78

The decision in *Tanner v Tanner* (above) specifically avoided a finding that the woman's right of occupation amounted to an exclusive irrevocable licence to occupy land which would have made her the tenant for life under the Settled Land Act 1925. However, in *Ungurian v Lesnoff* [1990] Ch 206 where insufficient evidence to infer a beneficial interest under a constructive trust existed, a tenancy for life under the Settled Land Act 1925 was found to have been created. In this case the woman, who was a Polish academic, gave up her career and the valuable tenancy of her flat in Poland. She came with her sons to live in a property in London purchased by the man in his sole name for joint occupation by them and her children. His children, who were being educated in England, were also to live there from time to time. He purchased the property and she and her sons did some repair and renovation work to the property. It was found that she undertook the work not on the basis of a common intention that he had bought the house for her, but on the understanding that she had the right to reside there and that there was a common intention to provide her with a secure home.

11.79

The consequences of this finding were that she was the tenant for life with the power to sell and have the benefit of the proceeds of sale during her life. In this case, given the man's promise was not found to constitute any beneficial share in the property, it was still open to the court to find a licence by estoppel or a contractual licence since there was consideration in that the woman had given up her nationality, home and career in Poland. The abolition of strict settlements, combined with the fact that this approach seems to have been confined to the unusual facts of this case, probably mean that a similar case would in future be decided using estoppel principles, rather than an imputed life interest.

14 Transfer and settlement of property orders for children

11.80

As was discussed in relation to tenancies and in Chapter 9, para 1(2)(e) of Sch 1 to the CA 1989 enables the court to order the transfer of property between parents for the benefit of the child. Any beneficial interest in the home, or any other property owned by one parent, may be transferred either to the child or to the other parent for the benefit of the child. This opens up the possibility of the court effectively ordering the transfer of the home to the residential parent. Paragraph 1(2)(d) empowers the court to order the settlement of property owned by one parent for the benefit of the child.

11.81

In both cases, only one such order can be made against a parent in respect of the same child. The criteria set out in para 4 of Sch 1 discussed above in Chapter 9, identify the factors to be taken into account by the court. However, courts have been reluctant to transfer property to children directly in matrimonial cases (see *Chamberlain v Chamberlain* [1974] 1 All ER 33) and this reluctance has been extended to the Sch 1 CA 1989 provisions as discussed in Chapter 9. In *A v A (financial provision)* [1994] 1 FLR 657, FD, an application by the female cohabitant for an outright transfer of the family home for the benefit of the child was rejected in favour of a settlement for the benefit of the child until six months after the child's 18th birthday or completion of her tertiary education. On appeal in *T v S (financial provision for children)* [1994] 2 FLR 883, FD, it was specifically argued that the court's powers under Sch 1 should be widely construed to urge a different approach to capital orders in favour of children to that decided in the matrimonial context. However, the striking similarity of the provisions with those of the MCA 1973 was interpreted as preventing a different approach. Here, the order made provided that the property to be purchased with a lump sum for the benefit of the children was to be held on trust until the youngest reached 21 and thereafter revert to the father, not be divided equally between the children as had been ordered at first instance.

11.82

Similarly, in *J v C (child: financial provision)* [1999] 1 FLR 152, whilst a substantial property was placed at the disposal of the child, her mother and half-siblings until she was 21, the property reverted to the father at that point in time, subject to an option in favour of the mother to purchase at open market value. In *Hammond v Mitchell* (above), capital provision for children of an unmarried couple was deemed inappropriate and only periodical maintenance payments were ordered in favour of the children, although lump sums in favour of children have been willingly used to compensate for failure to meet child support obligations (see eg *Phillips v Peace* [1996] 2 FLR 230 and *V v V (child maintenance)* [2001] 2 FLR 799) as noted in Chapter 9.

11.83

Thus, case law to date seems to indicate a definite reluctance to use the court's powers more liberally or substantially differently to the matrimonial context. Such case law as there is certainly favours settlements rather than outright transfers of property for the benefit of the child. Thus, at the end of the term, the property (or the relevant portion of it) is returned to the respondent unless special circumstances apply and as referred to in Chapter 9 extreme wealth is not such a circumstance (see *T v T* [2007] EWHC 883 (Fam)). Disability or other special needs might be.

11.84

It should also be noted that there is in any event no power in the schedule to order the sale of the property. Where, as often will be the case, the property is jointly owned or the non-legal owner claims a beneficial interest in it, it will be appropriate to combine any application under Sch 1 CA 1989 for a transfer or settlement of property order with an application for a declaration as to the beneficial interests, or an order for or restraining sale under s 14 TLATA 1996. Ideally all such cases should be dealt with by a court that exercises both Family Court and county court jurisdiction (*White v White (joinder of Trusts of Land Act and Children Act applications)* [2003] EWCA Civ 924, [2004] 2 FLR 321).

This is as near as it is possible to get to achieving a family law based consideration by the courts of a property dispute between cohabitants. All possible issues, including financial provision for the children, should be raised at the earliest stage so that the appropriate forum and procedure, leading to the quickest and most effective outcome, can be decided.

11.85

Transfer and settlement of property orders extend to any property owned by a parent in possession or reversion and therefore, as discussed in Chapter 9, are not limited to use in respect of the family home.

15 Legal aid

11.86

Any advice given to cohabitants concerning a dispute relating to the family home must include information about both costs, and where appropriate, the availability of legal aid, the consequences of the requirement to pay a contribution if eligible and the Legal Aid statutory charge under s 25(1) of the Legal Aid, Sentencing and Punishment of Offenders Act 2002 (LASPOA). Legal aid will only be available to a client who has provided specific evidence of alleged domestic violence/abuse (including financial abuse) or a child protection need. The LASPOA definition of domestic violence is any incident or pattern of incidents of controlling, coercive or threatening behaviour, violence or abuse (whether psychological, physical, sexual, financial or emotional) between individuals who are associated with each other. Thus, if the claimant (or defendant) cannot establish that s/he has been a 'victim' of domestic abuse, legal aid will not be available and s/he will have to be advised of the potential costs to trial and the possible costs consequences of being unsuccessful in their claim (or defence) at trial.

11.87

If eligible for legal aid, there is power for the Legal Aid Agency (LAA) to postpone enforcement of the charge where property recovered or preserved is to be used as a home for the assisted person or their dependants (reg 22(1)(a), Civil Legal Aid (Statutory Charge) Regulations 2013). Similarly, where a sum of money is recovered under such proceedings for the purpose of purchasing a home in accordance with the order or agreement, the charge may also be deferred providing the property is bought within a year of the order or agreement and the charge is registered (reg 22(2)); in both cases, the LAA has power to agree to the purchase of a substitute property to which the charge will be transferred (reg 22(3)). Postponement is always at the discretion of the LAA and is dependent upon the property concerned offering sufficient security for the sum charged.

11.88

The court order must also make it clear that the property or sum awarded is to provide a home for the assisted person or their dependants and it is critical that advisors ensure that this wording is included in the wording of the order or agreement. Simple interest on the charge accrues at the rate prescribed (currently 8%) on the charge as of the date of registration and an assisted person may at any time make repayments in respect of the charge which will be applied first to the outstanding interest (see reg 25(2)).

11.89

The Court of Appeal decision in the case of *Parkes v Legal Aid Board* [1996] 4 All ER 271 also makes it clear that where, as in this case, an order for sale is successfully resisted under s 14 TLATA 1996, even though the extent of the beneficial interests were not in dispute, as there had been a recovery of the exclusive right to possession which had previously been a shared right, this would bring the property within scope and the property would be subject to the statutory charge to the extent of the costs incurred under the legal aid certificate.

11.90

In proceedings under Sch 1 CA 1989, a child is able to apply for a legal aid certificate in their own name or alternatively the resident parent may apply, where they seek orders for the benefit of the child. If a court orders that the former family home, where the interests of the parents in the property are agreed or have been decided, is to be settled on the child or children, then, as the child has only recovered an interest in possession in a property of which he or she is not an owner, the statutory charge would seem to be avoided. Care must always be taken not to deliberately evade the charge and good reason must be provided for making payment in an order direct to a child, particularly if the order is made by consent. LASPOA 2012, s 25(1) provides that where the dispute or proceedings which result in a payment to someone other than the client, such as a dependent child or a creditor, but where the payment is for the benefit of the client (eg to repay a debt on behalf of the client) then the charge will still arise on that payment. Wherever a legally aided co-owner acquires through proceedings an exclusive right of occupation for a substantial period, this may mean that the statutory charge applies and could in theory at least apply to long-term occupation orders granted in respect of an owner-occupied property under Part IV FLA 1996, where the successful applicant has a beneficial interest in the family home.

11.91

Full consideration of the legal aid funding implications must be discussed with and communicated to the client at every stage and seriously taken into account when considering the possibility of settlement. It should be noted that where an agreement is reached in consequence of Legal Help advice, the statutory charge does not arise where the property is the client's main or only dwelling which may be significant where preservation of the home by agreement is a real possibility and the client is eligible for Legal Help advice (reg 5(3)).

16 Negative equity and mortgage arrears

11.92

Cohabitants facing relationship breakdown may face the added problem of dealing with negative equity and/or mortgage arrears. Given that co-owners are jointly and severally liable for a mortgage debt, it may often be difficult to get a mortgagee's consent to a transfer of property order in a negative equity situation. The attitude of mortgagees to this problem varies. However, where the repayment record is good and there is sufficient income (including Support for Mortgage Interest (SMI) payments paid as part of a property (co-)owner's state benefits which are made directly to the lender) available to meet repayment of the interest element, it should be possible to negotiate the desired outcome. It should be noted though that SMI came to an end on 5 April 2018 and has been replaced by a loan. As this loan will have to be repaid, it may be that lenders are disinclined to support any proposed transfer of equity to the loan recipient. Particularly where the property market is depressed, however, there is little for a lender to gain in forcing a sale in adverse conditions if the interest on the repayments is being made. Where a sale is the only option in a negative equity situation on relationship breakdown, it is generally financially advisable for the borrowers to take urgent action to sell the home themselves, as they are more likely than not to obtain a higher purchase price than the mortgagee selling in possession and where no other option is possible both parties, should agree to limit the damage to each of them. However, consent of the mortgagee to the sale is needed in a negative equity situation or the sellers will not be able to redeem the mortgage and secure the release of the charge on completion of the sale. If the mortgagee refuses, then the borrowers can apply to the court to order sale pursuant to s 91 LPA 1925 to enable the court to direct sale on terms that the court considers appropriate (see *Palk v Mortgage Services Funding plc* [1993] Ch 330, CA). Such proceedings must be issued in the High Court where the total mortgage debt exceeds £30,000.

11.93

One important factor to bear in mind, however, is that a sale by the co-owners prior to a possession order may make them intentionally homeless if they are in priority need and not eligible for assistance as a homeless person (discussed below). Tentative enquiries can be made to the local housing authority as to how they view homeless applicants in this situation. The 2006 Code of Guidance on Parts VI and VII of the Housing Act 1996 confirms that genuine inability to keep up with the mortgage repayments where no further financial help is available should not be regarded as intentionally homeless. It states that 'an applicant's actions would not amount to intentional homelessness where he or she has lost his or her home, or was obliged to sell it, because of (rent or) mortgage arrears resulting from significant financial difficulties, and the applicant was genuinely unable to keep up the (rent or) mortgage payments even after claiming benefits, and no further financial help was available' (para 11.18), although their ability to pay the mortgage when the commitment was taken on is to be examined (para 11.9). A misrepresentation of the applicants financial position when the mortgage was taken out may make them intentionally homeless and ineligible for accommodation under the homelessness legislation and the sale or loss of the home due to wilful refusal to pay rent or mortgage repayments (para 11.20 (ii)) will be a deliberate omission warranting a finding of intentional homelessness, although not if payment would leave them without the means to provide for the ordinary necessities of life (see *R v Hillingdon London Borough Council, ex p Tinn* (1988) 20 HLR 305, QBD).

11.94

Another matter to consider in a negative equity situation where there is an endowment mortgage of at least ten years' standing is for the couple to switch to an ordinary repayment mortgage and for the life policy to be sold to a specialist broker for a price much higher than the surrender value. The proceeds can then be applied to discharge or reduce the negative equity.

11.95

Where there are arrears and possession proceedings, suspension of any possession order should be made where it can be shown that the mortgagor will pay off the arrears and be able to pay the repayments after a 'reasonable period' (see s 36 Administration of Justice Acts 1970 and 1973 (AJA 1970 and 1973)). In *Cheltenham and Gloucester Building Society v Norgan* [1996] 1 All ER 449, the Court of Appeal held that in assessing a reasonable period the whole of the remaining period should be taken into account. Where, as may be the case with second mortgages, the loan is under £25,000 and governed by the Consumer Credit Act 1974, time orders under s 129 of the Act are available 'if it appears to the court just' to make one in respect of any sum owed to the lender at a rate which is reasonable taking into account the debtor's financial position. This is an easier hurdle to overcome than the AJA 1970 and 1973 test and the provision enables both further time to pay and the rescheduling of payments beyond the original term of the loan. It is also possible for the debtor under the 1974 Act to apply for the order without awaiting proceedings being issued by the lender.

11.96

Following sale, legal co-owners will remain jointly and severally liable for the balance of the mortgage debt not met out of the sale proceeds and, if there have been possession proceedings, then a money judgment may also have been obtained. Although the mortgagee can in theory seek to enforce the whole of the debt against either of the co-owners, an agreement as between the former cohabitants as to how this should be borne should be considered on relationship breakdown. Where there has been an agreement as to the proportions in which the mortgage repayments were made, then the debt would be shared between them in these same proportions.

17 Homelessness

11.97

If it has not been possible to preserve the home, the final remedy to explore where there are children or a vulnerable cohabitant who are now homeless, is the duty under Housing Act 1996 Part VII to secure accommodation for those who are eligible for assistance homeless, in priority need and not intentionally homeless. Local housing authorities are now under a duty to provide the statutory homeless with permanent accommodation (s 193(3) HA 1996 as amended by the Homelessness Act 2002, s 6, which abolished the minimum period (of two years) for which a local authority was subject to a duty to rehouse).

11.98

The relevant provisions of Part VII of the 1996 Act and the current Department for Communities and Local Government Homelessness Code of Guidance for Local Authorities published 24 July 2006 have already been considered in detail in Chapter 3. Where there are children or the homeless cohabitant is vulnerable within the meaning of the s 189 Housing Act 1996, there is likely to be a priority need. Where it has not proved possible to obtain long-term relief from the court, as a result of which the vulnerable cohabitant or family become homeless unintentionally, the local authority would owe them a duty to secure them accommodation. Where there are children who can reasonably be expected to reside with the applicant, there is always priority need for homelessness purposes. The local authority then has a duty to secure accommodation for the partner with whom the children are to remain.

11.99

An interesting issue is the likely reaction of local authorities asked to house cohabitants in priority need to the availability of enhanced remedies for cohabitants to secure occupation of the home. Where a cohabitant's former partner is likely to be in priority need themselves, due to their vulnerability or dependant children residing with them, then this should ensure that a cohabitant is not put under pressure to use their other legal remedies. However, the ability to apply for occupation orders where there is not a violent situation, and where the interests of the child have been given increased prominence, may make authorities more inclined to advise potentially homeless applicants to apply for occupation orders in the first instance and subsequently use their legal rights to secure long-term occupation of the home. Whether or not refusal to do so would amount to intentional homelessness would depend on the facts of the case but remains a possibility, albeit not necessarily a strong possibility, as para 11.23 of the Code states that 'where the applicant has fled his or her home because of violence or threats of violence likely to be carried out, and has failed to pursue legal remedies against the perpetrator(s) which might have prevented the violence or threat of violence, although these decisions (to leave the home and not pursue legal remedies) may be deliberate, the homelessness would not be intentional if it would not have been reasonable for the applicant to continue to occupy the home'. It is certainly possible that authorities would expect cohabitants (where no domestic abuse is being alleged) to use s 14 TLATA 1996 or the transfer of tenancy remedy in respect of the family home (Sch 7 FLA 1996) or perhaps even the settlement and transfer of property orders available under Sch 1 CA 1989 for the benefit of any child of the relationship. Refusal to do so once advised of this possibility, certainly without clear reasons, could arguably amount to failure to do something which has resulted in homelessness and provide a basis for an intentional homelessness finding. Certainly, if there is an agreement between cohabitants that the one of them with priority need should leave to attempt to gain accommodation under the homelessness legislation, this may fall foul of s 191(3) HA 1996, although to do so it must have been reasonable for them to continue to occupy the accommodation.

11.100

It is to be stressed that in cases where there is no right of occupation of the family home by the cohabitant in priority need and they have left and become homeless, temporary accommodation should be provided pending enquiries (s 188 HA 1996) and subsequently at the very least pending the outcome of any court proceedings taken to obtain either an occupation order or an appropriate longer term remedy.

11.101

Finally, where a cohabitant who is not in priority need becomes homeless on relationship breakdown, they are entitled to advice and assistance from the local authority in obtaining accommodation (s 192) and may be able to place themselves on the housing register. The local authority might, for example, provide assistance with a rent deposit or guarantee to help the applicant to obtain accommodation in the private rented sector, or advice on applying for an allocation of accommodation through the social housing waiting list or through another social landlord.

18 Personal property

11.102

Essentially the rules relating to the division of personal property of cohabitants on relationship breakdown are the same as for real property. The law of trusts can be used where the property is of sufficient value and either a determination of the parties' intentions as to beneficial ownership is required (see *Marr v Collie* [2017] UKPC 17) or it is alleged that a non-legal owner is beneficially entitled to a share of the property. Indeed, this was vividly illustrated in the case of *Rowe v Prance* [1999] 2 FLR 787. Here Mr Prance, a married man, had a relationship with another woman, Ms Rowe, over a 14-year period, promising to leave and divorce his wife but never doing so. However, when the matrimonial home was sold, the couple found a boat which was purchased in the Mr Prance's sole name with a view to the couple living together on it and fulfilling their plan to sail the world. Ms Rowe, who had found the boat to purchase, was told it was registered in the Mr Prance's sole name because she did not have an Ocean Master's Certificate. In reliance on his representations to this effect, she gave up her rented home, placed her furniture in storage and began living on the boat which was referred to as 'ours'. Eventually, Ms Rowe realised that Mr Prance was not coming to live with her and demanded her share of the boat. The court, accepting her evidence, held that Mr Prance had constituted himself an express trustee of the boat as no writing was required in the personal property context. Consequently, they had no need to find a constructive trust and applying the equitable maxim 'equality is equity' confirmed that Ms Rowe held a half share in the boat.

11.103

Generally, anything owned before the relationship or purchased by one of the cohabitants during the relationship remains the property of that partner. Gifts remain the property of the donee. A useful summary of the law on gifts is found *in Montalto v Popat* [2016] EWHC 810 (Ch), [2016] All ER (D) 118 (Apr). It seems that joint bank or building society accounts held by cohabitants and intended to be a common pool of funds will be deemed to be held as joint tenants in equity, regardless of any disproportion in the relative contributions, in the same way as is presumed in the case of a married couple (see *Bernard v Josephs* (above) and *Jones v Maynard* [1951] Ch 572). Severance of that joint tenancy by giving written notice to the other will result in the creation of a tenancy in common in equal shares of those monies. If the common pool presumption can be rebutted, by an express or implied contrary intention, then the funds will be held on resulting trust for the contributors in shares proportionate to their contributions. If there is a cohabitation contract or other written declaration which deals with the ownership of such funds this is likely to be conclusive.

11.104

Share ownership in joint names entails considerations similar to those relating to real property and discussed in relation to the family home. It seems that resulting trust principles are most appropriate here in the absence of any express declaration to the contrary.

11.105

As a matter of practical importance, it is always essential to alert the bank or building society of a dispute and, if appropriate, to alter the drawing arrangements to prevent the funds being drawn by the other party. Any dispute concerning personal property which is litigated by a legally aided client will again be subject to the legal aid statutory charge. Transfer and settlement of property orders can be sought where there are children as discussed above.

11.106

In terms of jurisdiction relating to personal property disputes, the general equitable jurisdiction given under s 23 County Courts Act 1984 enables applications for a declaration of trust in relation to personal property up to a current value of £30,000 to be heard in the county court, with claims relating to property of greater value needing to be made in the High Court. Where chattels owned in undivided shares, are concerned, s 188 LPA 1925 permits an application for an order as to the appropriate division to be made by the court. Again, the county court has jurisdiction up to a value of £30,000 and thereafter applications should be made to the High Court.

11.107

In all cases concerning cohabitants' personal property, consideration should be given to whether such applications should be joined together with applications for financial relief under Sch 1 CA 1989 and in relation to the family home under s 14 TLATA 1996 or Sch 7 FLA 1996, as suggested to be appropriate to avoid proliferation of time-consuming proceedings in *Hammond v Mitchell* [1992] 2 All ER 109, [1991] 1 WLR 1127, [1991] FCR 938, [1992] 1 FLR 229.

19 Proceedings under the Married Women's Property Act 1882 and the Matrimonial Proceedings and Property Act 1970

11.108

It is easy to overlook the possibility of proceedings under these two Acts when advising cohabitants, as they are likely to be relevant in a minority of cases only. However, an application can be made under s 17 of the 1882 Act for a declaration as to the ownership of disputed property where the parties had an agreement to marry (or ss 66–68 of the Civil Partnership Act 2004 where the parties had an agreement to enter into a civil partnership). The application must be made within three years of the termination of the agreement. Section 37 of the 1970 Act provides that where a spouse (which includes a partner in couples with an agreement to marry) makes a substantial contribution in money or money's worth to the improvement of property that person is entitled to a beneficial share. Section 74 of the Civil Partnership Act 2014 mirrors the provision available for civil partners (including those partners who have entered into civil partnership agreements). This avoids the need to prove common intention under a resulting trust and may therefore be advantageous.

PRACTITIONERS' CHECKLIST ON COHABITANT CO-OWNERSHIP DISPUTES

11.109

- Establish legal ownership of the family home and the rights of any third parties, including the mortgagee.
- Gather detailed evidence as to equitable ownership and look to what the intention was at the date of purchase and subsequently, including:
  - documentary evidence (eg title documents, written agreements);
  - correspondence, declarations of trust;
  - evidence as to express discussions between the parties;
  - detrimental acts by the non-legal owner;
  - the history of the relationship and the whole course of dealing between the parties during the period of ownership;
  - direct and indirect contributions made to the purchase price;
  - direct and necessary indirect contributions to the mortgage repayments;
  - details of who carried out improvements to the property and on what basis.
- Consider whether there is an express trust or whether resulting or common intention constructive trust case law is appropriate to establish the parties' respective interests remembering the different approaches to stages 1 and 2.
- Consider issues relating to proprietary estoppel.
- Quantify the share claimed, and consider the date of valuation and whether equitable accounting will be appropriate.
- Notify and liaise with the mortgagee where appropriate.

- Enquire whether the cohabitants are engaged to be married or have entered into civil partnership agreements.
- Consider whether mediation or any other forms of alternative dispute resolution would be appropriate.
- Consider whether an occupation order and/or injunction restraining disposition of the assets pending the hearing should be applied for.
- Consider the statutory provisions available and most applicable in relation to determining the shares in and disposition of the family home and other assets.
- Consider whether other provisions relating to chattels, personal property and financial provision for children are relevant and ensure that all proceedings are consolidated to enable the issues to be heard together in an appropriate jurisdiction.
- Consider the impact of costs (including whether legal aid is available and if so the impact of the statutory charge).

APPENDIX

Comparative overview of rights of married couples, civil partners and cohabitants

Spouses and civil partners	Opposite-sex cohabitants	Same-sex cohabitants
Family home (owned)		
Spouses and civil partners enjoy 'family home rights' (ie the right to reside in family home in name of partner by virtue of the marriage/civil partnership irrespective of the length of relationship/marriage/civil partnership)	No right of occupation and no legal or beneficial interest as of right irrespective of length of relationship/cohabitation. Would need to apply under the Trusts of Land and Appointment of Trustees Act 1996. May acquire right of occupation under s 36 Family Law Act 1996 (FLA 1996)	No right of occupation and no legal or beneficial interest as of right irrespective of length of relationship/cohabitation. Would need to apply under the Trusts of Land and Appointment of Trustees Act 1996. May acquire right of occupation under s 36 Family Law Act 1996 (FLA 1996)
Family home (rented)		
Automatic statutory occupation rights for non-tenant under s 30 Family Law Act 1996	No automatic statutory occupation rights for non-tenant – s 36 occupation order possible	No automatic statutory occupation rights for non-tenant – s 36 occupation order possible
Non-tenant spouse succeeds on death to assured periodic tenancy	Non-tenant partner succeeds on death to assured periodic tenancy – s 17 Housing Act 1988	Non-tenant partner succeeds on death to assured periodic tenancy – s 17 Housing Act 1988
Non-tenant spouse succeeds on death to Rent Act protected tenancy	Non-tenant partner succeeds on death to Rent Act protected tenancy – Sch 1, Pt 1 Rent Act 1977	Non-tenant partner succeeds on death to Rent Act protected tenancy – Sch 1, Pt 1 Rent Act 1977
Succeed on death to secure tenancy	Succeed on death to secure tenancy in England (s 86A Housing Act 1985). Succeed as 'member of tenant's family' if lived with them for 12 months in Wales (s 87 Housing Act 1985)	Succeed on death to secure tenancy in England (s 86A Housing Act 1985). Succeed as 'member of tenant's family' if lived with them for 12 months in Wales (s 87 Housing Act 1985)
Discretionary transfer of tenancy on breakdown – FLA 1996	Discretionary transfer of tenancy on breakdown – FLA 1996	Discretionary transfer of tenancy on breakdown – FLA 1996

Financial provision on relationship breakdown Right to apply for all forms of financial provision including maintenance, transfer of property, lump sum and pension sharing orders (from date of marriage/civil partnership)	No entitlement to financial provision, save in respect of any children of the family under Sch 1 Children Act 1989, irrespective of the length of cohabitation. Any claims in respect of property would only be permissible if a legal or beneficial interest can be established.	No entitlement to financial provision, save in respect of any children of the family under Sch 1 Children Act 1989, irrespective of the length of cohabitation. Any claims in respect of property would only be permissible if a legal or beneficial interest can be established.
Inheritance/Partner dies without leaving a Will Spouse or civil partner receives all personal possessions, the first £250,000 and one half of the remainder, such entitlement arising from the date of marriage. Any children of deceased will share the remaining one half (s 46 Administration of Estates Act 1925 as amended)	Partner would not be a beneficiary under s 46 (so no automatic entitlement), although children (if any) would share equally the estate of their deceased parent. Would need to make an application for 'maintenance' only under the Inheritance (Provision for Family and Dependants) Act 1975 if able to prove cohabitation of at least 2 years with the deceased. If there are no beneficiaries at all, surviving cohabitant, at the discretion of the Crown may receive provision out of the deceased's estate without having to apply under the 1975 Act. If the couple are not able to satisfy the court that they were living together in the same household as spouses/civil partners for the required period, then the applicant must show that, immediately before the death of the deceased, he or she was being maintained, either wholly or partly by the deceased (s 1(1)(e)) which requires an element of dependency by the survivor on the deceased.	Partner would not be a beneficiary under s 46 (so no automatic entitlement), although children (if any) would share equally the estate of their deceased parent. Would need to make an application for 'maintenance' only under the Inheritance (Provision for Family and Dependants) Act 1975 if able to prove cohabitation of at least 2 years with the deceased. If there are no beneficiaries at all, surviving cohabitant, at the discretion of the Crown may receive provision out of the deceased's estate without having to apply under the 1975 Act. If the couple are not able to satisfy the court that they were living together in the same household as spouses/civil partners for the required period, then the applicant must show that, immediately before the death of the deceased, he or she was being maintained, either wholly or partly by the deceased (s 1(1)(e)) which requires an element of dependency by the survivor on the deceased.

Spouses and civil partners	Opposite-sex cohabitants	Same-sex cohabitants
Children/Parental responsibility		
Human Fertilisation and Embryology Act 2008 (HFEA 2008), s 33(1) provides that 'the woman who is carrying or has carried a child as a result of the placing in her of an embryo or of sperm and eggs, and no other woman, is to be treated as the mother of the child'. The legal father is the man whose sperm fertilised the egg (although if the legal mother is married then the rebuttable presumption is that her husband is the legal father). In the case of surrogacy, the child is deemed to be that of the surrogate mother even if both the egg and sperm were donated (s 33(1) HFEA 2008). The couple can in this circumstance though apply for a parental order under s 54 HFEA 2008.	The most common way for unmarried fathers to acquire parental responsibility for their child is by joint birth registration, a parental responsibility agreement or the making of a parental responsibility order by the courts.	If a child is born to a same sex female couple as a result of assisted reproduction services provided by a UK licensed clinic for them *together* and they have both given written consent in this regard, the mother may agree that her partner is to be treated in law as the other parent (HFEA 2008, ss 43 and 44). For gay male couples wanting a child together which carries the DNA of one of them, surrogacy is probably the only course. The child is deemed to be that of the surrogate mother even if both the egg and sperm were donated (s 33(1) HFEA 2008). The couple can in this circumstance though apply for a parental order under s 54 HFEA 2008.

Index

[all references are to paragraph number]

www.ingramcontent.com/pod-product-compliance
Ingram Content Group UK Ltd.
Pitfield, Milton Keynes, MK11 3LW, UK
UKHW021036150926
475561UK00003B/134

9 781526 503046